THE GOOD OCCUPATION

THE GOOD OCCUPATION

AMERICAN SOLDIERS AND THE HAZARDS OF PEACE

SUSAN L. CARRUTHERS

Harvard University Press

Cambridge, Massachusetts · London, England

2016

Library of Congress Cataloging-in-Publication Data

Names: Carruthers, Susan L. (Susan Lisa), author.
Title: The good occupation : American soldiers and the hazards of peace / Susan L. Carruthers.
Description: Cambridge, Massachusetts : Harvard University Press, 2016. | Includes bibliographical references and index.
Identifiers: LCCN 2016014994 | ISBN 9780674545700 (cloth)
Subjects: LCSH: Reconstruction (1939–1951)—Personal narratives, American. | United States—Foreign relations—1945–1953. | Soldiers—United States—History—20th century.
Classification: LCC D825 .C274 2016 | DDC 940.53/144092313—dc23
LC record available at https://lccn.loc.gov/2016014994

For

JOSEPH ROMANO,

with love

CONTENTS

THE GOOD OCCUPATION

THE TROUBLESOME "O WORD"

Americans have long held contradictory views about military occupation. Often, it seems they would prefer not to acknowledge that the United States has ever occupied anywhere. But at other times, when outright denial seems less tenable or desirable, they assert that America has been a singularly virtuous overlord, with the beneficence of U.S. forces rescuing such ventures from proper consideration as occupation at all. Peter Sellers skewered this national conceit in the 1959 satire *The Mouse That Roared,* in which the tiny, imaginary European country of Grand Fenwick declares war on the United States—purposely seeking to lose. The duchy's leaders rest secure in the knowledge that defeat won't lead to national prostration but to rehabilitation "beyond our wildest dreams." The Americans, one of Sellers's characters explains, are a "very strange people. Whereas other countries rarely forgive anything, the Americans forgive everything. There isn't a more profitable undertaking for any country than to declare war on the United States and to be defeated. No sooner is the aggressor defeated than the Americans pour in food, machinery, clothing, technical aid and lots and lots of money for the relief of its former enemies." Needless to say, the plan goes horribly awry. Grand Fenwick's hapless military leader inadvertently captures the latest American superweapon, the Q-bomb, thus winning the war.[1]

Occupational "doublethink"—the belief that Americans excel at something they simultaneously hesitate to acknowledge—was on prominent display in the run-up to the invasion of Iraq in March 2003. President George W. Bush and other key architects of "Operation Iraqi Freedom" made frequent references to post–World War II Germany and Japan as they sought to build support for a military campaign to topple Saddam Hussein. His ouster would enable a democratizing makeover of not only Iraq but the Middle East more broadly, advocates of this undertaking claimed. To reassure doubters, Bush, Condoleezza Rice, Donald Rumsfeld, and others repeatedly drew historical analogies with the United States' occupation of defeated Axis foes after 1945, while Undersecretary of State John Bolton explicitly broached "a kind of de-Nazification" of Iraq. If such noxious regimes as Nazi Germany and imperial

Japan could be reconstructed as prosperous and pacific allies, then it would surely be possible to transform Iraq along similar lines.[2]

Bush made a memorable statement of this case in a speech at the American Enterprise Institute, repeated in a radio broadcast on March 1, 2003:

> Rebuilding Iraq will require a sustained commitment from many nations, including our own. We will remain in Iraq as long as necessary, and not a day more. America has made and kept this kind of commitment before—in the peace that followed World War II. After defeating enemies, we did not leave behind occupying armies; we left constitutions and parliaments. We did not leave behind permanent foes; we found new friends and allies.
>
> There was a time when many said that the cultures of Japan and Germany were incapable of sustaining democratic values. They were wrong. Some say the same of Iraq today. They, too, are mistaken. The nation of Iraq—with its proud heritage, abundant resources and skilled and educated people—is fully capable of moving toward democracy and living in freedom.[3]

Time would darken the president's predictions. A CIA report entitled *The Postwar Occupations of Germany and Japan: Implications for Iraq* had warned before the war was launched—some nineteen days after this speech—that an invaded and occupied Iraq would in no way resemble Germany or Japan after long years of thoroughly ruinous war. So it proved.[4]

Less commented on than the flawed analogy was the tendentious version of history that underpinned Bush's impressment of the past to service present-day needs. Even as the president extolled the postwar rehabilitation of Axis foes, he offered an elliptical characterization of those ventures that implied brevity as well as generosity. In the 1950s, few Germans or Japanese would have concurred that U.S. forces remained "not a day" longer than necessary. The occupations of Germany and Japan lasted formally until 1955 and 1952, respectively, with the island of Okinawa remaining under U.S. sovereignty until 1972. But even after the formal end of occupation, significant numbers of American garrison troops stayed on in Germany and Japan, as they did in South Korea and Italy: a sizable, and by no means always welcome, presence. Indeed, U.S. bases still remain in these locations—and many others—in numbers that fluctuate as geopolitical priorities pivot.[5]

Far from coming in a spirit of reconciliation, Allied troops entered Axis territory in 1945 with an expressly punitive mandate to deindustrialize and demilitarize their foes. If new alliances were subsequently forged, these partnerships developed more by chance than by design—a consequence of the rapid inversion of wartime patterns of amity and enmity that turned the Soviet Union into the United States' principal antagonist. As political elites in Washington found a common cause with their former foes in anticommunism, so Japan and West Germany were transformed into the regional bulwarks of American grand strategy. Although the United States did leave "constitutions and parliaments," the victorious Allies also left both Germany and Korea partitioned into two hostile states. These severances resulted from the increasingly quarrelsome superpowers' inability to undo jurisdictional arrangements intended as temporary postwar expedients. Germany remained divided for forty-five years. Korea's schism continues: a fate all the more striking when we recall that the peninsula was ostensibly not *enemy* territory when first overrun by U.S. and Red Army troops in 1945. After four decades of despised Japanese colonial rule, Koreans fully expected that the Allies' arrival would herald liberation and independence, not permanent division.[6]

This messy history is elided in the invocation of miraculous, democratizing makeovers that seemingly happened at the wave of a wand, with no lasting imprint of American military force. Strikingly, even while Bush conjured this anodyne vision, he used the term "occupying armies" only to deny that the United States had left them on former foes' soil. This reticence also characterized other key advocates of Operation Iraqi Freedom, whose lexical squeamishness continued even after coalition forces had invaded Iraq and constituted themselves as the country's governing authority. The administration still couldn't decide whether to call this venture an occupation. Paul Bremer, who headed the Coalition Provisional Authority in Iraq during its yearlong existence from 2003 to 2004, observed that occupation was an "ugly word, not one Americans feel comfortable with." But the issue was far from purely semantic. Plainspoken use of what Bremer jokingly dubbed the "O word" would entail a parallel acknowledgment of the formal responsibilities bestowed by international law on occupiers. And this status the administration accepted only rather circuitously.[7]

The challenge of how to rescue occupation from the term's ugly overtones was not new. A similar dilemma beset American leaders sixty years earlier. Some months before the United States entered World War II in December

1941, various civil and military agencies in Washington had already begun to anticipate the moment when Allied troops would occupy Axis territory. Preparations for the war's aftermath continued in tandem with strategic planning for the defeat of Italy, Germany, and Japan. But visions of postwar order and retributive justice varied enormously both within and between the "united nations," when that term still denoted a squabbling wartime alliance, not a permanent international organization. Total war would terminate, the Allies hoped, in the Axis powers' total defeat. But then what? Who would disarm and dismantle enemy war machines? What would be built in their place, and how long would the work of reconstruction take? The prospect of American troops occupying conquered nations for an indefinite period—or, indeed, for *any* period—after the war ended generated fierce controversy, intensified by the news in 1942 that the army had established a special School of Military Government to prepare officers for postwar occupation. The Hearst press, a late and grudging convert from isolationism, railed against this "School for Gauleiters," copied (its columnists claimed) from Nazi Germany. The "whole idea of this school runs contrary to the instincts of the American people and the principles of our government," the *Chicago Daily Tribune* charged. "The notion that our soldiers will be available for long-term occupation of foreign soil is absurd and it follows that the training of officers for this kind of pro-consular work abroad is absurd."[8]

It fell to defenders of the controversial school—and others eager to turn Henry Luce's aspirational "American century" into concrete geopolitical fact—to point out that U.S. forces had, in fact, occupied many places, often for significant stretches of time, throughout the nation's history. In 1942, Library of Congress information specialist Benjamin Akzin tallied twenty-one occupations since 1815. Afflicted by recurrent amnesia, Americans simply retained "no knowledge of this fact." So lamented Yale historian Ralph Henry Gabriel, dubbing this lacuna an "American Paradox." He set out to elaborate—for the benefit of students at the School of Military Government, his fellow historians, and American citizens—an "old tradition" extending from nineteenth-century New Mexico, and containing "many distinguished names . . . and outstanding achievements." Others tried equally hard to assuage anxiety that occupation was dangerously akin to, or even synonymous with, imperialism—separated only by duration from a phenomenon Americans preferred to associate with European powers.[9]

During the war, no one promoted the idea and the image of occupation more endearingly—or more enduringly—than reporter and novelist John Hersey. Major Victor Joppolo, hero of his 1944 novel *A Bell for Adano,* set in occupied Sicily, provided a prototype for the culturally sensitive occupation officer. Imploring readers to "get to know this man well," Hersey averred that nothing less than the United States' "future in the world" lay in the hands of "our Joppolos." Sons of immigrants, these thoroughly assimilated men of "wisdom and justice" could traverse cultural, ideological, and generational divides, implanting new-world values in the lands their parents had left behind. Recognizing the unpopularity of postwar occupation among wartime Americans, Hersey insisted that America's "after-armies" would have to stay the course. His message, along with his hero, would be rediscovered many times over subsequent decades.[10]

The reassuring belief that uniformed Americans are singularly adept, if also uniquely diffident, practitioners of postwar reconstructive surgery was already latent during World War II. But this conviction took hold only fitfully. Just as it required imaginative industry for the "worst war in history" (in Paul Fussell's phrase) to crystallize as the "good war," so it required strategic acts of omission and selection to turn what followed into a fitting sequel: the "good occupation." That Americans have come to see the reconstruction of Germany and Japan in ennobling terms is evidenced by the Bush administration's strategic harnessing of postwar history to build support for the invasion of Iraq. But it is salutary to note that Americans often struggled, during the war and in its immediate aftermath, to see their country's exercise of "military government" as either virtuous or necessary.[11]

Seventy years after the fact, it's easy to imagine that the reconstruction of Germany and Japan along liberal capitalist lines was a foregone conclusion. During the war, however, nothing about the treatment of the yet-to-be-defeated Axis powers appeared self-evident. Animosity toward Japan ran so high in wartime America that Gallup opinion pollsters in November 1944 offered respondents to the question "What do you think we should do with Japan, as a country, after the war?" the option of checking "Kill all Japanese people." Chillingly, 13 percent of respondents made that their selection. About one-third opted for Japan's destruction as a "political entity," while just

8 percent favored "rehabilitate, reeducate." And if it was thinkable that Japan would be wiped from the map altogether, then talk of postwar occupation was clearly redundant. Less vengefully minded American commentators questioned whether the United States should undertake something so far-fetched as the occupation of a completely alien state. In a widely discussed *Harper's* article, Nathaniel Peffer anticipated that Japan's defeat would be so crushing—its encirclement by hostile Chinese and Soviet neighbors so complete—that there would be no need for the United States to conduct a costly long-term occupation of uncertain outcome. Debates about Germany's fate were just as heated. Treasury Secretary Henry Morgenthau famously proposed that Germany should be "pastoralized" after the war: severed into two or more units and reduced to long-term agrarianism. Although Americans failed to entertain scenarios of apocalyptic detonation for Germany, they nevertheless talked seriously about mass castration or sterilization of the German population—a slower "phasing out" than instant annihilation, but elimination all the same. For his part, Franklin D. Roosevelt breezily announced, "We don't want to kill the people. We want Germany to live but not to have a higher standard of living than that of the USSR."[12]

Once it was settled that U.S. forces would indeed occupy Germany and Japan, it remained uncertain how long troops would remain, in what number, and in what combination with other Allied contingents. When those ventures began in 1945, *military* government was conceived by planners in Washington as a brief transitional phase before civilian agencies assumed control over defeated populations. At the very highest level of national policy making, fundamental questions about the character, composition, and duration of occupation were unclear at the outset, as they would remain for many months thereafter.[13]

These quandaries did not pertain exclusively to Germany and Japan, although those occupations alone have lingered in popular memory. Since the amnesia that Gabriel diagnosed in 1943 has persisted, it may surprise present-day Americans to discover how many territories U.S. forces presided over during and after World War II, whether "liberating" or "occupying" them: a distinction that (at least theoretically) separated the joyful fate of countries emancipated from Axis rule, like France and Belgium, from the draconian treatment of enemy territory proper. The future of erstwhile colonies under Axis control—in North Africa, Malaya, Singapore, Indochina, Burma, and the Dutch East Indies, among other places—was particularly contentious.

In rhetorical statements of wartime purpose, Roosevelt and Winston Churchill implied, if they didn't explicitly promise, a postwar world without colonies: a prospect as deeply desired by colonized peoples as it was scorned by imperial elites hoping to reconsolidate their power. In many places, the end of Japanese occupation led not to liberation but to the return of colonial authority—often materially aided by Washington—and a rapid resumption of war, this time against the French, British, or Dutch. The Philippines, captured by the Japanese in December 1941, returned to U.S. military rule as various islands were reclaimed in 1944 and 1945, pending a formal transfer of power from American to Filipino hands in July 1946.[14]

In Europe, U.S. forces first occupied Sicily and then southern Italy in the summer and fall of 1943. The occupation of Italy in its entirety lasted under the aegis of Allied Military Government until 1947, although Trieste, tussled over by Italy and Yugoslavia, remained under Allied control until 1954. American troops briefly occupied parts of Czechoslovakia in the spring and early summer of 1945, before turning these areas over to the Red Army. Austria, meanwhile, was subject to quadripartite occupation until 1955. In Germany, where the pocket of territory around Aachen was claimed as early as October 1944, U.S. military government came to an end in 1949 with the Federal Republic's inauguration, but American civilian high commissioners stayed in supervisory positions until 1955. Meanwhile, in the Pacific, U.S. Navy personnel exercised sole authority over several islands captured, or recaptured, from Japanese control: the Solomon Islands, the Gilbert and Marshall Islands, Saipan and Tinian. Guam, reclaimed from the Japanese in 1944, remained under U.S. military rule until 1950. Okinawa, largest of the Ryukyu islands, did not "revert" to Japanese sovereignty until 1972. As for the Japanese home islands, the first American troops arrived in late August 1945, greatly outnumbering units of British, Commonwealth, and Soviet forces that (by Washington's design) played a peripheral role in Japan's occupation. In September, members of the Tenth Army landed at Inchon. Greeted as liberators, American troops soon resorted to blunt force to repress South Koreans' aspirations to self-rule, a condition for which they were deemed "unready." Meanwhile, thousands of marines were sent to occupy areas of northern China, becoming transient participants in the Chinese civil war on the Nationalist side.[15]

Just as the war began at different times in different places, so "postwar" was an unevenly rolling phenomenon. One infantryman conveyed the incremental way in which territory was claimed and combat ended in a letter home from Germany written on April 12, 1945 (coincidentally the date of FDR's death). "It's now in the process of ending bit by bit each day," Milo Flaten noted, "when we occupy some more ground the war is over for that particular part of the continent. When we occupy it all, the whole thing will be finished." Yet even after Germany had been claimed in its entirety by Allied troops and the instruments of surrender were signed, whether the "whole thing" was over remained more indeterminate. What was required for such a catastrophic war definitively to be over? Civilians and soldiers, victors and vanquished, had different answers. They would likely have agreed, however, that achieving "normalcy"—whatever that may have been—was a more fraught and fitful process than the cessation of armed hostilities. Peace, many American commentators pointed out, wasn't won at a stroke but had to be secured by painstaking, sustained work. And prominent observers of the postwar landscape—scholars, journalists, photographers, novelists—weren't at all sure that Americans were "winning the peace" in the war's early aftermath.[16]

For their part, many U.S. service personnel harbored the conviction that the war would really end only when they came home and were able to discard their military uniforms. They were under no illusion that peace did not "break out" on May 8 or September 2, V-E Day or V-J Day. Instead, for millions of servicemen and servicewomen these dates (or earlier ones) inaugurated a different phase of military existence: membership of an army of occupation. For some, this interregnum lasted merely a few weeks; for others, several months or even years. Needless to say, even more lives were affected as objects of occupation. By the reckoning of political scientist Hajo Holborn, some 300 million people fell under U.S. military rule at the end of the war. One year later, 150 million remained under the control of Allied Military Government.[17]

Most Americans in uniform regarded occupation duty as a bitter coda to wartime service that had already lasted far too long, prolonging the state of suspended animation most had hoped would terminate with the Axis powers' defeat. Pervasive feelings of hostility toward the business of occupation may explain, in part, why this epilogue to the war—or prologue to peace—has largely dropped from popular recollection, except as a hollow abstraction. To many combat soldiers, occupation duty seemed a particularly deflating anticlimax. "Of the time following the cessation of hostilities little need be said," the Seventeenth Armored Infantry Battalion's regimental history noted curtly. General George S. Patton, commander of the Third Army in Germany and briefly military governor of Bavaria, found the war's aftermath so tiresome that, when he could be bothered to record anything in his diary at all, he repetitiously scrawled, "Nothing of importance happened." Military historians, fixated on combat as the preeminent martial endeavor, have tacitly adopted a similar position. Many of the richest and most detailed histories of soldierly experience during World War II come to an abrupt halt in May or August of 1945, as though GIs did in fact simply pack up and go home the very moment their enemies' unconditional surrender had been assured.[18]

The occupations that followed World War II have not gone unexamined, however. On the contrary, with interest reinvigorated by recent wars and occupations whose post-ness remains moot, numerous studies have appeared over the past decade and a half. The fate of "displaced persons" and other refugees, in motion and stasis after the war, has been richly documented and dissected. Historians of gender have anatomized the sexual politics of occupation, while others have explored the Allies' attempts to refashion the politics, culture, and mentalities of the occupied. "Postwar" itself has generated considerable attention, a high scholarly standard set by Tony Judt's sweeping volume of that name. Ironically, perhaps, some of these works of history were mined for contemporary relevance by State Department employees and others in transit to Iraq in 2003. Noah Feldman, an NYU law professor who spent a year working on Iraq's new constitution, noted that on his flight to Baghdad everyone seemed to be reading books about the occupation of Japan. John Dower, whose study of postwar Japan, *Embracing Defeat,* won a Pulitzer Prize in 2000, may have winced at this revelation. He had presciently warned the Bush administration in 2003 of Japan's inutility as a blueprint for Iraq.[19]

Some of the renewed attention to occupations past has been driven by a more or less explicit desire to assist the state in the production of repeatable results. In think tanks and political science departments, researchers have used comparative historical analysis in pursuit of "metrics" for occupational success: optimal troop strength to population size, for example, or the length of time required to transform an autocratic polity into an electoral democracy. One Rand Corporation publication from 2003, *America's Role in Nation-Building: From Germany to Iraq,* even boasts a back-cover endorsement from Bremer, praising it as "a marvelous 'how to' manual for post-conflict stabilization and reconstruction," which he had kept "handy for ready consultation."[20]

This pursuit of a magic formula for positive outcomes has tended to generate formulae that urge *more:* more planning, more troops, more money, more time. And indeed some pundits still maintain that outcomes in Iraq and Afghanistan would have been rosier had U.S. planners heeded the prescription for more of everything. The goal of this book, however, is quite different: not to offer a recipe for occupational success but to explore the alchemy that transformed the base metal of lived experience after World War II into the golden stuff of national legend. How, in other words, was occupation *made* good—as it occurred and in hindsight? Authors such as Fussell and Michael C. Adams have deconstructed the "good war" mythos, revealing that the moral clarity routinely ascribed to wartime America is largely an artifact of latter-day wishfulness. Scholars have yet to probe understandings of the war's aftermath with similar attentiveness. The virtuous aura around the post-1945 occupations remains undimmed, and has been if anything enhanced by comparison with the recent U.S. enterprise in Iraq, a project intended to mimic and reprise earlier reconstructive triumphs.[21]

Drawing on hundreds of unpublished collections of letters, diaries, and memoirs located in archives across the United States, this study places servicemen and servicewomen at the center of investigation. How did the executors of occupation parse its hazards and rewards? What self-understandings did they construct as they documented postwar experience in private journals and missives home? In the recent upsurge of attention to occupation, the subjectivity of soldiers themselves has received strikingly little attention in line with a broader deficit of attention to the psychology and phenomenology of victory. "Cultures of defeat," in Wolfgang Schivelbusch's phrase, have attracted more attention. Loss undoubtedly appears a more complex and wrenching condition than victory. What, one might wonder, remains to be said about conquest that the victors themselves haven't already said? Free to do as they will, they are also empowered to mythologize their prowess in prose and have their version stick; so, at any rate, Churchill's famous dictum that "history is written by the victors" would have us believe. Yet, in practice, the meanings and sensations of victory were as diverse as the members of the "after-armies" themselves. Americans in uniform, despite their postwar incarnation as agents of democratization, belonged to a profoundly hierarchical organization in which segregation prevailed. Some victors were indisputably more equal than others. But in different ways, servicemen and servicewomen of every rank were less inclined to regard themselves as all-powerful conquerors than as victims: of circumstance, discipline, or discrimination. The vaunted fruits of victory often seemed far less tangible in reality than in imagination.[22]

It speaks to a shared cultural presumption of postwar's uneventfulness that inquisitive infants are rarely imagined asking, "What did you do *after* the war, daddy?" Yet "What happened next?" is the quintessential "child's question," as British historian A. J. P. Taylor observed (a question he believed it was the historian's "first function" to answer). Taylor might, then, have appreciated J. D. Salinger's story "For Esmé—with Love and Squalor," published in the *New Yorker* in 1950, as a fictional illustration of his point. Esmé, an orphaned British girl with a preternaturally extensive vocabulary, entreats a GI she's befriended to write her a story from defeated Germany. "Make it extremely squalid and moving," she instructs, before pausing to ask whether the American sergeant is "at all acquainted with squalor." He is, he assures her, "getting better acquainted with it, in one form or another, all the time." Esmé would not have been disappointed with the letters many GIs penned home from the countries they occupied.[23]

Civilian America didn't learn of the squalidly transactional character of life under occupation from newspapers, the radio, or newsreels alone. Freed from the constraints of wartime mail censorship, occupation soldiers wrote home and told them "what happened next," sparing few details. "You'd be surprised to know what you can get for a bar of chocolate here in Augsburg," one enlisted man obliquely remarked to his aunt in Hickory, North Carolina. Or perhaps not, given the profusion of press reports about "fraternization" in occupied territory. Others provided more unguarded descriptions of female refugees offering themselves to soldiers for packages of C-rations in Germany, and young Italian boys pimping on behalf of barely older sisters in Naples. Some sons didn't hesitate to tell their mothers about the military establishment's attempts to suppress venereal disease, and brothers shared details of bargains to be had at Japan's geisha houses. More politically conscious GIs wondered aloud whether the Allies' promised root-and-branch overhaul of defeated regimes would come about, as they watched members of ousted elites reassume positions of privilege and listened to senior officers' anti-Semitic diatribes. Meanwhile, African American occupation soldiers had ample opportunity to ponder the contradictions of democratizing missions inaugurated by an institution in which racial discrimination was a matter of official policy from on high, buttressed by unofficial vigilantism from below.

American "postwarriors" were not simply passive bystanders to postwar flux. Although many thought they were doing very little of anything on a day-to-day basis, they participated in epic processes of relocating millions of

displaced people and encamping others, disarming troops and guarding prisoners, protecting (or pilfering) supplies, and adjudicating, on a microbasis,
questions of guilt and innocence, trustworthiness and treachery. Whose
present plight merited help, and whose past actions deserved punishment?
Occupation soldiers, at every level, constantly made such judgments, however unaware they may have been of how these snap decisions shaped the
larger postwar scheme of things. Members of the "after-armies" played vital
and varied roles in assuaging, and sometimes exacerbating, the catastrophic
aftermath of the most destructive war in human history.

Occupation personnel faced existence—and extinction—at its most extreme. Across Europe and Asia, they entered towns, cities, and villages devastated by war. Millions of lives had been lost; countless others ruined beyond
recovery or comprehension. Occupation was a thoroughly *embodied* experience.
Drawn into intimate proximity with both exposed bodies and raw human need,
occupying forces were responsible for managing extremity: burying the dead,
feeding the hungry, disinfecting those suspected of disease, shuffling bodies
into camps or onto trains. Wasted life—and human waste—pervaded the
pages of Americans' written accounts. In its initial phase, trainee occupation officers were warned, the work of military government "consisted of
nothing but basic human necessities. You fed 'em, you watered 'em, and
then you struggled like hell to dispose of the urine and excreta that resulted."
Drawing on what he'd observed in Sicily and Saipan, Malcolm MacLean (a
military government officer and former college president) continued: "You
treated the sick, you plucked shrapnel out of their hides and when they died,
which they do in very large numbers, you shoveled them under. You chased
cows, and pigs and chickens. You scrounged like a slum dweller for every
scrap of stuff you could find and every scrap was used."[24]

No wonder, then, that uniformed Americans sometimes insisted that
"winning the peace" was harder than winning the war. Postwar reconstruction required greater finesse than the wartime work of destruction. Governing
took more skill, patience, and insight than did killing. It was tougher, many
officers averred, to discipline one's emotions in peacetime than to keep the
enemy in one's sights in combat; harder to keep hatred properly directed,
and harder to know whom to trust. Telling who was on which side was no
easy business when individual identities, like uniforms, were so readily
switched in the chaotic aftermath of war—as demobilized soldiers from
Martin Guerre to Don Draper have long known.[25]

As occupation soldiers recalibrated their judgments of allies, enemies, and enemies' enemies alike, they sometimes found recent foes more sympathetic than either those alongside whom Americans had recently fought or the stigmatized populations persecuted by their wartime opponents. In every occupied territory, service personnel vascillated between revulsion and attraction to the people over whom they presided. Disgust commingled with desire. With their monopoly of armed force and abundant supplies of stuff, occupation soldiers enjoyed easy access to women's bodies—a reward of victory enjoyed by some and fretted over by others. How to reconcile the competing attractions of doing right and doing wrong amid the barrage of mixed messages about whether the work of occupation was primarily punitive or protective? At a more fundamental level, how to decide whether occupied people really counted as human at all?

Before U.S. undertakings in postwar Germany and Japan acquired the deflective patina of myth, Americans in and out of uniform thought very differently about the business of occupation. While the *O* word occasioned anxiety then as now, one signal difference in the 1940s was that Americans lacked overweening confidence in the outcome of their postwar mission. Despite wartime attempts to invent a venerable tradition of military government, previous long-term occupations had not been notably successful, whatever the yardstick of judgment: whether in the American South after the Civil War, Haiti in the interwar years, or the Rhineland after World War I. Proof of the last's failure lay in the recurrence of conflict—initiated, again, by Germany—just two decades after the war that was meant to have ended all wars. In 2003, while Bush acknowledged the possibility that remaking Iraq would take time, other enthusiasts were more insouciant. Ken Adelman, former assistant to Secretary of Defense Rumsfeld, blithely claimed that "liberating Iraq" would be a "cakewalk." American soldiers, insisted Vice President Dick Cheney, would be "greeted as liberators," and welcomed with "sweets and flowers."[26]

During World War II, no one entertained fantasies of occupational ease. Early experiences in liberated France and Belgium injected a jolting dose of realism. "We know that the initial ecstasy which greets our armies soon gives way to bitter disappointment," cautioned an Office of War Information report in April 1945. Occupation soldiers were repeatedly warned to expect resistance from the occupied. They would need to remain vigilant and comport themselves sternly in a role that was "difficult and distasteful." The surprise—sequentially repeated in Italy, Germany, and Japan—was that defeated populations behaved much better than expected. It was the victors who behaved much worse.[27]

To reconstruct postwar mentalities from intimate firsthand accounts is to appreciate how differently Americans thought about themselves, about the military, and about their place in the world during a time of unprecedented global and national transformation. While shouldering their state's call to arms, many members of the "greatest generation" loathed the military they were obliged to serve in and couldn't wait to resume civilian lives kept on precarious hold for so long. Tens of thousands so passionately resisted postwar service that they took to the streets of Manila, Tokyo, Paris, and Frankfurt to demand immediate demobilization in January 1946. Seventy years later, with hundreds of U.S. bases built into the postwar landscape, it's easy to forget that it was not always thus; nor was this development a seamless holdover from the war. While we've come to know a good deal about how citizens of the former Axis powers "embraced defeat," we know considerably less about the awkward and hesitant way in which Americans—in and out of uniform—embraced supremacy in the postwar world. Here, then, is victory's fractious history.

Chapter 1

PREPARING TO OCCUPY

"What fun this really is—a change that again stirs the old blood, revives the childhood zest," Malcolm MacLean enthused in a missive to his wife in January 1943. "All kinds of good things are happening inside us. We've walked more in four days here, I think, than in four months in recent years. We eat light and get hungry. We chat much with interesting and friendly men. We vision a job to do ahead that makes us wish for a lot of years to grow up into it." Although MacLean's exuberance suggested a camping trip undertaken in particularly genial company, the source of this exhilaration wasn't a vacation but rather a return to school. Days after his fiftieth birthday, MacLean had relinquished his position as head of the historically black Hampton Institute. Exchanging a college presidency for the role of student, he'd also swapped civilian togs for a military uniform, another source of unexpected pleasure. "It's fun to be dressed up smartly and yet feel easy—and even to shine shoes," the middle-aged soldier-schoolboy chirped. At Franklin D. Roosevelt's personal request, the educator and former chair of the Commission on Fair Employment Practices had embarked on a four-month program of study at the School of Military Government (SMG), operated under the aegis of the provost marshal general at the University of Virginia in Charlottesville. As "student and spy," MacLean's mandate was to ascertain how well this outfit was fulfilling a novel mission: preparing its recruits to govern defeated enemy territory and areas liberated from Axis occupation.[1]

Opened in May 1942, the SMG drew instant fire from critics across the political spectrum. Leftists regarded its existence as evidence of unbridled imperial ambition, the *New Republic* preferring Moscow's plan to train progressive German POWs for leadership roles in a postfascist Germany. Liberal internationalists, meanwhile, relished the prospect of ongoing U.S. world leadership. But some doubted whether men in uniform were best placed to coax democratic polities from the ruins of Italian fascism, German Nazism, and Japanese imperialism. Most vociferous in their criticism, however, were conservatives who had strenuously opposed intervention in another globespanning war throughout the 1930s, endorsing American entry only after Pearl Harbor and through gritted teeth. Hearst's *Chicago Daily Tribune* led the charge, branding Charlottesville a "school for Gauleiters" patterned on the Nazi model. "Evidently the high command in Washington was determined that we must ape our enemies at every degrading point," the paper railed. This provocative analogy likened SMG alumni to the despised Wehrmacht overlords of occupied Europe, "regional tyrants" as fond of spilling blood as of amassing treasure. Opposed to prolonged military deployments and enduring foreign entanglements, the *Tribune* found the prospect of "Yankee Gauleiters" disturbing on two fronts. An SMG portended the extension of federal authority on a global scale, with republican allegiances to small government and self-sufficiency abandoned along the way. But if the *Tribune* fretted for foreign populations who would fall under U.S. military rule, it also feared for citizens at home. Editorials warned darkly that "some people in Washington" perhaps anticipated that Charlottesville's graduates could "be used in due time to rule Americans rather than enemy peoples." Adding insult to injury, these New Deal schemers had chosen the University of Virginia—Mr. Thomas Jefferson's own campus—as the incubator for their embryonic plot.[2]

It was hardly surprising that the SMG should have sparked such animated discussion when its existence first became public knowledge. After all, the training of American military governors could not be uncoupled from contentious questions about the world after war and the United States' role in global affairs. Washington's machinery for "opinion management" struggled to provide positive representations of what the war was *for*—a much harder task than depicting whom and what it was fought against. Both FDR's "Four Freedoms" and the grandiose rhetorical flourishes of the Atlantic Charter, promising "freedom for all the men in all the lands," left the specifics purposely vague. In wartime discourse, "freedom" and "democracy" were blank signifiers, abstractions that individual imagination could fill with meaning—like the contours in a coloring book. Neither FDR and his cabinet nor the fractious United Nations had agreed which freedoms, in what measure, would be bestowed upon whom when hostilities finally ended. Throughout the war it remained unclear how long Allied personnel would occupy vanquished enemy states and what kind of regimes would eventually replace those of Mussolini, Hitler, and Hirohito. The fate of territories annexed by the Axis powers in Africa and Asia appeared even more uncertain. Whether the postwar world would be one with or without colonial empires had yet to be determined.[3]

Political complexity and geopolitical gravity, rather than a refusal to think ahead, explain why these issues went unresolved for so long. In its earliest incarnation, postwar planning was in fact a *pre*war enterprise in Washington. The judge advocate general first mooted a program of training for military government personnel as early as September 1941, three months before Japan's attack on Pearl Harbor. From the outset, however, this proposition stirred controversy. "Our military government plans have been attacked as unprecedented, un-American, imperialistic, grandiose and personally ambitious," lamented Provost Marshal General Allen Gullion in February 1943. He did not overstate. Several of FDR's civilian advisers harbored grave reservations about whether the armed services ought to be entrusted with such weighty responsibilities and so much political power. One product of Americans' historical antipathy toward large standing armies, rooted in aversion to the prospect of military dominance over civil life, was the insistence that soldiers must be thoroughly apolitical. Until 1945, officers were not permitted to vote; and during the war years conservative anxiety over enlisted men's radicalization remained so intense that various measures were enacted to keep GIs' reading material free from "political taint." In the opinion of civilian critics, ingenues in uniform—conceivably with high ambitions for office—were singularly ill equipped to impart democratic values to defeated populations. The unavoidable contradictions of imposed democratization appeared all the sharper if the imposers belonged to an authoritarian organization in which commands were issued from on high and hierarchies of rank rigidly maintained.[4]

No senior figure was more implacably opposed to the idea of military government than Harold Ickes. During a stormy cabinet meeting in October 1942, a "much alarmed" secretary of the interior decried "the germ of imperialism" lurking in Charlottesville. But by then the controversial school had already been in existence for some five months. The War Department had prevailed, despite qualms voiced by the president himself. No civil agency—or projected international organization—could counter the military's clinching argument: that the first priority was to secure the Allies' rear lines as the juggernaut of combat rumbled onward. Until war was categorically over, government had to be military. "It is one of those inescapable incidents of warfare, completely sanctioned by international law, that no victorious army can avoid even if it would," insisted Provost Marshal General Gullion. Only after it had become apparent that defeated people were thoroughly quiescent could men in uniform trade places with civilian administrators.[5]

Military necessity may have trumped every other card in wartime deliberations, but it certainly didn't stifle all doubts, nor did it end calls for the establishment of a dedicated civilian agency that would quickly assume charge over defeated populations. Criticism of the SMG extended beyond the long-term remit of the venture to presidential complaints about the "second string" caliber of faculty and students. Charlottesville quickly acquired a reputation as a "dumping ground" for third-rate officers who had proven too indolent or inept for more vigorous frontline duties. FDR's allies were also eager to alert the president to what they perceived as the school's retrograde political makeup—chock full of anti–New Deal Republicans. "It has been reported . . . that no friends of the Roosevelt administration need apply for assignment to this school," the president's administrative assistant Jonathan Daniels warned his boss.[6]

In August 1942, FDR requested that Secretary of War George Marshall furnish a breakdown of those attending Charlottesville to ascertain their ages and previous administrative experience, since the president continued to fear that the program, its management, and its student body were "all faulty." Officers in a segregated military, SMG trainees were uniformly white and, for the first two years of the school's existence, exclusively male. Minor variations in class, religious, and ethnic background leavened the overwhelmingly WASP student body. Among the first cohort, the median age was forty-eight, which Daniels feared was "a little advanced . . . to be learning the difficult business of assisting in the government of strange people in far places." Many had been reserve officers before the war, and a disproportionate number were lawyers: men of the "'professional veteran' type, organized patriots, political and social conservatives," in Daniels's characterization. Only 8 percent of the first class had any relevant overseas experience. Although the school's second in command, Colonel Jesse I. Miller (himself a former Washington lawyer), vigorously denied that his outfit was "training incompetents to be imperialists," neither the statistical data nor word-of-mouth scuttlebutt offered much encouragement about the proconsuls who would sally forth from Virginia to rule over "strange people" in distant locales. No wonder, then, that Roosevelt sent not one but two spies into the hornets' nest: MacLean and his son-in-law, Seattle newspaper publisher John Boettiger.[7]

Military government candidates at Charlottesville found themselves on a campus radically reshaped by wartime mobilization. President John Lloyd Newcombe had mandated physical education for all students in 1942, and within months around 1,300 of the university's 1,700 students were enrolled in some type of military program. "Few industrial plants have undergone a more complete conversion to war aims than the University of Virginia," claim the authors of a college history. Although SMG trainees supplemented a depleted student body, they were not alone in adding a martial air to Jefferson's bucolic campus. Men who had long since graduated from college, if they had attended at all, had to regain habits of study, putting in long hours in lecture halls and at the library. But recruits weren't simply mature students adjusting to campus existence. More awkwardly for some and enjoyably for others, they assumed a hybrid identity as scholar-soldiers. As MacLean's enthusiastic epistle documented, SMG trainees were required to wear uniforms at all times. Military courtesies, "saluting etc.," as abbreviated by the school's General Orders No. 4, were to be "carefully observed." There would be "no smoking in class," and students were required to trim and tone middle-aged girth, while learning (or relearning) how to march, drill, and handle small arms. As a *Washington Post* puff piece on the school put it, the students had all received some basic army training, "so that in a pinch they can leave their desks and fire a gun or direct a maneuver." This may have been true, but the *Post*'s assertion the trainees had all "met the same physical requirements as any doughboy" strained credulity.[8]

As the school matured, the median age of its students dropped while the range of their professional experience broadened. One graduate praised his cohort of 150 as "about as fine a group as I've ever known. There were a few duds—the most careful selection can't avoid mistakes. But at least 90 per cent of the men are really very superior." Hailing from thirty-six states, this group included "doctors, lawyers, manufacturers, businessmen, bankers, city managers, a Major or two, a congressman (T. V. Smith from Illinois), government workers from Treasury, Agriculture, Justice etc, a few educators and college professors and a number of regular army men—West Pointers with an army career back of them." Adding a dash of cosmopolitanism to the mix, there were also "three Polish officers, two Belgians, two Dutch, two British, and one Norwegian," representing their respective states or governments in exile.[9]

On paper, at least, the professoriate was yet more impressive. The SMG enjoyed its Charlottesville berth thanks to Colonel Hardy Cross Dillard, a

FIG. 1.1 At the School of Military Government in Charlottesville, officers attend a lecture in April 1943. Photographer: John Collier. Library of Congress, Prints and Photographs Division, FSA/OWI Collection [LC-USW3-022653-E].

West Point graduate who, as director of the university's Institute of Public Affairs, had brokered this arrangement at a nominal cost to the War Department of seventy-five dollars a month. Professors and visiting speakers included prominent scholars, mostly drawn from the Ivy League, in a range of disciplines across the humanities and social sciences. Students received numerous lectures on the "various countries which we and our allies hope to liberate or conquer—stretching around the world. Countries like Bulgaria and Burma got one lecture each; Japan, Italy, and Germany each got a whole series." Theories of race also featured on the curriculum, since it was intended, in the words of Colonel Miller, that students would "have an accurate understanding of the historical, political, geographic, racial and economic settings" in which they would later operate. Students thus learned from Yale's Arnold Wolfers "how to handle the Germans." This would call for "much vigilance and energy," as Germans were given to misinterpreting "self-restraint, politeness or even kindness as a sign of weakness." However, "fairness, decency and humanity" combined with "unyielding firmness" would do more to reeducate Germans than "any amount of propaganda could ever hope to achieve," Wolfers predicted. Pointers on "Japanese characteristics" were offered by Columbia professor Hugh Borton.[10]

Alongside lectures on military organization, international law, and history, students spent a significant amount of time working collaboratively on "problems." Small teams of men with different areas of expertise were tasked with drawing up detailed plans for the occupation of specific places. This exercise encouraged trainee military governors to anticipate every aspect of civic life they would later manage in conquered territories: from food supply to transportation, currency control to public health, sewage systems to schools. Initially, role-playing projections were based on purely hypothetical scenarios, with students instructed to plan the occupation of Charlottesville or California. But as the curriculum underwent serial modifications, the school's superintendents conceived these initiatives as opportunities to devise workable blueprints for the administration of cities and regions earmarked for Allied occupation. Successive cohorts of trainees duly devoted hours to studying maps, charts, and data sets intended to familiarize them with the basic layout and administrative setup of their putative destinations. This practical orientation helped assure critics in and out of government that Charlottesville was not excessively wedded to book learning.[11]

But the school's military overseers and civilian faculty wrestled with ongoing problems of identity and purpose that defied resolution. In part, these difficulties arose because vital questions about the length, character, and political objectives of postwar occupation remained in dispute in Washington and among the Big Three. Proposals continued to proliferate for a new civilian agency, or agencies, that would assume control over defeated countries as soon as war's post-ness became an incontrovertible fact. An Office of Foreign Relief and Rehabilitation under the direction of former New York state governor Herbert Lehman was founded in November 1942, and then subsumed a year later into the new United Nations Relief and Rehabilitation Administration (UNRRA). With forty-four contributor nations, UNRRA was nevertheless under U.S. stewardship, with Lehman at the helm. Meanwhile, Ickes and his associates continued to agitate for a specialized cadre of civilian administrators, since UNRRA's welfare-oriented remit took "care" to be something different from "control."[12]

Hitherto keen to insist that the military would be only too happy to transfer authority to civilian hands at the earliest possible moment, the Provost Marshal General's Office baulked, raising the specter of hopelessly tangled chains of command between uniformed officers and UNRRA. The War Department was particularly upset that military personnel stood to lose authority over distribution of food—a strategic weapon of the first order in managing foreign populations, as anthropologist Margaret Mead had pointed out. Key figures associated with Charlottesville began to issue more frequent and strongly worded reminders that "American experiences in the past disclosed an urge to terminate military control too soon." As evidence, they cited a "premature" decision to cede control of the Philippines to civil authority in the early 1900s, leaving the military to wage a protracted counterinsurgency campaign against Moro rebels.[13]

Periodic reminders about the dangers of premature withdrawal notwithstanding, the most consistent message to emerge from the War Department was that military government was a task men in uniform did not relish, nor were they best equipped for it, once the emergency conditions created by combat had subsided. To corroborate the point, senior personnel stressed that the armed forces were so averse to this particular mission that they had repeatedly neglected to prepare for it. Over the past 140 years, American armies had "conducted a number of military governments but never trained a single officer," the preamble to a four-volume *History of Military Government Training* asserted in 1945. Quickly forgetting each successive experience of occupation, the services never developed a coherent body of doctrine. As a result, the wheel had required reinvention numerous times—even though the official history of the U.S. occupation of the Rhineland after World War I (the Hunt Report) had made an express plea for greater preparedness. Irvin L. Hunt closed his account, noted the Provost Marshal General's Office, "almost with a prayer, that never again should the American Army be permitted to undertake such a task without having first trained a sufficient number of officers qualified for the work in those special duties that were involved in it." Hence the unique importance of the Charlottesville school in the eyes of its progenitors.[14]

This diffident posture resulted in an extremely narrow articulation of what occupation would entail. Recruits were tutored to conceive their role as a purely supervisory one: "government" without politics. Military government officers would not rule, they were taught, so much as exercise oversight: they would constitute an administrative carapace stretched over preexisting local arrangements. Only theater commanders were, properly speaking, military governors. Since Charlottesville's trainees were merely military government officers, it was not their job to make policy. Nor were they empowered to change local customs, laws, and traditions. Above all else, their function was to ensure that military operations and supply lines could roll on, unhampered by lawless civilians behind the advancing front. Military government's sole objectives, Thomas Barber informed his students, were "to prevent the population interfering with the army, to induce them to help the army, and to look after enemy property that has been taken or abandoned." Barber cautioned his class of prospective occupiers to keep out of the way of the occupied, since military government represented an "intolerable burden on the people." Any attempt to "spread sweetness and light" threatened to boomerang disastrously. There was, he warned, "nothing more irritating than being compelled to have sweetness and light spread over you, especially if you hate the guts of the spreader." "Best gov't is least gov't," student Richard Van Wagenen dutifully scribbled down.[15]

As SMG graduates would soon discover, the exercise of power by force of arms could never be anything other than political. Equally spurious was the insistence that the Hunt Report on the Rhineland had "slumbered in the archives of the War Department for many years," as Brigadier General Cornelius Wickersham (commandant of Charlottesville) claimed. While the school itself marked an institutional innovation, officers in the interwar years had received some instruction in military government. It would have been odd if this weren't so, given the number of occupations U.S. forces carried out in the twentieth century's first three decades. The Marine Corps' occupation of Haiti lasted from 1915 to 1934, while Nicaragua and the Dominican Republic were also occupied for significant periods. In 1920, Colonel H. A. Smith at Fort Leavenworth drew up a primer titled *Military Government,* and officers continued to wrestle with occupational "problems" throughout the 1920s and 1930s. Anticipating entry into a second global conflict, the

War Department issued a *Basic Field Manual on Military Government— Field Manual 27-5* in 1940. This became the "bible" of SMG novitiates, along with the Hunt Report.[16]

The military establishment's overstatement of its underpreparedness indicates a deep-seated ambivalence about occupation—one shared by the civilian population. Charlottesville's faculty faced particular challenges in attempting to invent a valorous tradition of military government, the better to instruct and inspire their students, while sustaining a resolutely anti-imperial self-image. More was at stake than just a defensive effort to rebut charges that the school was instructing "incompetents to be imperialists." The larger aspiration was to liberate occupation from any tarnishing association with imperialism, thereby affirming the virtuous identity of military government and the United States alike.

Instructors mined and melded historical material into a "usable past," informing students that American forces had occupied numerous places, sometimes for lengthy spans of time, over the course of the nation's existence. Indeed, without military occupation the United States' boundaries would never have reached their current extent. Territory acquired in the nineteenth century by purchase or conquest—Louisiana, Florida, New Mexico, and California—had initially been ruled by military governors before assuming statehood and gaining incorporation into the republic. Yale historian Ralph Henry Gabriel gave several lectures on these experiments in military government, lauding the sagacity of Winfield Scott in particular, an early exemplar of the tenet that good governors interfered only minimally with local structures, customs, and mores. Another of Gabriel's heroes was Leonard Wood, the physician-general who, as turn-of-the-century military governor of Cuba, had cleaned up this "pest-hole that was a menace to the health of American ports."[17]

Yet as Gabriel's invocations of an illustrious past suggest, it required an especially sharp semantic scalpel to sever military government from imperialism. Viewed from a different angle, occupation's extended lineage merely confirmed that the nation's history was, and always had been, an imperial one—in the Americas and beyond. The backgrounds of many key players in military government planning and training further evidenced the ruling elite's deep entanglement with empire. Tellingly, even those who decried Charlottesville as indicative of the military's empire-building ambitions pitched their counterclaims in decidedly colonial terms. Thus Ickes cited the

Department of the Interior's unique experience with "primitive people"—Native Americans, in particular—in championing his organization's fitness to furnish postwar administrators. "Superintendents of the Indian Reservations, men who have priceless experience in the actual administration of non-white peoples, could be asked to share their knowledge and experience," enthused Dr. Saul Padover, in a bid to translate Ickes's ideas into action. As for FDR, despite his vaunted anticolonial inclinations and preference for civilian rule, he had endorsed a Marine Corps recommendation that Haiti be placed under "unimpeded military government" after he visited Hispaniola in 1917 as assistant secretary of the navy. While there, Roosevelt had looked into purchasing a plantation, and later bragged, misleadingly, that he had personally written Haiti's constitution.[18]

Attempting to square the circle by shaking off imperialism's pejorative connotations, Gabriel and other Charlottesville instructors stressed the singular virtue of U.S. military rule overseas. American history "affords, to its honor, examples of the occupation of territory not for profit, not for the restoration of a previous sovereign, nor to compel the signing of a treaty or the payment of reparations; occupations where the motive of benevolence was predominant," boasted Lieutenant Colonel Paul Shipman Andrews. In Cuba, the Philippines, Haiti, and Puerto Rico alike, Andrews claimed, the United States had no goal other than to build "a capacity for self-respecting autonomy," with a view to leaving these countries "better than we found them." Ironically, these assertions of valor—with imperial rule conceived as a tutelary trusteeship of unspecified but finite duration—replicated standard self-justificatory claims of European colonial powers. Rarely, after all, have states ever validated others' exploitation by trumpeting greedy self-interest as their objective. But in burnishing occupation's humanitarian credentials, Charlottesville's instructors ran into another bind. Senior military personnel preferred to see themselves as vigorous men of action rather than "Good Samaritan internationalists," an identity with less robustly martial connotations. Whatever humane ends military government might incidentally serve, students were constantly reminded that its primary function was to establish order in the interests of speedier victory. Thus Colonel Dillard admonished new entrants, "You are not rehabilitation experts going out to build four-lane highways all over the world. Your job is a tough Army job with as its primary goal helping the Army win the war."[19]

Of the many struggles to shape unwieldy material into an affirmative model for postwar military government, none proved more vexing to SMG instructors than the historical chapter that was probably best remembered by residents of Charlottesville. Gabriel's claim that Americans harbored no recollection of occupations past was a national generalization that overlooked a significant regional exception. In the 1940s, southerners recalled quite vividly that various Confederate strongholds had been occupied by Union forces during the Civil War. Indeed, military government of recalcitrant southern states had continued (in some places) for years during the era of Radical Reconstruction, leaving unreconstructed white southerners to kindle bitter memories of tyrannous domination by "federal bayonets." The horror stories conveyed from one generation to the next would trouble some southerners who found themselves reluctantly occupying former Axis territory after the war. African Americans and white progressives, meanwhile, recalled the betrayal of emancipatory aspirations by federal troops who proved unable, or unwilling, to check the terrorism of white supremacist organizations and were hastily withdrawn. Howard Fast conceived his popular 1944 novel *Freedom Road,* set in the era of Radical Reconstruction, as a warning that extirpation of fascism overseas—a parallel venture to the eradication of homegrown racism—would require an occupation measured not in years but in decades.[20]

One southerner on whom Reconstruction had left a particular impression was Woodrow Wilson, himself an alumnus of the University of Virginia. Brought up on chilling tales of Yankee bayonets, Wilson deemed the effort to enfranchise emancipated African Americans "unnatural, ruinous, and utterly demoralizing and barbarizing to both races." That the federal attempt to uphold black citizens' civil rights represented an abominable upending of the proper racial order of things was the prevailing wisdom of Wilson's day, an idée fixe given intellectual respectability by Columbia historian William Dunning and his acolytes. Beholden to racialized notions of fitness and unfitness for self-rule, this interpretation of U.S. history deeply informed Wilson's vision of postwar order after World War I. His insistence that defeated Germany be governed humanely by its conquerors summoned the mythic depredations of military government in the postbellum South as a warning of what could be expected if vengefulness were given free rein.[21]

Wilson's understanding of Reconstruction as a grotesque bacchanal, with Yankee occupiers maliciously bent on destroying a venerable way of life, buttressed the precept that occupying forces must respect the norms and traditions of conquered territory. Enshrined in the Hunt Report, this nostrum was reaffirmed by the 1940 *Field Manual on Military Government* with its caution against changing "existing laws, customs and institutions" created by the local population and hence "best suited to them." In tandem with this injunction, Gabriel relayed the Dunningite version of history as gospel. Military occupation of the South had been "founded on vindictiveness and hatred," he warned, a disastrous attempt to "change the culture" by avaricious and spiteful northerners. "Held up as an instance of an unsuccessful military government was General Benjamin F. Butler's rule of New Orleans," recalled SMG graduate Justin Williams. "By confiscating silverware, showing contempt for the upper classes, and jailing women who insulted U.S. soldiers, he had outraged the South, stiffened resistance, and hurt his country's diplomatic relations with England and France."[22]

Today's historians tend to laud the postbellum application of military power as a progressive venture in "nation-building." But during World War II the United States' "best" occupation was understood as its worst: unassimilable to the ennobling national tradition that Charlottesville's faculty sought to create. Instead, Radical Reconstruction was the historical exception that proved the rule. The credo that military governors leave indigenous traditions intact owed less to what would now be called cultural sensitivity than to extrapolation from racially overburdened domestic history. But while their instructors circumnavigated the Civil War and Reconstruction, military government trainees could hardly fail to register the undead past in a small, unmistakably southern town dotted with "Confederate heroes standing about in bronze." Many lived off campus in rented rooms or apartments where they rubbed shoulders with Charlottesville's residents. Responding to local prompts, members of the second class coined for themselves the jocular nickname "overseasers" in preference to the epithet locals might have bestowed, "carpetbaggers"—a derogatory term for Yankees who flocked south after the Civil War looking to profit from railroad construction and other speculative ventures.[23]

"Overseas-er, Parlez Vous" was one of several ditties penned by Charlottesville graduates. Performed at commencement dinners, these verses were then preserved in class yearbooks. Other compositions offer equally suggestive clues as to how trainee military governors negotiated the barrage of mixed messages they received about the responsibilities, hazards, and rewards of occupation soldiering. While Undersecretary of War Robert Patterson declared "we have no use for imperialism" before one class of graduates, students gleefully cast themselves in the role of pith-helmeted pooh-bahs. A marching song (to the tune of "Over There") included the chorus, "Keep the natives active/The girls attractive/The lands extractive all our way." Another couplet ran: "Rule the natives gently, or their hair may come uncurled/Rule the tribes with kindness, though you're torn and mauled." Turning their thoughts from Gauguinesque South Pacific islanders to the Japanese home islands, the overseas-ers' fantasies assumed a more vengeful air, envisioning the day when the SMG rulebook could be thrown away: "Some day in Japan, I'll forget all I can/And take war laws in my own hand."[24]

The particular challenges anticipated in occupying Japan prompted a drastic expansion of the military government training program in 1944. Original plans for Charlottesville projected that the school would graduate 6,000 officers over its lifetime: a figure premised on the notion that military government was primarily an adjunct to combat operations. Once the "tactical" phase ended, occupation would enter a "territorial" stage, with officers passing the baton to civilian administrators. But several emergent developments challenged the War Department's initial blueprint. Most obviously, the lack of any single civilian successor organization left plans looking "grotesquely inadequate" given the sweeping extent of Axis territory that wartime planners imagined would fall under U.S. control, perhaps sooner rather than later. By 1943, the tide of war had turned decisively with Allied victory over Erwin Rommel in North Africa. The Red Army's success in breaking the siege of Stalingrad in February had also forced the Wehrmacht into retreat on the eastern front. Together these developments brought forward the predicted date of the Axis powers' defeat, prompting the War Department to push for the production of more military government personnel more rapidly.[25]

The need to train occupation officers for the Pacific theater loomed increasingly large in planners' minds. Even with a truncated program of instruction, cut from four months to eight weeks, and with class sizes greatly expanded, Charlottesville alone could not graduate enough officers at the desired speed. Under pressure, Henry Stimson modified his earlier stance that the rigors of life just behind the front line put women out of contention for military government work. This reversal paved the way for four "feminine students" (as the *Atlanta Constitution* put it) to join a class of 250 trainees at Charlottesville in July 1944. But their token presence, which may or may not have mollified professional women disgruntled by the War Department's discriminatory policy, did little to boost the overall graduation rate.[26]

From the Pentagon's perspective, another deficiency was more alarming than the paucity of female military government officers; namely, the fact that Charlottesville students devoted just a fraction of their time to language training. Five hours' weekly instruction was hardly enough to gain even modest conversational competence in Italian, French, or German. And it certainly would not suffice to produce officers who could make themselves understood in Japanese. Even if the goal wasn't to "turn out fluent speakers" but "to be able to keep the native interpreters from deceiving them," as Colonel Miller put it, a good deal of training would still be required before officers could unmask the treacherous intent promiscuously imputed to all ethnic Japanese. Numerous go-betweens would be required to translate documents, offer cultural orientation, and mediate interactions in a prostrate postwar Japan. But by the War Department's reckoning in 1941, just sixty white Americans were enrolled as students of Asian languages in college, causing Provost Marshal General Gullion to lament that "acquaintance with Far Eastern languages, institutions and points of view is practically non-existent." On the eve of war, the navy and army separately scoured the country for white citizens with relevant linguistic skills, whether acquired as the children of missionary parents, as venturesome students abroad, or as commercial entrepreneurs. Strikingly, the first four officers of the Women's Army Corps (WACs) to gain entry to Charlottesville included a lieutenant born to missionaries in Korea and another whose journalistic background included stints in Shanghai, Manila, Hong Kong, and Manchuria. But such individuals, who had also to be in reasonable physical shape and under the age of fifty, were exceedingly scarce. So too were bilingual "informants"—the military's loaded term for tutors who took their charges through daily hours of language drills.[27]

A solution lay at hand. Yet the most obvious remedy was also hardest for wartime planners to countenance. Animosity toward Japanese Americans ran so high that, despite the advantages to the wartime state of cultivating and capitalizing on their language skills, military authorities remained hamstrung by mistrust and racialized aversion. In November 1941, the army's Military Intelligence Department had opened a small language-training school at the Presidio in San Francisco. By that time, several thousand Japanese Americans had enlisted in the armed forces, and fifty-eight of the school's sixty students were Nisei. But when the Fourth Army, which ran the Presidio facility, was also charged with sweeping *all* Japanese Americans into War Relocation Authority (WRA) camps the following year, "the difficulty of training Nisei on a West Coast bereft of Nisei" became "insurmountable," one wartime student of Japanese pointed out. This predicament beset military and civilian institutions alike, though the distinction was increasingly blurred. At Berkeley, with Japanese American faculty members incarcerated, the university's distinguished resident Sinologist, a Dutchman by birth, was rebranded as a Japan expert. Koreans shouldered the burden of Japanese language instruction.[28]

Over time, the War Department moderated its approach. Several thousand Japanese Americans from Hawaii and recruits from WRA camps—after subjection to microscopic loyalty tests—were enlisted into military service, though not before Representative Karl E. Mundt of South Dakota had floated an inverted solution to the problem of America's unpreparedness for the occupation of Japan. Rather than letting Japanese Americans out of confinement into the armed forces, he recommended turning over WRA camps to the War Department for use as "a proving ground for training Army officers in the techniques of military government." In Mundt's plan, the government would eliminate the "terrific waste of money" currently spent on instruction in judo and go (a game like checkers), while military government trainees, in their new guise as camp commandants, would glean insights into Japanese psychology, honing their management skills for later application in Japan.[29]

Mundt's scheme to turn interned Japanese Americans into military government guinea pigs did not gain traction. Instead, the War Department expanded special programs of immersive language instruction for officers and enlisted men earmarked for occupation duty in Asia. A network of Civil Affairs Training Schools (CATS) was inaugurated at ten different universities across the country, along with Army Specialized Training Programs for enlisted men tabbed as potential officer material. While the navy established a Japanese language school at the University of Colorado, Boulder, the University of Michigan hosted the largest of these ventures on behalf of the army, with a student body composed of both Nisei and white American enlistees. The more promising candidates were then transferred to the Military Intelligence Service Language School, which was relocated first from San Francisco to Camp Savage and then to Fort Snelling, both in Minnesota. A former hostel for indigent elderly men, Camp Savage was remembered by its alumni as a "hellhole"—its identity clumsily concealed from curious locals because Japanese training programs remained swaddled in official secrecy.

Although Japanese American students formed a numerical majority of the trainee population, they inhabited separate and decidedly inferior quarters, relegated to tarpaper shacks on a former turkey farm behind the barracks. Still under suspicion of incipient treachery, Japanese American enlistees also found their diaries and letters subject to routine surveillance and confiscation.[30]

Life for those at Japanese language training facilities combined grueling twelve-hour days of study with military discipline of sometimes absurd ferocity. Donald Richardson, a student at Michigan and then Camp Savage, recalled being gigged for such infractions as a "dusty dictionary."[31] But he and his cohort of white students nevertheless received a variety of privileges denied to Japanese American students and enjoyed at their expense. When Richardson and his buddies mounted a musical revue jauntily entitled "Nips in the Bud," their amateur production was adopted as a fund-raising platform for war bond sales, with special performances staged at Ford's vast Willow Run factory in Ypsilanti, among other venues. Although Richardson's memoir fails to elaborate, it's hard to imagine many (if any) Japanese American classmates joined the exuberant chorus:

> When we get our chance at the Rising Sun
> It's not gonna be a dud
> And you bet your chips
> That we'll speed its eclipse
> We're those Nips in the Bud.

Richardson was, however, uncomfortably aware that he and other white "nippers" were the direct beneficiaries of institutional racism in the services: "the living symbols of Nisei discrimination at Savage, Snelling and subsequent postings," as he put it. Unlike their Japanese American peers, white students were eligible for commission. As a result, irrespective of their linguistic competence, it would be white officers who presided over Japanese American enlisted men in occupied Japan.[32]

Long before the language school at Fort Snelling closed its doors in June 1946, the first military government graduates had set sail for destinations unknown. The adequacy of their classroom lessons would soon be put to the test. In purely material terms, however, they were hardly underequipped for whatever lay ahead. One officer fresh from Charlottesville offered his loved ones a detailed self-portrait on the eve of embarkation in August 1943:

> You may picture me boarding the ship dressed in high army shoes and leggings, khaki trousers and shirt, open at the throat, a wide canvass belt and suspenders harness, with a pistol, first aid kit, canteen, and ammunition magazines slung from my belt, a canvas sack hung high on the suspenders in back and stuffed with impregnated long underwear, sox, coveralls, hood, and cotton gloves; stuffed into the same canvass bag, but protected by the cellophane in which I have wrapped the smelly impregnated clothes, is my mess kit. Under the flap of the bag and strapped tight to it, is my "trench coat". . . . Over all this, in a horse shoe roll, is half my tent with two blankets, a mosquito tent, and a sand fly-mosquito proof covering, and my ten tent pins, the tent being the wrapper. Hanging on my left side, slung from my right shoulder, is my gas mask in a canvas case. On my head is a steel helmet. In my right hand is my big suitcase containing the other half of my tent, and my dark uniform, field jacket, khaki changes etc etc. In my left hand is my well stuffed brief case. . . . On a truck are my bedding roll and barracks bag containing everything I won't need till I get settled somewhere.

With each officer lugging more baggage than could be comfortably squeezed into a paragraph, it's no wonder space on board naval transports was so tight that enlisted men often slept in bunks five tiers deep, sometimes rotating in shifts.[33]

On the far side of the Atlantic, some military government officers were sent off to liaise with their opposite numbers in Shrivenham, Britain's counterpart to Charlottesville. Others headed to North Africa, where Field Marshal Bernard Montgomery's Desert Rats had recently dispatched Rommel's Afrika Korps. High in the Atlas Mountains, a joint British-American civil affairs staging area was established at Chréa in Algeria. Nicknamed Shangri-la, this hilltop outpost in a former tuberculosis sanatorium—"beautiful with flowers and silver cedars and flowering locusts"—was "a perfect setting for tired officers about to emerge into history." Mountain hikes, drilling exercises, and outdoor calisthenics punctuated further periods of planning, along with regular visits from dignitaries who "added the zest of actuality to the imaginary world of military government in the process of becoming." Dwight D. Eisenhower himself dropped by to offer exhortatory advice, encouraging officers to use initiative and promising that inaction would be punished more severely than action—even if the latter didn't yield the best results.[34]

Beneath the cerulean vistas of Shangri-la, the Maghreb at sea level presented several shocks to Americans newly arrived in Algeria and neighboring Tunisia. These territories, prized away from German and Italian forces, were not the province of Allied military government proper, political deals having been cut with former Vichyites that restored French authority over North Africa. For Americans of a progressive persuasion, this expedient arrangement—justified by Eisenhower as sparing the need for 60,000 U.S. troops to "hold the tribes quiet"—was the first unpleasant shock. Long strings of German and Italian soldiers were being marched into captivity, yet North Africa remained under the control of reactionary French colonialists. The Allied bargain with Admiral Jean-François Darlan raised troubling questions, to those minded to pose them, about the war's larger purposes if a modus vivendi with fascism could be so easily brokered.[35]

By no means did all American soldiers experience jolts of disillusionment in response to Washington's first retreat from "unconditional surrender." Most, however, recoiled from their first advance into North Africa. With its vivid colors, jarring contrasts, pungent smells, and unfamiliar flavors, Algeria was "every bit and more than anyone's wildest imagination can conjure up," noted army medical officer Dean Fleming. American observers rarely wondered, or attempted to find out, what local residents made of the massive influx of Allied commodities, materiel, and men—often drunk, invariably well provisioned—into communities that decades of colonialism and months of war had "already pressed flat," as a character in John Horne Burns's heavily autobiographical novel *The Gallery* put it. However heedless of their contribution to local squalor, military government personnel registered the incongruity of their insertion into a decidedly alien setting. "It was rather an interesting sight to see a group of 15 or 20 officers sitting on the sand or on the stones around a little park, gravely repeating Italian phrases, while baggy Arabs sauntered up and pestered us for cigarettes," Lieutenant Colonel George McCaffrey noted in his diary, stunned by the temporal and cultural chasm separating leafy Charlottesville from dusty Oran. Soldiers' letters and diaries brimmed with references to grotesque beggars, covered in open sores, that buzzed around like flies; the unshakable swarms of treat-seeking children; "veiled mysterious women," whose half-glimpsed faces "hardly seem[ed] worth the trouble"; and everywhere crafty swindlers looking to pilfer pockets or empty wallets of their contents by other means.[36]

In the shimmering desert heat, Americans' self-image as generous bene-factors curdled and soured. Rather than earning appreciation from the locals, largesse—whether casually dispensed sticks of gum or crates of U.S.-manufactured goods—seemed only to encourage cupidity. And the more grasping foreigners appeared, the less Americans liked them. Perhaps, mused Fleming, foreign travel under military auspices wasn't a broadening experi-ence, but rather a stimulant to enlisted men's prejudice. "When they see so many good things coming here and being handled by no-good natives, when they hear from home how difficult or impossible it is for their own people to get the same things, even the best Christian attitude toward a supposedly unfortunate and deserving country takes a beating," Fleming wrote in a letter home from Algeria in February 1943. He continued,

> This is what happens as long as the US Army comes to these countries with the policy of saving them, of helping them by giving away freely and widely the so-called endless resources of Americans. These people, or at least the ones most soldiers see, so obviously play the US for suckers with no corresponding Chris-tian spirit, that the soldiers get disgusted. In order to make soldiers happy about being generous with their own supplies, they would have to come to these places as conquerors and absolute controllers, and make the local people pay on the line at the time for everything they receive. If it was obvious that the US was gaining something at the time it was putting out, then there wouldn't be so much misunderstanding.

Finding gratitude in short supply as payment for generosity, GIs would prefer the transactional character of U.S. policy to be candidly acknowledged and, better yet, fully monetized. How dispossessed populations would afford American products if not by capitalizing on Allied soldiers' appetites in ways the latter often found extortionate, however pleasurable, wasn't a consider-

ation Fleming pursued. But the day when Americans would land in fresh locations as "conquerors and absolute controllers" was not far off. On the night
of July 9, 1943, the British Eighth and American Seventh armies waded ashore
at different locations on the coast of Sicily. Operation Husky had begun.[37]

In Sicily, fantasies of "absolute control" bumped against awkward realities,
as did plans for what was initially termed Allied Military Government of
Occupied Territories. "Very uneuphoniously abbreviated to AMGOT," no
one seemed to like the acronym. *New York Times Magazine* columnist Herbert Matthews thought it sounded "too much like AMTORG or OVRA or
something else undemocratic," while the *Raleigh News and Observer* discerned
a hint "that the Allies have gotten something and may attempt to keep it,"
proposing ARCON as an alternative, Allied Assistance for Reconstruction
of Countries Overrun by Nazis. It was perhaps just as well that an anonymous (perhaps apocryphal) linguist soon let slip that the totalitarian-sounding
term meant "horse buns" in Turkish. Thereafter, occupation under combined
British-American auspices went by the castrated designation AMG.[38]

As a harbinger of the postwar world, AMG's progress was carefully moni-
tored by the U.S. press. Fittingly, then, it was a twenty-nine-year-old journalist, John Hersey, who would deliver the most abiding depiction of military
government in the form of *A Bell for Adano*, a durable template for the "good
occupation" that self-consciously sought to boost emotional mobilization on
the home front. Published "hot off the griddle of war" in February 1944,
Hersey's novel was soon adapted for the stage by Paul Osborn, becoming a
Broadway sensation before conversion to the big screen by Twentieth Century
Fox in 1945. With uncanny synchronicity, the "first novel of postwar," as one
reviewer dubbed it, was awarded a Pulitzer Prize on V-E Day, making Hersey
the only first-time novelist to have achieved that distinction to date.[39]

A Bell for Adano combined eyewitness observation with a substantial
dash of wishful thinking. Hersey had spent a week at Licata, near the scene
of the American landings at Gela, reporting on AMGOT's rollout for *Time*
and *Life* magazines. Returning home with a notebook of jotted impressions
and the pocket diary of Charlottesville graduate Major Frank Toscani, Hersey
transformed a feature written for *Life* into a full-length novel, produced in
three weeks of "angry haste." This propulsive energy flowed from Hersey's
dismay over the primacy AMG accorded to military necessity, spiked by a

FIG. 1.2 Twentieth Century Fox hopes to capitalize on the phenomenal popularity of John Hersey's novel with its 1945 release of *A Bell for Adano*, extolling its "superb drama . . . glorious romance . . . matchless emotion!"

more personal animus against General George S. Patton. The latter made a barely fictionalized appearance in *A Bell for Adano* as General Marvin—a "bad man, something worse than what our troops were trying to throw out." A device for Hersey to divulge through fiction what wartime censorship debarred from publication as fact, Marvin served as a foil to Hersey's hero, Major Victor Joppolo, loosely modeled on Toscani.[40]

Hersey's Victor embodies virtues—sincerity, generosity, and vitality—cherished as quintessentially American. By dint of his Italian heritage, Joppolo, a thoroughly assimilated Bronx sanitation worker in civilian life, is uniquely attuned to the local population's spiritual as well as material needs. He thus understands that what Adano's inhabitants crave above all else is a new church bell, the original having been carted off by the fascists to melt down for munitions. As de facto mayor, Joppolo gets the fishermen fishing, the flour mill milling, and the streets swilled of centuries of filth. He also administers rudimentary lessons in democracy, taking his place at the back of the breadline rather than elbowing to the front, as Adano's fascist rulers had. Tempted by the alluring blond belle of Adano, Tina, Joppolo exhibits commendable restraint; despite feeling "terribly lonely," he remembers his wife back home and Tina's fiancé in a POW cage. Finally, the ingenious major manages to procure a suitable liberty bell. But along the way, he falls foul of the general, countermanding an order that peasant carts must be kept off Sicily's main roads: a military necessity in the general's eyes but a failure of human sympathy in Joppolo's. Without mule-drawn transportation, Adano's residents would languish without food or water. The novel's bathetic conclusion has Joppolo receive his marching orders—just as the first chimes ring out.[41]

In this schematic confrontation between the "good man" and "bad," Hersey restaged the civil-military dispute over the character and ownership of occupation that had riven FDR's cabinet. His influential novel made a decisive intervention on behalf of civilian values while fudging the issue of who (if not sensitive officers like Joppolo) would uphold them in the precarious interregnum between war and peace. By compressing all the novel's action into a span of just two weeks—a foreshortening the casual reader might easily miss, given the proliferation of incidents in Adano—Joppolo is, both literally and figuratively, saved by the bell. And since the major didn't have to see the work of occupation through, his creator did not have to resolve the conundrum of who exactly would do what in occupied territory, or for how long. In a bludgeoningly didactic foreword, Hersey did, however, issue a plea for readers to embrace their national destiny as agents of postwar reconstruction, assuring Americans of their singular fitness to make occupation good and of the need to make it stick. "Until there is a seeming stability in Europe, our armies and our after-armies will have to stay in Europe. Each American who stays may very well be extremely dependent on a Joppolo, not only for language, but for wisdom and justice and the other things we think we have to offer Europeans." The sympathetic Joppolo represents nothing less than "our future in the world."[42]

On publication in 1944, few critics troubled over the novel's shortcomings: its reductive moral binaries and buffoonish Italian "types" whose manifold unfitness for self-rule kept in abeyance any qualms over military government's sweeping abrogation of local sovereignty. Diana Trilling's evisceration in the *Nation* aside, *A Bell for Adano* met with an overwhelmingly positive, often adulatory, response. While admirers lauded Joppolo as a cross between Woodrow Wilson and Jesus Christ, the Council on Books in Wartime adopted *Adano* as an "imperative": a work that engaged citizens *ought* to read. Boosted by this organization's promotional apparatus and popularized by magazine condensation, Book of the Month Club distribution, and radio, theatrical, and screen adaptations, the novel became a touchstone for subsequent discussion of occupation, a reference point of assumed familiarity. That a sentimental fable should have achieved near total cultural saturation says a good deal about wartime Americans' craving for confirmation that the war was indeed good and that, under benign American leadership, it would yield a future that was even better. Hersey's mailbag bulged with letters from fans who, like the fawningly appreciative peasants of Adano, wanted to kiss the master's hand. Of these effusive tributes, none was surely more gratifying to the young author than one from Albert Einstein. Praising Hersey for the "considerable service" he had "rendered to equity and justice," Einstein confessed that he had begun the novel at midnight and stayed up until five o'clock in the morning, unable to put *A Bell for Adano* down, such was the "indescribable pleasure" it afforded.[43]

If *A Bell for Adano* served a feel-good function for civilians, the perfect antidote to visions of American gauleiters and colonial satraps, it filled a more specific void for those military trainees who longed to understand the war, and their role in it, in progressive terms. Despite (or perhaps in part because of) its scathing depiction of Patton, the novel was adopted as an unofficial primer by enlisted men and officers alike. "The book is the talk of the town here," Margaret Clement informed Hersey, writing from Charlottesville, where her husband was a student. "You have done a good job and a worthy one too, for in choosing the novel as a vehicle for your account, you have made the facts more potent to the average civilian and soldier." Corroborating the point, Corporal Sam Pillsbury wrote Hersey from Camp Reynolds, Pennsylvania, to tell him that no fewer than fifty members of his Army Specialized Training Program had read the book in a two-week period "as regular reading for a course on Military Government": "All who read it agreed it represented a very fine piece of writing and that it analyzed clearly at least one main aim of this war. Most men in the Army have little or no idea of the war's real purpose. I think you will agree that the bland vapid generalizations that come out of Washington do little to clarify the average soldier's mind, either. Many of us are headed for Military Government and the picture of Major Joppolo will remain a vivid guide to use when we hit our particular Adanos."[44]

Military government personnel who had already hit their Adanos, some of whom had met Hersey during his brief stint in Sicily, tended to take a dimmer view of both the novel and AMGOT's initial excursion. Among them was Maurice Neufeld, a military government officer whose civilian background was in labor relations in the New York state legislature. On the eve of his departure from Sicily for Salerno in January 1944, Neufeld grimly concluded that "AMGOT has a C record and no more." Had he given Hersey's novel a grade, it would undoubtedly have been even lower. Neufeld and his wife, Hinda, an enthusiastic reader keen to hear from one of the novel's life models whether *A Bell for Adano* "rang true," had ongoing exchanges about the book that was making such a splash. Even before Neufeld read it, based on what he'd heard from both his spouse and the army's public relations section, he was thoroughly turned off: it "sounds like pure shit to me, sicklied o'er with the pale cast of sentiment at that." Warming his theme, Neufeld continued:

> Hersey, whom I did meet, must necessarily have been superficial. He doesn't know the first thing about military government and spent only a week in Licata with Frank Toscani who is an able officer but who could never teach Licatans or any Italians about democracy in three weeks. Teaching them democracy, besides, at this stage of the game, is not the important job, and it's not taught as such. It's taught by reestablishing their own pre-Fascist institutions and teaching them to work within those frameworks, by getting the schools started, by making their agricultural and labor organizations more efficient, by doing all those unsung tasks no nation, not even America, and no people, not even Americans, ever really honors.[45]

That the day-to-day work of occupation was largely thankless, decidedly unglamorous, and of daunting magnitude were recurrent themes of Neufeld's voluminous correspondence from Sicily and later from mainland Italy. Quite how one taught democracy—whether by practical demonstration or homespun homily—would continue to perplex officers taught at Charlottesville that reeducation was emphatically *not* their job. Of doubtful pedagogical value, one of Neufeld's first assignments was to clear human and animal excreta, along with the carcasses of dead horses, from Gela because, as Lieutenant Colonel Charles Poletti put it, "General Patton found the littered streets a menace to Army traffic and health and a distasteful reminder of the hygienically unregenerate ways of Sicilians." Deficient "hygiene" would be repeatedly decried by occupying Americans in Italy. Personnel trained at Yale had learned from portraitist and art historian (later "monuments man") Deane Keller to expect "some very peculiar toilet arrangements"—the Italians "preferring to squat and hold on to iron rails rather than sit to evacuate the bowels." "To us, this is not as good as mono-metal, tile, and porcelain work with accessories," Keller acknowledged. "But it exists, and must be accepted for the *moment* at least!" Elsewhere, too, Americans would gauge the civility or backwardness of local populations by how, and whether, they disposed of waste matter, most particularly that produced by the human body.[46]

Recounting sensations and experiences in Sicily, American officers routinely twinned "filth" with "sloth," locating backward Sicilian peasants in a different century, or even millennium, from the occupying forces. Although Neufeld attempted to sustain a progressive self-understanding, duly reminding himself that Sicilians—subject to serial occupations by Phoenicians, Greeks, Carthaginians, Romans, and Moors—strategically deployed dilatoriness as a weapon of the weak, he still struggled to suppress feelings of repugnance. "At times I find myself in despair, and almost hating them for their sloth," Neufeld confided to his wife in November 1943. When Hinda read her husband's Sicilian diary, what struck her most was the pungent whiff that lifted from the pages. "One never gathered that there was that much filth from Hersey's book," she marveled, speculating that the author's background, as the son of missionaries in China, might explain this omission rather than any deliberate attempt to prettify Adano. The "Orient . . . probably isn't very much cleaner," Hinda mused.[47]

Others trained similarly orientalizing lenses on the Sicilians. Men who landed on the island fresh from North Africa were apt to engage in comparative evaluations of the foreign populations they had encountered thus far. Sicilians often fared poorly, their whiteness and Europeanness insuffi-

ciently pronounced to spare them from stigmatizing judgment. Philip Broadhead (who briefly belonged to Toscani's team at Licata) couldn't understand
why the locals "find so much to complain about," blessed with bountiful or-
anges, lemons, and apples and abundant crops of almonds and walnuts—"all
this plus good scenery etc." Fleming, who had earlier decried Algerians'
grasping acquisitiveness, noted that in Sicily, "housing, roads, water supplies,
what railroads there are—all are in primitive shape, considerably lower standards than in North Africa. The people all know how to say 'Gimme' and
hang around all day, looking for handouts and pick-ups. Like WPA workers,
they have no special gratitude, but simply come back for more. The world, and
especially the USA, owes them a living." Just days after the initial landings on
Sicily, Fleming anticipated that, although there weren't any Arabs on the island, Sicilians would "probably be as bad once things quiet down." In the first
instance, however, the carabinieri, clergy, and dignitaries displayed an "almost
embarrassing readiness" to genuflect before the occupiers. Fawning shows of
sycophancy struck some members of their audience as even more distasteful
than rank ingratitude. The latter at least had the virtue of honesty.[48]

As in North Africa, officers tended to be more conscious of what Americans did for local inhabitants than the things occupying soldiers did *to* them.
But abuses were so common, and sometimes so egregious, that they couldn't
be completely ignored. Although Hersey relegated rumors of rape to the mar-
gins of Adano, with the oblique insinuation that they could be discounted
as a debased currency peddled by the former fascist mayor, Major Toscani's
notebook documented "many complaints regarding molesting of women by
American soldiers." So, too, did numerous weekly and monthly reports produced by AMGOT officers. Neufeld's terse initial diary entry on Sicily noted,
as the very first order of business, the need to straighten out "the matter of
two Americans soldiers robbing a carabinieri and shooting one. They then
entered the house, shot at husband, hurt father, and then attempted to rape
wife." Prevention and investigation of rape were not, however, subjects well
covered by the Charlottesville curriculum. One instructor, drawing on his
post–World War I experience in the Rhineland, even informed students there
that there was no such thing. With "such a plethora of extremely enthusiastic ladies" in France and Germany, Barber considered that "there would
seem to have been no sense in it." Although military government officers were
obliged to pursue accusations of rape, they "should always be unsympathetic
to the woman," he proposed.[49]

Following a pattern established in the past and later repeated in France, Germany, and elsewhere, occupation soldiers routinely viewed local women as easily available—their slatternly, voluptuous bodies a stand-in for the "taken" country as a whole. Poletti, a senior officer who came to Sicily fresh from a twenty-nine-day incumbency as governor of New York, gave voice in doggerel form to feelings of attracted repulsion toward Sicilian women, expressive of the deep ambivalence he and others felt about the objects, and objectives, of military government:

> A beauteous maiden, a smile on her face,
> With a breath of garlic, fouling the place;
> Listless housewife, no shoes on her feet,
> Washing and cooking right out in the street.
> I'm glad I came, but damn-anxious to go;
> Give it back to the natives, I'm ready to blow.[50]

Uncertain in their responses to sex taken by force, military government personnel were armed with proclamations that, among myriad other injunctions, forbade Sicilians from supplying it for money. Yet more sweepingly, women infected with sexually transmitted diseases were ordered not to have intercourse with occupation soldiers. But it was significantly easier to print such rules on large posters—in the hope that townsfolk would read and heed the occupiers' commandments—than to enforce them. Regulation of fellow soldiers' sexual activity, in its many permutations, was not a task for which Neufeld and others felt adequately prepared. The Supreme Headquarters Allied Expeditionary Force (SHAEF) *Civil Affairs Public Safety Manual of Procedures in Liberated Territories* further mandated officers to suppress "homosexual or other perverted or harmful practices," without offering guidance as to the remit of this instruction or its application. And what was an AMGOT officer to do when approached by a pair of Sicilian women for help in recouping two dollars earned from sexual transactions with GIs and then confiscated by British MPs? Neufeld instructed his wife to preserve this petition "for the files," finding it richly humorous, though perhaps Hinda was less struck by the hilarity of the officer's predicament than the poignancy of the women's determined pursuit of compensation.[51]

In broader terms, military government training failed to anticipate the extent of devastation Allied troops would both confront and create overseas.

Some Sicilian towns and villages had been pummeled almost flat in the course of battle and by aerial bombardment. Along the coast, whole communities had scattered and fled to the hills. Occupation soldiers found thousands of islanders living in caves, as they later would in Okinawa. With corpses decomposing in wrecked buildings and water supply haphazard, the specter of typhus loomed ominously. Aggravated by German scorched-earth tactics and Allied bombing, Sicilians' poverty was so profound that, as Neufeld noted in Marsala, even the doctor lacked shoes. No scenario postulated at Charlottesville had anticipated catastrophe of such magnitude. "Central problem: town must be rebuilt" was Neufeld's succinct take on the task ahead. Lectures by Charlottesville's Italophiles had conjured poverty as something altogether more picturesque; war as less thoroughly ruinous. Raw human need, as the occupiers encountered it, ennobled neither its sufferers nor those seeking to staunch it. Malcolm MacLean's report on his findings as "spy" for FDR noted that no specially trained military government officer "expected to find the Sicilians and Italians as dirty as they are, with as little sense of responsibility as they have, with as many techniques for chiseling and cheating and buck-passing as they have developed."[52]

Of Sicilians' many needs, none gnawed more pressingly than food. "Hunger governed all," journalist Alan Moorehead observed—with good reason. Military government officers were well aware that keeping stomachs filled was the dominant preoccupation of Sicilian life during the initial phase of occupation. Had they been seduced by local produce into imagining a land of plenty, American personnel could scarcely overlook the food riots that soon erupted across the island. Major Toscani, Hersey's native informant, made no reference to church bells in his notebook but commented copiously on problems of supply: the "disappearing" of dismantled motorized vehicles, endemic hoarding by farmers, and pervasive black market trading that put provisions out of reach of all but the wealthy few. During the first week of occupation, Poletti noted "such a complete lack of transport that a small consignment of flour which had to be sent from Licata to Palma to relieve a starving population was loaded into a none too sound city ambulance."[53]

As popular clamor for food mounted, along with labor strikes and other public demonstrations, it became increasingly clear that, unlike in fictional Adano, Sicilians were not people without politics, incapable of initiative and bereft of ideas about economic and social justice. Nor were they slow to make their feelings about the remaining fascist authorities clear. "Mayor was

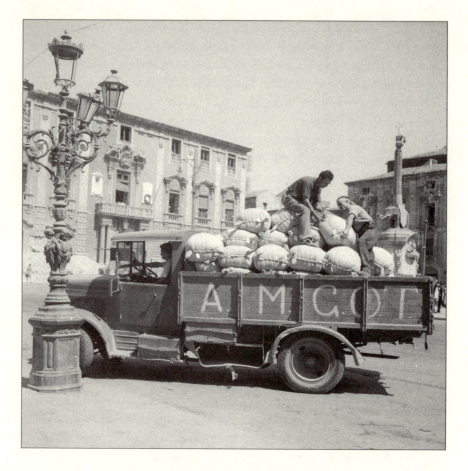

FIG. 1.3 An AMGOT truck delivers flour to a bakery in Sicily, where provision of food proved the most urgent priority confronting military government personnel, in September 1943. Photographer: Nick Parrino. Library of Congress, Prints and Photographs Division, FSA/OWI Collection [LC-USW3-040000-E].

clubbed out of town," Poletti bluntly recorded on July 17. "All government is evil to the peasant," he ventured, "and the worst feature of fascism is that there was such a lot of it." Military government officers' initial impression that Sicilians had been so completely cowed by the party and its overbearing minions that they were unable even to use the toilet without a permit gave way to more complex, often contradictory, readings of local psychology and politics. Densely crosshatched by monarchism, secessionism, and communism, Sicily's political geography proved especially challenging for AMGOT personnel to negotiate. Deciphering individuals' bona fides was all the harder on an island where organized crime syndicates had instilled codes of silence and habits of mistrust. Americans routinely remarked on what they perceived as a complete lack of fellow feeling among Sicilians, with insular communities tenaciously refusing to share hoarded supplies because "the people in one town do not care if those in the next starve to death or die of typhus so long as they themselves are fed and well." But military government officers displayed analogous tendencies, secreting and jealously guarding supplies in their own area to prevent poaching by their opposite numbers in neighboring communes.[54]

Since Allied officers often mistrusted one another almost as much as they did the Sicilians, and sometimes more, it's no surprise that leading players in AMGOT's cumbersome binational bureaucracy often disliked one another's political protégés. While British commanders tended to favor conservative forces, prominent American players aspired to cultivate more liberal elements—or at least wanted to be seen cultivating them, after the damaging political compromises of North Africa. Tensions between AMGOT's leading lights ran high. Its principal, Lord Rennell (Francis Rodd), a financier whose connections to prominent fascists in the interwar years were well known, was said by his subordinates to be in "open feud" with the most senior U.S. military government officer, Brigadier General Frank McSherry. The British aristocrat also drew particular opprobrium from Poletti. In an unguarded epistle to John McCloy, Poletti took aim at General Rennell, suggesting that he would do better to stick to grouse shooting:

> He doesn't know what really hard work at a desk means. He's always flitting about Africa or lunching with a Prince instead of being at his desk listening to discussions of specific problems and then deciding. He knows nothing of governmental administration. He is superficial in his analysis of problems and seems to carry a heavier load, than most people do, of pre-conceptions. Incidentally, they are of the kind that do not promote liberal democratic government. . . . General Rennell is the main cause of AMGOT HQ ineffectiveness. The leader sets the pace and it has been a wobbling shuffle!

Despite Eisenhower's admonishments to officers at Chréa to show initiative, Poletti and others deemed administrative verve one of AMGOT's scarcer

commodities. The old complaint that military government attracted medi-
ocrities, serving simultaneously as a retirement pasture for army duds, persisted. One wag reworked the acronym as Ancient Military Gentlemen on
Tour.[55]

Criticism, like the local wine, flowed freely all around. U.S personnel
chafed at British dominance of AMGOT, certain that "the British 'blundering through' is only a pose," as Leon David put it. While they complained
loudly about the Brits' "colonial" condescension toward the Italians, and
British officers grumbled about the Yanks' boorishness, Americans also took
frequent jabs at one another. Personal animosities were not contained by national kinship, with class prejudice sometimes trumping other affiliations.
Neufeld was aghast at how easily gulled by local elites his fellow countrymen
were: how impressed by status, how susceptible to flattery, and how quick to
equate means with merit.[56]

The prominence of Italian Americans in AMGOT stirred a good deal of
barbed comment in Sicily, along with some carping from the stateside press.
The gregarious Poletti was a particularly polarizing figure. Lionized in the
New York Times, and the subject of several flattering magazine features, some
likening him to Hersey's "Mister Major," Poletti was lambasted by the Hearst
press for having pardoned a number of "labor sluggers and goons" during his
three-week tenure in Albany. Worse yet, he was reported to have engaged
mob boss Vito Genovese as an interpreter—a rumor Poletti deemed libelous,
suspecting Fiorello La Guardia as its likely source. To detractors, Poletti was
variously "too anti-fascist," too hostile to the monarchy, too ambitious, and
too gluttonous for publicity. Far from establishing his fitness to build cross-
cultural bridges à la Joppolo, Poletti's lineage as the son of an Italian stone-
cutter was a positive demerit in critics' eyes. Kenneth Royall, visiting Italy
on a War Department reconnaissance mission in 1944, gathered numerous
reports that "high social Italians" disdained "Poletti and his ilk" as "poor
immigrants" unfit for seniority of command. Fellow officers denounced
his handling of people as "too rough." And, proving that the British held no
monopoly on condescension, an outspoken Texan complained that Poletti
was just "not the proper class of person." Royall concluded his visit by noting
that he had "never seen as much personal conflict in one organization."[57]

Many AMGOT insiders agreed. They were, after all, Royall's primary
informants. In their estimation, if not that of a generally more appreciative
American press, military government had flunked its first test. But diagnos-

ticians of the Sicilian malady, even those who traced its source to the same infection, offered divergent prescriptions. Where some observers perceived too much lenience toward the local population, others felt Italians were being "kicked around too much." Both tendencies were routinely blamed on Italian Americans, whether because they fraternized too freely (in the first scenario) or were determined to prove themselves a cut above the locals (in the second). Either way, contra Hersey, the contribution of "hyphenated" Americans to the project of occupation was called into question. At issue was whether Italian immigrants to the United States had failed to assimilate sufficiently, hence their eagerness to embrace ancestral allegiances, or just the opposite. Mandatory "Americanism" perhaps prompted Italian Americans in uniform to distance themselves so thoroughly from their ethnic roots that some bullied the local population to assert a new identity in need of constant revalidation. Similar questions would resurface two years later in occupied Japan—this time about Japanese Americans.[58]

Larger concerns about the mission of occupation, who was best suited to undertake it, and how they might most effectively prepare remained similarly unresolved. Critics disagreed as to whether AMGOT's numerous ills in Sicily—administrative inefficiency, political blundering, food scarcity, soaring inflation, endemic looting, and sexual violence—stemmed primarily from defective plans or deficient people, or some combination of the two. Reflecting on their experience in Sicily, several firsthand observers reached a paradoxical conclusion. Even as they bemoaned the deficiencies of their training at Charlottesville or elsewhere, men like Neufeld stressed the radically contingent conditions encountered in occupied territory. The ideal "first responder" was one blessed with unusual flexibility: someone capable of adjusting, with ingenuity and empathy, to rapidly shifting circumstances. But if war invariably generated chaos—on a scale that couldn't be known in advance, and to which occupation added further dislocations—then detailed postwar planning was arguably a fool's errand. And if the ability to manage unpredictability was the most desirable attribute of a good occupier, it remained unclear whether adaptability could be taught. Neufeld himself was adamant that occupation ought to be the province of carefully prepared civilian administrators. Others doubted it.[59]

Skepticism about training for occupation—what it should comprise, and whether it should even be attempted—was not confined to those who feared the postwar ambitions of "American gauleiters," rubbishing the very idea of occupation. Those who most ardently embraced the mission included the loudest champions of improvisation. Hersey, whose novel was regarded as a training manual of sorts by eager enlistees, had his protagonist tear up his lecture notes on page fourteen of *A Bell for Adano* and rely instead on a single sheet of "Notes to Joppolo from Joppolo." Twentieth Century Fox went a step further as it set about turning the novel into a motion picture. The studio preferred to see Joppolo as a combat soldier with no special training for military government who found himself unexpectedly thrust into the role. "I think he becomes a better and a somewhat more human character if he accomplishes this without having studied for it—if he doesn't particularly like the job he draws, and would rather have gone on with the invasion troops. In this fashion he does a good job just because he can't help doing a good job. I think it reflects something more of credit to our democracy, and to the Service," proposed Anthony Muto, Fox's Washington representative, addressing the head of the War Department's feature film section. Veterans of AMGOT, by contrast, were more inclined to see misplaced faith in improvisation as constitutive of the problem, not its solution.[60]

Fewer observers of wartime's emergent postwar scene questioned Sicily's suitability as a model for the occupation of Germany and Japan. Following Mussolini's ouster and the king's surrender, Italy became a "cobelligerent," engaged in a joint exercise to oust German troops from the north while under Allied occupation in the south. Cobelligerency meant "treating the Italians as friends and foes at the same time," one British diplomat dryly remarked, or like "an enemy on parole," in Max Ascoli's apt phrase. Italy's idiosyncratic status blurred the Allies' attempt to draw a rigid distinction between the Axis powers proper and territory wrested from their control. "Military government" would preside over Germany and Japan, while "civil affairs" officers would administer "liberated" territory. Since the terms referred to the same personnel, who had undergone the same training, the distinction lay in the two designations' semantic connotations. "Civil affairs" was purposely intended to imply more benign treatment than "military government." It's telling, then, that AMGOT was billed as a venture in civil affairs, signaling a less draconian occupation regime for Italy than the fate imagined for the other Axis powers. AMGOT could thus appear, in American journalists' eyes at least, as "a kind of alien Santa Claus in uniform, very severe but at the same time strictly fair and singularly generous" without provoking a hail of protest that the Sicilians were being coddled.[61]

As the war continued into 1944 and 1945, the Allies' commitment to imposing drastic terms on their principal foes deepened. The aftermath of unconditional surrender would be a total transformation of Germany and Japan under the aegis of Allied occupation. For an unspecified number of years, the victors would undertake invasive surgery on an unprecedented scale: destroying not only their defeated enemies' war-making capacity but also the desire of those states' citizens to make war. A reconstructive project of such sweeping ambition would call for control over every aspect of German and Japanese society. And if this was the formally proclaimed long-range goal of occupation, the mantra that military government was "a sort of superstructure preserving local customs and psychology as much as possible" would have to go. Experience in Sicily made plain what had been deliberately obscured in the course of training: that occupation invariably created new "facts on the ground." The task in Germany and Japan would require military government personnel to jettison the tenet they'd been taught at Charlottesville. Out went the idea that their job had "nothing to do with the post-war regimes of enemy countries," and hence "no politics in it." Changing local traditions and rooting out ideological impurity was, henceforth, precisely the point.[62]

Chapter 2

"THE LIFE OF CONQUERORS"

When General George S. Patton, commander of the Third Army, crossed from Luxembourg into Germany via a pontoon bridge on March 23, 1945, he marked both the moment and the turf by stopping to "take a piss in the Rhine"—a triumphal gesture immortalized in his diary. (A marginal "Whew!" emphasized Patton's exultant sense of relief, as well as pride of territorial possession.) With water passed under the bridge, the general stooped to "pick up some dirt on the far side as a seizin in emulation of William the Conqueror." Inhabiting the role of victor came readily to Patton. Inflated with a sense of his own world-historic significance, he airily invoked the expansive rights of feudal fiefdom enjoyed by conquering heroes in centuries past. Patton's spirits were doubtless lifted not only by casting himself as the Norman conqueror of England in 1066, but by savoring his entry into Hitler's Germany well ahead of many present-day rivals. "You can tell the world Third Army made it before Monty," Patton crowed in a telephone call to General Omar Bradley, referring to his British nemesis, Field Marshal Bernard Montgomery. United in their desire to defeat the Wehrmacht, Allied generals were also in competition with one another to claim the war's highest prize, Berlin.[1]

Strikingly, Patton's account of his arrival on enemy soil made no mention of any Germans encountered along the way—only of other Allied generals and their driver. Few lower-ranking American soldiers experienced equivalent euphoria on entry into Germany. While four-star generals could revel in winning decisive battles, against allies and enemies alike, GIs found conquest a more fraught and fragmentary experience. Triumph was certainly not synonymous with crossing the Rhine. The Wehrmacht proved a sometimes elusive but stubbornly obdurate enemy until the bitter end, and combat wore on relentlessly for weeks after it was clear (to the Allies, at least) that the Third Reich was crushed beyond any lunatic hope of recovery. Victory was neither instantaneous nor felt in isolation from the foreign bodies Patton's account so completely overlooked. The sensations, privileges, and dissatisfactions of conquest were experienced in the course of interactions with defeated Germans. GIs recognized themselves as victors not by seizing clumps of German soil or adding water to its tributaries, but by passively observing, or actively enforcing, others' submission to superior force. Wielding such power could be as uncomfortable for some men as it was gratifying to others.[2]

Captain Payne Templeton, for one, felt decidedly uneasy about the business of conquest. A superintendent of public schools in Helena, Montana, Templeton had volunteered as a military government trainee. He undertook basic training at Camp Custer before transferring to Yale for specialized instruction along the lines of Charlottesville's School of Military Government. On his own admission he "never did fully adjust with comfort" to life in uniform, though he derived some professional satisfaction from his subsequent work with a military government detachment in France and Belgium. When he crossed into Germany at Saarbrucken, his first job was to find food and water for 5,000 "restless DPs [displaced persons] corralled in a city park being minded by U.S. army units." After a few days, he and his unit moved on, traveling across Bavaria, the southern region of Germany that had provided Hitler's fledgling National Socialist movement with its most hospitable cradle. Through Heidelberg, Nuremberg, and then Munich Templeton's detachment passed. But progress through the last was slow. The roads were jammed with Allied soldiers prodding German and Hungarian prisoners out of the city into POW camps on its outskirts.

With nothing to do but observe this woebegone cavalcade, Templeton witnessed an incident that inverted Patton's triumphal gesture. "There was one picture which will not leave my memory," he later wrote, "of a poor little Hungarian soldier in a front rank trying so hard to urinate. His straight was desperate, he just had to go. His arms were up when we saw him, but somehow he had gotten two or three buttons loosened. We will let it go with that. Such a pathetic gesture of a war's end!" Where pissing in the Rhine symbolized victory for Patton, the Hungarian POW's miserably wetted pants struck Templeton as the humiliating emblem of defeat.[3]

Within an hour of encountering the POW parade, Templeton and his detachment had taken over two "palatial villas." This expropriation also occasioned some discomfort for Templeton. It felt wrong to be ensconced in plush billets "in a world of desolation, ruin and hunger." But his fellow military government personnel didn't see it that way. "A war had been fought and won; and why weren't the victors entitled to the best they could find?" Templeton's countrymen and countrywomen answered that rhetorical question in multiple different ways, just as they took to (or resisted) the role of victor with varying degrees of ease and satisfaction.

FIG. 2.1 Wehrmacht prisoners captured with the fall of Aachen march toward captivity in October 1944. NARA [260-MGG-1061-1].

When Allied troops entered Germany, chastisement, not rehabilitation, was the first order of business. A total war launched by the Third Reich would fittingly conclude only with its total defeat. That goal was enshrined in JCS 1067, the basic directive for Germany's occupation formulated by the Joint Chiefs of Staff in September 1944 and entrusted to General Dwight D. Eisenhower as supreme commander of the Allied Expeditionary Force. Eisenhower, the directive grandiloquently announced, would be "clothed with supreme legislative, executive, and judicial authority" in the area of his command: phraseology that conjured power as a kind of magic cloak.

JCS 1067 asserted categorically that Germany would "not be occupied for the purpose of liberation but as a defeated enemy nation." Unlike France, Belgium, and other European countries overrun and occupied by the Wehrmacht, conquered Germany would not be free to govern itself as Germans saw fit after the Third Reich's collapse. Instead, the victors would sequester German sovereignty for a period of years as yet undetermined. The purpose of this quadripartite venture—since the Third Reich's dismantling would also be overseen by French, British, and Soviet members of an Allied Control Council—was to realize "certain important Allied objectives." Of these, the preeminent goal was "to prevent Germany from ever again becoming a threat to the peace of the world." In line with the agreement that Germany would be "dismembered," reached in February 1945 by Franklin D. Roosevelt, Winston Churchill, and Joseph Stalin at Yalta, JCS 1067 decreed that the country would be simultaneously demilitarized and stripped of industrial capacity. Meanwhile, ideological disarmament would proceed with the outlawing of the Nazi Party and its various offshoots. The directive called for the "immediate arrest" of Nazi functionaries pending trial as war criminals.[4]

Washington's wartime planners hoped that, over time, Germans would be reconditioned so that they never would never seek to plunge the world once again into war. But democratization trailed behind demilitarization, deindustrialization, and denazification in the "3 Ds" that spelled out Germany's postwar fate. JCS 1067 broached only "an eventual reconstruction of German political life on a democratic basis," dropping its series of urgent imperatives in favor of more aspirational language. In the short term, the implements Germans had—or could no longer have—in their hands mattered more than the ideas in their heads. But the directive pointedly enshrined the controversial principle that Germans were collectively responsible for the war and its devastating consequences, settling (in effect) the long-running wartime debate over whether there was any such thing as a "good German." *All* Germans would be made forcefully aware of their guilt; none could evade responsibility for the "chaos and suffering" set in motion by the Nazis' bid for world power. This imperative carried particular force as many prominent anatomists of Teutonic character foresaw that Germans would resist acknowledging either personal or national culpability. In defeat, they were likely to pin everything on the Nazi high leadership, distancing themselves from any role in Hitler's rise to power and the party's longevity in office, along with the appalling atrocities committed during the war. Most experts predicted that Germans in defeat would lapse into a lachrymose morass of self-pity. Devoid of sympathy for the victims of Nazi atrocities, they would weep only over their own suffering, for which they would blame others. The sole fault an unrepentant superrace could be expected to acknowledge was having lost the war, not having started it.[5]

Faced with a daunting mission and an undaunted enemy, the army embarked on a multipronged campaign to educate the occupation's foot soldiers about their role in the Joint Chiefs' ambitious program to disarm the defeated enemy. Indoctrination materials emphasized the appropriate comportment of GIs toward the Germans rather than specific tasks soldiers would be required to perform after the Third Reich capitulated. An Army Signal Corps short issued in early 1945, *Your Job in Germany,* frontally assaulted what its creators regarded as U.S. soldiers' Achilles heel: a guilelessness that could easily shade into dumb gullibility. Directed by Frank Capra with a script by Theodor Geisel (better known as Dr. Seuss), the film issued a stern warning that amiable American boys were liable to be suckered into believing that Germans were really just nice, decent people not so unlike themselves. Vigilance was required: a message driven home by a narrator whose voice dripped with sarcasm in rubbishing German claims to innocence. That Germans, not Nazis, were responsible for a long history of war formed a mainstay of *Your Job in Germany.* Hitler was just the latest in a succession of führers dating back to Bismarck and Kaiser Wilhelm. GIs were also reminded that, not so many years before, U.S. troops had occupied the Rhineland after World War I—only to be seduced by the attractions of Germany and Germans: "We poured in our sympathy; we pulled out our armies." What fools an earlier generation had been![6]

The best way to avoid being fooled once again, the film urged, was not to allow Germans close enough to pull the wool over American eyes. This time the job of securing peace must be done definitively, and that meant maintaining a safe distance. "Don't clasp that hand!" was *Your Job in Germany*'s first commandment. Occupation troops were stationed on enemy soil neither to befriend nor to "argue with" Germans. "Don't try to change their point of view. Other Allied representatives will concern themselves with that," the narrator chided, hinting at a reserve corps of experts armed with psychology PhDs. Occupation soldiers were to exercise mute vigilance over their newly defeated foe. "You will be aloof, watchful, and suspicious," the film instructed, echoing the language of JCS 1067 that had stipulated that the supreme commander would be "just but firm and aloof." The film's warning against fraternization was unyielding: no hand would be shaken, no home visited, and no German trusted, irrespective of sex or age. *Your Job in Germany* issued its direst warning against the "most dangerous" group: young boys in shorts and knee socks, who would look every bit like American Boy Scouts were it not for arms outstretched in massed "Sieg Heil" formation. Their minds poisoned by lifelong Nazi indoctrination, German youth were "products of the worst educational crime in the entire history of the world." GIs should thus give children an especially wide berth. As for women, *Your Job in Germany* discreetly avoided any mention of German fräuleins, perhaps to avoid unintended subliminal suggestion. The film's injunction against fraternization did, however, pointedly stress no cordial interaction "public *or private,*" and though the accompanying image depicted a gemütlich family mealtime, Sunday lunch was undoubtedly not the form of intimacy most feared by senior commanders.

Soldiers also received a forty-three-page *Pocket Guide to Germany*. Prepared by the Army Information Branch in 1944, the booklet delivered many of the same messages while scrambling some of the intended meanings. *"There must be no fraternization. This is absolute!"* the preface warned on page two. The work of occupation, the booklet stressed, was in large measure simply that of being there: "Your very presence on German soil will serve as a constant demonstration to the German people, that the master race theory that sent them forth to bathe the world in blood, was just so much tragic nonsense. According to its own values, they should be occupying *your* home town instead of your occupying *their* soil." But what were readers to make of a subsequent section entitled "Health" that cautioned that should soldiers "become exposed to venereal infection"—in whatever agency-less way such exposure might occur in the absence of "fraternization"—they must "report for immediate prophylactic treatment"? This was followed by another paragraph, "Marriage Facts," that detailed the near impossibility of marriages between American soldiers and "foreign girls" for reasons more logistical than ideological. Transportation for war brides would not be available "for a long time to come."[7]

Flubbing the message about resisting outstretched German arms, the *Pocket Guide* issued a less ambiguous warning to GIs that they should expect armed resistance. "You are in unfriendly territory. Your life may be in more danger than it was during the battles." The booklet predicted that about 500,000 of Heinrich Himmler's trained killers would "discard their uniforms and disappear into the anonymity of civilian clothes." These projections weren't simply scare tactics conjured to instill a properly martial bearing in occupation soldiers. Senior Allied commanders took the threat of organized resistance very seriously. For some, the specter of a last redoubt of fanatical Nazis in the Alps and a guerrilla "Werwolf" organization became little short of an obsession. Not without reason, American commanders feared that elite members of the SS and the party's *Sturm Abteilung* (Storm Troopers) would not meekly acquiesce to defeat, even if the Wehrmacht had done so and the führer himself no longer remained alive. When military intelligence reports sought to dispel the myth of the Werwolf in April 1945, General Bradley and others of a like mind still deemed it more prudent to expect resistance than reckon on all-out surrender.[8]

Thus, on the eve of Germany's defeat, combat soldiers in the process of becoming occupation troops received an unending stream of reminders about how difficult and dangerous their job would be. This was also the dominant motif that American civilians found in newspaper stories. In March 1945, the *Chicago Sun* reported that "some correspondents contemplated bullet-proof windshields for their jeeps while the Reuter news agency reported that all correspondents would of necessity be issued machine guns. And in addition, the talk before entering Germany was filled with bereaved German mothers sniping from their second-story windows, German underground gangs silently throttling American sentries with wire cords and killing others with multitudes of devilish booby-traps and mines." As the *Sun*'s ironic intonation hinted, however, these dire forebodings were already beginning to look foolishly overblown in the light of what GIs had begun to encounter on enemy soil.[9]

Crossing into enemy territory marked a momentous turning point for American soldiers—a moment electrified with epochal significance. Military government trainees and those who landed in Germany fresh from Army Specialized Training Program courses were intimately acquainted with this terrain on paper, having spent months poring over maps, charts, and statistics. For these officers and NCOs, the Third Reich represented their targeted objective. Hanns Anders was one of them. The son of Austrian immigrants to the United States, "Friedl" had completed a German area and language course at the University of Nebraska before arriving in Germany at the start of April 1945. With portentous gravity, he wrote to inform "Mummel" that he had reached "that country for which I have been destined." Meanwhile, combat soldiers fought their way in, not knowing whether Germany would be the terminus of their military service or merely a staging post before dispatch to the Pacific or China-Burma-India theater. But irrespective of past training or future prospects, almost every uniformed American who was in the habit of writing home recorded initial impressions of Hitler's semiprostrate homeland. How it felt to "come as a conqueror" into Germany—in Ike's robust phrase—was undoubtedly something that folks back home wanted to hear. Setting this experience down on paper also provided an opportunity to sort out, and perhaps suppress, profound sensations of variously occasioned unease. Although military censorship forbade soldiers from mentioning specific places and landmarks they had passed (within a twenty-five-mile radius), the rules didn't prevent men from documenting either physical landscapes or psychological states.[10]

Julian Hayes opened a densely typed three-page record of this turning point by contrasting a typical Sabbath at home with the "cloudy Sunday morning that I entered Germany": a counterpoint letter writers often employed to accentuate the chasm separating the cozily devout sanctum of family life from the parallel universe of combat. "Back home you were perhaps cooking a big chicken dinner, or dressing to go to church very much as usual," Hayes mused. "However, you may be assured that nothing in Germany was very much as usual on that day. Instead there was a picture of destruction, confusion, despair and hopelessness."

Hayes marveled that infantrymen had managed to break through the notorious Siegfried Line, "a defense of 'dragon's teeth,' tank traps and fortified pill boxes." The onslaught appeared to take complaisant or underequipped Wehrmacht troops by complete surprise. "Destroyed tanks, guns and vehicles lined the roads. Some were still sitting in the roads so we had to drive around them, while others were turned upside down on the shoulders or burned out in the ditches." Personal equipment and articles of military clothing also littered the landscape of hastily improvised retreat, along with an amazing number of "dead horses and wrecked pieces of horse-drawn artillery—this the mechanized German army we hear about." Only later did Hayes and his fellow GIs encounter human remains: "When we got almost to the Rhine the dead soldiers lay among this wreckage. What a gruesome sight it was! Everything had happened so fast there had not been time as yet to even bury the dead. Thank goodness the weather was cold (snow still lay in small spots on the ground) so there was no odor. . . . Words cannot describe the horror of this picture. I'm sorry if you're shocked at this. Perhaps I shouldn't write it, but it's just the way I saw it and I can't pretend to find something pleasant here."

When Hayes finally encountered living beings, an elderly man and three little girls, they all appeared intent on ignoring the American troops, affecting not to notice the conquerors' presence. But he wanted to scrutinize faces, not turned backs. Seeking exterior clues as to interior states of mind, Hayes hoped to find evidence that Germans had properly grasped the totality of defeat. Yet they retained an "arrogant look of hatred in their eyes," he thought. Neither waving nor cheering, they "still had that haughty spirit and disdainful bearing that Hitler instilled in them. . . . Fraternize with them? I should say not! Sympathize with them? How can one sympathize with a gang of murderers who have killed innocent human beings, are proud of it, and would do it again if they had the chance!" Any treatment the Germans received would be "too good for them and more than they deserve." But Hayes also favored an all-out reconstructive effort—the "best American teachers and educators, the best priests and missionaries." This would be the only way to "protect our own way of life and the future happiness of all peace-loving countries." Although he presciently anticipated home-front protest against the prolonged absences this task would entail, Hayes saw no alternative.[11]

Many American GIs pouring into Germany in March 1945 shared Hayes's deep repugnance toward civilians who appeared altogether too well fed and insufficiently contrite. "A fellow could shoot them and feel good," one soldier noted. Others registered a sudden barometric drop on entry into Germany from liberated France, Belgium, or the Netherlands. Military government officer Maurice Kurtz, a professor of romance languages in civilian life, described the peculiarly oppressive atmospherics—in lines laid out as verse—for his French wife:

> So this is occupied Germany!
> How marked the change between a liberated country and an
>   occupied one!
> The moment you cross the border, a pall of heaviness and fore-
>   boding descends upon you. There's an extra load to carry: the
>   load of being surrounded by the enemy on all sides.

At the moment of first contact, occupiers and occupied maintained an uneasy, watchful distance, exchanging hostile glares or impassive stares if civilians didn't simply turn their backs. Like Hayes, many soldiers attempted to decipher whether Germans' physiognomy registered dejection or defiance. Watching the enemy was part of the occupation soldier's mandate, after all, and many soldiers seemingly stared at enemy civilians as hard and often as conditions permitted. But whether impassive faces signified sullen acceptance or unchecked arrogance was difficult to tell, and the Allies' headlong rush through Germany made the elusive business of emotional detection harder yet.[12]

Having breached the Siegfried Line, military traffic traveled at "almost breakneck speed," Kurtz related, "as if we all wanted to get as much German land as possible behind and away from us." Village after village, town after town, fell with minimal resistance or none whatsoever. GIs duly noted the eclectic assortment of white articles—sheets, bedspreads, towels, torn-up shirts—that civilians draped from windows to signal surrender. Where Nazi slogans remained daubed on the walls of municipal buildings, these haranguing calls for resistance unto death and contemptuous insults toward the Allies bled with unintended irony. Leo Bogart (then a twenty-four-year-old intelligence officer, later a leading figure in media sociology) listed an array of these hortatory slogans: "We will never surrender!," "First work, then victory!," and "For the Führer, your trust and duty!" In some places, American troops found Germans hastily whitewashing over the old slogans. Perhaps they hoped to distance themselves from the party, or wanted to avoid provoking the newly arrived conquerors into shooting up communities with no intention of firing back. Maybe both. But since last-ditch German defenses were surprisingly feeble, Allied progress was accordingly fast. One surly corporal in the 4265th Quartermaster Truck Company complained to his wife that this undue haste was typical army BS. "You go lots of places and never see any of it," Clarence Davis grumbled, as though rapid advance were yet another privation the brass had dreamed up purely to inconvenience and frustrate enlisted men. Most soldiers were doubtless more appreciative of the forward momentum.[13]

The dregs of the Wehrmacht, supplemented by hastily drafted young boys and older men, failed to put up much of a fight in many places. But the absence of house-to-house combat did not leave German towns and cities untouched by war. On the contrary, Allied bombers had done their work, and precisely what they had done attracted much awed commentary by American soldiers who traversed the country on foot or by vehicle. In the rush to keep up, some infantrymen even commandeered bicycles and pedaled after the armored columns. One city after another appeared leveled almost flat, leading many to speculate that these shattered sites would never be rebuilt. Some expressed gratification at seeing Germany reduced to a state of such thorough ruination. Describing the scene he'd found in Mannheim in April, Albert Hutler told his wife, Leanore, that "it was a beautiful picture of what an air force can do." Others grappled to find words for such cratered, postapocalyptic landscapes. Emphasizing the destruction of organic communities, places that had once pulsed with life, they described Germany's pulverized cities as "skeletal" or "carcasses," "with the hearts knocked out of them," or like something "the termites have eat [sic] all the insides out," as Corporal Davis characterized one "ghostly looking" structure. To some observers, partially destroyed buildings resembled stage sets or giant dollhouses, hinged sides ajar. With exterior walls gone but some inner partitions remaining, rooms and their contents gaped open, suspended in both space and time. Here and there a bed remained in place, a lampshade dangled. One GI was amazed to see a German inhabitant making use of a lavatory, now exposed to full public view, in a semidemolished building in Kassel. Surrealist art seemed brought to life in such places. But everywhere traces of death lingered. Spring arrived early in 1945, and with March days feeling more like May, the odorless corpses noted by Hayes began to rot under the rubble. What the eye did not see, the nostrils couldn't avoid. The stench of death saturated the air—an invasive, choking presence.[14]

In Germany's unbuilt urban environment, soldiers routinely wondered where all the people went at night. By day, women were out on the streets stacking rubble in orderly piles with what GIs regarded as typical Teutonic efficiency. In some instances, occupation soldiers ordered these *Trümmer-frauen* to undertake clearance work or lose their ration books, a forfeit calculated to instill obedience. Often, though, Americans arrived to find rubble sorting already well advanced. Remarking on this industriousness, John Winner took it as confirmation that Germans were "not a conquered people in humility or initiative . . . not discouraged but energetic." They would need to be taught a little more humility, have their "talents properly channeled." Amid the death and detritus wrought by war, life went on. But where exactly was it lived? Perplexed Americans could only presume that German city dwellers burrowed at night into cellars and basements or camped out in rooms that might lack a wall, a roof, or windowpanes. In the morning, they would resurface, surprisingly well dressed and neatly groomed.[15]

Where German cities appeared both depleted of residents and only spectrally inhabited by those who remained, the countryside presented a different set of contradictions. Here was a landscape of often breathtaking beauty. The lush Rhineland and picturesque Bavaria—with its soaring peaks, spruce forests, fanciful castles, and colorfully decorated cottages—surely belonged in a child's picture book, not in Hitler's Third Reich. Geraniums tumbled from boxes in every window, and flower gardens were lovingly tended. What a contrast from the putrid cities! With lilacs in profuse, woozily perfumed bloom, Germany "smells much like heaven," noted Sidney Eisenberg in a letter to his sister and family in the Bronx. Occupying soldiers repeatedly puzzled over such incongruities. "I simply cannot comprehend how these people can live in the midst of such natural beauty and still be such stinkers," marveled Donald Sheldon. What on earth had these people wanted? Staff Sergeant Alfred Rogers rhetorically inquired of his spouse. Why did Germans, possessed of such sparsely populated yet fertile farmland, need to wage war for lebensraum? Having passed through shattered and starving European countries on their way into Germany, infantrymen observed that Germans were far better off than their neighbors. Whence this insatiable appetite to despoil others with fewer riches to be plundered?[16]

Germany's roads presented a less bucolic picture. American soldiers in motion across the country were astonished by the sheer volume of people also on the move: hundreds of thousands, if not millions, of people trudging wearily home or shuffling from one location to another, hoping for better conditions elsewhere. While some Wehrmacht soldiers had surreptitiously shed their uniforms, hoping to melt back into civilian life, others were being rounded up and transported into vast makeshift POW camps. Bogart offered his family a snapshot of the scene on April 7, 1945, one month before Germany's final capitulation:

> The roads of Germany now present a truly fantastic sight. First of all there is our military traffic, the endless convoys moving up, and other convoys coming back, uncovered GI trucks packed tight with German pw's. They look grey and haggard and unshaven, and there is nothing for them to look or feel happy about, despite the joyous tone of our propaganda leaflets. The men seem to be middle-aged for the most part; they are in green Wehrmacht or blue-grey Luftwaffe uniforms, with some Volkssturm-manner in civilian clothes, and even an occasional woman packed right in with the rest. One looks in vain, either among these Germans, or among the remaining male representatives of the civilian populace, for any examples of the classic Aryan superman prototype. I think that even for the Germans that myth must be pretty well out of fashion by now.[17]

While POWs were being confined, German civilians who had sought refuge from Allied bombing in the countryside were now in motion, if they could circumvent military government's attempts to ground them. Like many other soldier-writers, Bogart noted the amazing variety of rigs—wheelbarrows, baby carriages, hand carts, boxes on wheels towed by humans or animals— that people used to convey their pathetic bundled possessions. Extremity kindled ingenuity. For one African American captain, a college professor from the South, Germany's clogged roads, uprooted throngs, and improvised wagons evoked a historical parallel. This was surely how "Southerners must have sought their homes at the close of the Civil War," Leonard Taylor ruminated.[18]

Meanwhile, men and women from elsewhere in Europe who had been forced into labor by the Third Reich were heading away from their captors as fast as they could. Bogart, who had traveled east across Europe into Germany, observed French and Belgians setting off for homes and loved ones he could vividly picture: "I feel myself now in the position of someone who sees the two separate sides of a play meet only at the end. In the towns of France and Belgium I have seen the women patiently waiting, waiting for their men, rising in hope through the lonely, loveless days,—and now to see these men, brown and worn and gaunt and weary, trudging west on the dusty highways, laughing and pulling their collective baggage wagons,—this is something I can never never forget." "Each of these individuals has his own story," Bogart concluded, "but all are merged in a great collective story of Europe in exile, transient, disorganized by Fascism."[19]

Not all these displaced persons got very far, however. Guzzling what they took to be intoxicating spirits, some died from poisoning. Outside Leipzig, a group of former forced laborers broke into a railroad tank car under the impression that it contained grain alcohol. According to one American soldier, they "drank quite a bit of it before they started to keel over and die," realizing only belatedly that the liquid in question was brake fluid "from one of the chemical factories there." Elsewhere, some DPs drowned in liquor where cellars had been raided and bottles or casks emptied to create a pool of alcohol supped on all fours.[20]

Awash with refugees, Germany had become a "nation of hoboes," in the words of Paul Mitchell, a public relations officer with the 362nd Fighter Group. "Kids riding between cars. Whole families sleeping in blankets atop freight cars." Railroad stations served as points of exchange where journeys and lives intersected; where mobile men in uniform encountered others' desperation at intimately close quarters. Mitchell recorded impressionistic sketches as his unit's string of cars pulled into a leveled train station at Regensburg:

> People, displaced personnel everywhere, on the platform amid
> their pitiful luggage, squalling kids, sad-faced women, frolicking
> teenagers, and strangely quiet old people. Others live in freight
> cars alongside, 10–20 in a wagon, waiting for some engine to drag
> them home—Where are they going? What do they return to?
> Uprooted—family ties strained and broken, herded like animals
> into a fantastic world of pointlessness, devoid of real purpose, a
> "tired" world of ruin and fog.
>
> All are hungry—and rush to meet each incoming troop train.
> Men beg for cigarettes and scoop up each castaway butt. Kids
> throng the open car doors, eyeing our rations. It's not safe to

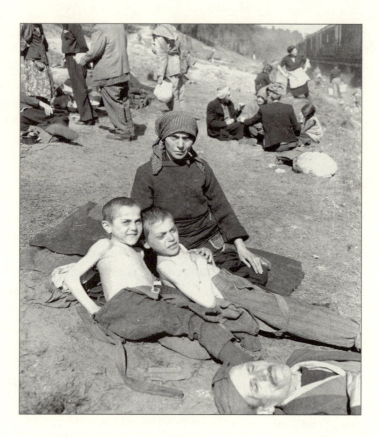

FIG. 2.2 "Malnourished unidentified Jewish ex-slave laborers wait for care from the United States Army and Red Cross," runs the original caption to this photograph dated April 14, 1945. United States Army Signal Corps/Harry S. Truman Library & Museum [61-173-19].

butter a cracker and munch it in open—you're immediately the center of attraction—and basic human envy. . . .

A middle aged woman begs Capt. Glazier for food—says she hasn't eaten in 3 days. He gives in to her tears—goes to her and gives her a cheese and crackers—she cries and kisses his hand. Moments prior she had bargained with GIs in [the] front car that for food she would "sleep with you until it kills me!"[21]

Such scenes were wrenching indeed: existence stripped to bodily need. But nowhere did Americans confront more visceral evidence of humans' tenacious will to survive—and more shocking evidence of the Third Reich's will to annihilate—than in the camps they began to encounter across the German countryside in April. Many incoming soldiers spent hours, and some passed days or even weeks, in former concentration camps: an experience that molded their initial bearing as occupation troops. Sometimes they entered mere moments after SS guards had fled or had exchanged their uniforms for inmates' attire. The disguise was rarely successful, however. No change of clothing could mask the guards' fleshy cheeks and ample girths. Their bodies bulked unmistakably large in contrast to the skeletal condition of those who had survived their captors' final frantic efforts to relocate inmates, or to force those still capable of hard physical labor to help burn documents and corpses. With Allied troops arriving, SS personnel hoped to save their own skins by passing for the very men they had earmarked for extermination. Naturally, survivors were quick to expose these cruelly ironic impostors.[22]

The SS masquerade was all the more brazen when performed to deceive the most senior Allied commanders. When Generals Patton, Bradley, and Eisenhower visited the newly liberated concentration camp at Ohrdruf, they were given a detailed description of various techniques of torture or murder, including a "whipping table" and "gallows where men were hanged for attempting to escape," strangled by piano wire. "One of the former inmates acted as impresario," Patton noted in his diary entry of April 12, which concluded with a cursory reference to the radio announcement of FDR's death earlier that day. Of the "impresario," Patton remarked that he "was such a well fed looking man that I had an idea he may have been one of the executioners." This intuition proved correct. A subsequent annotation in the journal confirmed that "2 days later this same guide was torn limb from limb by returning inmates." Ohrdruf was not the only camp in which inmates effected a final reversal of roles with their captors. In more than one instance, U.S. soldiers entered camps to find that survivors had just meted out justice to their former captors or were in the process of administering the coup de grace. On occasion, Americans in uniform also participated in these actions, sickened and infuriated by what they saw. On the back of a photograph of fellow soldiers at the newly liberated camp at Landsberg am Lech in Bavaria, Second Lieutenant Philip Broadhead recorded, "Shortly before this group arrived—some of the survivors of the camp recognized one of the former guards roaming around—as weak as they were they beat and clubbed him to death like a bunch of wild savages. Some of our group captured the camp commandant—he was turned over to 7 of the survivors for questioning and never heard of again—much quicker justice than Nuernburg [*sic*]."²³

The scenes found beyond the camps' bland exteriors beggared belief and hence defied description. Soldiers' letters, like journalistic reports, constantly stressed the incapacity of either words or images to convey what their authors confronted in the camps. "Too horrible to picture," Clifton Lisle recorded in his diary after visiting Dachau on May 10. "Piles of the new dead being sprayed with a hose, then buried. Masses of rotting bodies, stark naked. Thousands more dying in the wards. Other thousands in cage, almost naked." Yet however "unpicturable" its extremity, Nazi criminality also needed to be confirmed in, and by, writing. This too formed a point of epistolary emphasis, shared by soldiers irrespective of literary facility. "I am quite sure you in the States has no dought heard about these Nazie Consentration Camp that has staggered the imagination of everyone that has visited it so far," wrote Master Sergeant Joseph Jamison on April 25, 1945. Like other GIs, Jamison was determined to corroborate, and drive home, whatever loved ones might have heard elsewhere by providing his own account. There must be no skepticism—either about the camps' existence or their murderous purpose. American witnesses commonly doubted that stateside media had conveyed reality with even a vague approximation of its ghastly dimensions, simultaneously fearing that any description (however deficient) would be met with incredulity. "The stories you read are *not* propaganda but absolute facts," insisted Hayes with staccato emphasis.²⁴

Jamison established the scene, as many others did, by contrasting the "unbelievable beauty" of the landscape—"beautiful green hills, well kept farms, hedge growing all along the road . . . a lovely old castle . . . surrounded by lovely trees that were planted very artistically"—with the grotesque depravity beyond the camp's entrance: "Came to a crowd of GIs. Forced way to the front to see what was going on. About 75 to 100 men—or skeletons of men lying on the ground. Some shot, some killed with some blunt instrument; bodies a pale yellow or blueish color. Then came to a lime pit where bodies were destroyed by the Nazis after they'd been starved to death. In a house near by, 100s of bodies were piled up as if they were pieces of wood."²⁵

Jamison's impulse to make mass death real for those at home—so they would both credit other accounts and better understand the necessity of punitive measures—was shared by the SHAEF high command. Eisenhower was adamant that as many people as possible must inspect the camps in person: GIs, Germans, reporters, politicians, and other important opinion shapers of multiple nationalities. Various rationales underpinned the supreme commander's determination to make witnessing mandatory. Since army polls repeatedly showed that around a quarter of GIs failed to appreciate why the United States was at war, an intimate encounter with Nazi atrocities would (Eisenhower hoped) inject moral conviction into hitherto ambivalent soldiers. A stiff dose of "properly directed hatred" would serve the interests of Allied occupation by impressing on GIs the need to stay put and eliminate the organizations, personnel, and ideas that had produced such an unparalleled abomination.[26]

For German civilians, on the other hand, touring the camps would instill a better appreciation of their "collective guilt," a key tenet of JCS 1067. Eisenhower placed great faith in the power of face-to-face confrontation between bystanders and victims to dent Germans' moral conscience. To further stress shared culpability, American commanders sometimes compelled residents from adjacent communities to rebury the dead in more dignified graves than mass pits. No one could then claim to have clean hands—literally or figuratively. Cameras often recorded these scenes so that Germans farther from the camps could in turn be made to view images of other Germans burying the Third Reich's murdered victims. Not surprisingly, some resisted. One military government officer, exasperated by the throngs of civilians who jammed his office with petty complaints and requests, hit on a novel solution to dispel the crowds. He pasted up photographs of the concentration camps in the waiting area "for all the Germans to see." Since they preferred not to look, the crowds "thinned down to only one or two per hour."[27]

Germans' posture of innocence was one of the tendencies that most galled Americans in their initial dealings with residents of the Third Reich. No one, it seemed, had known anything about what went on in camps that often lay just a few miles from towns or cities. Such claims, repeated ad nauseam by Germans, defied belief. It might be true that inhabitants in the vicinity of camps had never been inside these sites of forced labor and mass death, but they had surely observed the arrival of trains, the pluming smoke from tall chimney stacks. No matter how blind an eye Germans had turned to whatever went on behind the camps' peripheral trees, fences, and barbed wire, they had undoubtedly smelled the charred, sickly aroma of grilled flesh or wafting currents of rotting matter. Eyes could be averted. But the nose, a more infallible sensory instrument, did not lie—even if its owner chose to. And it was often the putrid air of concentration camps that soldiers struggled hardest to convey in words, and then shake from nostrils and memory alike. "It was a smell like no other—as though the odors of all deaths, diseases and decays in that frightful establishment had been distilled into one distinctive, foul essence that shocked and revolted the senses," Major John Maginnis recorded in his diary, having just visited Buchenwald on April 29.[28]

German responses to the compulsory viewing and handling of victims of the Nazi regime remained opaque to American soldiers who enforced and observed these confrontations. Faces commonly wore a mask of impassivity, while displays of emotion could scarcely be trusted as reliable indicators of feeling. But whatever remorse, sorrow, or defiance Germans experienced as they were made to tour, and sometimes toil in, concentration camps, they surely knew themselves to be *defeated*—compelled by armed members of enemy armies to confront scenes, beings, and bodies they would have preferred to avoid. As for the American soldiers who presided over these forcible reckonings, they were perhaps especially conscious of their status as victors at such moments.

These encounters were not, however, the only situations in which occupying soldiers frontally impressed on German civilians their subordination to new masters. One of the first tasks of military government detachments, sometimes preempted by infantrymen's private initiative, was to requisition property to serve as administrative premises or billets. American soldiers approached the task in divergent ways. For Templeton, eviction of residents—with no regard for their political views or past records—constituted a "cruel act of war and occupation." Bogart, an acutely self-aware, Polish-born son of Jewish immigrants, also grappled uneasily with the absolutism that conquest required. "We are here as a conquering enemy; our safety and comfort involve suffering or discomfiture for Germans," he noted in a letter home on April 14, recording an incident in which he had ejected a German couple, along with a young refugee woman and her baby:

I know that we needed that house for our boys to stay in, I know
that the Germans whom we kicked out will find shelter elsewhere.

Yet it is not good to feel that even if only temporarily you have cut human beings off from their roots, from their home, from all the small loved amenities of life. Undoubtedly in the last half year my work has helped to break up many homes, to kill young men and bring agony to their women, but it has always worked through devious abstracted channels. Now I am personally an agent of woe, and this is no source of joy to me.[29]

But not all American soldiers experienced twinges of doubt or unease as they evicted Germans to make way for the occupying army or to accommodate camp survivors or other DPs. Milo Flaten, for example, offered his parents a lengthy account of how he'd booted Germans from their homes, remaining implacable in the face of inhabitants' manipulative tearfulness. In Flaten's story, the appropriation was entirely warranted by the weepy German girl's participation in an attack on downed U.S. airmen. The seventeen-year-old who dared to blub about losing her home had, Flaten related, not only refused to aid these Americans but spat on them. So informed sources said. "I asked her about it and she started to cry and mumbled sumpin about the war being bad or something so I hit her on the fanny with a rug beater and told her to stay out of my sight and that I was SS trooper. We usually give the Germans a better than fair deal but when we come on a town of out and out Nazis who are still arrogant and haughty well they'll soon change their ways."[30]

Other GIs similarly related expropriations in terms of unequivocal righteousness: a fate that Germans thoroughly deserved, just as American soldiers had every right to the best houses still standing. "If you see a house you like, you just tell MG and they'll requisition it," Sergeant Rogers told his wife, Norma. Fresh from experiencing Dachau, where he had been sick for days after guard duty required him to walk over piles of skeletons, it's hardly surprising that Rogers expressed a desire "to make it as uncomfortable for [Germans] as possible . . . to make them move out of their homes . . . no matter how fine they are, and live like kings for a change." What it meant to live the "life of conquerors" was a recurrent theme of soldiers' writings as Americans assumed occupancy of barracks and houses newly vacated by Germans, penning letters at the former residents' tables, sometimes even using their notepaper. These instant reversals—intimate occupations—could occasion unease, however. Certain places Americans stepped into felt indelibly tainted by their past occupants. Hutler, a Jewish military government officer in Mannheim, informed his spouse sardonically, "I sleep between pink sheets—in the front room of a nice apartment that belonged to a Nazi." At Dachau, Rogers had spent his nights in what had been the SS guards' quarters. To Norma he related only the comfy beds and convenience of a bath just outside the door. But dreams were perhaps not untroubled in such surroundings, no matter how good it felt to substitute a mattress for a foxhole.[31]

New domestic arrangements—with feather beds and flushing toilets—represented one of the most tangible fruits of victory, however bittersweet. Struck by the peculiarity of their position as temporary inhabitants of others' lives, occupation soldiers wrote in voluble detail, often on "liberated" letterhead, about the furnishings and decor of German homes. "We got a swell four story home, complete with practically new furniture, including tables, piano, chairs, beds, dressers, nightstands, etc.," Staff Sergeant Dan Self told a friend back in Mississippi. Like the three bears in "Goldilocks," GIs were quick to pass judgment on the mattresses in their new abodes. "Almost too soft," Self concluded. Meanwhile, in "ancient, low-ceilinged" peasant dwellings in the "undistinguished hamlet" of Gross Garz, Paul Haubenreich found the straw mattress as uncomfortable as every other aspect of this temporary resting place.[32]

Generally, however, American soldiers were more than satisfied with the domestic circumstances they had assumed. "Flowers bloom all over and the Germans take excellent care of everything. It's good to be a conqueror," Brigadier General Jack Whitelaw hurrahed in a letter home one week after V-E Day. Echoing the phraseology of Sergeants Rogers and Self, many men informed their interlocutors that as occupation soldiers they "lived like kings," enjoying regal luxury that not only far surpassed the wretched conditions of stateside training camps and privations endured by an army on the march, but exceeded anything yet encountered in civilian life. In some instances, enlisted men occupied lavish castles that had been commandeered as billets. Meanwhile, in Tyrol, Lisle steadily depleted General Hermann Göring's expansive (and expensive) wine cellar by consuming bottles of champagne with fellow officers on mountain hikes and "distributing, by ration, to all officers and EM [enlisted men] delectables such as . . . Veuve-Clicquot Brut . . . and Sandeman's finest port." Germany in the spring of 1945 was awash with both blood and wine.[33]

Some men self-consciously pondered the discrepancy between their own modest standard of living in the United States and the sumptuous perks they now vicariously enjoyed. If this was how it felt to "live as kings," how easy would it be to return to existence as a commoner? One month before the war with Germany ended, Bogart was already anticipating "reconversion blues." "It is hard for men who have weighed the precious essence of life in their hands to readjust to an existence of unregulated monotony (and to an appreciable degree, of lower living standards)," he mused. "The flying colonel who is offered his old job as an office boy, the Negro sergeant who has lived in a German castle and returns to the squalor of a cropper's shack—those are by now classic examples, but they are none the less to the point."[34]

The gap between FDR's promises of "freedom from want" and the reality of American poverty was not the only contradiction thrown into relief by the experience of occupying German homes. Many men noted a superabundance of Christian iconography—"last suppers etc."—and struggled to comprehend the chasm between Germans' apparent commitment to cleanly godliness and the terrible crimes they had collectively perpetrated. Aubrey Ivey, an infantryman from Augusta, Georgia, captured this bemusement in a letter to his spouse written on May 4, 1945:

> We are really in a nice house now and the furniture is beautiful they have a large clock that stands about 7 ft high with all kinds of chimes boy would I like to have it for our home. Darling the most beautiful pictures of Jesus are in every home you go into over here and in this home they are in most every room that is one thing I don't understand because every home you go in they have a crucifix in every room and they have large ones on all the highways and then on Sunday you see all the people flock to church.[35]

Others expressed deeper outrage. Noting that the Bible commonly ceded pride of place on the bookshelf to a copy of *Mein Kampf,* they couldn't help but wonder whether at least some of the ubiquitous pictures of Jesus hadn't hastily replaced portraits of the führer. More jauntily, Whitelaw turned the tables once again. He put his wife's photograph "in a frame that used to have a portrait of Hitler," assuring her that this substitution represented "a big improvement over Adolph." How flattering she found this compliment can only be guessed.[36]

The acquisitive eye with which Ivey admired the chiming clock in his new quarters hints at another pervasive feature of conquest: looting. Under military law, this was strictly prohibited, a point underscored in both the *Pocket Guide* and *Your Job in Germany*. The former insisted on its opening page that even "rifling of orchards and fields"—rather a petty misdemeanor in the GI scheme of things—was "contemptible and punishable by court martial." Had the army observed such scrupulous respect for German property, its personnel would have done little else besides attend drumhead proceedings. While a number of soldiers adamantly announced in letters home that "even though Germany is at our mercy we pay for things," many seized the opportunity afforded by chaotic situations to amass small trinkets, including the ubiquitous crucifixes, or more substantial booty. Germany presented itself to incoming Allied soldiers as "a world to be looted," writes historian Rick Atkinson, quoting a Twenty-Ninth Division unit report: "We're advancing as fast as the looting will permit." MPs who participated in this frenzy of acquisition earned the inevitable GI soubriquet the "Lootwaffe."[37]

Occupation troops accumulated Nazi paraphernalia with especial zeal. To seize party insignia, Hitler Youth daggers, and swastika-emblazoned banners was to stake a personal part in Hitler's downfall: a badge of victory in the here and now. But Americans also hoarded such items with a view to longer-term futures, anticipating the day when they would proudly show off these trophies to admiring grandchildren. Evidently not all loved ones were delighted to receive these articles, however, and they might have shuddered even more deeply had they known that nowhere was off-limits to looting. GIs even took "souvenirs" from concentration camps. Marion Davy noted that, on a visit to Buchenwald, his driver had made off with the mallet and apron "from the guy who removed gold from teeth of corpses before incineration"—"a momento," as Davy put it. Another GI tried to convince his wife, albeit through nervous laughter, that the stains on a Nazi armband he'd sent home were not what she thought—presumably the blood of a German killed by her husband. "I found it in some bombed out (ha ha) house. . . . The reason it looked so dirty was because I'd been carrying it around in my pocket for a while. Just throw it in the wash (ha ha)." Meanwhile, Flaten boasted, "I got me a kraut flag," before instructing his mom to "wash it up a bit" and "put some sort of a hem on it"—so long as she stitched it "without ruining the swastika."[38]

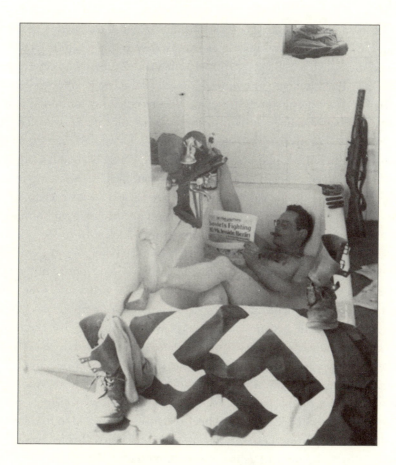

FIG. 2.3 An American soldier demonstrates the widely shared mania for collecting Nazi memorabilia as he reads about the Soviet occupation of Berlin. United States Holocaust Memorial Museum, courtesy of Monica Luke [93557].

Enlisted men were apt to protest that officers were the worst offenders when it came to collecting "souvenirs," as soldiers preferred to term their acquisitions. Collecting party memorabilia was, however, a mania shared by occupation soldiers irrespective of race, rank, class, or religion. Jewish GIs and officers were as ardent foragers as their gentile comrades in arms, sometimes incited to redouble their efforts by eager folks back home. Thus Eisenberg, a military government welfare officer, enthusiastically accrued swastika flags and other finds for his young nephew Bob in the Bronx, while seeing to it that his own newly acquired "officer's field coat" was fitted with a rabbit-fur hood. He considered the "most interesting war souvenir" an illustrated story penned specially for Bob by the former Luftwaffe corporal who served as his interpreter. But Eisenberg announced himself "completely flabbergasted that dad has a yen for a war souvenir," telling his sister that her son might have to relinquish a big Nazi flag. "It'll be the perfect souvenir for dad, who can hang it in his shop." For his part, Samuel Rosenfeld—a Ukrainian immigrant with a candy store in Philadelphia's Strawberry Mansion neighborhood—requested a different kind of memento from his soldier son, Jack, then serving in Germany. Writing to him in Yiddish in April 1945, Rosenfeld instructed, "If you meet a smart, respectable German pack him up in a box and send him to the Philadelphia Museum, and people will go there to look at him."[39]

Occupying soldiers did not restrict their collections to party emblems. The contents of German homes, vacated with two hours' notice or less, presented many temptations, as departing residents were well aware. One officer registered his amusement that the owner of a house he temporarily occupied had left notes beside her most treasured possessions asking that the Americans please handle her things with care because she "had lived in Brooklyn"— an entreaty they apparently honored. But many others refused the role of respectful houseguest. Even the punctilious Templeton, who regarded evictions as "cruel act[s] of war and occupation," noted in a revealingly passive voice that a "pretty little salt and pepper receptacle happened to find its way" into his topcoat pocket. Letters home often recorded this "light-fingered" behavior, whether by the writers themselves or by their uniformed compatriots. American soldiers' kleptomania quickly became a trademark feature of the occupation, well known to those on the home front from personal experience—as recipients of mailed loot—and from journalistic accounts. "Yanks' Looting in Reich Called Major Problem" ran a headline in the *Chicago Daily Tribune* one week after V-E Day, warning that "'souvenir' grabbing" was "apt to become a scandal." Soldiers would have to adjust to the "disappearance of all military excuse for commandeering and confiscation," warned the *Tribune.* Yet the work of occupation seemed not only conducive to acts of expropriation but positively to require them on scales large and small.[40]

The tall clock Ivey coveted for his Georgia family home presented an insuperable challenge to shipment home. However, almost everything portable that could be removed from office buildings, party headquarters, houses, farms, barns, and garages was fair game for the "Lootwaffe"—if the Red Army hadn't already staked prior claim by the time U.S. troops arrived. Since Soviet soldiers were obliged to "live off the land" by a military organization that did not equip its members with the abundant provisions Americans enjoyed, the former left little untouched in their eastern zone of occupation. Some U.S. observers believed their own countrymen did just as good a job of stripping Germany without the same imperatives of subsistence. Roi Ottley, the well-known African American journalist, was quick to point out how much exculpatory work euphemistic language performed. What was "looting" when enacted by Red Army soldiers was merely "souvenir hunting" when undertaken by their American counterparts.[41]

But license to loot was not unlimited. The army soon clamped down on mailing regulations to prevent stolen property being sent home, convening courts-martial to tackle more egregious cases in which soldiers robbed German civilians at gunpoint. Sometimes enlisted men assumed the guise of officers— with the benefit of props pilfered from superiors—to pass off armed theft as expropriation ordered by military government. "Soldier looting is great trouble," Lisle grumbled to his diary on June 16, 1945, noting that he was sending a private first class to a General Court on that charge. "He's alleged to have said he was an officer, a captain, and demanded a camera from the Burgermeister then struck him. At the time he was with a known Nazi whore. Too bad." In this case, the offender's behavior not only violated military law but also soldiers' own, more flexible code of conduct whereby items that could be loosely considered the property of an enemy army, rather than an individual's possessions, were fair game. According to this yardstick, it was acceptable to relieve newly captured Wehrmacht soldiers of their goggles, medals, watches, and so on, but a different matter to stop German civilians for "security friskings." "Taking watches was then clearly looting, not liberating," one member of the Eighty-Second Airborne Division would later recall.[42]

––––––––

Theft bulked large as a source of disorder during the final weeks of war and its immediate aftermath. Allied soldiers were by no means the only culprits. In bombed urban areas, German civilians adopted a survival-of-the-quickest mentality, rushing out into the streets after air raids to plunder shops blown open or pick through the contents of shattered homes. Adding to the mayhem were bands of former forced laborers—predominantly Poles, Ukrainians, and

Russians—in search of possessions, food, and alcohol. Columnist Dorothy Thompson likened roving DPs to "medieval landsknechte, killing game on preserves, carving out the steaks . . . stealing horses and having a wonderful time." But to most military observers, mass intoxication signaled latent menace. Entering the almost completely razed city of Nuremberg, Templeton found a scene of pandemonium with 30,000 displaced persons "on the loose—looting, injuring and killing, drinking themselves crazy": "The DPs were almost the only civilians around. As we drove along they would run happily to meet and greet us. Usually they were carrying bottles of champagne and other liquor, and sometimes they would throw these into our jeeps. Often the bottles would break, saturating the vehicle floor and parts of our clothing." For those in the vicinity, Templeton implied, the atmosphere wasn't one of carnivalesque revelry but bedlam charged with menace. Magnums of champagne may have been hurled in wild abandon, but the throwers' high spirits didn't blunt the shards of glass. Drunken mobs—often armed not only with bottles but also with guns—posed a life-endangering threat to themselves and others. If the streets of Nuremberg were bereft of civilians other than the marauding DPs, that wasn't because all German residents had fled from Allied bombers or advancing American troops. Civilians steered well clear of such scenes, or tried to, fearing for their property, and perhaps also their lives.[43]

In this maelstrom, military government personnel struggled to distinguish wild celebration from willful vengefulness; necessary acts of survival from criminal destruction. After years of forced servitude, DPs were raiding freely with a sense of unlimited entitlement. But Germans did not always surrender goods with passive acquiescence to the imperatives of postwar reparation, leaving occupation soldiers to adjudicate competing claims. In some instances their sympathies lay with DPs, especially when the latter found themselves violently challenged by German civilians. Bogart offered his parents a vignette in which "a couple of our boys" had "stopped a gang of Germans from lynching two Russians who had 'found' a chicken." His own situation ethics were clear: "A man is hungry and has no way of eating except by taking. That perhaps is fundamentally moral." Similarly, in Jena, Davy decided that former inmates of Ohrdruf had a superior claim to clothing hoarded by a German woman who sought American assistance against a crowd of ransackers.[44]

Other military government personnel arbitrated in favor of Germans, however. Some responded to the tug of ethnic kinship. Kenneth Clouse found that the population of Gau-Algesheim "looked and talked like the kind of people, the 'Pennsylvania Deutsch,' I had been brought up with in Reading. The bürgermeister of Schwabenheim, for example, bore a most striking resemblance to my grandfather, Henry Irving Clouse." Reminiscing years later about his experience as an occupation soldier, he acknowledged that he had "found it difficult to take the part of stern conqueror with such people," earning rebukes from his translator for undue "softness." Some white southerners justified lenience toward Germans with reference to the historical folk memories of Reconstruction on which they'd grown up, determined not to "act like the damnyankee soldiers and the carpetbaggers and scalawags." Others simply refused to accept that DPs' claims for compensation overrode Germans' property rights. Sheldon, in civilian life a school inspector from Arizona, wrote home on May 14 about a ruckus he'd encountered at a small store that was being looted by a group of DPs: "I kicked them out and a young boy asked me to come inside. There was a little old lady 86 yrs old and the boy. He said, 'She is the owner of the store and she wishes to 'Sie zu bedanken.' I shook her hand and tears were streaming down her face. I probably fraternized some by shaking her hand but I felt I did a good job for America." Like Clouse, Sheldon later concluded that he was "not built for being a conqueror," temperamentally ill suited to strict enforcement of military government edicts.[45]

The work of occupation required a good deal of emotional self-management: a discipline cultivated through the acts of letter writing and diary keeping. Wracked by the challenge of determining who owed what to whom in occupied Germany, introspective soldiers appreciated that the day-to-day business of reordering Germany required a strict marshaling of sensibility. Nothing in civilian life, and no amount of specialized training, had equipped military government personnel for the psychic demands of their task. Empathetic instincts had to be retrained. But imperviousness to civilians' pleas—from individuals who might have been personally blameless for the Third Reich's crimes—required a special kind of fortitude, as Bogart was well aware:

> Now that the Army stands deep in Germany, the term "enemy" is
> extended to civilians, and hostility must underlie all the casual
> little contacts in which all previous conditioning prompts one to
> be considerate and polite. The easiest way, unquestionably, is to

forget the larger issues and to treat individual Germans as ordinary humans. In the long run that doesn't work. I was by no means unperturbed when I had to detour an old blind man, his daughter, and her three or four young children (their eyes staring with curiosity and fear) from their customary shortcut home (which went near our area), but I don't doubt for a moment that I did the right thing.[46]

Instinctive kindness and prior socialization predisposed Bogart to make allowances for special circumstances, but he recognized that the dictates of occupation demanded unwavering sternness toward whole categories of people. There was neither time nor cause for fine-grained distinctions. Sensitivity to special cases would only impede military governmental efficiency. Kurtz, also an ardent supporter of nonfraternization, put the point more dramatically in a letter to his wife just days before Germany's final surrender: "Oh darling—we must hate these people, we know that. But it is not easy to hate. . . . Please don't think me facetious when I say, consciously and sincerely, that Johnny Doughboy's job of killing is less trying on the nerves, in many ways, than is mine."[47]

There were, though, many occasions when severity came readily to occupation soldiers—including Bogart and Kurtz. Obsequious German civilians who wore ingratiating smiles more often got an expletive-laden earful than a sympathetic hearing. Bogart angrily turned down two women who had the temerity to come to his office and complain that U.S. soldiers had taken their radio set without providing a requisition slip. Theatrical histrionics—special pleading accompanied by copious tears—were no more likely to achieve the supplicant's objective than displays of fawning deference. The thoroughly bilingual Anders, whose particular assignment was to dispense passes to civilians with a legitimate need to travel, formed the solo audience for many such performances. A couple of petitioners particularly enraged him, and he recounted these episodes in detail for his Viennese mother. One German woman, whose case for a pass Anders initially judged "pretty good," saw his hesitation and anticipated he was about to decline her request. "So she added, 'Oh, I make a plea on your sense of human understanding' (menschliche Verstandnis). God! When she said this I blew up—I told her she had a hell of a lot of nerve even to mention these words, after what misery the Germans had brought upon the world, and said NO in no uncertain terms."[48]

Face-to-face encounters gave military government officers the opportunity to confront unrepentant Germans directly with what they owed the Third Reich's victims. There could be a grim satisfaction in such work. Kurtz was particularly moved by the case of a "half-Jewish girl" whose parents had been forced to divorce, and who had spent the war years in hiding with her mother. The burgomaster, however, was now refusing to provide for them, and so the young woman had sought Kurtz's assistance. "In no uncertain terms the mayor was told that as a Jew she had priority over *every* and *any* German. He was instructed on what to give her and when," Kurtz related to his wife. After confronting the mayor, he had then driven the woman home, and was invited in to meet her mother: "A most distinguished grande dame met me at the door—of a barn!—I thought it was a joke, but said nothing. I was led up a shaky flight of stairs into a tiny room. There were two beds, beneath a roof damaged by the fire of SS troops, sniping from behind a rock opposite this 'house.' I bit my lip with anger at this sight. But anger almost turned to tears, for in the middle of the room was a small table, neatly set . . . home-made cake . . . tea." After this poignant social call, Kurtz summoned the mayor again, having heard that he'd prevented the mother and daughter from moving into a vacant property adjacent to his own: "I asked him whether he'd like his family to live in the same 'room' of this 'house.' He turned pale with fear. I told him that if he and his family were not in the room in the next house within 24 hours, I would personally order him and his family to live in the one upstairs room of the barn for a period of six months. In dismissing him, I ordered him to do the moving job himself. He must have been glad to get out from under my glare."[49]

The day-to-day challenges of determining what duties conquest demanded, and which of its rewards might be indulged, beset Allied soldiers arriving in Germany during the final weeks of the Third Reich's demise, as combat fitfully ended. At last, Wehrmacht generals signed the Allied instrument of surrender at Reims on May 7. Another version was then presented the following day in Berlin, after the Soviets protested that the initial document didn't match the finalized text that had been agreed on. With the war in Europe finally over, SHAEF proclaimed May 8 as V-E Day (May 9 in the USSR). Yet the initial phase of Germany's occupation remained incomplete from a U.S. military perspective. American troops had still not gained access to

Hitler's former capital. Indeed, the great prize for which all Allied armies had rushed would remain under exclusive Red Army occupation until the start of July—to the mounting vexation of French, British, and U.S. commanders.[50]

Frayed trust between American and Soviet generals, with ongoing disputes over who would occupy which districts of the city, kept the advance guard of U.S. military government for Berlin suspended in limbo for weeks after Germany's surrender. This group (a detachment known as A1-A1) proceeded to Halle, approximately one hundred kilometers from the capital, on June 18. They anticipated a swift entry into the capital itself, after months spent in France and Germany studying detailed plans of the city. Four days later, the progress of A1-A1 was halted by Red Army generals who insisted that the size and composition of their convoy exceeded the dimensions hitherto negotiated. According to the Russians, it was to comprise no more than 175 soldiers, thirty officers, and fifty vehicles. After downsizing a cavalcade designed to impress the Soviets with American military prowess, the Americans set off again, following a back-roads route the Red Army insisted on. "It almost seemed that the Soviets did not want us to be seen east of the Elbe," observed Major Maginnis (a senior member of A1-A1) in his diary. The absence of German civilians also struck him as noteworthy. The only inhabitants of this rural landscape appeared to be "gypsy-like detachments of Soviet troops guarding livestock in the fields," looking "more like partisans or insurgents than like regular army."[51]

The convoy's next disappointment was to find their progress blocked again at Babelsberg, a suburb that had been home to the prewar German film industry. Worse yet, rather than advancing into the capital to assume occupation of the southwesterly districts earmarked for U.S. military government, A1-A1 received a new temporary assignment: to make arrangements for the impending Big Three conference at Potsdam. Not until June 26 did the unit's commanding officers receive permission to enter the city, and then only for purposes of reconnaissance. Four days later, the detachment's final entry into the German capital lacked the triumphal grandeur to which the American governors of Berlin had aspired. On a drizzling night, fifty officers and 140 enlisted men found themselves on Berlin's periphery with nowhere to sleep:

> With no billets to go to, we wound up in the Grunewald, that
> great forest park in the southwestern area of the city. The cruelest
> blow of all was to have to set up pup tents in the mud and rain

and crawl into them for the night. . . . It was undoubtedly the most unimpressive entry in history to the capital of a defeated enemy nation, by the armed forces of a great conquering power. Right then and there in the feelings of the US forces to a man, there was instilled a feeling of resentment against the Russians that was really never to disappear.[52]

The commanding officer, General Frank Howley, professed not to mind the impromptu bivouac so much. A short while before, he had been billeted briefly in a former Wehrmacht *kasern* (barracks) outside Hanover whose most recent occupants had been DPs. On entry, Howley and his men found "human fecies [*sic*] and offal" on the floor and walls. In disgust, the general confessed to a "phobia over places that have been lived on and crapped on by people." With this experience still unshakeable, he preferred "a good clean forest" to "moving into filthy houses."[53]

Once ensconced in Berlin, Howley and Maginnis settled into handsome mansions in Dahlem, a prosperous suburb largely untouched by bombing. Enlisted men were less fortunate, however. Paratrooper Edward Laughlin, who had traveled to Berlin not in a highly polished motorcade but crammed into a forty-by-eight-foot boxcar, found himself billeted in a former German naval officers' barracks. Red Army soldiers had already removed most of the furniture, "except for a large, heavy, and ornate wooden table that was dark and highly polished. In the middle of this highly polished surface someone had defecated." This individual had also scratched words onto the tabletop. As translated by a Russian-speaking paratrooper, the message related the murder of the Soviet soldier's family by invading Germans. This fecal marker of victory—a cruder variant of Patton's triumphal urination—was also a testament to loss: elimination of life on a scale that mocked civilized mores. In occupied Germany wasted life and human waste remained all pervasive. As late as August 1945, Lisle evocatively noted that "under the shattered walls, the sickly smell of buried bodies still taunts the air."[54]

Chapter 3

STAGING VICTORY IN ASIA

The final act of World War II was staged on board a brand new 45,000-ton battleship, the USS *Missouri,* on September 2, 1945. Surrounded by a flotilla of American vessels and the hulks of sunken Japanese craft in Tokyo Bay, the *Missouri* played host to one hundred U.S. Army and Navy officers and representatives of nine Allied nations who gathered to accept the surrender of a party of Japanese diplomats and military officers. Lasting no more than twenty minutes, the ceremony was observed, documented, and recorded by a throng of reporters and cameramen along with thousands of U.S. servicemen. After two bound copies of the final surrender instrument had been signed, and a grandiloquent speech delivered by General Douglas MacArthur, hundreds of American fighter planes and B-29 bombers thundered overhead in formation—aerial annunciators of victory. One enlisted man, Sergeant Nicholas Pope, who observed the "big show" from the deck of an adjacent ship noted the potency of this display in his journal that night: "There has been talk of some diehard Japs starting trouble, but I don't think they will, too much power here, the Bay is full of Uncle Sam's fighting ships, and the sky is black with our Air Force. Its [*sic*] sure a good feeling to see our planes up there, with their stars standing out like a beacon just daring somebody to start something."[1]

A taunt to the Japanese, this demonstration of overwhelming American might offered welcome reassurance to Allied troops that their newly defeated enemy would have no choice but to submit to the occupiers' presence. Unlike the ceremony at Reims that marked Germany's surrender—so hastily improvised that the Soviets demanded a repeat performance the following day in Berlin—no detail of the *Missouri* ceremony was left to chance. With Japan's surrender, there was no margin for error. U.S. commanders regarded the stakes as significantly higher this time. Whereas Germany had been conquered by Allied troops pouring in from both east and west, Japan's home islands had yet to be invaded when Hirohito broadcast his acceptance of the Potsdam terms on August 15. But would Japanese civilians acknowledge that their country had been defeated without witnessing their military's capitulation? And would Japanese soldiers dutifully obey their emperor's injunction, or would they fight on regardless?[2]

On the eve of Japan's occupation, U.S. military personnel of all ranks feared the worst, as Pope's journal entry hints. Popular constructions of the Japanese as fanatical adherents of Shintoism, trained to regard suicide as more honorable than defeat, coupled with the knowledge that Japan had never "felt a conquering army's feet," did not inspire American confidence in their enemy's unconditional surrender. "One undisciplined fanatic with a rifle could turn a peaceful occupation into a punitive expedition," mused General Robert Eichelberger, commander of the Eighth Army, which had been earmarked as the primary occupation force for Japan. It was thus all the more imperative, in the victors' eyes, that the surrender ceremony impress the vanquished with the totality of their defeat. Japan's diplomatic and military elite would appear in humiliating walk-on roles—with neither names nor lines—in a stylized ritual of subordination.[3]

In his peroration on board the *Missouri,* MacArthur stressed the shared onus of rising "to that higher dignity which alone benefits the sacred purposes we are about to serve." Victors and vanquished did not meet in "a spirit of mistrust, malice or hatred," he insisted. But the supreme commander's hyperbole scarcely concealed the ways in which mistrust—if not also malice and hatred—shrouded the occasion. As for his invocation of "higher dignity," the ceremony was staged purposely to amplify the ignominy of defeat. Everything about the mise-en-scène accentuated the enfeeblement and powerlessness of the Japanese, right down to the fact that their copy of the surrender instrument was covered in humble cloth while the victors' was bound in handsome and durable leather. Moreover, by transporting delegates out to the *Missouri* rather than holding the ceremony on terra firma, the victors instantly reversed their disadvantage in numbers on occupied soil. A small reconnaissance party of U.S. officers had landed at Atsugi air base (twenty miles from the Japanese capital) on August 28. But despite round-the-clock airlifts of military personnel that began two days later in tandem with amphibious landings of marines on the shores of Tokyo Bay, the occupation force still numbered only about 11,000 by September 2. The Eighth Army had yet to enter Tokyo, and it was not until September 8 that MacArthur would take up residence in the former American embassy, having relinquished a dream of ousting Hirohito from his palace. At the time of the surrender ceremony, then, U.S. forces were a minimal presence largely confined to Yo-kohama (Tokyo's neighboring port city). But while the occupying army remained skeletal, there was nothing subpar about the flotilla of destroyers, battleships, and landing craft anchored in Tokyo Bay. The "greatest armada of all time," as Eichelberger described it, left no doubt as to who possessed superior strength.[4]

At every turn, the Japanese delegates were reminded of their chastened position. Passage from the destroyer *Lansdowne* that ferried them from the dock to the battleship was cumbersome. To clamber from one vessel to an-other was all the more fraught a maneuver under the gaze of thousands of sailors who crammed every inch of deck and craned from every railing. Mean-while, a battalion of photographers snapped rounds that sounded, to at least one Japanese participant, like "a rattling storm of arrows barbed with fire." All this was particularly taxing for the diplomat Shigemitsu Mamoru, who repre-sented the imperial government. Shigemitsu wore a wooden prosthesis, having lost a leg in a bomb attack by a Korean protesting against his country's coloni-zation in 1932. In the words of historian John Dower, the diplomat's awkward gait "conveyed an uncanny impression of a crippled and vulnerable Japan." Shigemitsu's pained progress and the evident discomfort of the Japanese delegates—kept standing for "about ten minutes" before MacArthur made his appearance—afforded an opportunity for schadenfreude that at least some Al-lied spectators relished. This tense interlude was, in the opinion of a senior American army officer, "one of the best parts" of the proceedings.[5]

The wait also ensured that the Japanese delegates had time to notice the framed flag hanging behind the table on which the documents would be signed. This was the standard with thirty-one stars brought to Japan by Com-modore Matthew C. Perry on his flagship *Powhatten* in 1853: a reminder that while Japan might not have been subject to thoroughgoing foreign oc-cupation before, it had been "opened" by American gunboat diplomacy al-most a hundred years earlier—by a naval officer from whom MacArthur was directly descended.[6]

The choreography of the event, from the gigantic scale of the battle-ship with its massed throngs of American sailors to the indignity of being ignored "like penitent schoolboys awaiting the dreaded schoolmaster," was calculated to impress upon the Japanese an inferiority of stature intended to signify inferior status. In the victors' "great morality play" (as Dower terms it) might and right appeared synonymous. Size did indeed matter, or so se-

FIG. 3.1 The motley appearance of Japan's delegates on board the battleship *Missouri* to sign the instrument of surrender on September 2, 1945, attracts much ridicule from American observers. Indiana Historical Society [MO783_BOX2_FOLDER38_SURRENDER_002].

nior U.S. officers seemed firmly to believe—in materiel as in men. The Americans' extreme body consciousness had already been evident two weeks prior to the surrender ceremony, when MacArthur selected General Charles Willoughby to meet the first emissaries of defeated Japan at the supreme commander's headquarters in the Philippines. Eichelberger noted in his diary that "the Japs proved to be a typically ill dressed and scrawny looking group of staff officers," wearing badly fitting, heavy uniforms and "ribbons without medals." Willoughby, on the other hand, "weighed in at about 220 and is 6′3″ in his stocking feet, making a fine contrast. The MP's guarding them were also a selected group of better than average size soldiers."[7]

On the deck of the *Missouri,* with massive twin sixteen-inch guns glowering down at an ominous forty-five-degree angle, everything about the

Japanese struck American observers as *lesser:* their size, their looks, their bearing. In pictures shot from scaffolding that gave photographers an aerial view of the proceedings, the Japanese looked diminutive, cowed, and ill at ease—as beleaguered representatives of the vanquished were bound to be in a sea of victors. They were also strikingly overdressed in comparison to the American commanders. MacArthur had decreed that attire would be informal, with neither ties nor ribbons—an insouciant gesture of a piece with his insistence that neither he nor any U.S. officer would carry a weapon when they disembarked at Atsugi. "If they intend to kill us, sidearms will be useless," MacArthur reportedly snapped. "And nothing will impress them like a show of absolute fearlessness. If they don't know they're licked, this will convince them." As one journalist put it, the dressing down on the *Missouri* represented the "master dramatist's touch"—"flamboyance, in reverse." With shirt open at the neck, the supreme commander demonstrated that he did not deem the Japanese sufficiently worthy adversaries to merit reciprocity of military respect. This studied casualness made the formal attire of the Japanese diplomats look all the more ridiculous. "The Japanese premier was decked out in tails, striped trousers, top hat and gloves," Eichelberger recorded in his diary, while his chief of staff, Clovis Byers, relayed another officer's quip: that this antiquated "get up" was "all that was needed to present a completely comic opera atmosphere."[8]

Despite overtones of Gilbert and Sullivan's *Mikado,* the mood was more grim than frivolous: a dark atmosphere intensified by the prominent place MacArthur accorded two former prisoners of the Japanese. When the supreme commander made his dramatic descent onto the deck, he was accompanied by General Jonathan Wainwright, who had surrendered the Philippines after the Battle of Corregidor, spending the remainder of the war in Japanese prison camps, and the British general Arthur Percival, who had endured the same fate after ceding Malaya and Singapore. The gaunt presence of these men offered a powerful reminder of the physical brutality Japanese captors had meted out to Allied captives. Their emaciation invited ongoing animosity toward the vanquished. In Byers's estimation, Wainwright's prominent position in the proceedings would sharpen Americans' enjoyment of the occasion by dramatizing how thoroughly power positions had been reversed. The Japanese were no longer able to dictate anything to anyone. On the eve of the surrender ceremony, Byers wrote home that "every American will rejoice at the prospect of seeing these little yellow devils brought to heel in the face of the man who had undergone so much."[9]

Byers's subsequent account of events on the *Missouri* corroborated this prediction. While other witnesses noted MacArthur's trembling hand and the ferocious glares he and General Walter Krueger directed toward the Japanese, Byers recorded that Brigadier General Lewis Beebe had expressed a desire to see Shigemitsu "knocked down." "How happy it would make me," he'd announced, recalling an occasion when Japanese officers had permitted a private to slap Wainwright's face seven times "just to demonstrate their position." Beebe's remark prompted an animated debate over how many of the Japanese representatives would subsequently commit "hari-kari," as Byers put it. He did not anticipate that a great number would take their own lives. But he was gratified that the climactic display of U.S. air power had made the Japanese dignitaries "realize at last that they had gotten themselves into a jam."[10]

Quite a jam, indeed. And its sweet taste was savored by Allied personnel on the *Missouri,* acutely conscious of their position as participants in an epoch-making event. For servicemen on board, the occasion was sealed by receipt of a special souvenir wallet card. Printed with a red setting sun backdrop, the commemorative card bore the facsimile signature of Captain Stuart Murray, the *Missouri*'s commanding officer, along with those of General MacArthur and Admirals Chester Nimitz and William Halsey. Like the thousands of Kodak snapshots taken that morning, this memento was to be preserved and treasured. A token of victory no bigger than a playing card, it offered tangible proof that the bearer had indeed been "present at the creation." It would be something to brandish in the face of skeptics or grandchildren in decades to come, should war stories one day encounter disbelief.[11]

———————

In his 1950 memoir, *Our Jungle Road to Tokyo,* Eichelberger gave the initial phase of Japan's occupation an ethereal air. Noting "an eerie feeling that all of us were walking through the pages of history," he invoked a sensation of floating unmoored in space and time while ink dried on parchment. But who had scripted this volume? And was Eichelberger an observer or a participant in the drama? The general's poetic turn of phrase left questions of agency and authority unanswered. But his private diary conveyed a less gauzy sense of how history was taking shape and who was shaping it. Eichelberger's journal entry for September 2, 1945, ended on a muted and discordant note at odds with that morning's triumphalism on the *Missouri*. "At 1700 I was called to General MacArthur's quarters for a conference concerning some reported rape cases on the part of Marines. There are also reports of some 'acting up' on the part of the 11th Airborne troops."[12]

"Acting up" was a considerable understatement, judging from letters that soldiers wrote home, free (after September 5) from invasive censorship exercised by commanding officers. One master sergeant told a friend that members of the Eleventh Airborne had gone "berserk" in the Japanese capital, "holding people up on the streets, raiding any place they could find including the Tokio Telephone Exchange, in which they robbed everyone in the place and raped all the women. To top things off, they broke into the bank of Yokohama and robbed it. 700 people are up for Court Martial for everything except murder." That this eyebrow-raising figure included "about ten C.O.s" arraigned for "organizing looting parties" suggests that the mayhem was a calculated program of avenging violence led by officers with a different notion of what MacArthur meant when he described arrival in Japan as "the pay-off." Another senior officer filled letters home from Japan to his wife with irate accounts of the "senseless looting" and utter havoc that American soldiers and marines had wreaked at the Japanese air base they occupied. Navy Lieutenant Harry McMasters's initial attempts to rationalize this behavior as a product of "hatred born of war" soon gave way to more outraged denunciations of the wantonness of a destructive frenzy that ruined equipment valuable to the occupiers. The marines' vandalism was, he noted, a "black eye on our forces' discipline." McMasters was also chagrined to learn that the first soldiers to arrive in Tokyo had simply walked into stores and taken whatever they fancied. "After all we have said about the Japanese looting of Nanking, Manila and so on, it certainly is a shame to realize that we are no better," he ruefully concluded.[13]

Such goings-on could now be privately conveyed by letter, mail censorship having been lifted on September 5, but they found no place in American public commentary on occupied Japan. With his sights set firmly on the White House, MacArthur maintained a tight grip on the press corps, as eager to maintain a pristine public image at home as he was to suppress unfavorable comment among the Japanese about the occupation. Rigorous censorship constrained both Japanese and foreign correspondents, including a sizable contingent of U.S. reporters. Americans who lacked contact with members of the occupation force but paid attention to reports from Japan in the fall of 1945 duly learned next to nothing of the rape cases and other varieties of "acting up" from their newspapers. The *New York Times,* for example, mentioned rape only once in connection with Japan in the fall of 1945. A story on September 10 carried a brief quotation from a pep talk MacArthur had given to his troops, reminding them that "looting, pillage, rape and other deliberate violations of universal standards of human behavior would but stain your own high honor." That some besmirching of reputation had already occurred was neither stated nor hinted by the *Times.* Eight days later, the *Atlanta Constitution* relayed verbatim the Eighth Army provost marshal's assertion that there had been "very few sex incidents," with "two of three 'rape' cases alleged by the Japanese" having proven groundless.[14]

In months to come, more negative press reports on the collapse of American troops' discipline and morale would surface. But, in the main, contemporary observers hailed the initial occupation of Japan as an altogether better-run and more laudable venture than the quadripartite mess in Germany. Commended earlier as a "good occupation," Japan has continued to receive accolades in popular American accounts over subsequent decades. "What is extraordinary in the Occupation and its aftermath was the insignificance of the unpleasant," John Curtis Perry rhapsodized in 1980. His verdict was later endorsed by Lee Kennett in *GI: The American Soldier in World War II.* Presuming to speak for Japanese citizens, Kennett claimed that the occupation soldier "came to symbolize a unique form of domination, one without any particular rancor or vengefulness."[15]

These assertions of uncommon virtue overlook a good deal of less than gracious behavior in Japan. They also require us to consider Okinawa—where conditions under occupation far exceeded the merely unpleasant—as wholly alien to Japan. For decades after the war, this attenuation of Okinawa from Japan constituted a geopolitical fact. The United States retained sovereignty over the island until 1972, twenty years after the occupation ended elsewhere in Japan. But in 1945 American policy makers had not yet settled Okinawa's longer-term postwar fate. They had simply decided that the largest island in the Ryukyu chain, a Japanese prefecture since the late nineteenth century, would become the springboard for the final assault on Japan's home islands, situated some 350 miles to the north.

The battle for Okinawa was among the bloodiest of the Pacific war. It commenced in October 1944 with months of aerial bombardment, during which Japanese authorities shipped out around 100,000 civilians from a total population estimated at 450,000, relocating many of those who remained from the south to the north of the island. Others fled to caves inland and around the southern coast, while men from fourteen to forty were forced—or actively chose—to assist in the island's defense, working in labor gangs or military units. When U.S. forces landed on the island's western shore on April 1, 1945, they were surprised to encounter almost no resistance, having received a grim warning that casualty rates might run as high as 80 to 85 percent. But the grace period did not last long. American commanders, together with those involved in planning this occupation, soon found that their projections had been mistaken. Based on faulty aerial intelligence and outdated demographic information, planners had imagined that northern Okinawa would be heavily defended but sparsely inhabited. Instead, they discovered that this area, which rapidly fell to the marines, was home to around 100,000 refugees—whose welfare now lay in the hands of underequipped military government personnel. Meanwhile, the Japanese military had turned the depopulated lower part of the island into a defensive fortress, as Tenth Army troops soon found on moving south. The war of attrition that followed would last until late June. By its conclusion, more than 49,151 Americans were dead or wounded, in addition to some 110,000 Japanese military fatalities. The number of Okinawan civilians who had lost their lives remained unknown but was estimated at approximately a quarter of the island's population: a total in excess of 100,000 lives.[16]

Among the casualties were a significant number of navy and army officers and enlisted men who had been selected as military government personnel for the island. Nowhere else did specially trained occupation troops incur such high fatalities or so many psychiatric casualties. Far from constituting an "after-army," many of these men disembarked with the first amphibious landings or arrived on the island shortly thereafter, after months of desultory drilling in Hawaii or study at the navy's military government school at Columbia University. Air raids were still nightly occurrences, and Japanese snipers posed a persistent menace to American encampments that consisted of pup tents and foxholes defended by jittery MPs or untrained guards. Both were apt to fire wildly at anything that moved, "even a block of grass moving in the breeze," one enlisted man noted, his friend having been shot through the thigh on their second night in Okinawa. "Don't hesitate to shoot any civilians who prowl at night," Twenty-Fourth Corps guidelines urged. "While it's true they may be innocent travelers, they may equally well be Jap spies. It's better to be wrong than dead."[17]

Schooled in the rudiments of public administration and well versed in the extended history of U.S. occupations, the majority of military government recruits were wholly unprepared for combat conditions. Some didn't even know how to fire the weapons they'd been issued for personal protection. One enlisted man noted bitterly after his best friend's death that they had never been told what "flak" was. Another officer failed to recognize the sound of artillery rounds. Wondering what all the commotion was about one night, he emerged from his tent in the middle of a firefight, dressed in white undershirt and shorts. To the amazement of those who saw or heard about this display of naïveté, he survived. But the episode was memorialized in official reports on the early phase of the occupation as emblematic of failures in military government preparation. Deficiencies in practical training were exacerbated by an uneasy division of labor between navy and army personnel. While the "taking" of Okinawa fell to the marines and Tenth Army, the island's administration was initially split between the navy and army. Naval unfamiliarity with army protocols contributed to further "friendly fire" fatalities. One young naval man was shot dead when he failed to recognize an army guard's commands to halt.[18]

American troops on Okinawa found conditions not only dangerous but unrelentingly bleak. "Christ A'mighty, what a hole!" one naval lieutenant wrote home to his mother in North Carolina, capturing his appalled reaction on first encountering Okinawa. The island was "probably the rectum of creation," Richard Rendleman proposed, echoing a line that John Hersey had overheard in Sicily. "The story is that we tried to give it back to the Japs, but they said, 'You took it away from us, now you can keep it.'" Until Quonset huts were built later in the year, accommodation was in tents or foxholes. These were uncomfortable enough in dry weather but campsites turned into miserable quagmires when heavy rain fell and typhoons buffeted the island, uprooting whole encampments overnight. Enlisted men rinsed their teeth from beer cans and washed from helmet liners. Latrines were rudimentary in the extreme or nonexistent, requiring those uninitiated in field conditions to acquire hasty expertise in use of the "entrenching tool."[19]

Meanwhile, food supplies soon dwindled. Subsisting on dehydrated C and K rations for weeks at a time, men fought off not just dietary tedium and hunger pangs but also signs of malnutrition. Rendleman, maintaining a jocular tone in letters home, "borrow[ed] a line from Damon Runyon's 'Little Miss Marker,' I'll bet my stomach thinks my throat is cut. What I've put in it the past two weeks hasn't been enough to feed a bird or fit for a dog." For his mother's benefit, he described what K rations comprised:

> As you open your parcel, you wonder whether or not you'll find cracker jacks and a prize or a batch of Japanese War Bonds. But after a month of it, I've found that most always a box of 'Dinner' contains the following items: a piece of cheese, some stale crackers, 4 lumps of sugar, a package of either nescafe or powdered grape, lemon, or orange juice mix, 3 cigarettes, 2 sticks of gum, 1 piece of candy, a book of matches, a water purification tablet, and several sheets of toilet paper. Now, brother, if you can make a meal out of that, I'm a port director.[20]

Next to food, mail formed a second mainstay of morale, and service on Okinawa was patchy despite the best efforts of Lieutenant Commander James T. Watkins IV. A political science professor from the University of Ohio with expertise in Japanese history, Watkins was one of a miniscule number of U.S. officers fluent in the language. But it was typical of military bureaucracy's inability to match individual skills with administrative need that Watkins found himself for several months tasked with running the postal office—a position in which he had no contact with Okinawans. Although he regretted the navy's failure to make better use of his expertise, Watkins took a personal interest in the well-being of enlisted men. (They were akin, in age and essential decency, to his undergraduates, he told his wife.) As the primary censor of their letters home, he was well aware of the depths of their demoralization, repeatedly urging his superiors to address a dangerous state of disaffection—to little avail.[21]

Watkins's failure to elicit results reinforced widely shared perceptions that military government's senior echelon consisted of arrogant, selfish cowards who set the men beneath them to perform demeaning tasks—latrine digging, KP (kitchen patrol), and guard duty—for the primary purpose of reinforcing the subordination of enlisted men and junior officers. Watkins noted one man's remark, "Here we don't work with the gooks, Bud, we are the gooks": a comment as revealing about attitudes toward Okinawans as toward the officer caste. These criticisms were made with particular vehemence against the commanding officer, Brigadier General William Crist, whose pusillanimity and imperiousness soon became legendary. For the first ten days after the initial amphibious landings on April 1, Crist refused to come ashore other than for brief daytime inspection visits. Once he did finally join the other military government personnel at their makeshift camp, he ordered enlisted men repeatedly to erect and move his tent—with an eye to his enjoyment of an unobstructed coastal vista—before they had had time to pitch their own pup tents. He then demanded construction of a personal air-raid shelter that he subsequently proved loath to leave.[22]

However harsh conditions were for American occupation troops, they were exponentially worse for Okinawa's surviving inhabitants. The island had been decimated by months of bombardment and wholesale population removals. Cities and towns had been razed. The majority of Okinawa's pigs, goats, and chickens had been, in military-ese, "irrevocably eliminated from the civilian economy." Most dwellings lay in ruins, their inhabitants having fled or died. Okinawa experienced such catastrophic devastation that monetary transactions ceased altogether. Survival was a matter of day-to-day graft amid conditions of wholesale ruin and bloodshed. Tens of thousands of Okinawans died as a result of bombing; others were immured in caves or ancient "turtleback" tombs in which they had sought shelter only to be sealed in and incinerated by American flamethrowers. An unknown number of Japanese soldiers committed seppuku (ritual suicide) rather than surrender or face capture by the enemy, while hundreds—perhaps thousands—of civilians threw themselves over cliffs or blew themselves up with grenades, whether because they regarded death as preferable to an uncertain future or because compelled to do so by the Japanese military.[23]

One American airman later recounted his perplexity as to where all the people were on Okinawa when he first arrived. Then, driven by a buddy to the spot where he'd poured gasoline into caves before igniting it to "drive the Japanese out," Ben Games looked over a cliff and saw a "pile of heads higher than I'm tall. . . . Someone had cut the heads off and piled them up before burning the bodies." On the beach "you would find seashells mixed in with human bones wherever you stepped." Others were more rapidly aware of the scale of human loss. One marine private wrote home in late April: "The stink and smell of dead bloated bodies [is] in the air everywhere. Dried up blood and bones are strewn around, and wounded people straggling around."

Urging his parents to get his letter printed in a hometown newspaper, Private First Class John Taussig also expressed a desire to "forget about all this that I've seen," including finding two buddies dying, tied and staked to the ground, "their guts cut open and their tongues cut out and their privates stuck in their mouths." Marines who landed on the island four months later found that their campsites were only feet away from decomposing Japanese soldiers' bodies.[24]

Most Okinawans who survived the battle were displaced from their homes—or, more commonly, uprooted from places where incinerated homes had formerly stood. Many had been separated from family members as communities were uprooted and shunted north by the Japanese. Thousands who had escaped these forced relocations and were roaming the northern area of the island during the months of April, May, and June 1945 found themselves corralled by U.S. troops desperate to secure their rear lines. With Japanese soldiers still at large and fears of sabotage running high, the Tenth Army sought to ring-fence Okinawan civilians, bringing them "under military government control." Soon the upper third of the island was "just packed with refugee camps," John Dorfman, a former naval military government liaison officer, later recalled.[25]

Since American planners had not expected to find 100,000 refugees in the north within days of the initial landings, their meager resources were immediately overwhelmed. Military government teams were hampered by a lack of supplies—tarpaulins, food, medicine, vehicles—and a dearth of experience in humanitarian relief work. No wonder, then, that magic seemed necessary to cope with this surfeit of human need. One career naval officer reportedly kept a collection of thin white sticks topped with big white stars behind his desk, marked "magic wand for creating trucks," "magic wand for creating supplies," and the like.[26]

But no amulet had protected Okinawans from either the ravages of battle or the privations of weeks or months spent living in caves. Paul Skuze (in civilian life a police officer from Boston) noted in a letter to his wife, Margaret, written as the battle was drawing to a conclusion in June 1945, that every day soldiers were bringing in hundreds of people from caves in the hills—predominantly women and children. "Most of the small children are covered from head to feet with sores, either impetigo or scabies." Like many other military government personnel, Skuze wavered between empathy and revulsion at the sight and smell of these unwashed, diseased, and lice-ridden survivors. But he was also astonished by the refugees' stoicism:

The most amazing thing is that you never hear a whimper out of them. The bones may be sticking out of their arms or legs from compound fractures, sometimes their eyes or part of their faces are shot away yet they never cry or complain. I never knew that a human being could suffer so much in silence. I sometimes wonder how we Americans would act under the same conditions. Some of the real little fellows and girls are heart-breaking sights. Especially those wounded who are orphans. They just sit by themselves with no one to comfort or take care of them.[27]

With a little girl of his own, Skuse was particularly moved by the plight of Okinawan children. He became all the more sharply aware of the chasm between his daughter's life at home and the abjection of those around him—and how little of this could be communicated to a seven-year-old—when she sent him a "drawing of a girl in a grass skirt, wanting to know if this is how people dress here, and if so, she'd like one." "These people are clad in the scantiest, dirty, torn rags that you could imagine," Skuse told his spouse. "They have had the same clothes on for months hiding in the hills and in caves without baths so try to imagine what they look like. They are all covered with lice in addition to their scabies, sores, boils etc. You can't get within 6 feet of them without gagging the stench is so bad." There was nothing exotic or enviable about Okinawan girls' attire or their circumstances, and certainly nothing to be sent home as a gift to Skuse's inquisitive daughter.[28]

The same spirit of quiet endurance that marked Okinawans' responses to physical injury also characterized their acquiescence to confinement in military government–run compounds—at least as American officers observed and deciphered their reactions. Bringing the civilian population "under control" meant enclosing Okinawans in camps that differed little from prisoner-of-war compounds, except that conditions were more rudimentary than those in American-run POW camps elsewhere. Skuse described a situation in which 25,000 Okinawans were crammed into a space "smaller than Boston Common," living under tarpaulin or without even that minimal covering. Yet an inspection tour of the premises with two local policemen had uncovered just one violation of the rules. "Imagine in America if we had 25,000 people crowded into such an area, police would make hundreds of arrests every night for every type of crime imaginable. Yet all I could find wrong was one fire!" Skuse marveled.[29]

If the inhabitants of these makeshift camps were uncomplaining, it was not for lack of cause. Not only were basic necessities in short supply but civilians, unlike POWs, were not subject to the Geneva Conventions and were thus more readily compelled to perform uncompensated labor—a practice impermissible for prisoners of war. In Okinawa's camps forced labor was the norm, though military government officers insisted that no compulsion was used to make thousands of Okinawans work for upwards of eight hours a day under armed supervision. Crist reported that all laborers had it explained to them by officers working through interpreters that each would receive "wages in kind, consisting of a K-ration box for his noon-day meal . . . in addition to the two meals each civilian refugee receives in camp." And if anyone should fret that the Okinawans went unpaid, well, there was as yet nothing "available for purchase."[30]

Long hours, strenuous toil, and harsh discipline applied to both sexes. Men were recruited for military construction while hundreds of women were sent in gangs to harvest sweet potatoes and other produce that had survived the battle. Those who succumbed to the temptation to squirrel away a potato or two from the field they had spent all day digging were punished severely. Since the imposition of fines was not an option, and forced laborers were already effectively incarcerated, military government personnel employed collective punishment as a disciplinary mechanism, turning the wrath of fellow workers against such offenders. "In a case like this," Skuse informed his wife, with reference to an old woman who had hidden two sweet potatoes, "the Court sentences her section of the compound to go without eating for one day. This section will usually consist of about 100 people. When they all get through with her you can be pretty sure that she won't hold out another potato. It may appear harsh to you, but keeping 25,000 people under control is no easy matter and, if you don't maintain rigid control, you are licked." This specter of latent disorder contradicted the impression Skuse's earlier reports on Okinawan submissiveness had conveyed, suggesting some defensiveness on the subject of collective punishment. After another episode, involving six secreted potatoes and 200 collectively deprived Okinawans, he touchily justified the practice as "common all over the Far East and very effective." He left unspoken the fact that the Japanese were among the foremost practitioners of this technique of control.[31]

As Skuse's letters illustrate, military government personnel occupied protective and punitive roles simultaneously. Struggling to provide field

medical care, food, shelter, and clothing refashioned from military uniforms, they were simultaneously the agents of further dislocation and distress
for those who survived the Battle of Okinawa. Even before combat concluded,
U.S. forces began work reconfiguring the island to fulfill its new strategic
assignment. A massive "Base Development Project" earmarked most of
Okinawa, including the bulk of its fertile land, for military installations:
airstrips, fuel tanks, ammunition dumps, and troop accommodations. In the
anodyne language of the official history of military government's first month
of operations, this plan "foreshadowed a mass movement of population necessary to turn rural Okinawa into a powerful fortress capable of serving as a
springboard from which to launch the final blows, by air, land and sea,
against the Japanese homeland."[32]

The report's statistical charts provided a stark sense of just how complete
the island's devastation had already been. For an estimated surviving population of 250,000, military government personnel judged that 3,700 houses
remained intact. One soldier related to a friend that the Okinawan capital,
Naha, with a prewar population of 60,000, now consisted of just seven gutted
public buildings. Other reports corroborated that in houses or compounds
that had hitherto accommodated families of five to ten, some fifty to one
hundred people were crammed. Now many of these refugees were to be
moved once again, as the island's middle and southern sections were turned
into airfields and camps. American personnel conducted these relocations
with such extreme haste—and such scant regard for the well-being of those
being moved—that some died of suffocation in the process. A memo from
June 1945 noted blankly that civilians had been so tightly packed into military
trucks—one hundred in a single vehicle—that three adults were dead on arrival at their destination. One corpse belonged to a sixty-five-year-old woman,
and then there were two others, "each with a dead infant in her arms."[33]

Military government officers were doing more "disaster relief rather than
governmental supervision," the official history concluded. This was undoubtedly true. But it was equally clear—if rather obliquely expressed in Crist's
report—that the disastrous conditions endured by Okinawans did not stem
from battle alone but also from "base development." What war hadn't accomplished in the way of obliterating an entire way of life, the Seabees' (naval
construction battalions) earth-moving equipment would soon complete. "The
very face of the island was being lifted," one officer later lamented. "A whole
ancient culture was disappearing. Town after town was being destroyed

and . . . even the country was being destroyed by bulldozers in making roads, airfields, dumps and campsites." But those undertaking the reconstructive endeavor were scarcely surgical in their precision, and there was little cosmetic about Okinawa's face-lift. "When I go home I can say that I saw the civilisation of Okinawa wiped out. We did it," another young officer bitterly noted in July 1945.[34]

Dwellings untouched by bombs were being torched at such a rate that the Tenth Army issued an order on May 12 prohibiting "indiscriminate and unsupervised burning of native structures." Eight days later, this injunction was supplemented by another, which prohibited demolition of "tombs or similar native monuments except in cases of compelling military necessity . . . construed as (but not limited to) construction of airports, building roads, and the opening of quarries." As the permissive parenthetical sweep of this formulation implied, "military necessity" was sufficiently expansive to cut a wide swathe through Okinawa's built environment, terraced fields, and pine forests. "It was during this period," wrote military government officer John Caldwell, "that we all learned the real meaning of 'military necessity,' a term which is relied upon by the military to support and justify many amazing things. We gave it a more accurate word: 'military convenience.' For example, if a highway was to be widened through a village, for some reason it was more 'necessary' for the military to bulldoze the dwellings on *both* sides of the road, not just one side." Entire towns and villages were erased in the process. One naval intelligence officer later described how, within the space of a month, Sobe, a "medium-sized village," simply ceased to exist. "There was not a trace of the village or the fertile green slopes that surrounded it. In its place was a tremendous gravel pit surrounded by a network of roads, and toward the beach were large areas that had been bulldozed flat and rolled to make various sorts of dump areas. All that could be seen was a great expanse of crushed rock."[35]

Little of this was known to Americans back home, where reportage from Okinawa was sparse, especially after the battle concluded in June. A rare two-page photo spread in the November 17, 1945, issue of the *Saturday Evening Post* provided an upbeat gloss on the remodeling of what it described as "a high priced piece of real estate"—obtained at the cost of "45,000 American casualties." One photograph showed Seabees in a featureless earthen environment constructing a four-lane Bailey bridge. Their efforts, the caption announced, reflected the "American passion for smoothly flowing traffic."[36]

This reassuring *National Geographic*–style treatment obscured all but the cost in American casualties to "obtaining title" to Okinawa. A number of military government officers were aghast at the island's despoliation, however. Foremost among them were Caldwell and Watkins (both political scientists in civilian life), along with their colleague Willard "Red" Hanna, Okinawa's self-appointed "monuments man." An American journalist who had lived in Japan and spoke the language fluently, Hanna decided to establish a museum dedicated to preservation of Okinawan artifacts. This collection would serve as a "means of propaganda"—aimed at "high brass and other dignitaries"—to "show them that Okinawa had once been something more than an island of broken-down farm houses and pig-sties." The island's cultural heritage was at as great a risk from American "souvenir-hunters" as from bombs and artillery shells, Brigadier General Crist reported. According to one enlisted man's account, based on conversation with the general's disgruntled Nisei interpreter, Crist knew this very well. He was among the throng of military personnel scouring the Okinawan countryside in search of guns, swords, or other valuables that might have been stowed in caves or abandoned in homes hastily deserted. Not for nothing did Hanna fear army officers would "make an afternoon's work of the museum."[37]

As the American military presence grew exponentially over the spring and summer months of 1945, swelling to around half a million by August, Okinawans found life yet more precarious. A military government report dated August 6, 1945, (coincidentally the date of Hiroshima's destruction) noted an "alarming increase . . . in cases of rape, attempted rape, assault, and similar offenses." With wave after wave of restless, anxious soldiers pouring into a shattered, typhoon-pummeled island—"nothing but one large mud hole," as an enlisted marine put it—"sweating out" the days until they would be sent to invade the home islands (or so they imagined), it was hardly surprising that rumors of Japan's surrender should have triggered a frenzied response on Okinawa. Numerous witnesses wrote home about the anarchic discharging of weapons on August 11, "every anti-aircraft gun going off, it seemed like. Tracer bullets flying everywhere." At the military government camp, premature word that Japan had surrendered prompted guards to begin firing wildly. "Pent-up emotions were loosed with a vengeance," Watkins told his family. In September, Lieutenant Jack Ahearn related to his aunt in the Bronx that "the only safe place here when the surrender news came in was a foxhole. There were a number killed during the celebration."[38]

American military planners took the implacability of Japanese resistance on Okinawa as indicative of what U.S. forces would face when the time came to invade the main islands. Fewer regarded the Okinawans' acquiescence to occupation as a sign that Japanese civilians might respond to defeat with less ferocity than their armies had shown in battle. "These Japs Took to Conquest," an American magazine story trumpeted in June 1945. This chipper verdict echoed the views of military government personnel, impressed by a stoicism they more often interpreted as innate docility than as a stunned response to catastrophic loss. "Treat 'em good and they're good people," ventured Private First Class Albert Villegas. But despite Okinawans' unexpected submissiveness, American commanders still extrapolated more from the battle than its aftermath—even when Japan's surrender made it clear that Allied forces would not have to mount the projected invasion. Indeed, the very fact that the Japanese (unlike the Okinawans) had not witnessed ground-level combat encouraged fears of mass resistance to occupying troops' arrival. Eichelberger's projections were pessimistic as he cast ahead to what the Eighth Army might encounter in Tokyo: "I look forward to a city considerably devastated by war with the remaining population under poor control, the public parks filled with homeless, and all suburban areas jammed with refugees. It may well be that the utilities will be out of commission and the remaining people in a nasty mood." Like many others, the general doubted that the Japanese—leaders and led alike—regarded themselves as irrevocably defeated. "There is nothing in the tenor of the notes exchanged by the two governments that would indicate the Japanese feel this is anything more serious than a temporary delay to their forward progress," he noted in his diary on August 19.[39]

Eichelberger's private speculation found a counterpart in the very public warnings that other commanding officers issued to their subordinates on board vessels sailing toward Japan in August and September 1945. One enlisted man on board the USS *O'Bannon* recorded, as the ship approached Tokyo Bay, that Admiral Halsey had issued an order stipulating how members of the Third Fleet were to behave toward the Japanese. "He said to have no intercourse with them and to treat them impersonally—act superior in ever-y [sic] way. He said they were treacherous and should not be admitted to society. We are to lay down the law and use force if necessary and see that we are obeyed," radioman Walter Lee recorded in his journal, before adding his own gloss: "Gad! he is an old Jap hater."[40]

Those who expected outright resistance from the Japanese were to be surprised. The first American reconnaissance team that touched down at Atsugi on August 29 found the Japanese authorities with whom they liaised to be models of courtesy and helpfulness. By then, many Japanese troops had been stripped of their weapons, planes shorn of their propellers, and households relieved of ancient samurai swords. MacArthur had mandated that Japanese authorities would oversee a nationwide process of disarmament prior to the occupying armies' arrival, leaving only the police lightly armed. Those soldiers and marines who still retained their weapons showed no sign of wanting to use them. Likewise, the civilians that the advance party of Americans passed on the streets seemed "happy to have us here."[41]

When MacArthur disembarked at the same airstrip on August 30, the only scintilla of insubordination he encountered came when a Japanese newsreel cameraman, eager to capture the scene, jostled aside an American photographer. Such importunate behavior wouldn't be tolerated. "You'll have to make him capitulate," MacArthur apparently told the irate American. But it was soon apparent to members of the occupying army that the Japanese understood well enough not to apply their elbows to the conquerors. As MacArthur's motorcade stuttered toward Yokohama in ancient vehicles mostly powered by charcoal, the supreme commander and his entourage found the route lined with Japanese police "whose duty it was to prevent any hysterical action on the part of the populace" (in the words of Eichelberger's chief of staff, Byers). Their backs were turned to the road. This, an interpreter explained, was a sign of great deference—hitherto reserved for the emperor alone. But there were no manifestations of hysteria for the police to contain. Likewise, at the Imperial Hotel, which had been commandeered for a couple of hundred Americans, the Japanese staff was almost preternaturally solicitous, "as friendly as could be."[42]

Many occupation soldiers struggled to know what to make of this apparent eagerness to please—or found themselves more enraged than reassured by the absence of animosity displayed by the Japanese. The gap between expectations of resistance and the experience of courtesy engendered suspicion. "The Japanese people are very friendly and smile," one nineteen-year-old corporal wrote home from Okayama to his mother in Chicago, "but deep down I guess they hate us." This skepticism was perhaps only to be expected.

The traits wartime Americans most commonly associated with their Asian foe were treachery and duplicity. No member of the occupation force entering Japan in 1945 had forgotten the events of December 7, 1941; Ie Shima, Iwo Jima, Bataan, and Okinawa were all fresh in the mind. Predisposed toward negative judgments, U.S. soldiers often reached for orientalizing tropes in describing the perplexingly cooperative and amiable behavior they encountered. Japanese faces were indecipherable; their psyches inscrutable. Who knew what feelings of vengefulness or dreams of domination lurked beneath the veneer of Japanese politeness?[43]

McMasters, an intelligence officer tasked with appraising the state of research and development in Japanese military aviation, wrestled with questions of trust puzzled over by many occupation soldiers. McMasters was unusual in that he'd spent some time in Japan before the war, but his attitude nevertheless typified the wariness occupation personnel felt toward people whose embrace of defeat seemed too ardent to be true. In a long letter to his wife written on September 10, 1945, McMasters struggled to sort out his responses. He was impressed by the Japanese military officers and aviation engineers he was working with, finding one in particular, Commander Otsuki, "so personally likeable" that it was "difficult to maintain any reserve." And yet,

> as news filters down about Japanese atrocities against prisoners
> and as we find increasing evidence that they have sabotaged some
> equipment we could have used, and when we find everywhere that
> their secret documents have been removed or burned, we grow
> more stern in our feelings. They are too ingratiating, they bow
> and smile and salute too much. It is a mask. It is not possible for
> any people who have been fed the propaganda of hate against us
> that they have for the last four years . . . to execute such an about
> face as on the surface they appear to have done. I mistrust them
> increasingly; through inexperience with them I was taken in for
> the first week or so, and I have no doubt that many of us have.
> But I am beginning to see through them.[44]

Many of McMasters's fellow occupation soldiers reached the same conclusion that outward signs of Japanese cooperation must be insincere. In military government circles, humorous anecdotes were rife—some perhaps apocryphal—about the skittishness of certain brass hats who refused to let down their guard. Donald Richardson, an interpreter with the Allied Translator and Interpreter Service, noted wryly that two colonels wouldn't take the elevator to the top floor of the NYK Building, where ATIS was located, because "they had heard that the operators were former kamikaze pilots." In time, much derisive comment would be made about the supreme commander's reclusiveness and why he was so loath to abandon the comforts of home even temporarily. Despite bold displays of fearlessness on arrival, MacArthur left Tokyo fewer than a dozen times in all the years he remained there.[45]

There were, however, no kamikaze attacks, nor any bids on MacArthur's life. Rumors about squads of diehard Shinto-crazed fanatics proved even more ill founded in Japan than did expectations of Werwolf resistance in Germany. How was it possible that such a ferocious foe was so quiescent in defeat? In the opinion of many occupation soldiers, if the Japanese submitted to defeat it was surely because the emperor had *commanded* them to do so. After all, they were "really experts at obeying people in power," a marine officer announced, expressing a view many shared. No less than the Japanese, Americans had also been subjected to years of wartime propaganda encouraging them to hate their foe in relentlessly racialized terms. The uniformity of Japanese compliance seemed to corroborate a dominant theme of American wartime propaganda: that the Japanese were stamped from the same mold, conditioned by the precepts of Shintoism to obey the emperor unquestioningly. An orientation film for troops, *Our Job in Japan*—like *Your Job in Germany,* scripted by Theodor Geisel—-conjured a metastasized "Japanese brain" as the real enemy to be disarmed in occupied Japan.[46]

Prompts like this reinforced a repertoire of stereotypes that had long structured Western perceptions of Asians. American soldiers applied these preconceptions most readily to women and children—assumed to have the most compliant of "Japanese brains." To their initial amazement, the occupiers found Japanese children, even "little kids," not only waving and smiling but giving them the V-for-victory sign "of all things," as one WAC captain put it. When another Marine Corps officer noted the children's tendency to "throw kisses" at the Americans, he could only assume that they must have been "drilled in what they were to do," dutifully obeying instructions to put their lips together and blow as the occupation troops streamed past.[47]

Women, by contrast, appeared first strikingly absent and then markedly reticent. American troops attributed both phenomena to the success of Japanese official warnings that women should remain indoors, away from

FIG. 3.2 A dozen inquisitive Japanese boys gather around a U.S. military jeep in the early phase of the occupation. Harry S. Truman Library & Museum [2015–3112].

the rapacious grasp of the conquerors. When women and girls resurfaced after a few days they were typically dressed in *mompei*—"hideous overall combinations in which the trousers look like ankle length bloomers," in one senior officer's description—not the colorful kimonos Westerners associated with Japanese women in general and "geisha girls" in particular. Americans assumed that they were attired in this way not for reasons of utilitarian wartime expedience but to make themselves as unattractive as possible to the occupying forces, again at the behest of Japanese authorities. But occupation soldiers were generally more interested in Japanese women's bodies and faces than in their clothing. Often they professed to find them "unappealing" and "bow-legged" in letters home crammed with descriptive detail about the peculiar country over which they presided and its unprepossessing inhabitants.[48]

Letter writing provided an opportunity to document initial impressions and exercise comparative judgments about the relative merits of here and there, us and them. In Germany, much had seemed familiar in cultural and ethnic terms to many GIs. But in Japan, almost all U.S. military personnel, some Japanese American interpreters aside, encountered the country as unquestionably alien: an enigma that defied decryption. For some inquisitive soldiers, this made Japan all the more enticing as territory for exploration. The thrill of discovery was heightened by the fact that privileged access was written into the very terms of Americans' presence. "The contrast between our ease and their discomfort was so marked that we often wondered at their stolid acceptance of such conditions," Jean Smith (a women's affairs officer with SCAP [Supreme Commander for the Allied Powers]) noted. Her observations on the "conqueror complex" exhibited by some fellow countrymen took aim at a pervasive sense of entitlement that was made rudely manifest, especially in settings where formerly communal amenities had been ring-fenced for the enjoyment of occupation troops alone. But the conquerors didn't always feel unassailable in so foreign an environment, and this frustration could lend an unpleasant edge to interactions between occupiers and occupied.[49]

Expectations of superiority afforded by membership of an occupying army—coupled with Americans' habit of imagining that larger physical stature conferred unchallengeable advantages of power—were undermined by the disabling effect of being unable to understand what was being said or to make oneself understood. For American troops to get by in Japan meant relying on brute force, gesticulation, the assistance of a Japanese American interpreter, or the superior linguistic facility of the occupied themselves, since Japanese familiarity with English was more widespread than American knowledge of Japanese. Verbal incompetence was a form of vulnerability that left some soldiers feeling dangerously exposed, certain they were being fleeced by "Japs" only too eager to part them from their yen and adept at taking advantage of these culturally disoriented easy marks. Major General Herbert Sparrow noted that six weeks into the occupation Japanese storekeepers were already selling "trashy 'souvenirs' at outrageous prices" to occupation troops. It was, he added, a "sickening business to attempt to be ethical in dealing with people who do not value ethics except as they can use them against us."[50]

In this frame of mind, lack of familiarity bred contempt. "No American will go home without a deep feeling of relief and gratitude that, with all its faults, his country is not like this, his people not like these," Sparrow concluded. Other journalistic commentators echoed this hypothesis that foreign travel—in its militarized postwar guise—would narrow the horizons of Americans exposed to alien Asian cultures and mores, invigorating nationalism rather than cosmopolitanism. "All the normal provincial prejudices of the American were magnified a millionfold in this vast enforced migration," noted Harold Isaacs in 1947 with reference to overseas deployment. "The American soldier was neither student nor missionary. He was an unwilling exile." And the occupation soldier was also often an amateur ethnographer, attuned to markers of difference. Measured by a Western yardstick, Japanese modes of existence, like Japanese bodies, struck many occupation personnel as vastly inferior. Occupation soldiers constantly noted the "midget" size of Japanese facilities, with homes "like neat doll houses," "so it almost looks like we're living in a miniature world." Tiny in scale, Japan was also located centuries back in time on the developmental ladder that was imagined to ascend from barbarism to modernity. Letters home brimmed with references to Japan's "backwardness," its "feudal" relationships between men and women, the "medieval" character of rural life, and "primitive" condition of buildings—particularly with respect to plumbing and sanitation systems.[51]

More empathetic observers wondered how much of the poverty and primitivism they witnessed resulted from wartime conditions rather than from the primordial stagnation Westerners so often ascribed to "the Orient." In the former imperial army and navy barracks U.S. troops occupied, as well as in civilian buildings, evidence of frantic efforts to fuel a dying war machine were unmistakable and ubiquitous. Radiators, pipes, condensers, and boilers had all been torn out. Every last vestige of metal that could be salvaged, every drop of fuel that might be saved, had been channeled to martial purposes. Almost every male in the country appeared to have no clothing other than a tattered uniform or garments improvised from military supplies. All this sacrifice—to lose a war! American soldiers who paused to consider the deep incisions that war mobilization had inflicted on the Japanese body politic wondered how their recent enemy had ever imagined they might win. And why had they persisted so long after it had surely become apparent that victory was impossible? Noting the "bug-eyed" way crowds of Japanese stared at the vast quantities of equipment and supplies pouring off U.S. naval vessels, occupation troops imagined that the defeated population was asking exactly the same thing.[52]

FIG. 3.3 Seaman Paul Gray explores the devastated city of Tokyo by bicycle in this undated Department of the Navy photograph. NARA [80-G-473728].

Overawed by American materiel Japanese onlookers may have been. But they did not strike most American observers as overwhelmed by their situation. Some GIs were impressed, as their counterparts had been in Germany a few months earlier, by their former foe's industriousness in setting to work on reconstruction. Surrounded by bomb damage that had flattened acre after acre of what had recently been residential neighborhoods, resilient urban dwellers had started to clear and sort the rubble, building makeshift shanties with what they salvaged. Even the smallest pockets of soil were now under cultivation. "Everywhere gardens, gardens, gardens," noted Sparrow, "vegetables growing into the Vs of road junctions, vegetables on the road shoulders, vegetables along the railroad tracks." Not "digging for victory," as wartime Britons had been entreated to do, the Japanese were digging to survive defeat.[53]

Occupation soldiers who ventured into the countryside were immediately struck by another facet of Japanese life apt to animate revulsion: the use of human excrement for fertilizer. This practice was also much commented on in letters home. GIs heaped scorn on the "honey carts" that collected fecal "night soil," shuddering at the noxious odor that permeated rural areas and clung to the collection vehicles. In Japan, as elsewhere in the postwar world, occupation soldiers reeled from such boundary-violating sights and smells. Visceral revulsion frequently colored judgments about bodies, race, and difference. Perhaps the fact that toilet facilities were "ridiculously inadequate" in the barracks they occupied made American soldiers recoil all the more from exposure to other humans responding to the insistent prompts of their bodies. "The average American will tolerate anything if he can only have clean toilet facilities [and] clean places where he may wash and bathe," ventured Eighth Army chief of staff Byers, noting how very rudimentary the arrangements were in Japanese barracks now occupied by Eighth Army troops.[54]

Although he himself occupied a luxurious private mansion, Byers's own tolerance was not boundless. Acutely conscious of Japanese bodies and bodily functions, he penned a long description of a visit to the Ueno train station, where he had witnessed parents holding diaperless babies downward at a forty-five-degree angle. "Nature then takes its course in open view. . . . It may be in the street, gutter, against the side of a building or just on the sidewalk and no one thinks anything of it." "Male members of the populace are apt to do the same thing," Byers noted, judging such indecency worse even than the "semi-inclosures [sic] which are common in Paris." Whether Japanese women were so lacking in modesty he wasn't certain. Few members of the occupation force appreciated that at least some public emptying of bladders and bowels, especially in devastated urban areas, wasn't typical behavior but a result of mass homelessness caused by bombing.[55]

In a popular account of the occupation published in 1947, the author, a former paratrooper, claimed that "the reaction of most occupation troops in Japan is that of a person suddenly handed a brimming bedpan and told to guard its contents carefully. It comes as a shock to the average American to find himself custodian of such a smelly and strange country." Elliott Chaze's analogy is telling, but also overstated. Not all soldiers were either so thoroughly averse to the assignment or so revolted by Japan and the Japanese. A few, like McMasters, specially volunteered for a mission of world-historic significance. Others thrilled to the prospect of entering Japan as part of a victorious army. To Sy Kahn, sailing into Tokyo Bay in September 1945 after combat in the South Pacific and Philippines was "one of the most exciting moments in the world"—"'even more exciting than nude women,'" he sardonically quipped to his buddies. And there were certainly those with no prior knowledge of the language or culture who found much to admire, seeking out opportunities to befriend Japanese civilians.[56]

But the initial weeks of occupation were filled with frustration for many occupation soldiers, despite, or even because of, the gentility they met from the Japanese. Those who regarded it as the victors' responsibility—or their "pay-off," perhaps—to remind the defeated of their subordinate status resented the dearth of opportunities for chastisement offered by a population that had so thoroughly adjusted to the new order of things, or at least *appeared* to have done so. How dare the Japanese act as though Americans were partners in some new business venture, or guests to be welcomed with endless cups of tea? Japanese politeness made some infuriated Americans want to treat them all the more rudely. "Their slavishness and obsequiousness is offensive," prominent journalist Teddy White opined in the pages of *Life* magazine. "It implies the meeting of two peoples on the basis of friendship, equality, respect and cordiality. It comes because we are stronger, because we beat them, not because they feel that they or their country have done anything wrong."[57]

By White's curious logic, whereby "slavishness" implied parity between those fawning and fawned upon, there could be no fail-safe method of humbling the Japanese. If the Japanese bowed only to superior strength without any acknowledgment of either inferiority or guilt, then further demonstrations of American power would presumably generate only more manifestations of obsequiousness: deeper bows by people who remained fundamentally unbowed. The same issue of *Life* noted, in a chilling turn of phrase, that Americans had not yet rubbed "Jap noses in the atomic dust of defeat." Animated by this nose-rubbing impulse, some officers regretted the lost opportunity to stage assault-style landings that would impress those watching with the victors' invincible might. Japan's surrender meant that American ships could simply sail unopposed into Japanese harbors and berth at their docks.

Where amphibious landings went ahead regardless, they tended to make American naval personnel feel more clumsily cumbersome than showily victorious. There was nothing dignified, let alone vainglorious, about wading through surf in drenched uniforms, holding rifles aloft in bedraggled ill temper while waves washed away the helmets of men who had stumbled, some of whom required rescue from drowning—all under the "impassive" gaze of a crowd of Japanese onlookers.[58]

In their attempts to teach the occupied their place, some officers replicated the tactics of the *Missouri* ceremony on a smaller scale. They kept Japanese officials waiting, making sure they knew American tardiness was entirely intentional, and choreographed meetings to maximize Japanese physical discomfort and awareness of their smaller stature. (The famous photograph that shows MacArthur towering over Hirohito during their first meeting on September 27, 1945, is merely the best-known example of this stratagem.[59]) In a letter home written less than a week after the surrender ceremony, McMasters told his wife that the Japanese were now "learning what occupation means." By this he meant, among other things, that they were constantly being given the runaround by overlapping layers of an American bureaucracy whose complexity and inefficiency daunted and infuriated even its own personnel. The Japanese bore it all "with extraordinarily good grace," McMasters recorded.[60]

American enlisted men might well have recognized many of the tactics with which senior occupation personnel announced their superiority over the Japanese. Their own experience of military hierarchy provided ample exposure to the full panoply of ways in which men vested with authority asserted status and attempted to ensure that enjoyment of perks was commensurate with rank. Increasingly, however, the foot soldiers of occupation were less inclined to accept egregious manifestations of the military caste system with good grace. It was all very well for officers to recommend that the victors deal with the Japanese by mimicking some of the latter's reserve, keeping in check a national propensity to become "soft-hearted and ingenuous suckers." "We should view this filthy abject race with loathing," counseled Sparrow, "and treat it with cold correctness." But further discipline, including self-discipline, was the last thing most Americans in occupied Japan wanted to exercise in the fall of 1945.[61]

Chapter 4

FROM V-E TO VD

From the moment Allied occupation troops entered Axis territory, two things became apparent: first, that GIs would waste little time in finding new sexual partners; and second, that with just as much gusto, American reporters and photographers would alert stateside audiences to these liaisons. What was arguably soldiers' overriding preoccupation became, and remained, a dominant focus of popular commentary on postwar Europe and Asia. No occupied territory excited greater, or more prurient, interest than the female body. Nor did anything more speedily tarnish the image of America's postwar occupations than the avidity with which U.S. servicemen of all ranks engaged in what was euphemistically termed "fraternization" with defeated former foes. In October 1945, *Time* reported a "striking number of higher-rank officers in residence with mistresses of vanished Nazi bigwigs." With Germans and "many a discerning G.I." referring to U.S. occupation rule as "the government of interpreters and mistresses," "Americans were losing face, Germans recovering their arrogance," *Time* warned. This story prompted one First Airborne brigadier general in Berlin to fume that he very much doubted there was "a single high ranking officer living with the 'Mistress of a Nazi bigwig,'" though some officers (he confessed to his wife) were certainly "shacking up with Kraut women." But whether *Time* exaggerated or not, the reputational damage was already done.[1]

A proliferation of images of American servicemen embracing foreign women heralded the war's conclusion, later coming to emblematize both the liberation of Allied countries and "fraternization" in conquered territories. *Life* magazine's first story from occupied Sicily in August 1943, featuring John Hersey's account of Licata under Allied Military Government, was illustrated with photographs by Robert Capa, one of which caught a GI with his "arm around a girl" as they waited for his buddy's shoeshine to be done. From the woman's smiling upturned face and the soldier's self-satisfied grin, there was little ambiguity about the charged character of their interaction. And from the photograph's whole-page size, there was little chance of readers missing it. Similarly, when servicemen landed en masse in France the following year, their exploits in a country popularly imagined—by American soldiers and civilians alike—as Europe's erotic epicenter did not pass unobserved. Photographs of GIs kissing French women, apparently all too grateful to be liberated, soon saturated American magazines. Ralph Morse's image of a soldier face-locked to a woman as they perched atop his half-track in Chartres, published in *Life* on September 4, 1944, drew some female readers' ire. Why were American men squandering kisses abroad that ought to be saved for home, and what was *Life* doing publishing such pictures?[2]

More alarming implications of soldiers' intimate encounters with foreign women were also apparent to those who followed the news. When one ex-army wag quipped in 1946 that "VD swiftly followed V-E," he overlooked the fact that rates of venereal infection among U.S. troops had been escalating for months *before* V-E Day, as attentive American civilians already knew, whether from newspapers or relatives in the forces. Soldiers and journalists both documented the alarming rise in cases of sexually transmitted diseases wherever GIs went, whether "occupied" Britain, the Pacific Islands, or North Africa. During his brief stay in Oran, Maurice Neufeld noted in May 1943 that, despite Americans' general revulsion with the locals, "the length of the prophylactic station lines were mute evidence that the houses were well patronized although the venereal disease rate is very high, running to 98% of the native population." From North Africa, infection accompanied Allied forces to Italy. "Naples has no Piccadilly Circus," noted a *New York Times* report in 1944, referring to London's best-known sexual marketplace, "but venereal disease lurks in the rooms of impoverished girls and women all over town."[3]

As Mary Louise Roberts's recent book *What Soldiers Do* makes clear, sex was an explicit reward for soldiering in France, where prostitution was sometimes actively facilitated by the U.S. armed forces. In Italy brothels also operated legally, alongside much selling of sex in unauthorized places, with GIs evidently boosting business in both lawful and illicit trades. One of military government officer Robert Hill's first assignments in Naples was to find accommodation for 500 to 1,000 prostitutes: " 'Just walls, ceilings, and water,' the commissioner said." But the military establishment intended that relations between soldiers and civilians would be different in enemy territory proper. In this regard Italy, as an idiosyncratic cobelligerent, didn't really count. There could be no mistaking Germany's status, however. American service personnel were expressly forbidden from fraternizing with Germans, of all ages and both sexes, in any way whatsoever. They were reminded about this prohibition at every turn, from the *Pocket Guide to Germany* to orientation films, radio spots, posters, and large billboards that lined the routes along which GIs poured into the Third Reich in the war's closing months. Germany *ought* not, then, have furnished more images of the sort *Life* had offered its readers from Italy and France. Romance was a by-product of liberation, kisses an emblem of gratitude (or so the pictures implied). In Axis territory, by contrast, the vanquished were no more expected to "embrace defeat" than the victors were permitted to embrace the defeated.[4]

At first, Germany—and German women—appeared suitably hostile or simply absent from the visual record of Allied conquest. In its issue of March 19, 1945, *Life* carried a striking, full-page image of an amused corporal cinching a female figure with a passing facial resemblance to Marlene Dietrich. But on closer inspection, her extravagantly arched eyebrows turned out to be the least improbable feature of this GI's inamorata: a mannequin wearing almost nothing other than a long wig topped by a Wehrmacht officer's cap. The caption explained that "American soldiers are forbidden to 'fraternize' with real German girls." Although the text went on to remark that fraternization was "hard to prevent," *Life* offered no further illumination. This would soon change.[5]

Four months later, the magazine devoted several pages to a photo story illuminating the "No. 1 gripe of American GIs in Germany, the official policy of 'nonfraternization'": a rule that meant "soldiers are forbidden marriage, visits, drinking, shaking hands, playing games, hobnobbing, exchanging gifts, walking, sitting, dancing or talking to the Germans." To show how egregiously the ban was being violated, *Life* devoted an entire page to a photograph showing a GI as he pinioned a young woman against the wall of a dreary apartment building, his body angled toward hers, their faces just inches apart. Caption: "In a back yard near Wiesbaden, U.S. soldier corners a pretty, laughing German girl. If caught, he would claim she was a displaced person." American servicemen evidently exercised considerable ingenuity in circumventing the prohibition. But the other photographs in this story served a rather different purpose: to show that the truly ingenious players in occupied Germany's game of cat and mouse were the fräuleins who set out to tease and ensnare guileless GIs. They, in effect, did the real pinioning. Wearing "flimsy" summer dresses—or even less at Germany's beaches and pools—they paraded their untouchable assets. "Girls flaunt themselves partly to taunt the Americans," *Life* explained, "but chiefly in order to get 'frau bait'

FIG. 4.1 Ralph Morse's photographs of German women apparently "flaunting" themselves in flimsy summer attire occupied several pages of *Life* magazine in July 1945. The LIFE Picture Collection/Getty Images [50626572].

of candy, gum and cigarets [*sic*]." *Stars and Stripes* published similar photographs of solidly constructed young women in two-piece bathing suits that both reminded GIs about what was off-limits and encouraged them to disregard the prohibition. "Verboten—but not too bad from this angle," ran one caption.[6]

The claim that women solicited their occupiers' attention—for both amusement and profit—quickly became a dominant explanation for the breakdown of soldiers' sexual restraint in occupied Germany, where fraternization was supposedly "Verboten" but everywhere apparent. This thesis was endorsed by no less an authority than Field Marshal Bernard Montgomery, who accused the country's female population of practicing a "new form of German sabotage by wearing fewer and fewer clothes, thereby undermining non-fraternization policy." Both Tommies and GIs were disarmed by this treacherous striptease, *Time* reported. "German girls in brief shorts and halters systematically sunned themselves in full view of U.S. engineers. . . . Military policemen . . . had their patience tried by a girl who patted her backside and whispered 'verboten' every time she passed. . . . The effect on [troops] was exactly what the Field Marshal feared."[7]

This story encapsulated pervasive contradictions that marked popular commentary on sex and the occupation soldier. On the one hand, nothing seemingly sullied the good name of U.S. military government more than illicit intimate contact between American personnel and foreign women. Fräuleins, after all, differed from the gratefully liberated women of France, Belgium, or Italy. As Percy Knauth pointed out in *Life,* they were "girls who used to go out with the guys who killed your buddies," had GIs chosen to think in those terms. That German women were "pre-occupied," the former lovers of party bigwigs or Wehrmacht small fry, made them all the more dangerous—or worse yet, all the more alluring. But however lamentable this sordid state of affairs, GIs were not wholly, or even primarily, to blame for sexual licentiousness in occupied territory.[8]

Since the "unspeakable" was also highly marketable, it cried out to be broadcast aloud, a source of salacious fascination. The very activities that were ostensibly so reprehensible occasioned indulgent winks. Magazine editors, popular columnists, and opinion formers invited civilian audiences to be variously (or simultaneously) horrified and titillated by the antics of their uniformed representatives overseas. Rarely did commentators on GIs' exploits in occupied Germany pass up an easy double entendre. When *Collier's* magazine published a story in October 1946 entitled "Heels among the Heroes," it illustrated Edward Morgan's essay with a photograph of three "comely German Frauleins" in bikinis protesting an "off-limits" sign planted at a beach. The GI they petitioned was dressed only in bathing trunks. "It takes a strong man to remain firm," the caption nudged.[9]

One troublesome word, "occupation," thus found itself inextricably entangled with another: "fraternization." It was an "awful big word for most GIs," an army field surgeon wrote to his wife from Germany in July 1945, but it "usually just means one thing to them." A much simpler, four-letter Anglo-Saxonism could readily be substituted for this cumbersome term— or it could be abbreviated to "frattin'" with no truncation of meaning. In Japan, Douglas MacArthur would write a concerned letter on the subject to military chaplains in 1946, regretting "a growing tendency to misconstrue the word 'fraternization'—to clothe it with the sole meaning of immorality." But what the supreme commander regarded as semantic clothing signaled hasty undressing to the occupation solder. "Fraternization is strictly a matter of sex," the author of an instant history of *America's Germany* announced with none of MacArthur's verbosity. So it had come to be, and so it would remain.[10]

When the first American-authored novels set in postwar Italy and Germany began to emerge, publishers routinely made lowered necklines and raised hems a selling point. From the jackets of mass-market paperbacks, GIs exchanged smoldering looks with daringly *déshabillée* and improbably proportioned women, even on the cover of the single novel to encompass gay sex between occupiers and occupied, John Horne Burns's *The Gallery*, published in 1947. In typical fashion, Hollywood played up the "blonde belle" of Adano, a role bestowed on Gene Tierney, in both the shooting script and promotional materials for John Hersey's made-over novel. When Billy Wilder's *A Foreign Affair* appeared in 1948—starring Marlene Dietrich as the object of soldiers' quadripartite desire in Berlin, and a former Nazi bigwig's girlfriend—his punning title merely underscored a nexus between intimate and international affairs long evident in occupied Germany. It was only fitting that Dietrich, who played an American officer's girlfriend on screen, was widely rumored to be having an off-screen romance with General James Gavin of the Eighty-Second Airborne Division.[11]

Neither before nor during World War II had U.S. military commanders hit on a reliable formula for constraining soldiers' sexual activity in all its unruliness. Prohibiting all social contact between conquerors and conquered was a radical measure, and, in the view of many senior officers, no more likely to succeed as a defensive perimeter than the Maginot Line. A ban on fraternization had been tried in Germany before, when American troops occupied the Rhineland after World War I. The prohibition failed, and was quickly rescinded. During World War II, soldiers overseas had become accustomed to having sex, with or without the military establishment's direct facilitation. It was inconceivable that troops—encouraged to regard vigorous assertions of heterosexuality as intrinsic to martial esprit—would cease and desist from all sexual activity on entry into Germany, no matter what stern injunctions SHAEF might issue. Recognizing this, one senior officer proposed that, if a ban on fraternization were insisted on, "we should import into Germany at the earliest possible moment our own women in as large numbers as may be."[12]

As this alarmed recommendation suggests, the ban on fraternization was not exclusively, or even primarily, a military device contrived to starve soldiers of sex. Dwight D. Eisenhower's order prohibiting all social contact, issued on September 12, 1944, the day after the first U.S. troops occupied a small pocket of southwestern Germany around Aachen, reflected the tightening of high policy in Washington on the so-called German Question. As such, the ban sought to impress on citizens of the Third Reich their "collective guilt" by force of complete ostracism. To help Germans "see the error of their ways," they would be "held at arm's length," as General John Hilldring, commander of the War Department's Civil Affairs Division, put it. His figurative expression would be made literal by the terms of Eisenhower's prohibition. Germans wouldn't just be held at arm's length; they wouldn't be held at all. Even hand shaking was ruled out. That more intimate physical contact was also impermissible was left unspoken but evident from the blanket ban on social niceties or even common courtesy.[13]

Washington's line on fraternization toughened under popular pressure: another product of ostensibly private behavior being made public. Soon after American troops occupied Aachen, photographs appeared in stateside newspapers showing soldiers enjoying the hospitality of German families—taking convivial meals together, with GIs' arms familiarly draped over children's shoulders. Within days, Franklin D. Roosevelt cabled Eisenhower about photographs "considered objectionable by a number of our people." The president asked that SHAEF both stamp out fraternization and ensure that "publication of such photos be effectively prohibited." Eisenhower responded that he had already insisted "that fraternization be suppressed completely," but the ban would henceforth be more total in its remit.[14]

Military commanders thus found themselves in the uncomfortable position of imposing a prohibition they believed unenforceable. Suppressing pictures was a seemingly simpler expedient, at least under wartime censorship regulations, because credentialed photographers' negatives were checked by military authorities as a matter of course prior to dispatch back to the United States. But the circulation of stories (if not also pictures) was hard to curtail so long as the illicit behavior in question was pervasive, and so very visible. Military authorities thus employed every conceivable argument to urge men away from contact with Germans, playing, in particular, on fears of contamination. Antifraternization propaganda construed German women as doubly dangerous: carriers of noxious ideological strains as well as sexually transmitted diseases. Posters presented a lurid image of female siren-saboteurs poised to infect American boys' minds with the bacillus of Nazism and their bodies with syphilis and gonorrhea. In the spring of 1945, after the concentration and extermination camps were liberated, antifraternization warnings also incorporated photographs of their victims to underscore the message that Americans must shun the perpetrators of these abhorrent crimes.[15]

Some soldiers needed no reminding that Germans had placed themselves beyond the pale of civilized society and, as such, could not be treated with ordinary social grace. But the terms of the ban were extraordinarily difficult to respect. This was true even for men who understood their military service in principled antifascist terms. Military government personnel whose work required them to interact with German civilians on a day-to-day basis found it especially difficult to sustain the brusqueness, or outright rudeness, the nonfraternization order mandated. On occasion, military government officers were rebuked by subordinates, including drivers and translators, for unthinkingly offering their hands to German civilians or returning salutes before they'd had time to curb reflexes to obey codes of military courtesy. Some checked their instincts but wondered whether they had been correct to do so. Major John Maginnis recounted in his diary on May 22, 1945, that he had gone to pick up some photographs from a small shop in Berlebeck: "In the normal European fashion, he [the elderly proprietor] courteously preceded me to the door and extended his hand as I departed. I did not take it and somehow it bothered me that I did not. Had I given him the customary brief handshake, would I have been fraternizing? Probably." Maginnis didn't pursue the logic of his unease further. But others certainly wondered whether the ban wasn't calculated to engender more hostility than remorse, particularly among Germans who had not been party members and bristled at the undifferentiated guilt Americans attached to the entire population.[16]

One particularly nettlesome question was whether children deserved to be stigmatized in exactly the same way as their parents and other adults. Sidney

FIG. 4.2 This U.S. Army handbill from May 1945 issues a grim warning to soldiers that they must not fraternize with a German population deemed collectively responsible for Nazi atrocities. United States Holocaust Memorial Museum, courtesy of Jamie Kirkebo [36965].

Eisenberg related to his sister and family in the Bronx a fleeting encounter, two days before Germany's final capitulation, that had rattled him: "As you know I take this non-fraternization business very seriously—far more than most. I slipped up once. I walk home from work every day—3 ½ miles—for the exercise and completely ignore the Herrenvolk en route. But the other day a sweet little girl—about 7 years old—dragging a tiny kid brother, smiled at me faintly—hopefully. I grinned at her efforts and she immediately broke into the loveliest smile imaginable—one I shall never forget tho I felt guilt about even this afterward."[17]

Eisenberg was not alone in finding it hard to maintain a posture of icy reserve toward German children, particularly those too young to have been conscripted into Nazi youth organizations or mustered into the final defense of the Reich. Some German teens did strike occupation soldiers, including Eisenberg, as filled with hate toward their conquerors. But toddlers and infants were another matter, and some soldiers let their observance of the ban lapse when they saw German children foraging through garbage cans or politely requesting candy. "The little Krauts are our worst enemies," one exasperated officer wrote home, feeling "like a heel" for taking down the names of soldiers whom he had found talking to children that morning. But "the soldiers can't mix with these people and must ignore the kids most of all."[18]

Living arrangements in the early phase of the occupation commonly brought soldiers into close contact with German civilians, making fraternization—in all its iterations—harder to avoid. "The set-up we have now it's almost leading the men to it," one enlisted man told his wife. Although billeting with German families was specifically forbidden under the terms of the nonfraternization order, it continued nonetheless. Occupation soldiers frequently filled letters with descriptions not only of the creature comforts they now enjoyed in German homes but also of their billets' former inhabitants. Some stayed put, becoming housekeepers, cooks, and laundresses to the American occupants.[19]

James Thompson, an army barber who loathed military discipline, appreciated the freedom that being quartered with a German family gave him. Not only was he spared the drudgery of guard duty and the dreaded KP, he enjoyed so much leisure time that he began a small business sewing cloth caps and selling them for the handsome sum of $4.50 apiece. Thompson also reveled in the fact that the female owner of his billet did all the cleaning and even decorated the place with fresh flowers. By June 1945, Thompson was spending "lots of time playing" with the owner's "cute two year old daughter." In letters home, he voiced amazement about his unexpectedly cushy and congenial situation. He couldn't imagine American families doing so much for strangers as his German "hosts" had. "Of course we're the conquerors and all," he acknowledged, "but still that doesn't mean the people have to do this for us." While they may have *had* to house GIs, Germans certainly didn't have to enjoy—or appear to enjoy—the conquerors' company so much. Thompson was far from alone either in striking up such friendships or in developing a cottage industry on the side. One medical supply officer, alerted to the fact that the niece of his billet's owner lacked American-style "feminine hygiene" products, set to work producing homemade Kotex with gauze and cotton batting swiped from military supplies. (Unfamiliar with American ideas of disposability, the recipient tried to wash them—to the enterprising manufacturer's chagrin.)[20]

If gemütlich family situations kindled friendships, they surely also fostered romance—or more transactional sexual encounters between soldiers and the women who assumed various domestic burdens around their commandeered homes. Hence the common GI quip that fraternization represented "the best solution to the laundry problem." Not surprisingly, more intimate relationships found a less prominent place in occupation soldiers' letters home. After all, the vast majority of mail—or certainly of those correspondences preserved and deposited in archives—was addressed to female interlocutors, whether mothers, wives, girlfriends, aunts, sisters, or former schoolteachers. On the home front, letter writing was women's work. The fact that commanding officers cast a beady (or more jaded) eye over their men's letters, taking an X-Acto knife to offending material, weighed heavily on some men. "I did not like to write a lot of personal things when I had a feeling that maybe the officers were sitting around making wise cracks about it," Corporal Clarence Davis told his wife just after censorship had been lifted from his quartermaster unit, then in Würzburg, on May 23, 1945. Conceivably, however, Davis exaggerated his officers' voyeuristic tendencies. In practice, mail censorship was as haphazardly undertaken as enforcement of the nonfraternization order. Certain officers evidently took the chore far more seriously than others, particularly where matters of reputation rather than operational security were at stake. In the spring of 1945, some soldiers freely described Germany's sexual landscape in terms that were often vivid and sometimes lurid, disregarding a ban on any reference to violations of the policy.[21]

Ban or no ban, American soldiers found Germany alive with sexual activity in the spring and summer of 1945. One particularly galling phenomenon to many GIs was the fact that German POWs were being released and returning home by the early summer. (The speed of the Wehrmacht's final collapse made it impossible for the Allies to accommodate all surrendered enemy personnel for a protracted internment.) "Darling it sure does burn the boys over here to see all the German soldiers walking down the road going home and then we have to stay here and watch them," Aubrey Ivey wrote to his wife from Landa on May 26, 1945. Worse yet, these demobilized veterans were publicly resuming their romantic lives, and seemingly flaunting their freedom to do so, under the disgusted gaze of the occupiers. On June 6, Leo

Bogart wrote his parents in Brooklyn on the subject with some feeling: "To the GI who is faithful to a woman back in the States, or who just wants to keep his nose clean and sticks to the non-fraternization rule, there is something extremely irritating in the sight of a Nazi soldier, in his uniform, walking slowly down the street of an evening in the embrace of a good-looking Fräulein." Doubtless some other GIs resented such scenes precisely because they did *not* stick to the nonfraternization rule and regarded "good looking Fräuleins" as the occupiers' sexual terrain, presumptuously encroached on by Wehrmacht returnees, men whom they had supposedly defeated. Either way, it was a bitter irony that the vanquished should be able to enjoy the comforts of home—the longed-for rapture of reunion—so far in advance of the victors.[22]

Former Wehrmacht soldiers weren't the only ones who apparently enjoyed an instant "peace dividend." Displaced persons, many of them former impressed laborers imported into Germany to work in factories and on farms, were "running loose." Amid the drinking and looting that bedeviled occupation soldiers' attempts to regulate rural German life, some female DPs were also running "miniature houses of joy," as one military government officer put it. "I broke that up fast for the two were Polish and therefore had to be shipped to a repatriation center if they weren't doing *useful* work," Maurice Kurtz informed his spouse, quipping that "useful" was all a matter of perspective. Predictably enough, the Poles' clientele wasn't limited to other DPs. Since the ban on fraternization did not extend to other nationalities, American soldiers quickly entered into liaisons with DPs. Although some commanding officers attempted to circumscribe these encounters too, their success was evidently limited.[23]

Consider this sequence of observations offered by an enlisted man to a male friend in the initial phase of Germany's occupation. In a letter from late May 1945, the author (Eddy) ruefully related, "Things aren't so hot here anymore what with non-fraternization and stuff like that. But you understand the Genus GI well enough to know that 'bars do not a prison make.' Also; 'Love will find a way . . . .'" He was not alone in expressing such sentiments. Many other servicemen wrote home to the effect that Germany was "crawling with good-looking Babes," as one officer put it, "which doesn't help on the non-fraternization business much." By early July, if not before, it was clear that "love" had indeed found a way. "We've got a nice deal again after our latest move," Eddy informed his buddy. "I'm shacking with the sweetest thing this side of a PW cage. It's the same with all the guys. All Germany is just one big Whore House. They don't even preach fraternization to us any more because it is a big joke. Then right in town with us we have over 1000 Polacks. Mostly women and girls. They're good for a dance two or three times a week. They're good for other any [*sic*] night of the week. The guys are drunk more often than not lately. 4th of July we had a big parade . . . it was a little doozey. No one could walk a straight line, even the Officers. C'es [*sic*] le peace . . ."[24]

Other occupation soldiers attested to the same situation, if not quite so crudely. By July 12, 1945, Thompson—manufacturer of the cloth hats—had concluded that nonfraternization wasn't "worth a darn." Of particular astonishment to him was the fact that, when his company decamped from Dessau to a new location some 300 miles distant, they had been followed by a number of DPs. These women had cycled all the way in order to find their GI boyfriends. "Camp following" of this sort became a widespread phenomenon.[25]

American soldiers did not limit their pursuit of sex to displaced women alone. Photo stories in *Life* and elsewhere were not mistaken in depicting GIs flirting, and more, with German women in the spring and summer of 1945— even if their emphasis on female initiation minimized male agency and obscured the role of coercion or brute force in some such encounters. *Life* also alerted its readers to the way in which GIs would spuriously "re-nationalize" women to circumvent the ban against fraternization, pretending that German girlfriends were actually Poles, Russians, Yugoslavs, or other nationals. "The boys never admit fraternizing, and it's always a French girl, or a Belgian, or a Russian, or a Pole involved. They're very cagey," Dr. Felix Vann informed his wife in late May. In an attempt to stamp out this ruse, headquarters of the Twelfth Army Group began issuing colored cloth armbands to DPs that would identify them by nationality: a practice uncomfortably redolent of Nazi insistence that persecuted populations literally wear their identity on their sleeve. Another unit tried something similar with lapel buttons. Predictably, these readily discarded markers of identity didn't prove a very effective impediment to GI ingenuity. Indeed, enlisted men's can-do entrepreneurialism simply ensured that a brisk black market developed in DP armbands and buttons.[26]

Officers were just as quick to circumvent the fraternization ban as enlisted men. But where the latter often required deviousness to maneuver around rules, officers simply bent them on a grander scale, maximizing the comparative advantages afforded by superior rank. Officers, after all, both devised and enforced the rules—or ignored them. Dr. Vann expanded on his observations about enlisted men's associations with DPs, or Germans they passed off as such, with equally scathing diatribes about officers. Many of them, he noted in July 1945, were "going off the deep end." Married and single officers alike routinely maintained relationships with women they had met earlier in France and Belgium, issuing themselves passes so they could return west at whim to visit their girlfriends. Unlike enlisted men, officers enjoyed the self-assigned leisure and mobility required to sustain long-distance romances. Others, Vann noted, were "shacked up with WACs and nurses," leading to another common complaint of enlisted men—in Europe and Asia alike—that their superiors monopolized all the available American women. Expressing a familiar refrain, Alan Sterling, a naval radioman stationed in Japan, complained to his sister in April 1946, "It would be too fruitless to try to find a nice American girl here. Officers' apartments are the most frequently used places to disrupt their morals and most of them seem very weak and soon show signs of preforming what was once dispised [*sic*]."[27]

With some officers openly pursuing affairs in Germany and beyond, enlisted men inclined to break the rules no doubt felt all the more vindicated in pursuing their own amorous adventures. In this permissive environment, punishment for violations of the fraternization ban was rarely severe, especially after V-E Day. Enlisted men faced fines of sixty-five dollars for fraternization, a sum equivalent to two or three months' net pay for most, but few offenders were actually docked. Officers tended to be especially lenient in excusing one another's "indiscretions." Maginnis's diary records his vexation that General Frank Howley failed to take a more serious view of two field-grade officers who had been openly "having social parties" with German women, letting them off with nothing more than a "good dressing down." Meanwhile, in the Bavarian Alps, Clifton Lisle tried to maintain the line by court-martialing an officer who had consorted with a woman Lisle described as a "notorious Nazi whore." (His diary noted his incomprehension over "such things," but not the verdict.)[28]

Despite some officers' best efforts, the line was not to be held. As army historian Earl Ziemke writes, "Nonfraternization did not end, it disintegrated." The first substantial retreat came on June 4, 1945, when SHAEF quietly released word that contraction of VD would no longer be "used directly or indirectly as evidence of fraternization," one indication that the ban had done nothing to curb escalating rates of infection. In fact, halfhearted attempts to respect nonfraternization had just the opposite effect. One army medic noted that, after Eisenhower's initial order was decreed, the bowl of condoms that had formerly sat at the end of the chow line was removed—with predictable consequences for the sexual health of soldiers and their partners. As infection rates soared, new initiatives were required to encourage men to use "Pro[phylaxis] Stations" and seek treatment without fear of punishment.[29]

These pragmatic rationales for rescinding the ban hardly made for the best PR, however. The public narrative, as spun for the home front, attempted to turn a negative into a positive by first authorizing friendly relations between military personnel and children. Eisenhower made this announcement on June 11, conjuring a heartwarming image of the generous GI to whom youngsters everywhere were irresistibly drawn. This surely elicited knowing chuckles from men only too well aware that it was hardly the dispensing of Hershey bars to infants that had ever preoccupied the high command. The new amendment also seemed almost to encourage GIs to set their sights ever lower, since interaction with young girls could now, however disingenuously, be justified by the official sanction given to friendly dealings with children. In this vein, *Life* tellingly captioned a photograph of a GI greeting a young German woman, "Goodday, child."[30]

What was left of the ban lasted only another month before Eisenhower announced that soldiers could henceforth engage German adults in conversation. Gamely, but also misleadingly, he asserted that this move reflected the great strides that had been made with denazification. By permitting verbal exchanges, the ameliorated policy would encourage yet more progress since (Eisenhower suggested) GIs would now be able to express their outrage to Germans about the horrors of the extermination camps. Few, one suspects, had either the language skills or the inclination to take up this opportunity. Rather than reflecting the success of denazification, the retreat from nonfraternization actually demonstrated how unworkable the hard-line policy of JCS 1067 had proven in practice. And as SHAEF's commitment to "collective guilt" ebbed, that hitherto elusive figure, the "good German," discursively resurfaced. In this rapidly shifting climate, the ban was eased further in August before being rescinded altogether two months later. Some commanders still tried to prohibit social engagements between officers and Germans, who were neither permitted into army installations nor entitled to army food. But the pendulum had swung so far in the direction of liberalization that, by early fall, marriages between GIs and Germans were being contracted, though still forbidden. "It seems wholly incredible to me," Lisle seethed in his diary. "We fight these beasts one moment, have our prisoners shot down in cold blood, see Dachau and the rest, then marry these creatures before the blood of our own people is off their hands."[31]

Some occupation soldiers noted an intensification of Germany's already febrile atmosphere as soon as the ban was lifted. Those who favored a tough line toward the Germans regretted that what had been widespread but furtive hitherto now became ubiquitous and shameless. One sergeant wrote home to express his misgivings:

> The very first day of the ban-lifting I was out in a jeep going somewhere and could tell just by riding along that something new had come about, especially with the broads after sundown. I've been accustomed to people in Europe giving GIs the once-over because at one time they were a rarity, not much seen, but it's gotten to a different stage now. I realize it's been nothing for the women to have babies for Hitler and throw themselves at the Kraut soldiers, but do they intend to keep on doing it to build the country back? And I'll bet in a few months there'll be so many with a child on the way, and it'll be some American's. I thought France was bad in this way, but they are good there compared to the Krauts.

Alfred Rogers wasn't alone in blaming German women's loose morals, coupled with their desire to replenish a severely depleted population, for the breakdown of military discipline in Germany. His portrait of fräuleins as the primary sexual aggressors replicated the image of the hyperideologized, hyperfertile, predatory female constructed in antifraternization materials and dominant in U.S. press reports from occupied Germany.[32]

Reporters greeted the end of the ban as tantamount to an order from Ike to copulate. At any rate, they announced that GIs had gleefully taken his "fraternization order" that way. Some officers agreed, infuriated that enlisted men were now quite openly consorting with German women in public. Indeed, according to Brigadier General Jack Whitelaw it was impossible to go outdoors in Berlin without tripping over fraternizing couples:

Yesterday [September 16, 1945] being Sunday, I took the afternoon off and went for a walk around the lake. The thing called fraternization is still going on there full blast in fact its increasing and I've about decided that I must find some other form of exercise. The climax as far as I'm concerned was finding two Kraut women wearing ETO [European theater of operations] jackets belonging to men from the 82nd Division and complete with division patches, distinguished unit badges and campaign ribbons. The clowns who owned the uniforms had gone to their barracks to get some army food to feed to these wenches—I suppose to make them strong enough for more and better fraternization. I made quite a scene and really am plumb disgusted with American manhood as we find it in this theatre. What I don't like is the way they act in public.

And yet, as Whitelaw had acknowledged to his wife in an earlier letter, other than making a scene, "you can't do anything to the noble soldiery for hugging a kraut wench." This ignoble behavior he ascribed not only to "blowsy frauleins" but also to the fact that most occupation soldiers were really "pen pushers and not soldiers." These unruly enlistees tried to "turn their uniforms into zoot suits and then act like the kind of people who wear such clothes"—presumably, in Whitelaw's mind, Chicanos and African Americans.[33]

The indelible association of fraternization with sex thus lingered even after the lifting of the ban freed the word, at least in theory, to return to a more conventionally fraternal usage. Revocation of the nonfraternization order did, however, sanction other kinds of *social* contact, prompting some officers to seek out "good Germans"—female ones in particular—whose company their men might safely enjoy in chaperoned settings. A flurry of socials, dances, parties, and visits to German homes ensued.

With social contact permitted, young, unmarried soldiers began to allude to, or more openly announce, dates with German girls in their letters home. Hanns Anders enthusiastically recounted for his mother's benefit a party at a German doctor's house in late July 1945. There was, he wrote, "a pleasant atmosphere since there was a piano player and accordionist. One room was cleared for dancing (and yes, I partook)." Sandwiches and drinks helped sustain this merriment until four thirty the following morning. By October, Anders had become serious about a twenty-two-year-old expellee from Silesia: a "girl who has made a bigger impression on me than anyone else." Even though she professed admiration for Nazi ideas, faulting only their poor execution, Anders—a dedicated reader of New York's progressive newspaper *PM* and an ardent antifascist—found her candor refreshing. No other German he'd encountered had admitted even a passing attraction to party ideology. Anders was smitten with the young woman who had managed a farm single-handed, trekked across Germany when dispossessed, and found work as a translator in his office. Her "common sense, her initiative and spirit are what made such an impression on me," he enthused a month later, expressing a desire that his mother should meet the remarkable Issi. (It was not to be, however. Anders was on his way home by the time he next wrote in December.)[34]

Some soldiers also divulged the uglier aspects of sexual behavior in occupied Germany, although they were notably reticent on the subject of rape, especially when perpetrated by fellow Americans. Dr. Vann, the medical officer who had freely described the mating behavior of officers and enlisted men, went so far as to tell his wife that he doubted there was "really any such crime as rape." There were, he wrote scathingly in May 1945, "entirely too many sluts and bitches running loose in Germany." In his opinion women's sexual availability precluded any *need* for rape: an expression of thwarted male libido, in his view, not misogynistic violence. Hence, according to Vann's syllogistic logic, rape did not occur. Such specious reasoning also found expression in American popular commentary on occupied Germany, authored by women as well as men. "Many kids who left the States at the hand-holding stage quickly learned what life was all about by being chased into a bush and taught by experts," opined New York *Sun* correspondent Judy Barden. "If there was any rape, it certainly wasn't necessary." The military justice system viewed things differently, however. Between January 7, 1945, and September 23, 1945, the U.S. Army tried 187 rape cases in Germany and convicted 284 soldiers. Doubtless, the number of rapes far exceeded the number of courts-martial.[35]

German women were also raped by members of the other Allied occupation forces, a phenomenon that occasionally made its way into soldiers' letters home. Bill Taylor, an enlisted infantryman, referenced a mass rape in Stuttgart, purportedly carried out by French North African troops, and was taken aback that his parents hadn't heard anything about it. More surprising, perhaps, is how little American soldiers had to say about the tens of thousands of rapes committed by Red Army soldiers in eastern Germany and

Berlin. Given the speed with which many senior officers soured on their former Soviet allies, initial estimations of Russian discipline and behavior in occupied Germany were remarkably positive, and sometimes downright indulgent, as historian Atina Grossmann has pointed out. "Maybe they were just too drunk," speculated Whitelaw in a letter home on April 12, 1945, reflecting on Red Army troops' comportment. But "maybe they're what I think they are and just too good natured to be intentionally cruel." Despite spending the months from August to December 1945 in Berlin, Whitelaw made not one mention of rape—though he made many disparaging references to GIs' unseemly fraternization with fräuleins.[36]

If rape was either too sensitive a topic for discussion or too readily dismissed altogether, the violence that arose as rigid ideas about race coincided with flexible sexual mores received somewhat more candid comment. In an essay on the "Americanized Mannheim of 1945–1946," historian David Brion Davis quotes extensively from letters he wrote his parents during his service as a teenage security policeman with the First Armored Division. One incident he recounts at length involved an altercation—complete with gunshots and flesh wounds—at a nightclub, precipitated either by black soldiers' encroachment on a white establishment or vice versa. Mirroring the bifurcation of the U.S. armed forces, places of entertainment were segregated along racial lines—at American, not German, insistence. Irrespective of whose trespass had triggered this particular dispute, Davis had no doubt that the "racist hostility certainly centered on blacks dating or dancing with white German girls."[37]

White officers and enlisted men who shared the same prejudices colluded in the establishment and maintenance of a racialized hierarchy of access to German women. Often, formal army practices regarding segregated social space converged with informal vigilantism, as white enlisted men made plain to black soldiers—sometimes at gunpoint—what was either officially or unofficially "off-limits" to them. Resentment and anger flowed in both directions. Some white enlisted men complained about the way in which black soldiers' readier access to army supplies, "frau bait," as *Life* put it, conferred an unfair advantage in sexual competition. Ironically, this privilege was a product of institutional racism, which consigned most African American soldiers to menial, noncombat roles. In Quartermaster Company positions, they trucked military supplies across Germany and were thus well placed to siphon off goods into private channels.

For their part, black soldiers were enraged by racist abuse made all the more galling since members of a segregated force—subjected to constant aggressions both micro and macro—also had to endure endless puff about America's mission to democratize Germany, accompanied by denunciations of Nazi racial doctrines that often seemed entirely hollow. If they fared better with German fräuleins than their white peers, then the explanation lay less in the abundant enticements at their disposal than in their more respectful mode of courtship. So, at any rate, journalist Roi Ottley proposed in an interview recorded in 1946 by Lawrence Reddick (curator of New York Public Library's Schomburg Collection). "The cycle, Ottley said, was that of the Negro GI offering a girl a can of Spam the first day; the second day, chocolate; the third day, a date. The White GI would begin at the end of the cycle by tapping her on the shoulder: 'If you don't give, I won't.'" Only one of Reddick's interviewees, Wilbur Young, offered a contradictory account, relating how the "white fellows treated us like brothers"—a confraternity that permitted a "Southern colored boy from South Carolina and a Southern white boy from Georgia" to visit two German sisters together. "We all managed to fraternize despite warnings to the contrary," Young averred.[38]

Reddick's veterans stressed the uniform enthusiasm of German women for the generous and genial black Americans they encountered. But, unsurprisingly, given the insistence with which Nazi racial theory had been promulgated, some Germans held black soldiers in contempt—particularly those who appeared in public with white women. Unlikely alliances, grounded in shared racial antipathy, arose across lines of nationality and ethnicity. One telling episode was related by Jack Rosenfeld, who composed passionate once-, twice-, or thrice-daily love letters to his beloved "bubala," Sylvia Solov, in Philadelphia. That their missives always bore the ardent motto "Our Love Is As Strong As Our Desire to Crush Fascism" attests the strength of Rosenfeld's political convictions, which also prompted his growing concern over fraternization. June 3, 1945, found Rosenfeld steaming:

> Babe, I've got to tell you this little "incident" that, altho I just bit my lip and ground my teeth it almost made me "shit"—one of the fellows in our section, a Jewish boy, related this story on the way to the game—he was walking with his date, a German girl (yes fraternizing—plenty of that going on) and they saw another German girl walking with a Negro soldier—the Jewish non-aryan

and the German aryaness were astonished and displeased—the German girl didn't like that one bit—beat that. That's the kind of incidents that makes a guy say "what the hells the use knocking your brains out trying to teach people anything or trying to make a better world for people like that to breathe in"—I better be coming to you real soon cause so damn much of this stuff going on is going to make a hell of a cynic out of me.[39]

Occupied Germany was undergoing rapid social transformation, but how liberal this liberalization was remained unclear. Writing home to Nebraska from Hofheim in November 1945, Leland Hiatt documented a more alarming occurrence: "An American Negro soldier was killed by some Germans in a small town about 8 kilometers from here, for going with one of the German frauleins (girls)." Unlike Rosenberg, however, Hiatt's primary concern in telling this story seemed to be to register his disgust over the sexual behavior that had *prompted* the murder, rather than the killing itself, and to fret about his own personal security. "I shall endeavor to keep my door locked every night, and a pistol near my bed," Leland informed his sister Claire. Ten days earlier, Hiatt had reported that two German women had been beaten "royally"—but not undeservedly in his opinion—by German men. "The girls had been seen with negro soldiers, which is indecency in anyone's eyes." "Too bad they can't send a load of negro wacs here," he concluded.[40]

In postwar Asia, official policy on fraternization differed from one site of occupation to the next. Only in Okinawa was a thoroughgoing ban promulgated in the early months of American military government. Although this prohibition outlived its German counterpart, lingering on into 1946, it was no more successful in restricting social interaction or sexual intercourse between men in uniform and local civilians.

The reasons for the ban in Okinawa differed, however, from the tangled political, moral, and ideological considerations that undergirded policy in Germany. There, the guiding impulse was to drive home "collective guilt" for the horrors of Nazism, predicated on a belief that German citizens had enthusiastically embraced the Nazi Party, sustained it in power for more than a decade, supported the waging of aggressive war overseas, and turned a blind eye to the atrocities committed both on German soil and abroad. In Okinawa, by contrast, the ban on fraternization owed little (or perhaps nothing) to any conviction that the island's population was too complicit with Japanese imperial criminality to merit civil treatment. Rather, the injunction against any civil interaction with the local populations was announced, reannounced, and defended in the name of maintaining security and gaining respect. Both these concepts were grounded in pernicious ideas about race and racial difference.

In April 1945, two months before the Battle of Okinawa ended, Twenty-Fourth Corps Headquarters issued a paper entitled "About the Okinawans," a primer in occupational affect that rhetorically asked what the "American soldier's attitude towards the Okinawans should be." Prior "inappropriate" behavior had evidently prompted this pronunciamento. However, the particular *forms* of fraternization singled out in this document weren't those that preoccupied American commanders in Germany but offenses such as offering rides to civilians in military vehicles. "There is no reason to give them rides—they've been walking since birth," the memo cautioned, unmoved by the fact that thousands of Okinawans, very young and very old alike, were being forcibly relocated by the U.S. military to facilitate the vast Base Development Project. Likewise, the paper stressed that soldiers should desist from friendly gestures like smiling or waving because, in Okinawan eyes, the wave was a "sign of weakness." "Jap soldiers beat and shot these people to establish respect," headquarters bluntly asserted, with the implication that "respect" could be sustained only by force. Worse than a tactical blunder, affability was scorned as a violation against immutable laws of nature. "There is no reason to make friends with them—they are not our race."[41]

That Americans must remain aloof because Okinawans were racially inferior rather than ideologically tainted was a pervasive theme of military pronouncements on fraternization in Okinawa. Over the coming months, more and more directives poured forth warning occupation soldiers against "improper actions" and the importance of a "correct attitude" toward a population regarded as irredeemably Other. Prohibited from offering rides to Okinawans, GIs were also barred from performing any work for them. "Orientals do not respect conquerors who perform menial tasks for the conquered," a directive from the commanding general of the Tenth Army announced in May 1945. Embellishing the instructions formulated a month earlier, this document stressed that service personnel would not return salutes or V-signs, nor would they dispense food, cigarettes, or candy. Lest anyone take these warnings too frivolously, the memo ended with a sharp reminder that all American energies must be "devoted to our primary mission of killing Japanese soldiers." Those who disobeyed were threatened with the stockade.[42]

If the animating impulse behind Okinawa's nonfraternization ban differed from that in Germany, so too did the will to enforce it. The contempt with which many senior commanders viewed the Okinawans galvanized their determination that Americans would eschew any reciprocation of courtesy toward the local population. And if soldiers weren't to be friendly with Okinawans, they certainly could not be *photographed* in convivial settings. Thus Brigadier General William Crist took particular umbrage at a photograph, shot in May 1945 and circulated via the military NewsPix service, that featured two U.S. officers drinking tea with Okinawan women. Particularly outrageous was the fact that the men had removed their shoes, following local custom. This, in Crist's view, was no way for the conquerors to gain and maintain respect from "Orientals." Nor would enlisted men's commitment to nonfraternization be boosted if officers were shown "going native." Before leaving the island to serve elsewhere, Crist made fraternization the subject of a final homily to his long-suffering senior staff, not all of whom shared his attitudes. With evident distaste, Jim Watkins recorded Crist's finger-wagging "lecture" on the offending photograph: " 'These people are not your class. You wouldn't invite them for tea at home. Why should you do it here? Moreover, they are the enemy.' " Here, the brigadier may have substituted class for race, but his point was just as blunt.[43]

Crist and other commanding officers thought in terms of totalizing racial binaries: Occident and Orient should not meet, greet, or drive in jeeps. When they asserted Okinawans' racial "unlikeness," these men invoked an American identity of pristine whiteness. In so doing, they ignored two salient features of occupied Okinawa's ethnic topography. First, the occupation force included hundreds of Japanese American interpreters, without whom military government would have faced an impossible challenge in making its orders understood, other than by the bluntest of force. Some of these soldiers were Nisei from the mainland United States, plucked from internment camps for specialized training. Others hailed from Hawaii, sometimes encountering friends or relatives in Okinawa—for the second fact that assertions of an absolute dichotomy between "us" and "them" overlooked was the presence of many Hawaiians on the island, some of them U.S. citizens. Distinctions between citizen and alien, friend and foe, American and "oriental," were thus much fuzzier than Crist and his ilk wanted to believe.[44]

Japanese American enlisted men were unlikely to be deterred from wooing local women by officers' assertions that they were "not our race"—a claim as dismissive of their military service as it was demeaning of the Okinawan population. And sure enough, a number of Japanese Americans quickly found local girlfriends, to the dismay of the nonfraternization lobby. But if the latter had imagined that white American soldiers would have no interest in islanders racially unlike themselves, they were mistaken. Judging from the frequency with which senior commanders felt compelled to reassert the ban, servicemen were obviously "fraternizing" with abandon—in a variety of ways. In early July, Colonel Charles Murray (Crist's successor) reaffirmed that "CBs [Seabees] will not drive through villages throwing out cigarettes and candy to the passing civilians. MPs will not, as they guard marching lines of refugee 'gooks,' walk with the prettiest girl. Units will not make mascots of children."[45]

As in Germany, the attempt to outlaw social and sexual contact failed dismally. Okinawa, devastated by months of the most brutal warfare, was also a site of sexual opportunity for many American servicemen, irrespective of their ethnicity. Sex was variously had by consent and through coercion; paid for and taken by force. The battle for the island was barely over before military government reports noted an increasing "rape problem." On Okinawa, as elsewhere, rape was primarily ascribed both by locals and by white officers to African American troops, as transpacific racisms converged. Meanwhile, at headquarters, officers "shacked up" with WACs and nurses. (To Watkins's dismay, parties at the colonel's house were invariably drunken affairs with couples sprawled in sozzled abandon over the couches.) Elsewhere, at military government's rural outposts, officers and enlisted men slept with local women. Prostitution flourished. This trade was, at least in part, a legacy of Japan's militarization of the island in preparation for its final defense: a process that included importing hundreds of Korean "comfort women" to provide sex for Japanese soldiers. Many of these impressed sex workers remained on Okinawa after Japan's defeat. Awaiting repatriation to Korea, they constituted "a constant source of trouble in the districts," one official report peevishly complained.[46]

But prostitution was certainly not the exclusive preserve of Korean women brought to the island with Japanese soldiers' "comfort" in mind. Watkins was aghast to discover that, when military government headquarters relocated to a site closer to Okinawan inhabitation, commercial "fraternization" increased apace. According to the enlisted man who filled Watkins in, "The approach is to accost some boy or old man and indicate by gestures that what you want is 'push-push.' 'Geisha?' he will ask. You nod assent. He motions you with both hands to be seated and wait. Then he goes to the village and brings you the desired partner. Apparently the warm earth of the nearby fields provides all the couch you need." Watkins professed utter amazement. How could HQ's *Parc aux Cerfs*—a reference to Louis XV's trysting place (literally "stag park")—"give the necessary privacy"? But obviously privacy wasn't a prerequisite as far as some military government personnel were concerned. One former army officer, M. D. Morris, subsequently noted the army's covert facilitation of prostitution: "For the common good, some wiser, saner heads worked out an off-the-record arrangement whereby all interested girls were assembled in a single area in which drinking, money, medical examinations, and an orderly movement of actually thousands all were controlled closely without creating any disturbance from the outside." So much for the attempt to outlaw fraternization on Okinawa.[47]

In Japan "proper," MacArthur avoided issuing a formal ban. Acutely publicity conscious, the supreme commander no doubt wished to avoid the kind of embarrassment Eisenhower suffered when his nonfraternization order became, as many contemporary commentators put it, the most widely disregarded policy since Prohibition. MacArthur later explained his decision with reference to a lesson instilled by his father, who had taught him never to give an order unless certain it would be carried out. "I wouldn't issue a no-fraternization order for all the tea in China," MacArthur was quoted as saying in an *Esquire* profile in 1967.[48]

However, this reluctance to prohibit fraternization did not mean that GHQ (General Headquarters), the occupation's headquarters, and the Eighth Army command (under Robert Eichelberger) adopted a laissez-faire attitude toward interactions with the Japanese. SCAP's disapproval of amicable dealings with the former enemy was plainly understood by officers and enlisted men alike. At least some members of the occupation force worried about the ethical implications of cordiality with Japanese officers or civilians. Naval intelligence officer Harry McMasters expressed such concerns to his wife, just three weeks into the occupation: "My conscience troubles me a great deal about this fraternization, for such the drinking of tea with Japanese naval commanders and their wives undoubtedly is. I condemned it roundly on the part of our troops in Germany, and here fall in with it myself in Japan. When

I think of the men who fell on Saipan and Iwo Jima and all the other islands, it seems traitorous. I am afraid that the Japanese are unrepentant and
their only regret is that they lost. Unless we are stern with them, can we reeducate them?" It did not take long, however, before Eichelberger and his
chief of staff were enjoying the hospitality of various Japanese princes, who
were eager to introduce the American occupiers to the delights of net-
ting—and then eating—duck among other traditional pastimes.[49]

Such esoteric cross-cultural pursuits weren't available to enlisted men, but
the most popular erotic form of fraternization was. With regard to sex, Mac-
Arthur's high command initially adopted a pragmatic approach, facilitated by
the Japanese government's decision to establish brothels for the occupation
troops' use. The rationale for this policy was that prostitutes, by satisfying
the sexual needs of American troops, would buffer "respectable" Japanese
women from the rapacious attention that Japan's leaders believed would
otherwise be directed at them. The "comfort stations" were conceived as a
"bulwark *(bōhatei)* against the danger posed by foreign servicemen," explains
historian Sarah Kovner. A special government agency, the Recreation and
Amusement Associations (RAA), with a budget of one hundred million
yen, set out—just a week before the first occupation troops arrived—to recruit sex workers who, unlike the coerced wartime "comfort women," were
paid. Ikeda Hayato, head of the Finance Ministry's tax bureau (and later
prime minister), noted that the money would be well spent if it helped "protect the pure bloodline of the Yamato race." Some estimates reckon that as
many as 70,000 women were employed by the RAA at the height of its operations, with many thousands more working in the informal, streetwalking
sector of "pan pan" girls.[50]

By the time the first American reconnaissance officers arrived in Japan,
a handful of RAA establishments were already open for business. When A. E.
Schanze, assistant chief of staff to the Eighth Army, landed in Japan on
August 29—one day in advance of the Eleventh Airborne—he was surprised to pass a modern, glass-fronted structure in which "girls filled the
entire side of the building, five or six to a window." Asking his interpreter
Mr. Suzuki, a representative of Japan's Foreign Office, what this establishment was, Schanze was told, "That is a present from the Japanese government to the officers in the United States Army." It didn't take long for the
recipients to enjoy this gift. Indeed, Schanze's unpublished memoir suggests
that the very first customer was the sergeant he had tasked with guarding

the establishment, later observed through the same plate glass with four Japanese women, "naked as jaybirds."[51]

Senior commanders were also inclined to accept and make use of the Japanese government's "present." Eichelberger noted in his diary on September 11, 1945, that he and his circle of senior advisers had decided not to deter men's "usage of houses of prostitution." While the army could not "become involved in any sanction or operation of individual establishments," it would exert "strong pressure" via the Japanese police to "maintain cleanliness and order," stationing MPs in the vicinity of brothels to rein in disorderliness. (This move was, in part, a response to reports of rape—dismissively referred to by Eichelberger as "extracurricular activities"—by members of the Marine Corps.) In some ways, then, licensed prostitution appeared the best available solution to the "problem" of soldiers' perceived need for, and entitlement to, heterosexual sex. As Eichelberger's diary entry reveals, military commanders tended to believe that ready commercial access to women's bodies would inhibit rape, which they understood to result purely from repressed libido, not more violent impulses to dominate or degrade. Moreover, since workers in officially regulated establishments were (at least in theory) easier to surveil than women at large, they could be—and, in occupied Japan, were—subjected to regular medical examinations. Prostitutes infected with venereal disease were then quarantined from soldiers until cured, or thrown out of work. These measures, U.S. military officials hoped, would help ensure soldiers' fitness for military service by reducing their exposure to sexually transmitted diseases.[52]

Another imagined advantage of this system—had disease prevention actually worked—was that demobilized soldiers would cease to imperil the sexual and reproductive health of their wives: a further reason to sacrifice "disreputable" foreign women in the interests of more highly prized American womanhood. The very idea of servicemen going home infected was, in the words of one army medical report from June 1945, "tragic in its import."[53]

There were, however, drawbacks to such arrangements. The most obvious was that military-authorized brothels required secrecy. American armed services could hardly be seen by civilians back home as condoning, let alone organizing, brothels for their men. "I did not want to put myself in the position of being the big boss of a chain of houses of prostitution," Eichelberger noted in 1948, gathering thoughts for his subsequent memoir. But screening these establishments from public view wasn't easy, even at a considerable geographic remove and despite GHQ's close scrutiny of the press. Few matters are harder to keep secret than those pertaining to sex. This was especially true when the men in question weren't *supposed* to be having any: married men because they were married, and unmarried men because they were not. Even before Pearl Harbor, soldiers' unrestrained carnality—or (differently viewed) their susceptibility to corruption—was already the subject of anxious discussion in the United States. Freed from the restraining influence of mothers and wives, military recruits were viewed as easy marks for bad girls on the make. At the prompting of purity campaigners, the 1941 May Act outlawed prostitution from areas near training camps. Three years later, when it came to light that the army had effectively presided over brothels in some French towns, public outcry forced the military to back away from its pragmatic participation in the commercial sex trade.[54]

These were not new issues for the U.S. military in its overseas ventures. Something else MacArthur might have learned from his father, besides the unwisdom of issuing unenforceable orders, was the difficulty of shielding putatively private arrangements to supply soldiers with sex from public scrutiny. In the early twentieth-century Philippines, MacArthur senior (as governor) had to publicly deny and denounce the brothels that were flourishing under the aegis of the American armed forces.[55]

Military-sanctioned prostitution had a recurrent tendency to become troublesomely visible. It also failed to suppress venereal disease. Rates of infection rose apace in every site of U.S. occupation during and after World War II, from Italy, France, and Germany to Okinawa, Japan, and Korea. The reasons for this failure, despite the wartime innovation of penicillin as a remedy for sexually transmitted disease, are not hard to fathom. Young, often drunk soldiers didn't systematically make use of Pro Stations any more than brothel owners complied with mandatory regimes of medical inspection of their workers. American officers and local authorities were no more successful in confining all commercial sex work to licensed brothels, although halfhearted attempts to do so were made in Italy, Japan, and Korea.[56]

Sex, and sex workers, proved uncontainable. The existence of licensed brothels did nothing to stunt the growth of "uncontrolled" prostitution around, and even inside, military barracks. Attempting to curb prostitution, and VD along with it, proved to be a Sisyphean task. Whenever military physicians and public health officials thought they had a handle on the situation, it always seemed that more women had entered the sexual workforce.

GIs in Italy noted that boys of about ten or eleven were openly soliciting on behalf of their barely older sisters. Sweeping measures to confine, medicalize, or criminalize prostitutes, or women suspected of being such, were attempted. In occupied Italy, exasperated American military commanders talked of "waging unrelenting war on prostitution," discussing both tactics and the enemy in terms analogous to those of more conventional battlefield campaigns. "Any attempt to compromise with prostitution, only adds impetus to venereal infection," fumed the chief medical officer of the Peninsula Base Section in southern Italy, enraged by both the British army's failure to install sufficient Pro Stations in its area of occupation and the fact that hospitals to which infected women were confined had themselves become sites of uncontrolled carnality, three women sharing a single bed in one hospital in Pace. "These incidents in Allied Army History are not new, but are unprecedented in their enormity. There can be no weak and vacillating stand taken on the VD situation. Its widespread prevalence demands radical measures to control it just as a widespread conflagration requires radical measures be resorted to in order to control it—dynamiting if necessary. Venereal disease (prostitution) must be conquered if the army is to remain sufficiently strong to do the military job allotted it in the present struggle." But V-E was a victory more readily, or certainly more decisively, won than the campaign against VD.[57]

In Japan, the only aspect of sexual activity obscured from American public view was rape. Prostitution, and "fraternization" more broadly, received a good deal of attention in public commentary and private correspondence alike. In November 1945, a navy chaplain, Lieutenant Lawrence Lacour of Oskaloosa, Iowa, created a stir with a letter published in the *Des Moines Register* that discussed how the navy permitted sailors free access to Japanese brothels and even installed prophylaxis stations in them. So popular were these Tokyo establishments—the largest nicknamed "Willow Run" after the vast Ford factory in Detroit—that MPs kept watch over lines of men "four abreast almost a block long." Lacour charged that rates of infection among the workers in these brothels ran at 95 to 100 percent, lacing his moral critique of prostitution's degenerative influence on sexually naive young men with a vicious assault on the corrupting women themselves. In "beauty or sexual charm, none of the Japanese prostitutes could compare to the lowest streetwalker in the States," the chaplain asserted. Some had "open sores on their faces and feet," and had "previously been exposed to leprosy." Lacour further alleged that a number were "doubtless infected with certain varieties of venereal diseases, frequent in the Orient, which are said to be difficult or impossible to cure, even with the new drugs." This jeremiad was quickly picked up elsewhere in the press. The *Washington Post* devoted an editorial to chaplain's claims, denouncing "the insidious effect of gold-braid on the human intelligence" because the navy had adopted the "astonishing policy of trying to solve the venereal problem by encouraging its men to risk infection."[58]

Lacour's widely circulated letter attests not only the publicity given to prostitution in Japan but also to a fixation with Japanese women's bodies, conjured by the chaplain as grotesquely destructive, lethally "Oriental." Commercial sex—and the women who purveyed it—was part of American public storytelling about the occupation of Japan from the outset. As early as September 8, 1945, *Stars and Stripes* reported that GIs were greeted on arrival by "Jap welcomers . . . directing every lonesome looking American to the grand opening" of what looked like a giant USO club but turned out to have a much more diverse bill of fare. Prostitution in Germany, by contrast, received far less attention than the fraternizing fräulein: an "amateur," whose payment was generally depicted as a candy bar or cigarettes.[59]

Occupation soldiers in Japan wrote more, and differently, in their letters home about Japanese women than about German fräuleins. Admittedly, GIs spilled much ink on the "fraternization" situation in Germany, not infrequently issuing general pronouncements about the attractiveness of German women. Remarks to the effect that "some of these Kraut babes are damn nice looking," as one infantryman put it, peppered soldiers' letters. But precisely *how* German women were good looking, as opposed to how good they looked, was rarely elaborated on. Soldier scribblers took it for granted that the "Kraut babe" could readily be summoned in the mind's eye, "Krautness" having little to do with German women's appeal beyond a certain stereotypical cleanliness, sturdiness, and blondness.[60]

Japanese women, by contrast, mesmerized occupation soldiers, whose scrutiny combined ethnographic and pornographic impulses. Everywhere they went in Japan, American military personnel noted differences in scale; differences in customs and culture; differences in landscape and architecture; but most particularly differences between American and Japanese *bodies*. With regard to female bodies, black and white soldiers alike cataloged markers of phenotypical difference, simultaneously judging Japanese women's sexual desirability against standards of American female attractiveness. Members of the occupation force often exercised this possessive prerogative with so little self-consciousness that they thought nothing of sharing their appraisals with wives and girlfriends. Such musings could be passed off as the product of inquisitiveness "entirely natural" to American explorers in exotic territory. Or titillating descriptions could be justified with reference to the *lack* of body consciousness ascribed to Japanese women themselves. If the latter didn't fully conceal their bodies, failing to appear "modest" in familiar ways, why should American men cover up the nakedness of their own curiosity?

Many occupation soldiers duly wrote home to wives and mothers about the exposed breasts they saw, particularly in rural areas of Japan or in public bath houses where it was common to encounter naked men and women together. This kind of anatomical candor had already surfaced in letters written from Okinawa. Paul Skuse, for example, observed that many Okinawan women were naked to the waist, especially when working in the fields. Even older women, long past childbearing age, put their breasts to use as "pacifiers" for infants. "I've seen nothing but teats since I arrived. All shapes and sizes. It is disconcerting at first," he joked. But he also assured his wife that there was precisely no erotic content to these observations. "A fellow would have to be pretty hard up to get interested in them however as they sit around in their spare moments picking lice out of each other's heads. Such a sight tends to dampen one's ardor."[61]

American men often adopted the default position that Japanese women were unattractive for reasons of both racial difference and calculated ugliness, as the female population had been warned by local authorities to stay away from occupation soldiers, who could be expected to rape and pillage their former enemy. It thus warranted particular mention when that rare bird—an attractive Japanese woman—presented herself in public. McMasters, who just a week earlier had informed his wife that the Japanese were so "dirty, wizened and ugly" that he could "hardly imagine a man so lowering himself" as to visit prostitutes, wrote home enthusing over an "exceptionally attractive" woman he had just seen while "zooming along in a weapons carrier." This was an occurrence "sufficiently unusual that I can devote a paragraph" to it, McMasters explained, before detailing the woman's neat attire and use of makeup that "enhanced the natural beauty." But this vision of loveliness was, he insisted, an exception. In general "the middle aged women are wrinkled and old as you hardly ever see American women wrinkled. There may be pretty girls, but the one we glimpsed today is the only one I have seen." Two weeks later, McMasters would encounter another woman whose exposed breasts he appreciatively pictured for his spouse: "Riding back through Zushi we were startled to see a young Japanese woman coming along

FIG. 4.3 John Florea's photograph, dated October 1, 1946, captures an American GI staring intently at a Japanese woman's legs. The LIFE Picture Collection / Getty Images [50503748].

the street bare to the waist. She had exceptionally nice chichi for a Japanese. What did your husband do? He stopped the car and started backing up for another look! How she scurried; she ran away as fast as she could. I don't know what she thought, but I think I know." The fact that he had alarmed this pedestrian, causing her to imagine him a potential assailant, seemingly enhanced McMasters's frisson of enjoyment. His wife perhaps found both the incident and the register in which her husband described it rather less droll.[62]

Men of all ranks, from General Eichelberger on down, offered their spouses—and, on occasion, mothers—similarly candid estimations of the Japanese female form. The Eighth Army commander took a dim view of Japanese women, referring to one waitress as "the usual bow-legged homely type," and another as "looking like something the cat dragged in," in letters to his wife, invariably referred to as "Miss Em." He particularly disapproved of women who adopted Western dress. "Their legs and figures did not fit readily into our type clothing. . . . Why they tried to imitate the American girls is more than I have ever been able to understand because they just can't do it," Eichelberger sighed. That he saw fit to comment regularly on the looks of waitresses is telling—both about the circumstances in which officers encountered Japanese women and about their fascination with the latter's physical appearance.[63]

Unlike in Germany, few enlisted men in Japan lived in Japanese homes alongside their former occupants. Most officers, however, lived in either requisitioned mansions or hotels, where Japanese women cleaned and served meals. Some men evidently took considerable care over the selection of their domestic employees, hiring them on the basis of their attractiveness, a practice that prompted suspicion about exactly what services these women supplied. Eichelberger wrote a huffy letter to Miss Em on the subject on May 20, 1946: "I have never tried to bring in any of those pretty little Japanese girls as waitresses. I realize they are decorative but I feel that the Japanese men like Mr. Komori would resent having a lot of little girls around. Also, they would be a temptation to the young men of the house—and I don't mean the non-commissioned officers only. At some of the places I go, they have managed to collect some beauties." Attractive Japanese women were, Eichelberger conceded, "collectible" rarities—like "dolls," as other soldiers often put it. But trophy hunting of this kind was primarily regrettable, his letter suggested, because Japanese men would resent a foreign army that had appropriated sexual property rightfully *theirs,* as had occurred in Germany.[64]

Many soldiers writing home about Japanese women, officers and enlisted men alike, filtered their impressions through the lens of the "geisha girl." These kimono-attired female entertainers were one of very few aspects of Japanese life—along with tea ceremonies and flower arranging—with which Americans were glancingly familiar. Madame Butterfly, the quintessential courtesan unceremoniously abandoned by an American lieutenant in Puccini's opera, assumed the same prominence in mental maps of Japan as Mount

Fuji did topographically. Consequently, this exotic foreign species had to be described for the folks back home, just as sightings of the iconic snow-capped peak did. Discussion of "geishas" was facilitated by the element of plausible deniability as to whether such women were prostitutes. Emphatically they were not, pronounced Lindesay Parrott in the *New York Times* in November 1945, noting (less than reassuringly, for some female relatives of servicemen overseas) that GI's "geishas" weren't in fact traditional geishas at all, a verdict shared by Peyton Gray in the *Afro-American*. Playing on this ambiguity, occupation soldiers often narrated their impressions of Japanese women in a humorous vein, intended variously to amuse, tease, or taunt the female recipients of their letters. John Walters, shortly after arriving in Sasebo, told his spouse about his first trip into town: "We forgot to go over to the Geisha district (ha! ha!) tho' we were close to it." His next letter informed her that some men in his company had been guarding the "geisha district," and that "some interesting stories have been told about the girls and the district." But he hastened to assure his wife that she alone was the object of his desire. When he had experimentally chatted with a couple of teenage shop girls, he'd shown them photographs of her and their baby daughter over which they "ah-ed." In a similar vein, Atlanta attorney Louis Geffen, poised to begin work prosecuting Japanese war crimes, flattered his wife that she could "surpass any of them, and I am waiting for the time when you can exhibit your prowess," bridging separation with airborne fantasy.[65]

Other men related their encounters with geisha girls as hilarious comedies of cross-cultural miscommunication: a mode of emplotment that extended into the 1950s with Vern Sneider's *Teahouse of the August Moon* and beyond. Captain Randolph Seligman, an army doctor with the Seventy-Seventh Infantry Division, penned humorous accounts of his adventures in Sapporo, Hokkaido, for First Lieutenant Mary Jane Anderson, a nurse serving elsewhere in the Pacific. One vignette conjured a party involving ten officers and two geisha girls at a local restaurant, the merriment fueled by sake and facilitated by a "little booklet published by the War Department in 1944":

> Most of the phrases have to do with military matters and are useless for conversational purposes. For example. "Are you a parachutist?" or "Throw up your arms and surrender!" or "Where can I get my brakes adjusted?" . . . We asked one of the Geisha girls, "What is your surface wind velocity?" and, pointing to her chest, "Are you familiar with this region? Are there any strong

points?" "Are there pot-holes?" Rather silly I'll admit, but it helps
enliven an evening. I don't know whether the Geishas really
appreciated this sort of humor, but they responded with uproar-
ious laughter anyway.[66]

Clovis Byers, Eichelberger's chief of staff, similarly told his wife about being
served dinner by three geisha girls who "looked like prints of Japanese dolls,"
and whose "efforts to say in English, 'Do you desire rice' brought great gales
of laughter from everyone present." Another variant of this mirth over mis-
pronunciation was occasioned by idiosyncratic Japanese translations into English. One medical officer gleefully recorded a sign at a geisha house, which
he claimed to have visited purely to take photographs, "All Woman Full of
Customer," and another that elliptically entreated GIs to "Come in with
rubber boots on."[67]

Both Seligman and Byers stressed that the women in question belonged
to the "general class" of "highly if artificially schooled professional entertainers of impeccable moral standards," as Byers stiffly put it. Seligman's
definition was more jocular: "The true Geisha is not to be confused with another type of entertainer called 'Joro,' or prostitute. The Geisha is a respected
person in Japan, comparable I imagine to a nightclub entertainer at home.
She sings, dances, plays an elongated string instrument resembling a guitar,
makes jokes, and fills your glass when it's empty. She also snitches cigarettes
at every opportunity."[68]

Some soldiers were remarkably unguarded in writing home about encounters with the other "class" of geisha girl. Corporal Marvin Reichman,
whose occupation duty involved playing the bugle every other day—a "swell
deal" by his own admission—wrote home regularly from Okayama to Chicago. On his nineteenth birthday, in November 1945, the "loving son" saw
fit to tell his mom that the military had instituted a "great system here to
prevent VD," with girls "inspected every day so there's very little chance of
getting infected." Perhaps he imagined she would consider this nugget merely
informational since his letters bristled with diatribes against the Japanese. "I
honestly wish the Air Corps had dropped Atomic Bombs until every island
in this group had been sunk," he wrote ten days after his birthday, raging
against the fact that the Japanese were "getting cocky." "I'm not going to
play nursemaid to these slant eyed, two faced——," he seethed. "Until the
time I get home I've stopped speaking to them. I don't want any part of these
people." But just a week later, Reichman wrote his brother about the "pretty

good deal" to be found at geisha houses: "It costs $2 for an hour and if you want to spend the night it costs 150 yen or $10. It's a hell of a lot of dough but you have a good time. Jap women have nice figures. One thing that got me was taking a bath with the girl. I've never taken a bath with a girl before and that was really nice." Bathing wasn't all that Reichman had paid for at the geisha house, he let his brother know in graphic detail.[69]

Four months later, Reichman had so thoroughly forgotten his vow not to talk to the Japanese that he was taking language lessons. "I thought it would be nice to know what these Japs are saying about me," he quipped to his mom. Without spilling any geisha house secrets that might have shed different light on his enthusiasm for conversational competence, Reichman also began to extoll the virtues of Japanese women. They were "very faithful" and would "never even look at another man after marriage," the teenage authority on Japanese gender norms expatiated. American girls, by contrast, "like to have a fella chasing after them and as soon as the girl is sure she has him, she grows tired and starts looking for a new toy to play with."[70]

Japanese women, often disparaged on physical grounds, were increasingly extolled by occupation soldiers for their virtues of loyalty and submissiveness. This implicit or explicit critique of the emancipated, emasculating American woman pervaded soldiers' public and private writings alike. Major Harold Noble of the Marine Corps embroidered the theme at length in a 1946 volume entitled *What It Takes to Rule Japan.* "The Japanese woman cannot fail to appeal to the American soldier. Her queer clothing and strange tongue may not please him; her dumpy figure will turn his thoughts to home," Noble ventured. "But her unfailing humor, thoughtfulness and sincere attempts to make man's life pleasant and comfortable is bound to affect the GI." Unlike their American counterparts, women in Japan "have been brought up to believe that this is a man's world, and that women's place in it is to make men happy." Feminine pliability made the otherwise unedifying task of ruling Japan immeasurably more appealing. "It will be quite an experience," Noble promised the uninitiated. Reservist Bill Hume's "Babysan" cartoons, which first appeared in the *Navy Times* and featured a beguiling Japanese woman of Barbie-doll anatomical improbability, suggested the same, although Hume's creation was also a wily manipulator who bamboozled hapless GI Joes into believing that she was their faithful "onrri."[71]

Winsome Babysan was a far cry from occupied Germany's most (in)famous cartoon creation, Veronika Dankeschoen. Drawn for *Stars and Stripes* by a twenty-year-old soldier, Don "Shep" Sheppard, Veronika Dankeschoen lacked the curvaceous allure of Babysan. A little too fond of her candy bars, the amply padded, slatternly fräulein favored a low-cut basque and dirndl skirt embroidered with hemline swastikas. Like Hume, Shep figured his fraternizing female as a cunning schemer, preying on the gullibility of American soldiers, whose good-natured credulousness could be presumed. But "V.D." represented a different order of threat from that of Babysan. The latter might charm a few extra yen or PX goodies from her American "boyfriends," but Veronika Dankeschoen was depicted as both a venereal and an ideological menace—an unreconstructed Nazi whose noxious beliefs threatened to contaminate the GIs with whom she consorted. ("Oh Ja, Papa was in the Party—but chust as a social obligation," one caption read.) In this regard, Shep's scurrilous creation was of a piece with army propaganda warning soldiers against "fraternization."[72]

The cartoon character's toxicity also chimed with broader currents of popular commentary. German women's stubborn adherence to Nazism was a recurrent theme of American press reports and instant histories of the occupation. Some commentators posited a one-to-one correlation between rising rates of venereal infection and the "readiness of the average officer and soldier to spout the enemy propaganda line," as Tania Long put it in a front-page *New York Times* report published in September 1945. "Treated too long as a joke," fraternization imperiled both the soldier's body and his beliefs—if not necessarily his heart and mind. "Right now Germany has hundreds of thousands of conscious or subconscious propagandists at work in the girls with whom our men associate," Long bluntly warned. Finding German women "politically quite apathetic," the *Times* reporter characterized them more as host bodies for residual strains of Nazism than as assertive campaigners. But since American commentators generally failed to ascribe any political identity to Japanese women, active or passive, the latter weren't construed as ideological contaminants in the same way. In popular discourse and cartoon iconography, Babysan and her ilk represented a hazard primarily to the occupation soldier's paycheck. If Japan's geisha girls spoiled GI Joe for his wife or girlfriend back home, it would merely be through excessive and unaccustomed pampering—the remedy for which wasn't penicillin but more regular doses of TLC.[73]

In some American minds, intimacy between GIs and Japanese women raised the specter of impossible marriages, biracial babies, and inadmissible brides. Yet despite (or perhaps in part because of) fears of "miscegenation"—conceived as a dual threat to racial bloodlines and national boundaries—liaisons between American men and Japanese partners proved more readily countenanced than those between GIs and Germans. Japanese sexual mores, presumed by many American observers to be looser than those in the United States, could be attributed to cultural difference. One paratrooper ventured that "the reason Jap morals were so flexible was because of the way they dressed, in kimonos and pajamas. They're always dressed for bed." GIs' adaptation to these norms revealed their susceptibility to local prompts, but if they "did things differently there," then it could be assumed that American men would revert to doing things "normally" when they returned home. What had happened in Yokohama would stay in Yokohama. That, at least, was the mindset Walt Sheldon (longtime resident of Japan and employee of the Armed Forces Radio Service) ascribed to the typical American occupationaire in Japan. "Sexual promiscuity was something to be practiced in a place like this, far from home, not adopted in the long run as a way of life."[74]

Given the openness with which many GIs wrote about "geisha girls," they may have also assumed that folks at home would judge their Asian affairs with tolerance—precisely because such encounters *couldn't* result in the bringing home of a foreign bride. Not, at any rate, until SCAP changed the rules to accommodate these unions, and Congress amended anti-Japanese immigration restrictions later, in the early 1950s. If soldiers' sexual indiscretions with Japanese didn't really count, this greater willingness to trivialize or exoticize such relationships reflected the fact that the women in question were understood to matter differently, and less, than those in occupied Germany.[75]

Popular commentary in the United States figured sex as both occupation soldiers' premier reward and their principal hazard. With easy access to women's bodies regularly touted as the age-old bounty of conquering armies, some GIs eagerly brandished the promissory note that seemed written into the terms of occupation soldiering. Fresh recruits sailing from Seattle to Japan in the fall of 1946 made this clear by waving, in the words of one eye witness, "crudely drawn signs appropriate to the hour: 'Tokyo or Bust,' 'Tokyo Here We Come,' and 'Gotta See a Geisha Girl.'"[76]

On arrival, some men undoubtedly enjoyed the sexual advantages conferred by membership of an occupying army, whether they slept with local women or merely savored the ease with which they *might*—and the opportunity afforded by open acknowledgment of this easiness to turn the tables on women back home. Throughout the war, many men in uniform had entertained grave doubts about the faithfulness of wives and girlfriends left behind, kindling one another's insecurities about sexual fidelity through communal circulation of "Dear John" letters and constant rumors of betrayal. Of course, a significant number of men serving overseas were hardly blameless in this regard themselves. Paul Fussell's contention that GIs were "drinking far too much, copulating too little," neglects how much of both many soldiers managed to do, even in seemingly unpropitious circumstances. Conditions in occupied Europe and Asia *appeared* to reverse that deficit. And the relish with which some GIs anatomized foreign women, evoking the overcharged atmosphere "over there," suggests a certain eagerness to taunt women with the specter of betrayal. Irked by his wife's nagging doubts about his fidelity in Italy, Neufeld promised he would tell her if he slept with another woman, sparing her the uncertainty of not knowing, "even though it might almost kill you."[77]

In different ways, sex could be a problematic source of pleasure for occupation soldiers—for both those who indulged and those who abstained. A number of men in uniform desperately hoped that American military government would remake a better, more politically progressive world. Mindful of their personal stake in securing a just and lasting peace, they aspired to be ethically scrupulous agents of a "good occupation." Others fretted about "frattin'" for rather different reasons, vexed that sexual privileges were so unequally divided, like everything else apportioned by the officer caste. One former occupation soldier recalled a mimeographed map of Matsuyama, showing "the Red Light district enclosed in a dotted line and one house marked with an 'X' reading 'Officers Only.'" Although the map's provenance was never verified, it was taken to be "a practical joke of some Enlisted Men on the Officers," Captain Philip Hostetter speculated. Some may have found this jollity uncomfortably close to the mark, since officers were widely rumored to frequent elite geisha houses off-limits to the lower ranks, and doubtless some did so.[78]

Still others struggled with the competing attractions and compensations of doing right versus doing wrong. For every nineteen-year-old who, like Reichman, told his brother geisha house tales out of school, there was another anxious teen pondering the value or worthlessness of his virginity under the constant sway of peer pressure. George Cronin was one such occupationaire:

a country boy who spent his nineteenth year in Korea, widely agreed by GIs to be the Siberia of all postwar outposts. Throughout 1946, Cronin maintained a daily record of his terrible, wonderful year overseas. ("Abandon all hope, ye who read these leaves," he warned trespassers on the flyleaf.) In his diary, Cronin chronicled worries about whether he'd be able to operate the complicated telephone exchange switchboard adequately, while anguishing over separation from both his best buddy and his beloved camera. Over the course of many weeks, Cronin also sustained a running monologue about whether to sleep with the prostitutes his friends regularly visited. What initially appeared reprehensible to him became more acceptable as the Koreans in question assumed ever-greater prominence in the soldiers' daily lives—visiting their billet, chatting, flirting. (That they made meals, sewed, and swept was an added bonus.) Finally, Cronin slept with a woman, after a number of "close shaves," thereby losing the virginity that had become such a burdensome asset. "Well, this was it. Sunday of all days," he confided to his diary with a mixture of pride, shame, and relief.[79]

Cronin's tremulous tone was hardly that of the presumptuously possessive conqueror, though he clearly regarded his Korean companions more as playthings than as individuals who were capable of being hurt, forming attachments, and feeling abandoned, as he did. In that sense, Cronin—like many others—remained oblivious to the power position he occupied in occupied Korea, where a few C rations went a very long way. But to read this teenager's diary, in all its naive unself-consciousness, is also to be reminded that junior enlisted men were hardly all-powerful, however privileged in their dealings with Koreans. Trapped on the lowest rungs of military hierarchy, young conscripts like Cronin understandably tended to be far more aware of their powerlessness than of their privilege. Although he and his buddies enjoyed a good deal of latitude to set up house, with a shifting cast of young Korean women in attendance, they remained unable to make more consequential decisions about what kind of work they did and, most importantly, when they got to stop doing it and go home. Enlisted men in an army of occupation were both conquerors and subalterns. If they felt amply deserving of whatever measures of pleasure might come their way, this sense of entitlement was perhaps as expressive of what enlistees thought about the men above them as about the women below them.

Chapter 5

DISPLACED AND DISPLEASED PERSONS

"The Germans certainly mixed up a lot of people in Europe!" Major John Maginnis marveled in his diary on September 16, 1945, pondering the irony that the Third Reich—so lethally committed to notions of racial hierarchy and Aryan purity—should have uprooted, transported, and reshuffled people of diverse ethnicities across the vast continental landmass hitherto occupied by the Wehrmacht. Maginnis's remark was prompted by a visit earlier that day to the displaced persons camp at Teltower Damm in Berlin's Zehlendorf district, located on the largely unscathed southwestern periphery of the city. Its wide, still tree-lined streets were home to many American occupation officers, billeted in grandiose nineteenth-century mansions, along with a sizable transient population of DPs. The facility at Teltower Damm had been in existence for just one month at the time of Maginnis's visit. Already, 200 new arrivals were passing through its doors every day. Refugees were deloused, examined, cleaned up, clothed, and, if pronounced "disease free," sent on their way. Their national origins, like their onward destinations, were numerous. Germans formed the sole population group debarred from Teltower Damm. Although millions of ethnic Germans were being ejected from central and eastern Europe in the fall of 1945, U.S. military government did not categorize "expellees" as DPs. Displaced persons were entitled to Allied assistance. Expellees, on the other hand, constituted a problem left to local authorities. German communities would have to absorb their ethnic kin as hostile neighbors ejected unwanted residents: a policy of mass expulsion sanctioned by the Big Three at Potsdam.[1]

Reflecting back on his months in Berlin, Maginnis observed that the DP problem had "almost become a way of life in Civil Affairs/Military Government for it was always with us." Dealing with millions of people who had been displaced before, during, or after the war constituted one of the most challenging, and most pressing, assignments for U.S. military personnel in the initial phase of occupation—in Europe and Asia alike. That the war would leave countless refugees in its wake had been anticipated by Allied officials mindful of the population upheavals that swept Europe in the swell and backwash of World War I. UNRRA was established in 1943 to handle the projected postwar refugee crisis. But this agency, still struggling to recruit its multinational staff and undecided as to what exactly "rehabilitation" would entail, was in no position to assume immediate control over refugee administration when the war ended. In the first instance, DPs were a military government responsibility. They were, however, expected to be just briefly—not *always*—with the victorious Allies: less a "way of life" than a temporary logistical problem.[2]

Reordering mixed-up populations represented an American ambition of stupendous, unattainable scope. The sheer volume of people who were "out of place," and the variety of factors responsible for the disarray Maginnis observed, was staggering in size and complexity. German and Japanese imperial projects had entailed the dispatch abroad of hundreds of thousands of administrators, farmers, engineers, and military personnel to regulate, tax, mechanize, police, and retain newly conquered territories. While German and Japanese settlers had followed their nation's flag overseas, the Axis powers treated colonized populations as a readily exploited, thoroughly expendable labor pool to be impressed and conveyed as expediency dictated. As wartime conscription depleted the industrial and agricultural workforce in Japan and Germany, millions of people in Axis occupied areas were forced into service—as soldiers, sex workers, machinists, miners, and field hands—and transported wherever their bodies were needed. The most comprehensive historical survey of forced labor in the Third Reich has tallied 13.5 million foreign workers, including impressed civilians, POWs, and concentration camp inmates, of whom 11 million survived the war. With respect to Japan, an Office of Strategic Services report predicted in late June 1945 that around two million non-Japanese, the majority from Korea and Formosa, would be in need of "liberation, protection, or segregation from the Japanese" when Allied troops occupied the four home islands.[3]

The victorious Allies agreed that returning forced laborers home, along with speedily repatriating former prisoners of war, constituted postwar imperatives of the greatest urgency. "Displacement" seemed to have a ready solution. Once hostilities ceased, people torn from their communities to service the Axis war machine would be dispatched back to their places of origin. On paper, mass repatriation appeared both a simple and a just expedient. American officials presumed that displaced people would *want* to go home, having been unwillingly conscripted into the service of Japan or Germany. As *The Wizard of Oz,* released in August 1939 just days before Germany invaded Poland, memorably asserted, there was "no place like home"—a sentiment to which millions of American servicemen and servicewomen heartily subscribed.[4]

But this blithe assumption that people could readily be re-placed, and would invariably wish to return home, overlooked several complicating factors. Washington's tendency to treat foreign and forced labor as synonymous minimized the thousands of Poles, Ukrainians, Balts, and others whose work for the Third Reich had not been entirely involuntary. A substantial number of eastern Europeans baulked at returning to their countries of origin, whether fearful that the Soviet authorities would treat them as "fascist collaborators" or drawn to the possibilities for individual reinvention afforded by western Europe. For these displaced persons, former places of residence did not beckon as a hallowed destination or place of protection. "Home" evoked less sentimental nostalgia than premonitory tremors of dread. Some Red Army soldiers, newly released from German POW camps, also feared that their journey east might end in a labor camp, prison, or worse. But Allied policy agreed on at Yalta had mandated that all displaced Soviet citizens be repatriated, including the large number captured in *German* uniforms. Thus, for some months after the war ended, the bulk of U.S. soldiers' work as "people movers" in the European theater consisted of corralling groups of Poles, Russians, Ukrainians, and others into makeshift assembly centers before packing them onto boxcars heading north and east.[5]

If British and American planners underestimated the depth of resistance toward postwar repatriation, they also failed to anticipate the particular needs and aspirations of Jewish survivors of Nazi genocide. Jews who had survived the Third Reich's campaign of annihilation, Atina Grossmann notes, were "the people both the Allies and the Germans had least expected to have to deal with in the wake of National Socialism's exterminatory war." The Allies liberated approximately 90,000 Jews on German soil in 1945. Almost a third of that number died within weeks, and very few of those who lived through both the camps and their liberation wished to remain in Germany. Polish Jews who returned to Poland soon after the Third Reich's collapse—traveling from Nazi camps or wartime exile in far-flung parts of the Soviet Union and elsewhere—were quickly disabused of the notion that former places of residence would welcome, or even tolerate, their return. Anti-Semitic violence and pogroms remained rife, culminating in vicious massacres in Kielce in 1946. The search for a safe haven propelled Polish Jews back to Germany—an unlikely refuge for Europe's surviving Jews. By 1946, occupation authorities reckoned Germany's Jewish population at around a quarter of a million, predominantly concentrated in Bavaria and Hesse in the U.S. zone.[6]

For American occupation personnel, the plight of Jewish survivors starkly exposed the shortcomings of a policy premised on automatic repatriation. Where Jewish DPs would settle was a transnationally vexed question. Palestine, a national homeland in the making, beckoned as a longed-for sanctuary for most of Europe's surviving Jews. But admission hinged on the British government's willingness to permit Jewish refugees into its increasingly turbulent mandate, and this will was signally lacking. Alternative New World destinations also proved reluctant to adjust immigration quotas. In the United States, as elsewhere, admissions criteria reflected stubbornly ingrained hierarchies of ethnic preference inauspicious for eastern European Jews. They also privileged putative entrants' productive capacity over moral claims to entitlement—to the detriment of the infirm and elderly.[7]

The Allies' determination to orchestrate demilitarization alongside decolonization in defeated Axis territories augmented the volume of human traffic in motion after the war. Italy was stripped of its colonies in Africa and the Dodecanese Islands along with its former protectorate Albania, a process that galvanized the exodus of Italian settlers from these overseas territories. With thousands of Italians leaving the northeastern region around Trieste, bitterly contested with Yugoslavia and under protracted Anglo-American governance, Italy also became a "land of refugees."[8]

"Unmixing" people in Asia occasioned even greater levels of dislocation. Not content with repatriating the 3.7 million Japanese military personnel who were overseas when Japan surrendered, U.S. policy aimed to remove ethnic Japanese from Manchuria, North China, Korea, Formosa, the Philippines, and elsewhere, irrespective of whether they had ever resided in Japan or wished to move. In Korea, U.S. occupation authorities hastily began registering all Japanese in September 1945, organizing the repatriation on a "priority system" that removed military units first, followed by "undesirables" (a category that encompassed Shinto priests and "geisha girls" along with other perceived troublemakers), before turning to the evacuation of Japanese civilians and demobilized soldiers and their families. By the end of 1946, over five million Japanese had been transported from around Asia to the four home islands. At the same time, American and British Commonwealth occupation forces set about clearing Japan of those deemed foreign. Koreans were removed to Korea, while Okinawans—assigned a distinct identity as Ryūkyūans—were conveyed to Okinawa, despite the complaints of naval military government personnel that an island almost bereft of housing was in no position to receive thousands of refugees. But within sixteen months of the war's end, more than one million people had been removed from Japan. This attempt to eliminate "minorities" by putting people back where they were presumed to belong—in states where citizenship, ethnicity, and nationality neatly aligned—was as heedless of long histories of human mobility and entanglement as of individuals' present-day wishes. But in neither Europe nor Asia would people meekly consent to being moved, as occupation soldiers and UNRRA staff soon discovered.[9]

For some U.S. military personnel, dealing with DPs was work that redeemed the otherwise unedifying business of occupation, a chance to assist those in grievous need. For others, it was an almighty "pain in the neck." But however they felt about the assignment, the magnitude of the task remained undeniable. Managing humanity in flux—former camp residents, newly encamped DPs, those who resisted confinement, and those in transit to destinations rightly or wrongly labeled home—constituted an epic undertaking in the months that followed V-E Day and V-J Day. It was also "terribly difficult, certainly as hard as anything in the army just now." "Nothing, absolutely nothing, was simple or turned out as expected," concluded Payne Templeton, who had chosen to join a DP detachment primarily because he thought this branch of military government would wind up earlier than other assignments, meaning that he too might return home sooner rather than later. His expectations of ease and speed soon proved unwarranted. "From the beginning all was confusion from hour to hour, and no one knew what tomorrow or tonight might bring. Plans were made, unmade, remade."[10]

Policy was reformulated as the western Allies' original presuppositions about displacement and its management met various forms of resistance. Moods turned just as quickly. The victors' sentiments toward their defeated enemies, as well as toward those whom the latter had oppressed and persecuted, fluctuated dramatically over the summer and fall of 1945. Displaced people—including occupation soldiers ever more dissatisfied with their lot and increasingly anxious to be on the move themselves—became more vocally "displeased persons," as a common UNRRA quip had it. Fraught encounters between the displaced and displeased would in turn shape the larger political contours of occupation.

Who exactly *was* a DP? Occupation personnel expected to be able to tell at a glance. As soon as U.S. troops entered Germany, they were struck by dense throngs of people "clogging" the roads, as soldiers often put it. Of course, not everyone in motion was a camp survivor or former forced laborer. German city dwellers who had headed to rural areas to escape Allied bombing raids were on the move, although not officially permitted to travel, as were "expellees" pouring into Germany from various points east. But many American military personnel assumed that those who appeared most wretched must be DPs, implicitly trusting outward appearances to make identity legible. In some cases, survivors were "still in their striped fatigues worn at Dachau or another concentration camp," Templeton noted in Munich in July 1945. But clothes—even uniforms—could be misleading. Army technician Theodore Inman felt aggrieved that U.S. Army surplus, stripped of insignia, was being given to DPs, making it hard to distinguish a slovenly soldier from a displaced person.[11]

Some more neutrally acknowledged the difficulty of telling who was who. Describing Germany's thronged roads to her family, WAC officer Anne Alinder confessed that "which ones might be DPs and which Germans returning to their homes I don't know," in a letter from Hochst dated July 6, 1945. Betty Olson, another WAC officer, was taken aback on her journey into Frankfurt to see that DPs near the railroad yard were "living in boxcars!" Echoing Alinder, she observed that at the main railroad station—packed with people "milling about or just lying on the ground"—it was impossible to tell if they were "German or DPs because everyone is equally as shabby looking." But in the WAC mess itself, a displaced person whom Olson had mistaken for a German set her straight:

> There are four or five little old cleaning women around the
> building. They are little and bent and old. I thought they were
> German and wouldn't smile or say "good morning" or anything.
> So one morning one came up to me, pointed to herself and said
> "No Deuche—Yougoslavic." I realized they were all displaced
> persons. They work like fury all day and fill our "requisitioned"
> vases with flowers and I'm afraid all they are getting to eat is soup
> and bread. Jeepers, we'd all gladly give up some of our food to the

DPs—but no Germans. But here I was the one who said we can't feed all of Europe.

As these expressions of distaste, confusion, or awkwardness reveal, DPs not only troubled Americans' notions of order but also tested their empathy.[12]

On paper, it was easier to identify a DP—but not necessarily any easier to eliminate the moral ambiguity that shadowed this new postwar person in American minds. SHAEF's *Guide to the Care of Displaced Persons in Germany,* issued in May 1945, defined displaced persons as "civilians outside the national boundaries of their country by reason of war," people "desirous but unable to return home or find homes without assistance." In addition to forced laborers from the Soviet Union, those who hailed from "enemy or ex-enemy territory"—countries such as Czechoslovakia, Poland, Hungary, Bulgaria, and Romania that were annexed or occupied by Germany—were also categorized as DPs, eligible for temporary care and help in returning to their places of origin. SHAEF's civil affairs branch assumed that these "ex-enemy" nationals would wish to be repatriated, although the booklet glancingly mentioned that non-Germans who had collaborated with the enemy would also be treated as DPs and repatriated. Displaced person status was not, then, synonymous with persecution or victimhood, although the category did exclude certain undeserving claimants. "Stragglers, deserters, self-demobilized personnel and others informally discharged from enemy military or paramilitary organizations" fell into a different category. Such individuals would be detained and turned over to "the appropriate Allied demobilization authority," the Big Three having confirmed at Yalta that quislings, traitors, and war criminals would, without question, be sent back to meet whatever punishment their betrayed homeland deemed appropriate.[13]

With unwilling repatriates relegated to a caveat, the "displaced person" designation rested on a common denominator of removal from home, presumed to be involuntary. By returning people to their homes, UNRRA and military government personnel would restore the "national order of things." This presumptuous logic brooked just one exception: those who, in the terminology of SHAEF's handbook, had been "persecuted because of their race, religion or activities in favor of the United Nations." Victims of persecution, it was conceded, might not wish to be repatriated. Irrespective of citizenship, they would be "cared for as UN DPs," including those of German nationality—the booklet's sole nod to Jewish survivors of Nazi genocide.[14]

Without shelter, employment, or other means of subsistence, DPs would depend on external support both for immediate sustenance and to travel home, or so U.S. and UNRRA personnel commonly supposed. And if it required capable others to do for the displaced what they could not accomplish themselves, DPs could readily be conceived as both passive and appreciative recipients of relief, rehabilitation, and repatriation—a third R missing from UNRRA's title but not from its mandate. Yet the SHAEF handbook also attempted to dispel illusions that DPs would either willingly follow orders when issued or be grateful for assistance. A prefatory paragraph predicted displaced persons' likely mindset on initial contact with military government personnel: "The experiences which they have undergone during the past few years may make them difficult to control; they may have little initiative[;] their desire to take revenge may result in looting and general lawlessness and their pent-up feelings against their former oppressors may express themselves in resentment of any type of discipline or authority." This characterization conveyed mixed messages about the appropriate attitude military personnel should adopt toward their putative charges. DPs were marked by undefined "experiences" at the hands of "oppressors." But if mistreatment was implied by this oblique phraseology, compassion for its sufferers was not. DPs were expected to be apathetically devoid of "initiative," yet also prone to avenging violence and aggressively mistrustful of anyone who presumed to manage them. Control was, however, military government's first order of business. Thus it was as unruly impediments to postwar order that soldiers commonly approached DPs.[15]

Far from lacking initiative, many former forced laborers did not listlessly await Allied direction as the Third Reich collapsed. Without means of subsistence, they couldn't, after all, simply sit and wait for incoming Allied soldiers to arrive, take charge, and dispense dehydrated rations. Instead, they set about taking household possessions, clothing, and food from German homes, shops, and farmland. "They do a thorough job, a finished masterpiece of robbery and pillage," exclaimed Albert Hutler, a social worker from Chicago in civilian life, then serving as a DP officer with the Seventh U.S. Army military government detachment in Mannheim. Looting was a necessary survival strategy, not simply an expression of vengefulness. Some occupation personnel, including Hutler, understood this and sided with DPs against Germans in disputes over property. But while acts of appropriation may have had both necessity and retributive justice on their side, unauthorized expropriations posed a challenge to Germany's governability, just as DPs' possession of weapons contravened military government's intended monopoly over armed force. Mannheim and its environs, noted Hutler, existed "in a polyglot state of nature, raw and threatening." Encounters between DP gangs and German civilians often struck occupation soldiers as charged with murderous potential, and some didn't hesitate to threaten—or employ—lethal force in response. Kenneth Clouse recalled that the officer who briefed his unit on military government work had "said that if anyone gave us any trouble, we should take them into the woods and shoot them." Vexed by roving groups of armed Polish DPs who were raiding farms in the area under his authority, Clifton Lisle grimly warned his diary that he would "hang a few" if he could catch them.[16]

Curbing lawlessness was one reason why American personnel sought to confine displaced persons in camps as quickly as they could in the spring of 1945. Some remained in the factories, sheds, and dormitories where they had hitherto been confined as forced laborers, running them as self-governing communities. Others roamed the countryside, camping in barns or abandoned Wehrmacht barracks. In cities, DPs bivouacked in parks—impromptu camps that occupation troops tried to formalize and enclose. Some of the earliest military-run DP camps were crude replicas of POW camps where razor wire was simply run around the perimeter of a field or park. Not surprisingly, given the military's rough methods of emergency management, the distinction between enemy prisoners of war and displaced persons could appear notional to soldiers charged with immobilizing both populations. Alarmed by this indiscriminate hostility, military government officer Maurice Kurtz told his wife that "Capt. A. would like put all foreigners in jail, all Displaced Persons," likening him to the "wop"-bashing Captain Purvis in *A Bell for Adano.* Other soldiers were more sanguine about shepherding stray bodies into camps. "We made containment areas by stringing barbed wire over large open areas, then established road blocks at strategic points and collected DPs into the camps," recorded William Puntenney, noting the strategic use of food as an enticement. Hungry people mostly "did as they were told."[17]

Another pressing reason to bring DPs into the ambit of military government stemmed from anxiety over public health and the spread of infectious diseases. With memories of the influenza epidemic that followed World War I still vivid, military epidemiologists and civilian relief workers feared another postwar catastrophe. The conditions in which many DPs lived or from which they had recently been liberated—calculated to degrade the human body—appeared perfect incubators for disease. Typhus and dysentery had swept many concentration camps, ravaging inmates already brutalized, emaciated, and exhausted, hence all the more susceptible to infection. Fears of contagion were amplified by experts' disparaging views of displaced persons as strangers to hygiene, sanitation, and cleanliness by dint of ethnicity, poverty, or both. The places from which DPs came—or whence American observers imagined they hailed—were envisioned as primitive, pestilent backwaters: farms, shtetls, or ghettoes mired in dirt and crawling with germs.[18]

Disgust formed a leitmotif of American reactions to DPs. No phrase recurred more regularly in official reports and private correspondence than "filthy beyond description." "Filth" served as a shorthand—left to the reader's imagination to fill in or block out—that encompassed every kind of detritus and waste. It was, however, human excreta that the euphemism most commonly implied, as though politeness dictated this evasive phraseology. But even if they substituted "filth" for "feces," many soldiers' letters, diaries, and memoirs leave little doubt that what most disturbed Americans about displaced persons was their seemingly ineradicable preference for relieving themselves wherever the urge overtook them and their failure to clean up the results. Harold Berge, a medic in Templeton's unit, drew an explicit connection between the overflowing toilets found in a facility for Jewish DPs in Nuremberg and the "most miserable days" of his army career, though he managed to shirk the order to sanitize the building by compelling German health workers to do so.[19]

Military government personnel recoiled from a variety of "excremental assault[s]." As historian Frank Costigliola has documented, American prisoners of the Wehrmacht released into Soviet hands often found "especially upsetting" Russian "practices for the disposal—or rather the nondisposal—of human wastes." In fact, under whatever circumstances they encountered their Red Army counterparts, American soldiers commonly remarked on the apparent lack of familiarity "Ivan" displayed with flushing toilets. By the same token, few occupation soldiers in Asia failed to offer the folks back home—in tones oscillating between horror and humor—a pungent whiff of the "honey carts" that collected human waste in Korea and Japan. Brought into intimate proximity with DPs, American military personnel routinely expressed heightened sensations of defilement and fears of contamination. No wonder, then, that the SHAEF handbook devoted several detailed paragraphs to the construction of latrines, including precise measurements for how far apart stalls should be placed, the optimal degree of separation between urinals, and preferred ratios between numbers of users and facilities to be constructed.[20]

Horror over the human body—its functions, dysfunctions, and degradation—was particularly evident in American soldiers' responses to survivors of Nazi concentration and extermination camps. Entering the camps, servicemen were often aghast at both the emaciated condition of those still alive and the staggering evidence of mass killing all around. When they tried to verbalize the horrific scenes they'd witnessed in letters home, many expressed simultaneous rage toward the perpetrators and pity for their victims. But some also recoiled from camp inmates whose physical state and traumatized condition animated revulsion. Immobile, skeletal beings appeared eerily corpselike. Differently alarming (or inspiring) were those survivors who, without waiting for the tardy wheels of military justice to grind, were executing their erstwhile SS captors.[21]

Even if they recognized that Nazi policy had deliberately set out to starve, brutalize, and break camp inmates, some servicemen struggled to view survivors as fully human. Frederick Kroesen likened the former concentration camp he encountered in Bavaria to "an insane asylum, where the inmates were in charge." Others used more dehumanizing language. "Can you imagine what would happen if 2,500 hungry, starved pigs were turned loose?" Wilbur Berget rhetorically asked his family in May 1945, having just encountered DPs en masse for the first time in an unnamed Bavarian town. "They were everywhere, lousy and sick as they were; took whatever they could lay their hands on, ate garbage like I'd eat ice cream and three men even took the pants off a German as they approached him on the street. They cleaned out everything there was in the town to take—the civilians were lucky to have left the clothes they were wearing. At least one didn't escape with that." Yet, despite likening camp survivors to ravenous pigs, Berget categorically rejected compassion for the German locals stripped of possessions and pants. "I have no sympathy for those civilians that would allow those things to go on for six years. Even so, one had the gall to present us with a bill for what they'd taken from him. Others cried to us for help for protection from the

Jews—the same Jews that they'd tortured since 1939." These radically con-
flicted views of survivors of Nazi persecution—abstractly deserving but personally repellent—would figure prominently in U.S. military responses to
encamped DPs.[22]

Occupation personnel did not respond to all survivors of Axis camps alike.
It perhaps goes without saying that they handled newly released American
prisoners of war with far greater consideration than they typically showed
DPs. Especially tender treatment was reserved for those who had endured the
war years in Japanese captivity. Uncertain just how pernicious Japanese treatment of camp inmates had been, Allied commanders feared the worst based on
rumor and projection. Tokyo's failure to subscribe to the Geneva Conventions
governing the treatment of prisoners of war, coupled with Japan's reputation
for wartime savagery, occasioned grave alarm. As a result, British and American generals in the Pacific theater made it a priority to locate, liberate, care
for, and speedily dispatch home former prisoners, whether military or civilian internees of the Japanese.

The urgency of this quest was written into the very terms of Japan's surrender. On August 19, 1945, Douglas MacArthur ordered that the Japanese
delegation summoned to Manila to settle terms must furnish all available
information pertaining to POW and civilian internment camps "wherever
located, within Japan and Japanese controlled areas." This imperative was
reinforced by SCAP's first directive to the Japanese government, issued on
September 2, which decreed that the "safety and well-being of all United Nations Prisoners of War and Civilian Internees" must be "scrupulously preserved" until the occupation authorities assumed direct responsibility for
camp inmates. The process of locating and recovering prisoners was to be ex-
pedited by specially trained recovered personnel detachments (drawn
from U.S., British, and Commonwealth forces) that would accompany the
occupying army into Japan. Primed to drop supplies and parachute into liberated Japanese camps, one "mercy team" was allocated to every 500 prisoners.
In an unpublished memoir, A. E. Schanze conveyed the solicitousness of
these efforts to locate prisoners, living and dead, and treat them with due
dignity and dispatch: "There was more to be done than just driving up to a
camp and saying, 'Boys, here we go, you're free.' There had to be graves reg-
istration groups to locate any American or Allied graves near the prison

compounds so the bodies could be disinterred and returned to the United States. Needed were doctors, nurses, hospital corpsmen and ambulances to give emergency care to the sick prisoners and to transfer them comfortably back to Yokohama." Four hospital ships were docked there ready to transport former prisoners back home, a mission overseen by Harold Stassen, a former governor of Minnesota who had been handpicked by the secretary of the navy for this role.[23]

These elaborate preparations were not always necessary, however. As in Germany, some camp inmates liberated themselves if they were able to overcome their guards or if the latter fled in the hope of avoiding capture and indictment for war crimes. Members of the reconnaissance team sent into Japan in late August 1945 to survey conditions before General Robert Eichelberger arrived with the first wave of occupation troops were amazed to encounter four Americans who had managed to walk away from captivity. The self-liberated prisoners had simply boarded regular trains and ridden into Tokyo, then hitchhiked out to Atsugi airstrip. In compartments crowded with Japanese civilian travelers, the Americans "were utterly astonished to see everyone jump up and offer them seats," Clovis Byers (Eighth Army chief of staff) wrote home to his wife, Marie. "You've never seen such courtesy and consideration as they reported having received."[24]

Military personnel who greeted fellow citizens on release from Japanese captivity were more apt to regard them as ennobled than debased by the brutalizing treatment they had endured. Eichelberger devoted "constant attention" to former prisoners' well-being, making frequent visits to meet incoming train cars as they conveyed former prisoners to Yokohama. His responses to these "very moving" reunions were unabashedly emotional, in person and on paper, as were those of Byers. "It is a difficult sight to watch these men as they observe for the first time the care which is to be theirs at the hands of American doctors and nurses," Byers told Marie. The pathos of these anticipatory homecomings engendered deep feelings of empathy, tinged by tearfulness, as senior officers embraced comrades who were no longer the robust specimens they had been in 1941 when they'd been taken prisoner in the Philippines. Their wasted bodies, distressing and enraging to behold, failed to animate visceral disgust of the sort sometimes triggered by encounters with DPs. Although wasted, hollow cheeked, and "in tatters," former prisoners remained (in their welcoming peers' eyes) recognizably kindred beings—men who had been starved and abused, not rendered subhuman. If shared

FIG. 5.1 General MacArthur embraces General Jonathan Wainwright in Yokohama's new Grand Hotel on September 2, 1945—their first meeting since they parted in embattled Corregidor four years earlier. Harry S. Truman Library & Museum [98–2448].

nationality was not the sine qua non of sympathy, it undoubtedly heightened Americans' reactions to prisoners. On one occasion, Eichelberger was surprised to find that the "trainload of returnees" he'd gone to greet "turned out to be mostly Javanese." It was, he told his diary, "still a stirring sight," but evidently fellow feeling was less intense.[25]

On September 20, 1945, barely two weeks into the occupation, Eichelberger was again on hand at Yokohama Station, this time to welcome—and wave on—the final trainload of former prisoners as they arrived to the accompaniment of two military bands and a throng of occupation dignitaries. In just eighteen days, Allied troops had liberated prisoners from all the Japanese camps in Honshu, Hokkaido, and Shikoku: a total of 23,985 people. Soon they were sailing home.[26]

Eichelberger then set about converting the emptied camp at Omori, a tiny island thirteen miles north of Yokohama, into a prison for Japanese war criminals. Responsive to the suffering of former inmates, the Eighth Army commander was also highly sensitive to criticism reaching him from home that the occupation was too soft on Japan's wartime leaders. "So he has come to the conclusion that if he puts all Japanese, high or low, in a camp formerly occupied by POWs the people back home cannot criticize him for being too lenient with the Japanese," Byers confided to his spouse. The general was "trying to lean over backward" to satisfy home-front vengefulness—too far, in his chief of staff's estimation. Inside the cantonment of tin-roofed, plywood buildings at Omori, Byers found conditions intolerably crude: no furniture, just parallel wooden platforms covered by tatami mats and a dirt floor. Except for a "community tub," washing facilities were outdoors. Replacing these un-satisfactory ablution arrangements with American-style plumbing was the only significant alteration the Eighth Army proposed to undertake at the camp. As Byers explained the symbolism to Marie, "Our goal in the treatment of these war criminal suspects is that they shall use the same simple Japanese facilities which were made available to our men when they were prisoners. The diffi-culty comes in the standard of sanitation which we are going to compel. This will be at the best American concept of cleanliness. We hope in this fashion to show them something of our ideas in an effort to make them realize they are worth striving for." Here, as elsewhere, occupation officers conceived hot showers and flushing toilets as the standard-bearers of civilization. Improved personal hygiene would, Byers intimated, work its own ameliorative magic on the incarcerated war criminals.[27]

American convictions about the healthy minds that surely inhabit well-scrubbed bodies were perhaps lost on war criminals awaiting trial and exe-cution. As shrewd PR, however, Eichelberger's stunt worked. Noting the imminent relocation of twenty-three Japanese prisoners, including General Hideki Tojo, to "one of the pesthole camps in which Allied prisoners of war suffered atrocities," the *New York Times* relished the "touch of poetic justice" involved in housing Japanese war criminals at Omori—the camp from which "the Allied world first learned of the atrocious conditions in which Japan kept the captives." The Japanese would get a taste of their own medicine, minus the vermin "now being exterminated by application of DDT." On October 6, the *Times* reported that the new inmates appeared to be settling in with remarkable equanimity. Half an hour after arriving, General Homma Masaharu, who had commanded the Japanese invasion of the Philippines, had been spotted "squatting on his bunk crosslegged reading—in English—*It Can't Happen Here*."[28]

Omori was not the only Axis camp to undergo a radical role reversal at the victors' hands. In their zone of Germany, American occupation forces turned various concentration camps into prisons for suspected German war criminals. But a straightforward turning of the tables wasn't invariably the operative principle. Several former SS-run camps also served to accommodate displaced persons—sometimes living side by side with imprisoned war criminals, as was the case at Landsberg in Bavaria, one of the largest camps for Jewish DPs. (Before the war, the prison attached to the military barracks in Landsberg am Lech was better known as the location in which Adolf Hitler and Rudolph Hess had concocted *Mein Kampf*.) Transforming concentration camps or Wehrmacht barracks into fit places for DPs' inhabitation was work that some conscientiously antifascist American officers regarded as a practical lesson in reeducation for German civilians. Taken aback one day in June 1945 by an unexpected call informing him that 1,300 DPs would shortly arrive in the Bavarian town under his command, Kurtz gave its residents an ultimatum. "Practically the entire town's population was 'sweating it out', everyone contributing utensils, dishes etc.," Kurtz told his wife, Laya. "It was a comforting sight to see the city's prettiest gals and most dutiful former Hitler Jugend, to see them on their knees scrubbing floors for their former slave laborers. All I did was give the order to the Burgomeister to have all in readiness within 48 hours. To do this, he had to enlist the active assistance, willing or otherwise, of the city's 15,000." Kurtz informed the mayor that this represented "his city's first opportunity to prove that they can rid themselves of the Nazi plague, namely by working, in their turn, for those who once slaved for the Germans . . . and not so long ago, at that. He saw the point. Result: within 48 hours, 4 large buildings were made livable."[29]

Fixed on mass repatriation, U.S. military government personnel set out with the assumption that most DP camps would have a restricted life span befitting their narrow purpose. SHAEF planners, after all, did not conceive facilities for DPs as semipermanent communities but as way stations through which transients would fleetingly pass as they embarked on the journey home. Tellingly, SHAEF's *Guide to the Care of Displaced Persons in Germany* spoke only of "assembly centers," not camps. These were intended to provide emergency clothing and shelter; curb the spread of disease through inoculations and DDT sprayings; and register individuals, having verified their nationality and weeded out possible war criminals.[30]

In the spring and summer of 1945, some U.S. Army–administered facilities functioned much as SHAEF had envisioned. Military government officers who elected DP work as their chosen field set to work at a frenzied pace on entry into Germany, weeks in advance of final victory. "Lady it is a job," exclaimed Hutler on April 3, 1945, having just arrived in Mannheim. "It is the most immense piece of work I ever expect to do for the rest of my life . . . unbelievably stupendous." Hutler, like others, was awed by the scale of human displacement, the diverse origins of his petitioners, and the profundity and variety of their needs, from finding a way to Palestine to locating their next meal. "I'm not dealing in a few human beings but in hundreds of thousands—in Russians, in Greeks, Frenchmen, Italians, Hollanders, Belgians, and any others there may be in our area. I've talked to Hindus, to Russian officers, to everything imaginable. Every day is different," he explained to his wife, Leanore.[31]

And every day was exceedingly long. Hutler detailed shifts that began at dawn and continued until midnight or one in the morning. Overseeing a bailiwick "as large as Illinois," containing 28,000 displaced people housed in six different camps, his first priority was to find transportation to convey French DPs home. Their repatriation was conducted at breakneck speed. On May 7 Hutler reported that 36,218 French men and women had been bundled west in trains, having been registered, deloused, medically examined, and billeted in "a fine apartment house from which we've evicted the Germans." Not until late June did he relate that the pace of work had "begun to slacken a bit," on-duty hours dwindling to twelve. By early August, however, Hutler's DP assignment was "about over."[32]

While Hutler and his three-man team hastily transported French DPs west, other military government detachments directed eastern Europeans of different nationalities into separate camps before sending them off in the opposite direction. Some departed in festive high spirits. In the Tyrolean resort of Kufstein, just on the Austrian side of the border with Germany, Lisle was struck by the exuberance of departing Soviet DPs who had bedecked a freight train with red flags and nailed green spruce boughs all over the sides. In terms of ethnicity, the homeward-bound crowd was, he judged, "a mixed grill of everything, many Mongolians"—common derogatory shorthand for those hailing from the Soviet Asian republics.[33]

Others strenuously resisted repatriation. It seemed that "move" was always a transitive verb: something done *to* them. Over the summer and fall of 1945, protest mounted, particularly among Russians, Ukrainians, and Balts, a significant number of whom had no wish to return to Soviet-controlled territory. As DPs became more obstreperous, Soviet military authorities demanded greater control over bodies they claimed as inalienable national property. Red Army liaison officers insisted on gaining access to camps in the U.S. zone to ensure they weren't harboring errant Soviet citizens. They also complained to American occupation authorities that camps had become politicized battlegrounds in which former Nazi collaborators were ruthlessly intimidating DPs who wanted to return home, forcing them to stay put and remain mute. With pressure on recalcitrant DPs to return intensifying from both Soviet and U.S. authorities, some took increasingly drastic measures. A number of displaced persons committed suicide or tried to provoke American soldiers to shoot them rather than be herded into boxcars. After a series of what the United States' Political Adviser for Germany Robert Murphy gingerly called "unpleasant incidents involving violence"—DPs' strenuous resistance to repatriation at gunpoint, and a number of mass suicides—U.S. policy began to shift away from compulsory repatriation.[34]

Disturbed by the unwanted role of armed enforcer, some occupation personnel voiced misgivings. Hutler was among them. His assignment with French DPs at an end, Hutler's next task was to deliver a group of Ukrainians into Soviet hands. "Yesterday in attempting to move some Ukrainians that the Russians classify as Russian, I found out what it can mean to be moved from one place to another; to fear, to be petrified," he told Leanore. "Our orders were to move these people to a Russian camp. The people refused to go; they barricaded themselves in their buildings; women knelt and prayed to soldiers not to take them; soldiers fired in the air. People screamed and confusion was everywhere." The obdurate Ukrainians were, Hutler conceded, "really not good people"—but "people all the same."[35]

What was to be done with these particularly "displeased persons" was a vexed question for U.S. military government. As American prisoners reappeared from areas under Red Army control, willingness to force eastern Europeans onto trains at gunpoint dwindled, since concerns for POWs' speedy return had contributed significantly to Washington's initial support for involuntary repatriation. By late 1945, the headlong rush to shunt DPs out of Germany was over. The residual "hard core" of DPs, as they were bluntly labeled, constituted those who could not, or would not, be repatriated. Locating suitable destinations for "non-repatriables" became the overarching goal of U.S. policy. This objective required high-level wrangling as Washington attempted to cajole often reluctant foreign states into easing immigration restrictions. None proved more obstructive than Clement Attlee's government, which adamantly refused admission into Palestine of 100,000 Jewish refugees—a quota pressed by the Harry S. Truman administration from August 1945 onward. At the same time, the president tried, and initially failed, to persuade Congress to modify the United States' own reluctance to admit displaced persons in any number. A Displaced Persons Act wasn't passed until 1948. Even then, its terms favored Baltic refugees over Jewish survivors of the Holocaust.[36]

For U.S. occupation soldiers, the nature of the DP assignment changed markedly over the fall of 1945. In the first instance, their job had been conceived more in logistical than humanitarian terms: gathering and sorting displaced people by nationality, recording names, issuing identity papers, and jamming bodies into trains as quickly as rolling stock could be found. *Clearance* was military government's first order of business, with DPs conceived as war's human debris—another kind of hazardous matter to be neutralized and removed. Speed and mass wrote depersonalization into the terms of military engagement with the displaced. "I find that when one begins dealing in masses one is prone to forget the individuals," Hutler confided to Leanore—acutely aware that some of those seeking his help must have hesitated to knock on an office door marked "A. Hutler." But he had been jolted from this numbed state of unresponsiveness. "Ever since a little Polish girl, a Jewess, who pestered me to help her, until I sort of lost patience, told me that I had become too big to think of individual problems, I've thought this over. (This sentence is why I carried Ds as grades in Rhetoric). She made me feel like a stuffy buck because I know she was right."[37]

Not all occupation personnel experienced the same epiphany, however. Indeed, antipathy toward displaced persons became more pronounced over the fall as the DP "problem" altered from assisted mobility to protracted encampment. Military government had entered what Dwight D. Eisenhower termed its "static phase." No longer staging grounds for imminent departure, assembly centers solidified into semipermanent settlements. Implicitly, camps promised to render their residents more easily controlled by overseeing authorities. But soldiers often found something very different, frequently responding to these disorderly spaces, and their wayward residents, with shuddering distaste. Viewed through military eyes, DPs could appear willfully obstructive—"sullen, bedraggled, suspicious, non-cooperative," in Templeton's characterization. The task of classification—one of encampment's primary procedures—was challenged by people who asserted fictitious national identities in the hope of evading compulsory repatriation, as did some Ukrainians and Poles by claiming to be from the Baltic states. Trying to verify nationality was made no easier for American soldiers by the multitude of languages spoken in DP camps. Military government officers in this line of work had to hope that their subalterns understood (and, better yet, could speak) some Polish or Russian.[38]

DPs' resistance to classification—their disinclination to be managed and disciplined by military authority—extended far beyond the matter of obscured national identity. In camps, human bodies and bodily functions appeared particularly exposed, upsetting many soldiers who interacted with the residents. John Wortham, a division medical supply officer in Bavaria who made regular inspections of camps, recoiled from this "uncategorizability." His abhorrence lingered decades later in an unpublished memoir written for his daughters. Of Hungarian DPs, Wortham remarked, "Decadence wasn't a word to them but a way of life. Some were alcoholics, some were drug-dependent. Many were homosexual and many were promiscuous. Apparently no one fit into just one category. They slopped over into several others. The women were chic, educated and were generally attractive but, to me, very scary." Wortham's brush with these attractive-repulsive "degenerate" Hungarian DPs clearly upset his notions of respectability. He was also, he informed his daughters, so committed to his own chastity—and so perturbed by the specter of venereal disease—that he forswore any sexual activity as an occupation soldier. All the more reason, then, to recoil from polymorphous, promiscuous sexuality openly displayed in DP camps. Wortham's response to unregulated, "irregular" DP intercourse was not, however, purely idiosyncratic. Animated by a similar mistrust of categorical sloppiness, military physicians targeted female displaced persons in campaigns to eradicate, or at least reduce, venereal infection via programs of mandatory genital inspection, a mission entrusted to often reluctant UNRRA medical personnel.[39]

U.S. military government's treatment of Jewish survivors soon became the most hotly contested dimension of DP policy—in occupied Germany and the United States alike—fueled by Truman's order to Eisenhower on August 31, 1945, that Jewish DPs would henceforth receive separate, and superior, treatment. Among other things, the president instructed Eisenhower to requisition more "decent houses" for DPs rather than relying primarily on camps for accommodation. "This," Truman proposed, "is one way to implement the Potsdam policy that the German people 'cannot escape responsibility for what they have brought upon themselves.'" Underscoring the imperative, Truman quoted the report that had prompted his instruction, written by Earl G. Harrison (former dean of the University of Pennsylvania Law School) after a monthlong inspection tour of conditions for Jewish DPs in Germany: "As matters now stand, we appear to be treating the Jews as the Nazis treated them, except that we do not exterminate them. They are in concentration camps in large numbers under our military guard instead of S.S. troops. One is led to wonder whether the German people, seeing this, are not supposing that we are following or at least condoning Nazi policy."[40]

Harrison's 8,000-word report appeared verbatim in the *New York Times* on the same day as Truman's order, exposing attentive Americans to the full gamut of mistreatment condemned by the special investigator. Harrison began by excoriating the fact that the "first and worst" victims of Nazi persecution had been "liberated" only in a narrow military sense. Not only did many thousand survivors remain confined in camps, some were living in the very same camps where they had witnessed their loved ones' mass murder, including "some of the most notorious of the concentration camps." (Harrison made particular reference to 14,000 Jewish DPs accommodated at Bergen-Belsen in the British occupation zone.) Many lacked adequate clothing. Some were "obliged to wear German SS uniforms," while others possessed only the garb provided by their erstwhile captors, producing a "rather hideous striped pajama effect." Languishing in idleness, fed on little more than large, unleavened quantities of "black, wet and extremely unappetizing bread," Jewish survivors gazed out from their sites of confinement at better nourished, better clothed Germans going about their business freely. They had also witnessed the frenzied activity that propelled hundreds of thousands of other displaced persons into motion on their way home. Contrasting this brisk tempo with the torpor of their own situation, "unrepatriable" Jews despairingly wondered when—and whether—they would reach their longed-for destinations in Palestine, the United States, Britain, or South America.[41]

Harrison took aim at the widespread contention that Jewish DPs should *not* be treated as a distinct, and distinctly entitled, group. "While admittedly it is not normally desirable to set aside particular racial or religious groups from their nationality categories, the plain truth is that this was done for so long by the Nazis that a group has been created which has special needs," his report stressed. "Jews as Jews (not as members of their nationality groups) have been more severely victimized than the non-Jewish members of the same nationalities." Here, Harrison skewered a tendency prevalent among senior occupation officers to argue that treating "Jews as Jews" ran against the grain of Americans' traditional concern for the individual human. Accommodating Jewish DPs in isolation, critics contended, would replicate the discriminatory practices of the Nazis—though their implication that segregation was necessarily stigmatizing was a curious one. The U.S. military itself, after all, operated on the principle that there was nothing inherently prejudicial about segregation on racial lines.

Senior occupation personnel regularly argued that preferential treatment of Jewish DPs risked provoking an anti-Semitic backlash among Germans. An analogous fear of "overplaying" Jewish suffering structured how U.S. officials represented the Nazi camps, their victims, and survivors in early newsreels and documentary films. These pictorial records of Nazi atrocity, while intended to place the industrialized mass killings beyond all possible doubt, resisted forthright acknowledgment that Jews were, as Harrison put it, the "first and worst" victims of a policy aimed at complete annihilation of European Jewry. The most important such film, *Die Todesmühlen (Death Mills)* told viewers that the corpses they saw belonged to many nationalities and religions. Filmmakers rationalized this evasiveness in terms of a desire to avoid stirring up anti-Semitism. Some unrepentant Germans, they ventured, shown irrefutable evidence of a genocidal onslaught against Jews, might regret only the incompleteness of the Nazis' work—not the persecution, torture, and mass murder. By universalizing the camps' victims, Allied documentarians hoped German viewers would experience the intended epiphany, realizing that they shared collective moral responsibility for nebulously defined "crimes against humanity."[42]

Confronted with Harrison's blistering report, Eisenhower protested that he had already authorized the requisitioning of some German homes for DPs' inhabitation. His subordinates were working hard to improve the quality and variety of food, just as they were striving to ameliorate the sanitary conditions of camps that did, in fact, separately accommodate groups along national or religious lines. However, while not exactly untrue, these claims obscured a good deal. Earlier in August, Ike *had* ordered George S. Patton (in command of military government in Bavaria) to oversee a wholesale improvement of conditions at Jewish DP camps. But Eisenhower neglected to mention that some senior commanders raised the specter of German anti-Semitism as a rather flimsy mask for their own prejudice. Their real quibble, in other words, wasn't with the idea of differential treatment but with the idea that Jewish DPs deserved more calories and better accommodations. Regrettably, the general to whom Eisenhower entrusted the ameliorative mission was outspokenly of this opinion himself. "If for Jews, why not Catholics, Mormons, etc.?" Patton testily asked his diary on August 29, 1945.[43]

Despite having witnessed conditions in Nazi camps firsthand, Patton exhibited no empathy for survivors whom he described as looking "exactly like mummies and . . . on about the same level of intelligence." His journal and letters home registered much deeper revulsion toward DP camps than toward Ohrdruf, which he had visited shortly after its liberation on April 12. Others present recorded that Patton had been nauseated by what he saw there, retreating behind a hut to vomit. In his own writings the general made no mention of his body's involuntary recoil from Nazi atrocity. Yet he reveled in describing symptoms of nausea prompted by conditions at Jewish DP camps. After visiting one camp in Bavaria with Eisenhower to participate in a Yom Kippur celebration, Patton lingered over its recollection, savoring the bilious piquancy of his own prejudice:

> We entered the synagogue, which was packed with the greatest stinking bunch of humanity I have ever seen. When we got about

half way up, the head rabbi, who was dressed in a fur hat similar to that worn by Henry VIII of England, and in a surplice heavily embroidered and very filthy, came down and met the General. A copy of the Talmud, I think it is called, written on a sheet and rolled around a stick, was carried by one of the attending physicians. . . . The smell was so terrible that I almost fainted, and actually about three hours later, lost my lunch as a result of remembering it.[44]

Patton routinely used diary writing as a whetstone to sharpen his anti-Semitism. Two days earlier, he had taken umbrage at the idea that "the displaced person was a human being, which he is not," adding that "this applies particularly to Jews, who are lower than animals." The immediate trigger for this toxic emission was receipt of Eisenhower's order that Jewish DPs were to be afforded distinct and better treatment—a policy Patton argued would produce a "severe pogrom." He would follow Ike's command, he mockingly announced, by placing Jews in "sort of improved ghettoes." In practice, Patton willfully disobeyed both the spirit and the letter of Eisenhower's injunction. A few days later, he told a fellow general to photograph the homes of thirty-two "rich German families" before moving "these animals" in. Documentary evidence might prove useful should the DPs damage the dwellings or remove the owners' property. To minimize that possibility, Patton further instructed his colleague to "move the Germans with as much consideration as possible" and to "give them transportation to move as much of their decent property out as they could"—a violation of Eisenhower's stipulation that Germans be permitted to remove only their bedding and a modest amount of clothing.[45]

Germans, unsurprisingly, did not respond with equanimity to either the prospect or the fact of eviction. The surrender of homes for the victors' inhabitation was a predictable consequence of defeat shouldered with grim acquiescence, judging from soldiers' accounts of these initial ejections. But the American demand that Germans trade places with the Third Reich's erstwhile victims was more unpalatable. For dislodged Germans, this reversal of roles simultaneously constituted an accusation of culpability, a demand for reparation, and an intolerable pollution of domestic purity. German communities in the vicinity of DP camps made American officers well aware that appropriation of homes would spell trouble. Rumors of forced relocations electrified the atmosphere in such places, a phenomenon recorded by Major Irving Heymont in letters home from Landsberg to his wife, Joan, in New York.[46]

In this small Bavarian town near Munich, the twenty-seven-year-old officer oversaw a Jewish DP facility that now accommodated approximately 6,000 people under the day-to-day management of UNRRA and representatives of the American Joint Distribution Committee. Although Heymont favored requisitioning homes, he also experienced firsthand the mayhem that could ensue, blaming both DPs for their premature possessiveness and German townsfolk for provocation. The first mass eviction he presided over, on October 4, 1945, turned into a melee as DPs gathered around the locals' homes while they were being vacated. According to the lengthy account Heymont sent Joan, the camp residents began objecting to the volume of possessions that Germans were removing, asserting their own greater need:

> The Jewish DP camp cops appeared on the scene and started to examine what the Germans were taking out of the houses. Soon the Jews started to go directly into the houses even before they were vacated. . . . Before long they were looting and pillaging all the houses in the vicinity of the camp. At first I started to try to control them through their own police. I soon realised that some of the police were doing the looting. It is to their credit that many of the police were trying to enforce order. Fearing that the situation was getting out of order I turned out every available man and every available truck and cleared the town of all Jewish DPs, police and all, and moved them back into the camp.

Heymont, who had hitherto allowed DPs to guard the camp rather than army personnel, reversed track, reimposing military control over Landsberg. Having confined residents overnight, he then instituted a pass system to control their movements the next day. Despite these draconian steps, the town remained abuzz with "the wildest rumors." The "most popular" of these fantastic projections, from what Heymont heard, was that "the entire town of Landsberg was to be turned over to the Jews," and that "from the hours of 1100 to 1300 all Jews were going to be turned out of the camp to loot and pillage at will." Meanwhile, Heymont's commanding officer, Captain Rein—"an excitable ass" whose sympathies lay with the townsfolk—was "going frantic and burning up the wires to Munich claiming that I had turned the Jews loose on the Germans."[47]

Burned by this experience, Heymont handled evictions differently thereafter, making sure to keep camp residents well away from residential areas until the premises were empty. To quell rumors of looting—by both DPs and his own men—he also insisted that before military personnel entered German homes, they remove all personal jewelry, watches, and money. Inspections of Heymont's soldiers would demonstrate that no German property had been illicitly removed. But these measures didn't dispel the cloud of rumor that darkened Landsberg. On November 7, the town erupted again with word that the Jewish DPs were to be "let loose to plunder the Germans" the next day—calculated retaliation for the Kristallnacht pogrom seven years earlier. When an UNRRA official ordered that a sewing machine be removed from a requisitioned home for DPs' use, townspeople took this as a signal that the "alleged looting had started." An angry mob quickly gathered, refusing to disperse on the UNRRA officer's command. By the time Heymont arrived on the scene, only fifteen or so Landsbergers remained. He promptly arrested them, issuing a stern warning to the burgomaster that there would be no looting and "if there was any more trouble in the village the whole village [would] be punished."[48]

Heymont's responses to both his senior commanders and the camp residents under his authority offer particularly revealing insights into occupation officers' fraught responses to Jews, Germans, and one another. Like many of his colleagues, Heymont struggled to recognize Jewish DPs as fully human. On first arrival at Landsberg in September 1945, he was overwhelmed by conditions "filthy beyond description," noting that residents "represent the worst among the Jews . . . beaten both spiritually and physically." "Most of the best Jews had been killed off by the Nazis," he added parenthetically. Subsequent letters home frequently elaborated on the camp's woeful sanitary situation, which included constantly clogged latrines and DPs relieving themselves in the corners of dormitories, corridors, stairwells, and even the larder of the kosher kitchen. This emphasis on the excremental also pervaded some U.S. newspaper reports, notably when editors sought to exonerate Eisenhower by suggesting that Harrison had overstated the case against the army or minimized the contribution DPs made to their own parlous situation. "Blame UNRRA and Jews for Filth of Camps," ran one accusatory *Chicago Daily Tribune* headline.[49]

Like many other officers, Heymont judged camp residents with assumptions about better and worse classes and nationalities that hewed closely to the hierarchy of ethnic desirability enshrined in the U.S. immigration quota system. Thus he deemed Lithuanians the best educated and admired the more prosperous Polish "infiltrees" who began arriving in the U.S. zones of Germany and Austria, and the American sector of Berlin, in large numbers in the fall of 1945. This new influx of Jewish refugees sparked considerable debate about whether they should be permitted entry, and whether those who had spent the war years in the Soviet Union were eligible for DP status. This dispute was settled in the affirmative, but not without a good deal of griping from some disgruntled officers who regarded these Palestine-bound "infiltrees" as undeserving profiteers—anticipating a binary between voluntary migrants and political persecutees that would soon come to structure the postwar international refugee regime. "Most all officers were afraid to oppose these people for fear of being attacked as anti-semitic," General Frank Howley grumbled in his Berlin diary. "There was much unofficial talk condemning the people who were, in fact, well fed and well clothed and quite different from the original DP's who had been victims of Fascism."[50]

Like many fellow officers, Heymont found working with DPs a source of persistent frustration, leavened by moments of intense gratification. Despite the major's hectoring admonitions that Jews elsewhere managed to live in cleanliness, and his lectures on the redemptive power of hard work, camp residents simply wouldn't do as instructed. Yet threatening to use force made Heymont uneasy. Other mechanisms of compulsion—like cutting rations for DPs who refused to work—were equally problematic in their redolence of Nazi methods. Above all, Heymont struggled to understand why residents of the densely overpopulated Landsberg camp proved so resistant to being moved to a less crowded, more spacious camp nearby. At Föhrenwald a mother and child might even enjoy a room to themselves. It defied reason, as Heymont saw it, that DPs would stubbornly refuse to budge when dorms flimsily partitioned by fabric hangings cramped any possibility of a dignified existence. Like the toilet situation, sleeping arrangements constantly distressed Heymont, who was troubled that several adult men and women should share the same room, with the number of bodies exceeding the number of beds. "Again we find men and women sleeping together in more than one bed and rather happy about it. We have plenty of beds available but they are not particularly interested," he complained in late October.[51]

FIG. 5.2   Peter Carrol's October 1945 photograph of Jewish DPs at Feldafing Camp depicts crowded conditions. The original caption noted that residents were soon to "be removed to better German homes that have been requisitioned." Peter Carrol/Associated Press [4510050125].

When Heymont kept his affronted viscera in check, however, he glimmeringly recognized that much of what he initially regarded as evidence of indolence, indifference to cleanliness, or stubborn willfulness was better understood as the result of extreme suffering, "spiritual and physical." Indeed, the edition of Heymont's Landsberg correspondence printed in 1982 offers an "improved" version in which the author's latent intuitions about the Holocaust's traumatic imprint on Jewish DPs have been rendered explicit. In the letters' published form, Heymont recasts DPs' resistance to outdoor toilets as a consequence of the lethal peril involved in walking outside at night to latrine blocks in Nazi camps. Similarly, he interprets residents' refusal to transfer to less-crowded Föhrenwald as resistance to *being* moved—triggering flashbacks to Nazi transports—as well as stemming from an attachment to Landsberg, a community where new allegiances had been formed, new families started, and new possibilities imagined. Heymont also came to appreciate that the DPs' apparent "shamelessness"—conducting in public behavior that was properly private—was primarily a function of the indecent exposure of the DP camps themselves. Subject to constant, often unannounced, inspection by visiting generals, journalists, politicians, and others, Landsberg afforded little respect to residents who were often treated as inanimate exhibits—a situation that, perversely, was aggravated after the Harrison report prompted more frequent and invasive tours.[52]

As the original letters make clear, Heymont sought to assist camp residents' regeneration in numerous ways, supporting the camp committee's efforts to stimulate Jewish cultural life and intellectual development by establishing schools, a university, and a newspaper. He also looked favorably on Zionist activism among Landsberg's residents and battled with superior officers for permission to assign German farmland to kibbutzim eager to cultivate both the land and their agricultural skills. The major advocated on behalf of the camps' residents in multiple ways, earning their respect and gratitude. When Heymont departed from Landsberg in December 1945, he was hailed by one UNRRA officer as Landsberg's very own Major Joppolo—though he confessed to his wife that he would have to read Hersey's ubiquitous novel, *A Bell for Adano,* to discover what tribulations his fictional counterpart had faced and whether they offered any approximation of Landsberg's challenges.

The UNRRA official's likening of Heymont to Joppolo was perhaps more apt than he appreciated. In the novel, Joppolo's success stems from the cultural heritage the Italian American major shares with Adano's residents, allowing him to appreciate why they yearn for a church bell above all else. Heymont was also a Joppolo figure in terms of shared kinship—but secretly so. Throughout his four months at Landsberg, Heymont concealed from both military colleagues and camp residents that he was Jewish. A career army officer, he had kept this identity hidden throughout the war and continued to conceal it afterward. In letters home, Irving fretted that if the DPs knew he, too, was Jewish they would subject him to more intensive petitioning, which would be harder to resist. Beset by conflicting pressures and prejudices, Heymont dreaded discovery or betrayal by what he regarded as his telltale features: "my beaked nose, recessive chin with fat, and my protruding adam's apple." When a photographer shared images captured during a red-letter day at Landsberg—the visit of Zionist leader David Ben-Gurion—Heymont was alarmed when fellow officers joked, "Major, you are beginning to look like a DP!" His secret remained safe, however. Leo Schwarz's pioneering study in 1953 of Jewish DPs and those who aided them, *The Redeemers,* described Heymont as "a spare, intelligent, idealistic New Yorker of Protestant faith."[53]

Heymont's reluctance to "let the mask slip," as he put it, obliquely attests the pervasiveness and virulence of anti-Semitism among senior officers. Alert to anything that smacked of "special pleading" on Jews' behalf, several of Heymont's superiors behaved indulgently toward local German residents, including SS prisoners housed on the periphery of the Jewish camp at Landsberg, which was later the site of execution for twenty-two Mauthausen war criminals. The alarming proximity of these two encamped communities, as well as the preference shown to SS prisoners, deeply perturbed Heymont. As the first postwar winter approached, Heymont was infuriated that his nemesis General Sidney Wooten refused permission to have SS prisoners to chop wood for the DP camp, insisting that DPs should do it themselves. Overridden by a superior, Wooten then insisted that the SS outfit would work only "union hours." Adding insult to injury, Wooten introduced sports and leisure activities to the SS camp—teaching Nazi war criminals baseball, to Heymont's outrage—while denying the Landsberg DPs even a film projector for entertainment.[54]

And yet, despite these many troubling episodes, Heymont remained a regular army officer, proud of a professional affiliation that anchored his sense of self. He therefore bristled at what he considered excessive and undeserved criticism of army handling of DPs in the press back home. "I don't think the army should have to take the rap because after so many years in concentration camps the Jews have no marked desire or spirit to work or live clean. We can't be expected to reform them in no time flat after what they have been through," Heymont opined in the wake of the Harrison report. For all his superiors' insensitivity toward DPs and indulgence of Germans, Heymont didn't think the army was handling an impossible mission so badly. This verdict was endorsed by Hutler, who encouraged Leanore to inform their friends that "much more has been done for these people by Jewish soldiers and officers than by any organized aid." Neither UNRRA nor the Joint Chiefs of Staff had accomplished as much as "our own boys in their own silent ways." Hutler had enlisted with Jewish welfare in mind, convinced that soldiering, at least in its military government guise, could be compatible with humanitarianism. But Heymont took a different stance, emphatically stressing that the army had no aptitude for, nor any long-term future in, postwar welfare work. Like many other military men, he could hardly wait to transfer DP camps to UNRRA's exclusive control.[55]

Americans' tendency in Germany to find defeated foes more sympathetic than those whom the latter had victimized found a parallel in Asia. Under occupation, Japanese soldiers and civilians proved pleasingly tractable. At first this surprised U.S. military personnel who had expected their Asian nemeses to be as ferocious in defeat as they had been in battle. Such fears quickly evaporated, however. USMC Brigadier General Fred Beans later reminisced, with disarming bluntness, "You had trouble taking prisoners, that's why you shot so many. . . . But once you got them prisoners they were very well behaved." Viewed through military eyes, Japanese exhibited some of the same virtues as Germans: cleanliness next to orderliness at the apex of preferable attributes. Indeed, Japanese soldiers and sailors proved so cooperative that American officers entrusted them with a good deal of unsupervised responsibility in the epic task of "unmixing" people in Asia. They accorded Japanese naval officers, along with civilian welfare agencies, increasing authority to manage the shipment back to Japan of fellow nationals from scattered ports in Korea, Formosa, China, Indochina, Singapore, and Malaya. By March 1946, the U.S. Navy had handed over one hundred Liberty ships, eighty-five landing ship tanks (LSTs), and six hospital ships to expedite the process of shipping various ethnic groups to and from Japan. Before long, repatriation ships sailed under sole Japanese stewardship.[56]

As a result, most members of the U.S. occupation forces in Asia came into less extensive contact with displaced persons than did their counterparts in Europe. At Sasebo, one of the largest Japanese ports, the repatriation center was staffed by 650 Japanese, two U.S. Army officers, and thirty-five enlisted men. Senzaki, another major entrepôt where emptied ships conveying Japanese from Korea were loaded with Koreans being propelled in the other direction, was run by members of the British Commonwealth Occupation Force. Where Americans did encounter Asians in motion—or stalled in camps—they frequently judged them according to a racialized scale of value, much as their peers did in the European theater.[57]

These taxonomies of difference almost always privileged the defeated Japanese over populations the Allied occupiers had "liberated" from them, Koreans in particular. Marine Corps Lieutenant General James Berkeley, who ran a repatriation center at Yokosuka, unself-consciously reprised this classificatory mentality in an oral history interview conducted in 1973:

> The Japanese barracks were for people coming from the west and back to Japan. They would move in the barracks, they were spotless. They were moved in, even the civilians, in military fashion, somebody in charge, they slept there, neatly cleaned; they left the next day after they'd been processed, and it was spotless.
>
> The Chinese going the other way would come in, and they were fairly clean: they looked like what I would expect a Chinese troop train to look like—it wasn't too bad. But the Koreans, it looked like pigs that lived in the damn place. Some of them didn't even know how to take care of themselves. They knew nothing about toilets at all.

Embellishing the point, he added that on LSTs, Koreans "didn't even know what the plumbing was for; they used the deck." His disdain echoed what many of his peers in Europe felt toward displaced persons in general, and Jewish DPs in particular.[58]

Berkeley's demeaning view of Koreans was far from anomalous. SCAP's "Basic Initial Post-surrender Directive" instructed occupation troops that in Japan they would "treat Formosan-Chinese and Koreans as liberated peoples," but only "in so far as security permits." The caveat proved more consequential than the affirmative language. Relegated to a zone of indeterminacy, Koreans could be flexibly deemed friend or foe as the occupiers saw fit. But as popular resistance mounted to an avowedly emancipatory occupation that promptly forestalled national self-determination, Koreans were more often seen as troublemakers to be put down than as liberated people to be raised up. American personnel in Japan and southern Korea shared a jaundiced attitude toward Koreans as less civilized, less educated, and less pliant than the Japanese. Touching down in Tokyo in October 1946, army officer Orlando Ward registered in his diary that "the officers here talk as if they were Englishmen speaking of Ireland" when they discussed Korea. On arrival there days later, Ward added that the Koreans were "very independent. So called Irish of the Orient."[59]

This ubiquitous appellation wasn't intended to connote anything positive about the Irish, the Koreans, or their anti-imperial struggles; rather, it served to signal their stigmatized status as colonial subjects. One former occupationaire later wrote that "the Japanese image of Koreans was prejudiced in every sense of the word: automatic, irrational dislike with the reasons for it invented after it had already been expressed. Koreans, in the Japanese eyes, were idiots, thieves, and garlic eaters. They never had been, and they never would be, of any account." But American ventriloquists of Japanese slurs often blurred the line between replication and validation, as Ward's diary hints.[60]

An Office of Strategic Services (OSS) report issued in June 1945, "Aliens in Japan," reproduced the full panoply of Japanese complaints about Koreans. They were "of low social position . . . very poor, uneducated, and unskilled, even by low Korean standards." In language, culture, and custom they were "quite different from the Japanese," and tried hard to remain so, resisting Japanese attempts at assimilation. "Koreans do not possess the Japanese fever for hard work, and to the energetic Japanese Koreans appear to be slow moving and lazy," the report continued. "The brevity of their stay in Japan makes them seem shiftless and lazy. The thrifty and austere Japanese also are appalled by the Korean fondness for food, elaborate ceremonies, impractical clothing, and gaudy decorations." The Japanese further deemed the Koreans "not as conscious of cleanliness" as themselves, living under "miserable conditions" because "they know nothing better." Failing to stress the self-serving and self-fulfilling character of Japanese racism, the OSS report's recitation of stereotypes did as much to endorse as to critique an imperialist mentality that rationalized Japanese colonial rule over Korea. Pernicious conceptions of racial difference also naturalized exploitation of Koreans within Japan itself, hundreds of thousands of these "lazy" good-for-nothings having been impressed as cheap labor for Japanese mines and construction projects. When the OSS recommended that occupation forces would need to "protect and segregate" the two-million-strong minority in postwar Japan, it did so anticipating not only vicious scapegoating of foreigners by the defeated Japanese but also retaliatory violence by Koreans toward their former oppressors. Which community would enjoy a greater claim to American postwar protection remained to be seen in June 1945, but preferences soon became clear.[61]

The American attempt to engineer ethnic homogeneity in Asia eliminated neither disorder nor discrimination. Instead it kindled exclusionary impulses. Confounding SCAP's expectations, many Koreans in Japan preferred to stay put. Although Korean repatriation, unlike the mandatory program to relocate overseas Japanese, was billed as voluntary, U.S. and Japanese authorities made life increasingly difficult for those who chose to remain. Koreans residing in occupied Japan were assigned a liminal status as Japanese "nationals." Denied voting rights, Koreans dangled between citizenship and exclusion: a designation comparable to the position of "Guamanians" relative to U.S. citizens, SCAP legal officer Jules Bassin pointed out.[62]

Yet despite marginalization in Japan, thousands of Koreans who had initially accepted repatriation soon attempted the journey in reverse. Some placed themselves and their savings in the hands of traffickers who operated "secret ships" across the Sea of Japan. Untold numbers of Korean refugees did not survive this hazardous passage, whether capsized from overloaded craft or killed by pirates. One attack in December 1945—lethal enough to make front-page news in the United States—left only one survivor, a woman, from a group of 250. That thousands risked death to regain entry to Japan indicates how bleak conditions in occupied Korea had become. The south was roiled by protest over American military government's abrogation of Korean self-rule, while movement across the thirty-eighth parallel had frozen due to deepening antagonism between U.S. and Soviet occupation regimes. This presented a severe challenge to Korean repatriates who originated from the northern half of the peninsula. By 1948, only 351 returnees had managed to make their way into the Soviet-occupied north.[63]

Political strife aside, the most pressing reason why so many Koreans set sail again for Japan was simple. They soon ran out of money. The occupation authorities permitted departing Koreans to take just 1,000 yen out of Japan, leaving all other savings and possessions behind: a sum equivalent in value to twenty packets of cigarettes. Barely enough for a week's subsistence, this pitiful allowance was certainly no foundation for a new life.[64]

Repatriation and expropriation went hand in hand—for Axis nationals and "liberated" peoples alike. The millions of Japanese shipped to the home islands in the fall of 1945 were prohibited from taking assets with them, limited only to "the amount each person could carry." In Korea, U.S. military authorities laid claim to possessions left in warehouses by departing Japanese who imagined they would one day be permitted to reclaim their belongings, having been issued receipts by American soldiers. A SCAP report in February 1946 documented that "all items suitable for sale as souvenirs were sold to the military at prices ranging up to 100 yen, in this category, among other items, were kimonos, obis, lacquer, in-laid pearl boxes, vases and pearls." Meanwhile, on arrival at Japanese ports, repatriated military personnel and diplomats found that confiscation of property had a more degradingly public aspect. Occupation authorities subjected newly landed Japanese returnees to invasive personal inspection—under the gaze of American dignitaries who sometimes treated this spectacle as a carnivalesque entertainment. Eichelberger gleefully informed Miss Em, before one boatload of Japanese diplomats was scheduled to dock, that the Eighth Army would have to "fluoroscope everyone to see if they have swallowed any diamonds." Japanese women were given what Lieutenant General Berkeley called "lady-type physical exams": ostensibly a precaution against the smuggling of jewelry. "They had nurses down there and so on," he added. "It was a little beyond the pale in my opinion, but . . . that's the way they did it."[65]

Berkeley and others expressed fewer scruples about the plight of dispossessed Koreans. SCAP personnel paid scant attention to the reasons *why* many repatriates refused to stay put, although military government officers in Korea candidly admitted that it was "impossible" for returnees from Japan to "reestablish themselves" on 1,000 yen. Instead, recrossing from Korea to Japan was criminalized. The lexical proximity of "stowaway" and "smuggler" in Japanese eased a collapsing of categories whereby infants of one or two could be arrested and deported for "smuggling." With illegal immigrants stigmatized as bearers of bodily contagion and contagious ideas, Koreans were routinely typed as both communists and criminals: a literal and figurative menace to the Japanese body politic. Like DPs in Europe who looted and bartered to subsist, Koreans found pilferage treated as a shooting offense. Twenty years after the fact, Beans still bemoaned the trouble he'd confronted in Japan with disbanded regiments of Korean forced laborers, left unpaid at the war's end: a nuisance dealt with by putting trip flares in a cave to stop them plundering the rice stored there. "The Koreans around there would risk their life to try to get an extra bag. That was our worst trouble." The interviewer's attempt

FIG. 5.3 Japanese repatriates at the port of Busan stagger under the weight of their human and material burdens, forbidden by U.S. occupation authorities from removing more than they could carry on deportation from Korea to Japan in December 1945. Frank Filan/AP Photo [451211037].

to point out that life had always been very difficult for a lot of Koreans "persecuted by the Japanese" elicited only an unimpressed "hmm" from Beans. Similarly, in the U.S. zone of Korea, troops used lethal force to protect livestock left by departing Japanese soldiers, "firing at Koreans," one American military memoirist recalled, "while guarding materials that we didn't really want or need."[66]

In Japan and Germany, U.S. occupation authorities hastily rearmed the police forces of their former foes, in large part to tackle looting and clandestine trade by, or ascribed to, DPs or minority populations. In both countries, American and local officials were united in their growing concern over black market activity. And those same "outgroups" were vilified as the major participants in illicit economic trade, although black market activity was pervasive—among occupiers, occupied, and displaced alike. "Eighteen months after the 'war of liberation,' the Koreans find themselves blamed for Japan's black market and the increase in crime and accused of being the carriers of disease, of paying no taxes, of having secured a financial stranglehold on Japan," David Conde observed in February 1947. Similar attacks were made by Germans against displaced people, and against Jewish DPs most pointedly. Excoriation of the black market provided a postwar outlet for the rehearsal of age-old, anti-Semitic slurs. As Heymont regretfully noted, some fellow officers used Jewish DPs' participation in black market trade as an excuse for armed raids on the camps that, on occasion, led to residents' deaths.[67]

U.S. military personnel of every rank lent increasingly voluble support to their former foes' prejudice against, and abusive treatment of, racialized Others. In Japan, General Eichelberger made a notation for his memoir that Koreans were "our allies in theory," but in reality were "small traders and black market people" who had "intimidated the police in many areas." Lieutenant General Berkeley more damningly related, "Anything illegal going on in Japan, you could count pretty much a Korean was going to be mixed up in it." Meanwhile, in Germany, an army survey of GI attitudes conducted in January 1946 found that anti-Semitic sentiment was on the rise. Twenty-two percent of the 1,700 men questioned said "they believed the Germans under Hitler had 'good reasons' for the persecution of the Jews." Another 10 percent announced that they were "undecided on the issue of German anti-Semitism." While press commentary on this phenomenon favored a diagnosis of sexual transmission to explain how American boys came to be infected with their German girlfriends' noxious views, it seems just as probable that the virus lurked within. Some senior officers' evident preference for the put-upon Germans, whom they claimed were being swindled and starved in favor of DPs—as a result of "pro-Jewish influence" in military government (in Patton's phrase)—surely emboldened some enlisted men to speak out along similar lines. Lisle, a DP officer, was galled to hear, shortly after release of the Harrison report, that back home it was being said that "we over here are mistreating the Jews worse than the Germans did." Truman had been "so informed by some fellow named Harrison. I suppose the Jew vote is back of it all but it disgusts me. Surely these wretched people bring most of their woes upon themselves." A few weeks earlier he had written in his diary, "I can see more and more each day how these people plotted to destroy Europe. The worst of it is that what Hitler said of them seems so largely true. I see the same traits in the Jew enlisted men and officers with me."[68]

As summer turned to fall in 1945, these voices grew increasingly shrill, anticipating the hardship that cold weather would bring—not to residents of unheated camps but to German civilians. "Winter is coming on; of seventy million people not a one is to get a pound of coal to heat his house; and already typists are fainting at their desks and I've seen old men part of a labor gang unloading trains scrape up flour off the floor of a car and eat it," Brigadier General Jack Whitelaw complained to his wife in Michigan. "To straighten all of this out we permit only the politically clean to hold office. That means as a rule old or inefficient people. This may be what our country wants. I only hope that the people back home know what they're getting."[69]

By the time winter arrived, however, the most pugnacious proponent of such views was silent. In September 1945, just days after Truman ordered the improvement of conditions for Jewish DPs, Eisenhower removed Patton from command of the Third Army. He had made particularly provocative comments to a group of American reporters about denazification, likening antagonism between Nazi and antifascist Germans to partisan sparring between Democrats and Republicans at home. And if (as Patton saw it) Nazis were just run-of-the-mill politicians—98 percent of whom were "only pushed into it anyway"—there was no need for any fuss over his employment of well-known National Socialists in the postwar Bavarian administration. For Eisenhower, already under fire for mistreatment of DPs, this was the last straw. Patton's outspokenness, verging on open insubordination, could no longer be tolerated. The Third Army commander was moved, ostensibly sideways, into a position where he would oversee production of an operational history of the war. But contemporary observers all understood this mark of demerit as a demotion. None felt its humiliating sting more acutely than Patton himself, who insisted that the offending remarks had been needled out of him—and then further distorted in print—by a coterie of Jewish newspapermen bent on his destruction.[70]

Patton made this case noisily to his diary, his wife, and the many admirers who offered words of compensatory adulation. In his self-representations, the general was the victim of both a Jewish conspiracy and Ike's eagerness to curry political favor in Washington, driven by misplaced ambition for high office. ("Ike will never be president!" he crowed in a letter home.) The reason for his dismissal, as Patton perceived it, stemmed from his championship of German civilians as the *real* victims of U.S. policy in occupied Germany, punished in order to cosset DPs or line the pockets of "carpetbaggers" in military government. Like-minded officers shared the diagnosis of Patton's martyrdom and German victimization. The general's de facto sacking, followed swiftly by his death after a car accident, did not silence these dissenting voices in U.S. military government so much as amplify their crescendo of righteous indignation.[71]

"Belsen and Buchenwald were nothing when you consider the plight of *all* of Germany," Whitelaw railed from Berlin in November 1945. "Americans can't look much longer at these gaunt old men and women of twenty-five and keep their reason. Maybe they won't have to look at them much longer for it's getting colder every day." Yet just three weeks later, as the brigadier general was about to depart for good, one of his final letters home quietly recorded, "Germans are doing more and more work for us. They write the letters, file our papers, drive our trucks, repair our billets, take care of our communications, cook our food, maintain our automobiles, and guard our installations." If the contradiction between the litany of grievances and the reality of rehabilitation struck Whitelaw, he gave no indication.[72]

Visiting Germany in 1950, Hannah Arendt was appalled to find that Germans routinely expatiated on their own losses when confronted with evidence of what the Nazis had done to European Jewry, proceeding, as she put it, to "draw up a balance between German suffering and the suffering of others, the implication being that one side cancels the other." Persistent denial was exactly what many American experts on German psychology had predicted during the war. What had not been anticipated, however, was how readily the victors themselves would endorse—and enable—their former enemies' sense of victimization. Nor was it foreseen how quickly American military personnel would come to regard *themselves* as victims. It took Patton only a few weeks to switch his brash self-image as conquering hero for that of helpless prey, alighted on by "a very apparent Semitic influence in the press." "The more I see of people," he complained to his diary, "the more I regret that I survived the war." For his part, Eisenhower (by Patton's account) said they were both "victims of bad PROs"—public relations officers.[73] But soldiers of every rank tended to assume the role of victim with greater gusto and self-consciousness than they did that of victor. They, too, were displaced persons. And like most DPs, many occupation soldiers were increasingly dis-pleased by their prolonged displacement. As 1945 concluded, vociferous de-mands to be on the move home culminated in mass protest across Europe, Asia, and the United States: "over here" and "over there" united in the call for immediate demobilization.

Chapter 6

DEMOBILIZATION BY DEMORALIZATION

"I'm telling you that I find peace is hell," Harry S. Truman quipped to members of the Gridiron Club in December 1945, inverting General William Tecumseh Sherman's well-worn aphorism. Beset by a wave of strikes at home, deepening rifts with former allies abroad, and detractors on Capitol Hill, the president's lament was more heartfelt than flippant. He was not alone in this sentiment. Many of the five and a half million Americans still in uniform, some sweating out their occupation duty overseas, surely agreed with Truman—about peacetime's hellishness, if nothing else. And on January 22, 1946, Dwight D. Eisenhower may have reached the same verdict, for it was on this day that the general found himself ambushed by a superior force and backed into a corner from which there was no graceful exit. As the press reported with some glee, the "military genius" who had "brought the Wehrmacht to its knees" was "routed" by a rambunctious posse of "irate war mothers."[1]

From as far afield as Seattle and Pittsburgh, these women had gathered in Washington, DC, to spearhead a grassroots campaign that had been gathering momentum for weeks. Their objective was to force Congress to expedite the demobilization of men—more particularly husbands and fathers—still actively deployed in the armed services. In November 1945, mass letter-writing initiatives had crystallized into more formal organization of local pressure groups. Across the country "Bring Back Daddy" clubs embraced a variety of tactics to pressurize lawmakers into accelerating the War Department's demobilization program. Female activists wielded a potent source of symbolic power: the image of the fatherless child. Exploiting the pathos of this figure to manipulative effect, they encouraged club members to send their children's photographs to members of the Senate Military Affairs Committee. These pictures "should carry the inscription, 'Please bring my daddy back,' or a similar legend," instructed Mrs. Harold Macy, "chairman" of the club's Chicago chapter, which boasted 600 members. Meanwhile, congressmen found themselves bombarded with babies' booties inscribed with these plaintive mottoes. Senator Elmer Thomas (D-OK), the recipient of forty pairs—some nearly new, others badly worn—announced that the women who'd sent these items were "doing destitute Europeans a favor." He would be donating this unexpected windfall to a charity that collected clothing for people in "devastated areas" of Europe.[2]

The dozen or more women gathered on Capitol Hill in January 1946 were determined to make their views known in person. With Eisenhower scheduled to appear before the House Military Affairs Committee to testify on the demobilization issue, the single hottest potato on Truman's heaped plate, the Bring Back Daddy activists seized their chance. Encircling Eisenhower outside the office of committee chairman Andrew May, the protesters informed Ike that they wanted to talk to him, and promptly unleashed a volley of questions. The general could do little besides request that the petitioners present their arguments in a more orderly fashion and then listen to complaints spanning the gamut of female unhappiness with protracted military service in general and occupation duty in particular. It vexed the women that shipping, which might have been used to transport their husbands home, had been assigned to convey European "war brides" to the United States. Earlier that month, the *Washington Post* had reported that 56,000 war brides would be in the United States by July. These foreign newlyweds had somehow elbowed their way past American women's husbands with a superior claim to shipment. But the protesters' rhetorical trump card was that absent men needed to resume their conjugal and paternal duties as soon as possible, restitching the fabric of family life ripped apart by wartime obligations. "We don't want more money; we want our husbands. Our children need them; we need them; they belong at home." So Eisenhower was sharply reminded.[3]

While the vulnerable child represented the most powerful weapon in the protesters' arsenal, it was the specter of male sexual infidelity—and marriage's concomitant fragility—that more obviously clouded this encounter. When Mrs. Dorthy Galomb stepped forward as the group's spokeswoman, she emphasized the soaring postwar divorce rate. One in three marriages was now ending in divorce, she informed Ike. All the talk of "fraternization" overseas, lavishly illustrated in the pages of *Life* magazine, had taken its toll on strained marital bonds and overstretched nerves. "Declaring that mothers, while trusting their husbands, look with alarm at pictures of fraternization of servicemen overseas, she asked General Eisenhower: 'How do you think we mothers feel? Marriage won't stand this isolation,'" recounted the *Christian Science Monitor*. Since the general himself was rumored by men of every rank to have formed an intimate attachment to his driver Kay Summersby

FIG. 6.1 Three-year-old Margaret Lou Salas, "cute representative of the 'Bring Back Daddy' Club[,] enlists the aid of Philadelphia's Mayor Bernard Samuel in Returning Servicemen from Overseas," runs the original caption to this press photograph taken on January 22, 1946. Acme Newspictures Inc.

while commanding the Allied forces in Europe, he had more than one reason to emerge from this ordeal "mopping his brow and confessing his experience to have been 'emotionally upsetting.'" The fraught encounter also made him ten minutes late for his committee hearing. But in both settings Eisenhower reiterated the same message: that demobilization was proceeding as fast as it possibly could without jeopardizing America's postwar objectives overseas, faster, indeed, than the War Department had initially envisioned. Although he joked that if he could only discharge all the fathers at once then two-thirds of his "troubles would be over," the general was also adamant that, bereft of the 700,000 uniformed men with children, there would be no army. By the end of the year, five million soldiers had already been discharged, along with more than a million sailors.[4]

The tale of how SHAEF's supreme commander had been outmaneuvered by a "bunch of women," in Congressman May's dismissive phrase, garnered front-page coverage. Photographs showed a beleaguered Eisenhower surrounded by animated assailants who didn't appear to like Ike one bit. The episode lent itself to ironic treatment—Gulliver pinioned by a mob of matronly Lilliputians. But trivializing press coverage notwithstanding, pressure for speedier demobilization was a serious business by January 1946. Not only was the president beset with emotional appeals that were hard to resist, so too were military commanders on the ground in occupied countries. The Bring Back Daddy movement represented a home-front counterpart to soldier activism overseas. Throngs of servicemen had already taken to the streets to demand immediate return home in the days before Eisenhower's entrapment.[5]

January 1946 saw a rash of demonstrations by U.S. military personnel—in France, Germany, the Philippines, Guam, Korea, Hawaii, and Japan. Some GI protesters also assembled at Wright Field in Dayton, Ohio. The immediate trigger was a War Department announcement that the rate of demobilization would be temporarily slowed down due to the more precarious "international situation"—an allusion to worsening relations with the Soviet Union—coupled with a shortfall in the number of men being inducted into the military as replacements. This deceleration called into question an earlier commitment that all men who had served two years would be discharged by March 1946. As *Time* put it, the earlier plan "was now only a pious hope, unlikely of fulfillment." Men who had initially hoped to be "home by Christmas," subsequently consoling themselves with the conviction that they would cer-

tainly be back for Easter, now had to reckon with an extension of their occupation duty. The prospect of being suspended in agonizing limbo for an
unknown length of time was more than enough to ignite the dry tinder of GI
discontent. Although the War Department claimed that the 1.55 million
men affected by this slowdown would be home within six months rather
than three, few enlisted men placed great confidence in official promises.[6]

Tempers were further inflamed by Secretary of War Robert Patterson's
lack of familiarity with how the "point system" that determined eligibility for
discharge operated. Points were amassed according to time in uniform, overseas service, combat decorations, and number of dependent children. Those
with the highest scores would, in theory, come home soonest. However, since
the point "clock" had stopped ticking on September 2, 1945, members of
the occupying armies gained no additional credit for *postwar* overseas service,
their scores frozen at the moment of Japan's surrender. Yet the secretary of
war himself appeared unaware that priority for demobilization was determined solely by an individual's wartime record and his family situation.
When Patterson displayed this ignorance about the September 2 cutoff in
public, it stunned both civilians and soldiers, few of whom accepted his subsequent claims to have been misrepresented by reporters. How could the
secretary of war have failed to grasp details of a system that everyone with a
family member in uniform knew inside out? From his unhappy posting as a
public relations officer in Frankfurt, Howard Silbar raged against this "utterly stupid statement." It was, he wrote to his mother on January 12, 1946,
"entirely obvious that the Army knows what to do with itself when life is
cheap and it can spend this commodity without thought of individual concern." But, absent "matters of life and death," the military was clueless about
management of human capital. "Forgivably this job of a peacetime army of
occupation is new," Silbar lamented. "Unforgivably are poor planning, poor
statements, and poor execution."[7]

Calculating point scores became an obsession—for soldiers and civilians
alike—as more and more citizens succumbed to what Silbar diagnosed as a
"raging epidemic of redeploymentitis." Just after V-E Day, Bess Katz wrote
from Philadelphia to Jack Rosenfeld in Germany, telling her brother that "the
chief topic of conversation is the new 'point system.'" In Bess's account, it
was "not an uncommon sight . . . coming home from work to watch people
with pencil in hand calculating the earned points of their friends and relatives in the service." In her office, Bess and her coworkers had "loads of fun"

trying to devise ways of "scaring up points" for her husband, with some play-fully suggesting that she adopt twins to give his score a much-needed boost. Across the country, similar conversations went on, getting louder and angrier as the weeks after V-J Day rolled by. Overseas, a GI version of the popular hit "Don't Fence Me In" made the rounds:

> Oh give us points, lots of points, we need just bout 85
> Don't fence us in . . .
> Oh make our score grow up like a blooming flower
> Send a request to General Eisenhower
> Release Sergeant Jameson and Corporal Jack Power
> Don't fence us in.[8]

Not surprisingly, Patterson was the target of much venom in the protests that erupted in January 1946, with the reclaimed Philippine capital, Manila, serving as the primary locus of activism. Two days after the contentious War Department announcement, a "wildly enthusiastic" crowd marched on the commanding general's headquarters and met in mass rallies, with placards making the sources of mass discontent thoroughly legible. One slogan, "Ya-mashita, Patterson, They Didn't Know," made a pointed comparison between Patterson's professed unawareness of the point system cutoff and General Ya-mashita Tomoyuki's claim not to have known that men under his command had committed wholesale atrocities in the Philippines. His military trial had ended in a death sentence one month earlier, ignorance deemed inadmissible. In Manila, according to an Associated Press report, the "angry" crowd, to-taling approximately 20,000, had to be dispersed by military police. But other full-throated demonstrations sprang up, and in Batangas leaders of the protest movement raised $3,700 to buy full-page advertisements in fif-teen leading U.S. newspapers. These bluntly demanded Patterson's resigna-tion. Meanwhile, in Honolulu 1,500 "cheering, jeering soldiers" gathered in what the *New York Times* characterized as a "noisy but orderly protest," having been warned against "mob action" by Lieutenant General Robert C. Richardson, Hawaii's senior military commander.[9]

Protests were not restricted to the army. On Guam, 3,500 enlisted naval men staged an overnight hunger strike to make their dissatisfaction known. The wave of defiance also swept far beyond the Pacific. In London, protesters sought out Eleanor Roosevelt, who happened to be staying at Claridge's

FIG. 6.2 U.S. soldiers assembled near city hall in Manila on January 7, 1946, in a mass protest after the army's announcement of the slowing down of demobilization. AP Photo/United States Army Signal Corps [345055568064].

Hotel. Granted an audience, a small committee of GIs elicited a promise that the former first lady would use her personal influence to help secure their early demobilization. Across the Channel in France, a group of about 500 servicemen marched by night down the Champs-Elysées to the U.S. embassy, carrying flares and shouting "We want to go home," while larger demonstrations were held outside the USFET (United States Forces European Theater) headquarters in Frankfurt on January 9 and 10. The first, and more heated, of these gatherings was "stopped at bayonet point by guards." Demonstrators yelling "We want Ike" were to be disappointed. Eisenhower was already on his way to testify on Capitol Hill.[10]

From a command perspective, the situation was particularly tense in Japan. Patterson was on a world tour when the demobilization slowdown was announced, and his itinerary landed him in Yokohama just as the protests reached their peak. With the secretary of war having been burned in effigy on Guam, Eighth Army officers were particularly fearful about GI insubordination getting out of hand when irate soldiers came face to face with the man they held personally responsible for their ongoing ordeal. Colonel Charles Mahoney, provost marshal of the U.S. Army service command in Yokohama, reproached members of the Eighth Army who yelled "We want to go home" at Patterson with a reminder that they were "insulting a man who was a soldier before you were born." In case this infantilizing invocation of seniority didn't sufficiently impress the "hotheads," he impugned their masculinity for good measure, asking whether "they were soldiers or boy scouts." "If you want lace panties, I'll get them for you," he taunted. Evidently, in Mahoney's eyes, only a *girl*—and a frilly, feminine one at that—would be so eager to get home.[11]

Seventeen miles from Yokohama in Tokyo, Chief of Staff Clovis Byers was minding the fort in Robert Eichelberger's absence. Like many other senior commanders, the general had flown back to the States for an extended two-month holiday—another source of embitterment as enlisted men watched "brass hats" realize the former's cherished aspiration of being "home by Christmas," while subalterns were told to expect months-long delays. In a long, emotional letter to his family, Byers described January 9 as "beyond question . . . one of the most serious days I have ever spent in my life. It was filled with much more worry than any day that I remember in the recent period of war."

With a mass meeting in Tokyo scheduled for the following day, Byers envisioned a calamitous scenario in which Japanese renegades might take advantage of the disorder occasioned by occupation troops' unruliness:

> There are about four-hundred Japanese for every American in this theater. If the Japanese should feel that our men would not fulfill their missions in any orders given by duly constituted authority, the Japanese might decide to throw us off the island. I don't really believe they could, but our units are so badly disorganized, and our leaders in the lower echelons so inexperienced, that any attempt on the part of the Japanese to overthrow our work

would result in some very unpleasant weeks for everyone in this theater, and I'm afraid some of these boys who are so upset for having to wait a month or so to get home might suddenly discover that they would never reach anything but their heavenly home.

Here, Byers conjured a familiar imperial nightmare: the specter of beleaguered outposts being overrun by an indigenous population that has realized its vastly superior strength in numbers. His elliptical final line hinted darkly at the bloodshed that would accompany such an uprising. But Byers left unclear whether he imagined American boys would be sent to their "heavenly home" by insurgent Japanese or by judge advocates general of the Eighth Army intent on quelling a mutiny.[12]

The apocalypse Byers feared was averted, however. Two days later, he explained to his wife how a courageous "Jewish boy" had mounted the hood of a truck, addressing a "few exceptionally well-chosen facts" to the small group of 200 or 300 uniformed malcontents who had gathered in protest:

> He said that the meeting had been authorized for a purpose, that that purpose had been attained, that if they remained in such a group some irresponsible individual might attempt to start something which would get everyone in trouble, that if anyone had a good reason for another meeting his request to the Commanding General would be approved at once, and that he recommended they break up and go home at once. Someone attempted to interrupt in the course of these remarks, and his clear voice stilled all comment as he said, "G—D—it! I'm risking my neck to say this and you're going to listen without interrupting!" The meeting broke up at once, and nothing more has been heard from the group.

Byers, meanwhile, sought out the young man—"a Jewish boy by the name of Goldman in one of our ordnance companies"—to commend his fearlessness and shake his hand. Crisis averted.

Yet Byers clearly remained rattled by the tidal upsurge of protest and evident depth of feeling that animated it, musing to his wife on how much harder the work of peacetime soldiering was than combat. "Now everything is so different. I guess it's the fact that you have so much more time to worry that makes this period so hard to take. While in battle you had to make up your mind and work so hard to get things done and there were so many fundamental things that had to be done that when you finished them and could get a few minutes for sleep, you fell off before worries could start." With its more expansive remit and extended duration, occupation's tempo dragged in comparison to the urgent quickstep of war, and anxiety rushed in to fill the vacuum. At least in his appreciation of time's worrisomely elastic properties in occupied territory, Byers was at one with the enlisted men of the Eighth Army.[13]

Where did this antimilitary militancy come from? Some commentators, including Eisenhower, identified "homesickness" as the primary impetus. But more candid observers of the postwar landscape, including discontented GIs themselves, knew very well that there was more to displays of intemperance than mere impatience. To excavate the roots of the January 1946 "near mutiny" (as the protests were commonly dubbed) requires a return to mid-1945, for the demobilization crisis began, in effect, as soon as the war ended— if not before. Secretary of War Henry Stimson complained, as early as August 9, 1945, that it seemed "as if everybody in the country was getting impatient to get his or her particular soldier out of the Army." This pressure intensified in tandem with a precipitous collapse of morale evident across the European and Pacific theaters in the latter half of 1945. Demands for demobilization and demoralization were "two halves of the same walnut," to borrow a figure of speech from Truman. Men who thought of nothing but getting home with all due haste weren't always the most conscientious or scrupulous occupation forces: a point playfully signaled by the men in Captain Philip Broadhead's photograph of the self-announced "Homeward Bounders."[14]

American soldiers' morale slumped as soon as fighting ended in Europe in the spring of 1945. Far from experiencing a moment of exuberant triumphalism, many men and women in uniform felt deflated and let down, imagining that back home in America victory had surely been celebrated with the party to end all parties. To be in Germany in May 1945 was "like remaining in a ballroom after the ball is over," one young officer observed, hinting at the desolation and aimlessness that he and millions of other service personnel now confronted: a tawdry scene suddenly thrown into unflattering illumination. The battle against Nazism may have been over, but their deployment was not. "Soldiers say 'After the war' all the time but what they mean is,

'After I am out of the Army,' " noted Corporal John Bartlow Martin, writing for *Harper's* magazine. "They still say 'After the war,' though the war is over." Victory may have been synonymous with peace in civilian usage, but not to soldiers, whose expectations that the cessation of combat would spell demobilization were soon dashed. "Is it peace or ain't it? Am I coming home soon or ain't I? These are the questions of the moment," infantryman Bill Taylor informed his parents, writing from Germany in August 1945. With these demands still unanswered in November, he seethed that "morale here is lower than a snake's belly."[15]

Military psychologists had long predicted that "fighting spirit" would suffer a devastating blow once there was no more fighting to be done. But they were nevertheless astonished by the speed and scale of morale's landslide slump. Almost overnight, it seemed, American servicemen and servicewomen had reverted to civilian ways of thinking and acting. Having done so, they couldn't wait to shed the chafing uniforms that denoted ongoing indentured servitude. One of the earliest outward signs of demoralization was widespread "sloppiness" in matters of dress and military courtesy. Officers who attempted to reverse this decline by emphasizing "spit and polish" were widely disdained.[16]

Who exactly were highly polished boots and neatly pressed uniforms meant to impress? enlisted men wondered. Edward Laughlin found himself sent to Berlin in mid-1945 to join a group of "show troops": "polished up to be and look more military (than like a bunch of seedy and unkempt combat types)." Spending his days in close-order drill, rigorous physical training, and exacting inspections, Laughlin reviled the honor guard—"a dressy garrison type outfit to be held in contempt by all seasoned combat veterans." He also doubted that the "show" had its intended effect on German civilians. It surely wasn't lost on the paratroopers' neighbors, Laughlin imagined, that the honor guard was quartered in barracks formerly occupied by the SS. From there, the conspicuously outfitted American paratroopers often ran through the city in formation with rifles. "The Berliners would stop on the sidewalks and stare. I thought they must be thinking, 'I have seen all this before.' " Laughlin himself was decidedly unimpressed when three fellow honor guards died in a parachute jump made under unpropitious conditions to mark the one-year anniversary of D-Day and intended to dazzle General Eisenhower on a visit to Berlin's Tempelhof Airport. These needless deaths struck Laughlin as yet another way in which attempts to "create an impression" backfired. Nor were ceremonial stunts gone awry the only way in which servicemen continued to die after the war was over. Alcohol poisoning and vehicular recklessness—often not unrelated—were two common causes of postwar fatality.[17]

With military attire and etiquette confining reluctant bodies, soldiers often construed their predicament in carceral terms. Occupation duty was like a prison sentence—only worse. After all, prisoners are generally confined for specified terms. Members of the occupying armies imagined themselves more akin to death row inmates, for whom the uncertain duration of confinement constituted an additional torment; life itself was suspended, but not the sentence. Some soldiers accordingly regarded the military as a custodial institution that trapped reluctant inmates, surveilled their every move, and subjected them to myriad forms of regimentation more sadistic than corrective. Rules were capriciously enforced or randomly disregarded with characteristic lack of uniformity. Excessive discipline, already a source of discontent during wartime, became all the more intolerable once the need for unquestioning obedience to officers' dictates, however petty, dissolved—at least in the eyes of those who received orders. Milo Flaten's complaint that "we are virtual prisoners here with the company area our walls. Everything we do is outlawed," resonated widely.[18]

Like prisoners, enlisted men—and some officers—frequently complained of indolence in their letters home. Time itself seemed to yawn and dawdle. Hours distended by idleness felt longer than those constructively filled. K. S. Mason complained to an aunt in North Carolina that there was nothing to do "but lay around and dream of hamburgers." Men too young to have known any other employment than military service but old enough to remember the Depression heard about the chronic shortage of jobs back home, where "reconversion" was occurring at breakneck speed. They feared coming home only to join an ever-growing unemployment line—one among millions of internally "displaced persons." African American troops, the vast majority of whom were assigned to service functions, had acute cause for concern over delayed homecoming after the War Department announced in May 1945 that labor battalions would be in high demand for redeployment to the Pacific and subsequent occupation duty. Langston Hughes's character "Simple"—a regular in the *Chicago Defender*—decried the inequitable division of labor under occupation, whereby white soldiers loafed, then left, while black troops did all the heavy lifting: "When every last white GI that wants to come home is home—and every last good job in the USA is taken—they still gonna have

the colored soldiers patrolling the natives over yonder in Guam or somewhere, and unloading ships, and digging drains around air-bases. . . . The
white man does not want that kind of work, and that is what they are going
to give to colored. The white man just wants to soldier and shoot—and
then come home. He does not care nothing about no occupation."[19]

But young men of every ethnicity worried that military service might
render them unemployable, ruined by inactivity (or too much of the wrong
kind of activity) for anything that required initiative. A teenage naval rating
stationed in Yokohama informed his old high school English teacher in Lynd-
hurst, New Jersey, that all he and his buddies did was "eat and then go right
back to the sack." As a result, he predicted that guys coming off the ship
would be "so lazy when they get back to civilian life that it will take them a
year to get enough energy to get a job." Flaten, miserably stalled in Germany,
agreed. "The army really makes a bum out of you."[20]

While enlisted men pressed to know when their time would be up, senior
commanders themselves remained uncertain as to the temporal scope of occupation. Responsibility for high policy resided in Washington. By the end of
1945, Truman had announced that the State Department would assume responsibility for the occupation of Germany the following June—a transfer
subsequently delayed—but no firm dates of termination for any of the occupations had been given. Even though the Germans and Japanese both appeared far more amenable to reconstruction than planners had anticipated,
the implicit long-range goal of securing American hegemony in the postwar
world was starting to look less certain for reasons other than defeated populations' intransigence.[21]

In the estimation of leading figures in the U.S. foreign policy establishment, Moscow was embarking on a dangerous program of postwar expansionism, an alarming trend validated by the expert authority of George
Kennan in his "long telegram" from Moscow in February 1946. Not only
was the Kremlin capitalizing on the Red Army's dominance over eastern and
central Europe to "sovietize" states on the Soviet Union's western periphery,
it was also seeking to exert control over the anti-imperial forces in Asia that
had turned their attention from fighting Japanese occupation to combating
the restoration of European colonial rule. In China, Mao Zedong's People's
Liberation Army was gaining ground on Chiang Kai-Shek's Nationalists, despite the long-term assistance the U.S. government had supplied to the
latter. This new constellation of forces, as perceived by the State Department

and its overseas outposts, heightened the geopolitical urgency of reorienting Germany and Japan along liberal capitalist lines as a bulwark against Soviet expansionism. "World communism is like a malignant parasite which feeds only on diseased tissue," Kennan warned. Improved "self-confidence, discipline, morale and community spirit" would be necessary if Washington was to exercise the constructive world leadership required to block communism's cancerous development. "Many foreign peoples, in Europe at least, are tired and frightened by experiences of the past, and are less interested in abstract freedom than in security. They are seeking guidance rather than responsibilities. We should be better able than Russians to give them this. And unless we do, Russians certainly will."[22]

This worldview—soon dominant in Washington—did nothing to shorten the anticipated duration of occupation. But the magnitude of the power-political stakes of occupation intensified fissures of opinion within and between the estranged Allies about how control over former enemies was best effected. Estimates of just how long, and how many, troops would remain overseas differed as widely as the particular visions of postwar order that informed these speculative timetables. In mid-1945, Field Marshal Bernard Montgomery had talked of the Allies remaining in Germany for six to ten years, while many U.S. policy makers and public commentators sometimes gestured toward occupations that would last decades or even "generations." These expansive estimates left those who wagered on short-term, finite missions in a minority. When General Eichelberger rashly ventured to reporters in September 1945 that the occupation of Japan—at least in its military incarnation—"would last not more than a year," he received a sharp rap on the knuckles from Washington, hastily retracting a remark critics saw as grist to the demobilization protesters' mill. Douglas MacArthur was similarly rebuked by the State Department for suggesting that, within six months, only 200,000 occupation troops would be required in Japan.[23]

Ike confused matters further with testimony delivered on Capitol Hill in January 1946. Explaining the need for a large peacetime military, Eisenhower drew an analogy with the fire service. Just because firemen were to be found "playing checkers sometimes" didn't mean you sacked them, Eisenhower pointed out. After all, the firefighters "may be vitally needed a few minutes later." So it was with occupation soldiers. Yet he also announced that an inspection of "every camp and post" in the ETO (European theater of operations) would be conducted to determine which men were "inessential" and could be sent home "without delay." At least some soldiers were starting to ask which blazes they would be asked to douse on whose behalf. And if they weren't all necessary for postwar firefighting, how would Eisenhower determine who was "essential, and essential to what?" the *New Republic* inquired.[24]

––––––––––––––––

Questions of time and toil underlay the demoralization crisis. Haziness over both the length and the nature of the postwar mission contributed to the peculiar atmospherics in occupied territory. Soldiers dwelt mentally in the short term, but all around the American presence showed signs of ever-greater permanence. On a grand scale, occupation was billed as an unprecedented attempt to reconstruct former foes politically, economically, and (in the more metaphysical inflection of the day) spiritually. Germany was to be emancipated from the Nazi Party and its noxious ideology, while Japan was to be freed from nepotistic privilege, emperor worship, and feudal vestiges, its women empowered and peasants transformed into landowners. Yet these lofty ambitions seemingly failed to generate lengthy to-do lists. "Occupation" implied a purposefulness often conspicuously absent from soldiers' lived experience of postwar service. Space was occupied—not time. The mass presence of stationary American bodies was intended to make a bold statement to the occupied, but serving a demonstrative purpose didn't satisfy the great majority of underemployed enlisted men. "After a while one becomes dead from the neck up," complained Taylor.[25]

The discrepancy between occupation's momentous ambitions and its monotonous air was nowhere more paradoxically felt than in Nuremberg, where the trial of Nazi war criminals began in November 1945. Here, too, a pall of tedium clouded the proceedings. British writer Rebecca West captured this odd disjuncture between occupation's world-historic significance and its practitioners' dissociative lethargy in her eyewitness reports for the *New Yorker*. The courtroom itself, she remarked, was a "citadel of boredom." The protagonists were caught in a "tug-of-war concerning time." While the Nazi defendants hoped to string out proceedings as long as possible, thereby deferring their own deaths, everyone else thought only of "going back to life" with what West characterized as "savage impatience." West likened the Allied officiants' desire to depart to the ferocity with which a "dental patient enduring the drill" wants to "leave the chair." Alert to this agitation, Herman

Göring—the highest-ranking defendant and most skillful courtroom performer—needled his nemeses by cracking a joke about their palpable eagerness to depart. Taking aim at the charge that the defendants had engaged in a "conspiracy" to wage aggressive war, Göring protested that the German high command had never been asked its opinion. "One way to prevent war might be to ask the generals if they want to fight or go home," Göring jocularly proposed. American columnist Janet Flanner (Genêt to readers of the *New Yorker*) registered "strained laughter in the court at this want-to-go-home jibe at the Americans."[26]

Military government personnel whose ennui oozed through every pore, like those at Nuremberg, were not necessarily either inactive or engaged in busywork dreamed up solely to keep idle hands occupied. The Nuremberg trials were far from inconsequential in terms of their contribution to normative international law; and, in a variety of ways, occupation troops who decried the utter tedium of their existence were sometimes performing work that mattered a good deal in the greater scheme of things. Taylor, for example, played a personal role in the mass repatriation of Soviet DPs while complaining of brain death. Protestations of boredom and indolence, in other words, might reveal more about occupation soldiers' *psychological* condition than about their physical state of activity. What disgruntled soldiers sought to register was the repetitious nature of their work, its unpleasantness, and their desire that—if routine tasks had to be performed at all—someone else should be conscripted so they themselves could return home. "Boredom" provided an idiom for expression of this urgent longing for release from military indenture.

Undoubtedly, however, the volume of work performed by occupation soldiers had dwindled during the latter months of 1945. More and more tasks initially handled by military government detachments were delegated, or surrendered altogether, to civilians—whether locals or Americans. Servicemen and servicewomen willing to remain overseas could become civilian employees of the army after a monthlong furlough in the United States intended to lure those with particular expertise back into military government. In other cases, soldiers simply stepped out of uniform and joined a different organization, such as UNRRA, which paid more money for essentially the same work that officers in the "DP business" had hitherto undertaken in the army. "As time passes, it becomes more and more obvious how little there is yet to be done," Hanns Anders told his mother in August 1945. "The work becomes more and more routine, the only real function being now that of making out reports showing what the civilian agencies are accomplishing." Like many of similar rank and sensibility, Anders contemplated going to work for UNRRA rather than returning home when his point score permitted. But like most others, he soon decided against it.[27]

Soldiers fluent in German enjoyed options. Some also found that the inaugural phase of military government had its rewarding moments. Sidney Eisenberg, for one, derived considerable satisfaction from his personal contribution to Germany's denazification in Straubing. On August 13, 1945, he wrote jubilantly to his sister and her family that he had received the first four applications from professional associations seeking to organize unions. "The very first? This will kill you—the city police!!! (Now everyone will be buying dance benefit tickets, draped with sauerkraut and schnapps.) You understand—these will be the first unions in Bavaria. Are you proud of your brother?" But even Eisenberg deemed occupation "distasteful" and "unnatural." And he was well aware of how things looked to low-ranking soldiers. A few weeks earlier, he had distributed cards to the enlisted men in his unit asking them to specify their preferred branch of military government work. Most, he told his mother, had written down "'going home—I have 93 points'—or something to that effect." The immediate postwar whirlwind having abated, the work of occupation—such as it was—appeared to many enlisted men to comprise either despicable busywork of the spitting and polishing variety ("chickenshit" in GI slang) or tedious, sometimes distasteful chores.[28]

Guard duty bulked drearily large in the life of enlisted occupation soldiers. In former enemy territory, there was a lot of "surplus" to be guarded: bodies in the form of POWs or DPs, spent equipment, and munitions slated for destruction. When the object to be secured by force was nothing more than waste food, guard duty could occasion uncomfortable pangs. Private Edward Sausville, of the 544th Engineers, wrote to Miss Marghita Macdonald, his former teacher at the Newburgh Free Academy in upstate New York, about his assignment in Wakayama, a rural prefecture in southern Japan. "The main purpose of guard here is to keep the Nips away from the garbage pails and mess lines. They are so hungry that they eat the garbage. More fuss, running them down. Deep down, I didn't like to do it—but, after all, we were at war and they get treated too good as it is." Like other soldiers closely acquainted with postwar abjection, Sausville had to work hard to suppress stirrings of conscience. With an awkward blurring of tenses, as he switched from present to past and back, the young private turned hungry scavengers into the enemy in a war that was not (in his mind at least) decisively over. Wanting reassurance that he wasn't doing anything wrong—or at least not unconscionably wrong—in chasing destitute Japanese away from leftovers at gunpoint, Sausville employed a form of relativism common to occupation soldiers. What would the "Japs" have done had *they* been victorious? Measured by the yardstick of Japan's record as an occupying power, U.S. forces appeared incontrovertibly better, their treatment of the defeated population "too good."[29]

Not all soldiers were convinced that defeated people needed such close supervision, or that it required two and a half million Americans to police quiescent populations—the interim force level for mid-1946 decreed by the War Department. "Our aimless piddling in the mud is becoming disgusting to me as well as to most others," Bob Titus informed his father, writing from Okinawa on August 28, 1945. He and his company had been set to work constructing hospitals. But where, he wondered, would the casualties to fill these facilities' beds come from now the war was over? "Our reason for being here apparently ceased to exist when the Japs surrendered." To "guard" victory, in larger strategic terms, surely didn't require such sizable forces as the United States planned to maintain in Japan and Germany; or so many servicemen asserted, echoing Titus's embitterment. They were accordingly dismissive of attempts to valorize occupation duty, whether undertaken by army Civil Information and Education Section officers or civilian opinion shapers.[30]

Anne O'Hare McCormick, doyenne of American foreign correspondents, attempted to do just that in a number of op-ed columns written for the *New York Times* at the height of the demobilization "psychosis," as fellow reporter Hal Boyle termed the "mental epidemic" afflicting the services. Commenting in November 1945 on the demoralization of occupation troops who complained about being insufficiently occupied, McCormick combined admonishment with exhortation: "Here [in Frankfurt] it appears that too many American boys lack resources in themselves to enable them to endure a spell of disagreeable duty with philosophy and profit. They lack understanding that this duty is as heroic and imperative as war service. This is the proof that they really did not know what they were fighting for, and this in turn means failure somewhere to make the issue so clear that they could not question the cardinal importance of the watch on the Rhine." When she reiterated the same points two months later at the height of the GI protests, Mc-Cormick was taken to task by "boys" whose commitment she had maligned along with their maturity. That Americans were "crying to go home"—"cry babies," more insultingly put—was a common motif of the protesters' critics, not so far removed in its insinuated "sissiness" from Mahoney's "lace panties" taunt.[31]

McCormick received numerous complaints from men in uniform as well as civilians who shared their discontent. One undated, unsigned letter made its way to her from Japan via a third party. Its author noted that "Miss Mc-Cormack," being a woman, had obviously received kid-glove treatment from the brass in Frankfurt. As a result, she had seen things "from the top," the only vantage point from which the "big picture" was perceptible in all its Olympian grandeur. "Just let her live with the boys for a while, and she'll find out why the men are unhappy," the letter-writer proposed, before elaborating his point about occupation's redundancy:

> The job of controlling the Japs is simply no job. It's less trouble
> than controlling the good people of Detroit or Peoria. I have
> yet to hear of a single incident involving violence to an American.
> A Yank can go anywhere, any time, without the slightest danger.
> If there's anything "heroic" about that sort of duty, I wish Miss
> McCormack would elaborate. Miss McCormack is all wet—
> what she's griping about is the very thing that makes America
> great—namely the great distaste toward sitting still or doing
> something that could be done equally well by the dull, unimagi-
> native members of the Regular Army. If she feels a crusade coming
> on, let her go out and recruit our dolts and sluggards for the
> Regular Army and send home the wide-awake lads who know
> what they're missing by being stuck over here in occupation.

This complaint was widely shared by young men in their teens or early twenties. Their lives, relationships, and ambitions—whether to attend or complete college, find a partner or return to one, get a job, or run wild for a while—had been placed on hold for two, three, or four years by wartime service. In their eyes, the military was a "thief of time," turning energetic young men into unwilling procrastinators. McCormick's interlocutor concluded with the suggestion that the *Times'* columnist acquaint herself with the history of "every war and occupation." She would then realize that "an occupying army carries in its very mission the seeds of its own disintegration"—evidence of which was apparent in the "sloppiness" of men's dress, their indifference to discipline, and the fact that officers and enlisted men alike "gripe openly about the inefficiency or crookedness of their superiors." Occupation's extended duration did more than corrode morale, in this writer's mind. It undid the very venture of postwar remaking.[32]

McCormick quoted this letter, along with several others, in a later column published on January 19, 1946. (Privately, she confessed that its author had "made a deep impression.") This time, McCormick extended her critique beyond the army that had failed to impress GIs with "the importance of this tedious and glamorless duty." Equally to blame for the demobilization debacle were America's impatient citizens. Heedless soldiers abroad merely echoed the domestic hue and cry, she claimed. Her rhetorical inquiry, "Who acts at home as though this were the hardest and most critical phase of the war?" would be answered, after a fashion, four days later by the Bring Back Daddy lobby on Capitol Hill. Eisenhower's ambushers gave every appearance of rejecting McCormack's characterization of occupation duty as a vital continuation of war by other means.[33]

Agitation for early demobilization had deeper, and more tangled, roots than the ignorant irresponsibility to which McCormick ascribed it. Those who insisted that "high points" troops be brought home quickly did not always reject the larger geopolitical purposes of occupation. Some protesters were adamant that they fully understood the importance of "staying put" as a postwar obligation incurred by a victorious United States. "I don't believe any of the soldiers are disgruntled (as you put it) at the thought that there will have to be an Army of Occupation," Silbar corrected his mother. "Certainly anybody who has seen the wreck which Europe has created out of itself will be reasonable enuf to hope that maybe something new might be a solution to this awful, age old problem." The protesters' complaint was rather that combat veterans should not be required to shoulder this additional burden when new enlistees—who had *never* served overseas, or had merely spent a few months in Europe—were being sent home. Instead of letting the machinery of conscription run down, the military establishment should require draft boards to keep pumping new recruits into the ranks. "If the draft is continued intelligently, each kid would serve a maximum of one year in the army, 6 or 8 months of which would be spent overseas," proposed Bob LaFollette (teenage grandson of the Wisconsin senator and Progressive Party leader Robert LaFollette) in an epistle from Manila. "This would work out wonderfully for everyone, as it will come at just the right time in their lives." Viewed in this way, occupation duty was the perfect "gap year" filler between high school and college.[34]

Other protesters challenged both the institution charged with democratizing the Axis powers and the larger interests served by long-term occupation. At their most blunt, these critics indicted the U.S. military as a "Fascist army"—as one emphatic veteran underscored the point in another letter to McCormick rebutting her diagnosis of the GI malady. This former soldier, fresh from four years' overseas service, was far from alone in assailing the "caste system" that structured military life. Demands for early demobilization were routinely accompanied by attacks on the unfair perks enjoyed by a power-abusing officer class. Antimilitary populism of this sort transcended left-right allegiances. A soldier did not, in other words, have to label the military "fascist" to denounce an institution in which senior officers led—or often appeared to lead—lives of pampered privilege at the expense of their subordinates. In the Philippines, where GI protests achieved their greatest velocity, demonstrators drew attention to one general's ten-room mansion staffed by thirty servants. In other locations, gradations of status were so finely parsed, and so fastidiously maintained, that they encompassed even the most basic of human functions. "The caste system works overtime in the matter of latrines, too," observed Lieutenant Colonel Robert Neville, a former editor of *Stars and Stripes* in North Africa. "It perhaps reached its finest flowing at Maison Blanche Airport at Algiers, where there were partitioned off and carefully marked a general officers' latrine, a field officers' latrine, a company-grade officers' latrine, a latrine for nurses and WAC officers, another for enlisted WACs and a final one for enlisted men."[35]

Anger over egregious manifestations of class privilege fueled the demobilization movement in a variety of ways. Many enlisted men regarded the War Department point system as rigged to favor officers. It struck many combat veterans as a gross unfairness that more points accrued to widely distributed "battle participation stars" than to the combat badges earned by men on the front line. By rewarding longevity of service, the system seemed to offer an unfair advantage to the "chairborne" elite who had enlisted early and then sat out the war ensconced behind stateside desks.

To the extent that seniority of rank correlated with age—often but not invariably the case—officers were also more likely than junior enlistees to

"Yer combat badge don't count. Ya need more of these battle participation stars."

FIG. 6.3 Bill Mauldin's cartoon, published on June 15, 1945, makes plain combat soldiers' frustration over the inequitable distribution of points that determined eligibility for discharge. Bill Mauldin Estate.

be family men. Each offspring under the age of eighteen earned his or her father twelve points. A Purple Cross or Bronze Star Medal, by contrast, was worth only five. While Bess Katz in Philadelphia joked with her coworkers about adopting twins, soldiers on occupation duty bemoaned the fact that they could do nothing to bump up their score on the paternity front—or nothing that would earn them extra points. (Babies begotten as a result of "fraternization" obviously didn't count for purposes of War Department tabulation.) Men without children could only bemoan their low-point predicament and quip wryly, as John Winner did, about donating his meager collection to the Salvation Army. Never had so many adolescent males cultivated such wistful fantasies of fatherhood. Fittingly enough, one chorus of the GI version of "Don't Fence Me In" ran, "Oh give us battle stars and we don't mean maybe/We'll take twelve points for that new born baby."[36]

As this humorous lyric also hints, a yet more vexing source of officer privilege lay in senior commanders' superior access to decorations. In the chummy upper echelons, old boys rewarded one another for deeds not necessarily so valorous. (That, at any rate, was a common subaltern perception of how the commendation system worked.) Since medals meant points, the more "fruit salad" an officer had pinned to his chest, the likelier he was to head home at an early date. But some enlisted men entertained different fears about unscrupulous superiors. Since rank and salary ascended in lockstep, officers were sometimes suspected of prolonging their tours of occupation duty, along with those of their underlings, to gain further promotions and the plumper paychecks that rewarded higher status. In Okinawa, Jim Watkins was dismayed to find that junior naval ratings believed that he and a handful of other midranking officers were digging in for selfish gain: "The depth of feeling on the part of the younger officers borders on hatred for us who are older and of higher rank. It comes pretty close to rank insubordination. The most poisonous arrows are directed against the half-dozen or so of us who stayed on to hold Military Government together. 'If a few lieutenants hadn't wanted to be lieutenant commanders—and to stick around making more money than they ever knew before,' so the complaint goes, 'Military Government would have folded up in December and none of us would be here now.'"[37]

Watkins bitterly resented their characterization of his motives. In aggrieved diary entries he insisted that he, and like-minded Japanese-speaking officers, had stayed on for the most altruistic of reasons: to establish a governing council of Okinawans that would help protect the islanders' interests when the army assumed responsibility for military government in the Ryukyus. A scathing critic of abused power, Watkins did, however, exhibit sympathy for frustrated enlisted men forced to endure the "indignities visited upon them by their officers" and never properly informed about the humanitarian necessity of occupation to aid a population ravaged by war. Had

they been treated "like self-respecting, intelligent individuals with some capacity for action, imagination, and responsibility," Watkins suspected more
enlisted men would have accepted their lot.[38]

Where some officers appeared to prolong the agony of occupation duty
unnecessarily for personal profit, others adopted just the opposite tack. Some
particularly impatient individuals were apparently going AWOL purposely to
get kicked out of the services. Harry McMasters observed a number of his
fellow officers pull this stunt in Japan. When three acquaintances spent an
unauthorized week enjoying themselves at a resort hotel at Karuizawa, their
illicit vacation terminated with a one-way ride to Pearl Harbor. This, McMasters remarked to his wife, was "just what they wanted." Enlisted men who attempted to do likewise were far more likely to wind up in the stockade than to
receive an instantaneous (if dishonorable) discharge like McMasters's peers.[39]

Among the most glaring injustices of the demobilization process was the
discriminatory treatment of African American service personnel. Some black
soldiers with enough points for discharge found their passage home stalled by
bigoted naval officers who refused to let them travel on board "unsegregated"
ships. One such case, largely ignored by the national papers of record, made
the front page of the *Chicago Defender* in December 1945. Correspondent
Venice Spraggs related that "123 war-weary GIs" had been effectively detained at Le Havre, a French port on the English Channel that was home to
notoriously grim "replacement depots" where men awaiting shipment bided
their time. These soldiers had been debarred from the USS *Croatan* "because
there were no jim crow facilities aboard the aircraft carrier redeploying army
personnel from the European Theatre of Operations," and Captain Charles
Griffin reportedly knew "from conversations with white army officers that
they were accustomed to jim crow facilities for colored troops." In deference
to these officers' racist proclivities, the 123 African Americans were transferred
to the *Thomas Johnson Victory*—"a slower ship," the *Defender* pointed out.[40]

Griffin's actions elicited a rebuke from Secretary of the Navy James
Forrestal, who publicly reiterated the service's "non-discriminatory racial
policy." But discrimination was an inescapable condition of life in a military
segregated by race. A mere handful of integrated units existed by the end of
the war, and these under white officership. Among other discontents with
the demobilization system, Bob LaFollette noted the "outrageous" fact that
in the Philippines certain senior officers were apparently denied promotion
because they had commanded black troops, considered "by top brass, not

worth a damn." Meanwhile, not just at Le Havre but across the Pacific, black soldiers protested over separate manifests for shipment home marked "white troops only" and "Negro troops only." In Okinawa, African American troops with sufficient points for discharge sat in camps grimly awaiting ships that never docked. "Okinawa seems a forgotten land," one man informed his girl-friend in November 1945, four years and two months into his term of mili-tary service. "Most of the ships go on to Manila or Tokyo with the 'Rock' as a by path. . . . The slogan of the men here has become 'no boats—no votes' to the big wigs in Washington."[41]

Institutionalized racism loomed large in the minds of many of those who branded the armed services "fascist." But the most radical critics didn't take issue only with the military's stratification along frequently convergent lines of class, color, and rank. Communist and socialist labor organizers among the GI activists, including David Livingston, Ewart Guinier, Jack Hall, and Norvall Welch, condemned the geostrategic purposes of postwar occupation as a vehicle for aggressively expansionist U.S. imperialism. Rejecting expla-nations for the demobilization slowdown that stressed logistical snarls with shipping, they countered that Truman was manipulating popular impatience to have men brought home to promote a bill for universal military training. This mechanism would have ushered every American eighteen-year-old male into the armed forces for a twelve-month term, thereby securing a ready supply of new recruits to replace existing occupation soldiers. (For that reason, it enjoyed some support among personnel deployed overseas.) But why, rad-ical protesters asked, did the United States need to maintain more than one million men in uniform, if not to protect American corporate interests as they extended across the globe, filling vacuums left by the evaporation of Axis power? Perhaps, theorized African American soldiers in the South Pacific, who sent an "affectionate" letter of dissent "To the American People" by way of the *Cleveland Call and Post,* their function was as a "show army" to "im-press certain other nations in the great game of world power politics."[42]

But whatever symbolic significance occupation troops may have had simply by "being there," at least some men in uniform were also required by the U.S. military to shoulder weighty burdens overseas—African American labor battalions carrying a disproportionate load. Radical activists drew atten-tion to, and strove to foster, global crosscurrents of subaltern militancy with a view to persuading soldiers not to perform work that served elite class interests. Working to coordinate GI demonstrations with a National Maritime Union strike in the United States, they also linked American protests to uprisings against resurgent European imperialism. In January 1946, members of the Royal Air Force staged sit-down strikes in solidarity with nationalists in India, Egypt, and Palestine. The following month, Indians conscripted into the Royal Indian Navy staged a mutiny against their British commanders. And across southern Asia, anti-imperialist forces in Indochina, Malaya, and Indonesia— fighters who had waged guerrilla campaigns against Japanese occupation during the war with the backing of British and American special services— were beginning to battle against the reimposition of French, British, and Dutch colonial rule.[43]

Far from supporting these struggles for self-determination, Washington did just the opposite. American military materiel was deployed to aid the restoration of colonial rule. This support was lent somewhat surreptitiously, with the Truman administration requesting that the "American label" be removed from equipment supplied to British, French, and Dutch armies. Truman's predecessor had, after all, endorsed freedom for "all the men in all the lands" as an Allied war objective even before the United States was formally a combatant. Yet it wasn't lost on GI protesters that naval transportation— supposedly too scarce to bring high-points men home with due dispatch— could be found for purposes of colonial reconsolidation. In the radical analysis, the U.S. military had become an instrument of transnational class power, employed to quell anti-imperial militancy on behalf of business and financial elites in Europe and North America. This materialist critique barely surfaced in the progressive press in the United States. But Roi Ottley offered readers of the *Pittsburgh Courier* a stinging denunciation of the way in which black troops were being used to build airports and infrastructure across North Africa, the Persian Gulf, and the Middle East. The purpose of defending the "thousands of little spots in the world that must contain a U.S. Army garrison" was, he proposed in February 1946, to protect the penetration of "big business" into new regions of Asia, North Africa, and South America. "This is the reason that the U.S. imperialists are alarmed by the GI protest—for actually it endangers their newly won possessions overseas."[44]

Washington's aspirations to global dominance also explained why 60,000 marines had been dispatched to China soon after Japan's surrender. Ostensibly their postwar mission was to locate and dispose of American war materiel while overseeing the surrender and demobilization of Japanese soldiers. But in reality, anti-imperialist critics argued, the marines' primary task was to ensure that equipment didn't fall into the hands of the People's Liberation Army. In essence, the Marine Corps' venture was undertaken in support of Chiang Kai-Shek's Nationalists as China's protracted civil war reached its zenith. Why were American troops running the railroad between Tientsin and Chinwangtao? some men asked. With seemingly greater prescience than the State Department, these soldiers anticipated which way the wind was to blow in China. "When we leave, the Communists will take it anyway—so why not let them have it now?" These points were boldly articulated by Technician Fourth Grade Fred Zeller before a rally of GIs at the Schofield Bowl, Hawaii, on January 10, 1946. Zeller criticized the use of American ships both to land Chinese Nationalist troops in North China and to transport supplies to the Dutch East Indies. "He also commented on the fact that American Marines were fighting side by side with puppet troops and Japanese troops against the Chinese communist forces"—a reference to the fact that, rather than repatriating all surrendered soldiers from Manchuria, the United States had effectively sanctioned Japanese involvement in the Chinese civil war on the Nationalist side.[45]

In turn, it wasn't lost on senior military commanders in the Philippines and Hawaii that militant labor organizers were among the demobilization protest leaders. That some were avowed members of the U.S. Communist Party was enough to taint others as "communist suspects." Zeller's contribution to the Schofield Bowl rally, quoted above, was transcribed and reported to General Richardson by the four counterintelligence agents he had tasked with monitoring the event. The general's suspicions had been aroused by an open forum on socialism conducted by Zeller at the Schofield Barracks' library two days before the demonstration. In response to rising activism, Richardson banned criticism of "persons in authority," heedless of the ammunition he duly supplied to critics of the "fascist army." He also took steps to clamp down on the soldier press, particularly peeved by *Stars and Stripes'* reference to him as "Number One Public Enemy."[46]

Richardson's interpretation of who and what his nemeses were—insubordinate rabble-rousers, in all likelihood "communist agitators"—found a responsive audience in Tokyo and Washington alike. MacArthur's GHQ, preternaturally alert to the "red menace" whether in Soviet, Japanese, or American guise, feared the same. MacArthur's press office, together with the Eighth Army publicity machine, took pains to brief receptive American correspondents on this worrisome development, stressing that even if the GI demonstrators themselves were not communists, their actions would surely succor and encourage America's foes. Just five months after V-J Day, SCAP didn't have to spell out that the enemy in question was the USSR and its local proxies. Conservative columnists needed little encouragement to promote the anticommunist line. The *Chicago Daily Tribune*'s coverage of the GI protests prominently headlined "reds" as the "sparkplug," and the reinvigorated House Un-American Activities Committee began an investigation into communist subversion among soldier protesters and progressive veterans' organizations.[47]

Across the Pacific, senior commanders shared an animus against not only "reds" but also a different perceived enemy within: the soldier press that provided a ready outlet for enlisted men's "gripes." Sometimes these two sources of menace appeared identical. In Japan, Eichelberger worked to remove an editor of *Stars and Stripes* believed to be a communist, while the Manila-based *Daily Pacifican* also came under fire. Staff of the latter were ordered to stay away from the GI rallies and instructed that their paper could print only wire-service accounts of the demonstrations. As far as they dared, military commanders in Hawaii, the Philippines, and Japan attempted to suppress coverage of GI militancy, both irked by the personal invective heaped on them and fearful of a "copycat" effect, with tactics and energy circulating from one location to another. Needless to say, soldiers noticed and resented this curtailment of news.[48]

Senior officers' irritation with the enlisted men under their command, yet insufficiently under their control, mounted in Europe too. In the ETO, the *Stars and Stripes* came under constant fire. Patton considered it a "scurrilous yellow journal" that had contributed to his downfall. Other officers objected strenuously to its "B Bag" column, which provided a forum for GIs' grievances. They also found its cartoonists' irreverence especially intolerable. Bill Mauldin, awarded a Pulitzer in 1944 for his "Willie and Joe" strip featuring two hangdog GIs with keen noses for officers' BS, was as thoroughly disdained by the brass as he was beloved by enlisted men. This was doubtless just as the twenty-four-year-old would've wanted things. But it certainly did nothing to endear Mauldin to senior officers that his name was so easily (and often) rendered as "maudlin," their preferred pejorative for the lachrymose condition of men agitating for early demobilization. In Berlin, Brigadier General Jack Whitelaw blamed the collapse of soldier morale on Mauldin—"with his filthy looking soldiers"—and on "the B-Bag in the *Stars and Stripes* of which many officers here in Europe are really afraid." Whitelaw couldn't fathom why "Ike doesn't clamp down on the men." When his wife demurred, Whitelaw took her to task for not properly appreciating that Mauldin represented a "threat to a realistic national defense policy." By stirring up demobilization sentiment, the cartoonist had encouraged the home front to "yap for the return of Willie and Joe," turning the army into an unruly mob of "homesick people." With unself-conscious irony, however, Whitelaw issued a sustained howl against his own predicament, trapped in rubble-strewn Berlin, surrounded by rampant—and all too public—"fraternization." Reminding his chastened spouse how much he hated "dancing on the carcass of a dead whale on a beach . . . especially when the dancing is jitterbugging," Whitelaw added, "I don't like Germany nor its occupants; so I say to hell with it. I want to go home." A familiar refrain indeed.[49]

Career officers were often particularly aghast at talk of a "caste system," which they considered complete hogwash. To its beneficiaries, entitlement often tends to be invisible. Many senior commanders preferred to regard military hierarchy as simply the ladder down which orders were conveyed and up which respect was (or ought to be) returned. Rank was thus naturalized as a necessary function of command rather than an inequitable configuration of power and its concomitant privileges. However, with sections of the press harping on the issue of officers' excessive perks, some conceded that they had a "perception problem" on their hands, if nothing else. When Whitelaw mailed his wife photographs of the mansion he inhabited in Berlin, complete with its staff of "thirteen domestics," he warned her not to let these pictures get into the wrong hands. Even though "we're supposed to live like conquerors," as Whitelaw put it, leaving unclear whether he meant "we Americans" or just "we brigadier generals," the "boys of the press" sometimes pretended otherwise. Reporters, those perennial hypocrites, were living "just as well, forever demanding better quarters, private automobiles etc.," Whitelaw complained.[50]

In Japan, Eichelberger shared this frustration with antiofficer "muckraking" encouraged by wealthy press barons. Fulminating against a February 1946 issue of *Life* that had given Neville license to explain "What's Wrong with Our Army"—juxtaposing reenlistment posters with Mauldin's cartoons—Eichelberger let rip in a private gripe session directed to Miss Em and against Henry Luce: "The caste system in the Army doesn't compare with the caste system in *Life*. When one contemplates that great lot of beautiful homes in Connecticut in which their leaders live, and the private dining room on the floor below the Rainbow Room in the Rockefeller Center where the officials eat, one realizes that they have not taken into their bosoms the younger people who eat in the restaurant around the corner."[51]

As Eichelberger's diatribe suggests, repudiation of caste coexisted with acute awareness of class. Not surprisingly, however, men of this patrician mold didn't understand themselves to be class conscious any more than they acknowledged the military to embody a caste system. Their unreflective assumption was that class antagonism existed purely among the lower orders, animated by the plebs' *ressentiment*. That West Point Brahmins' condescension toward subaltern untouchables might have contributed to the rising tide of popular rage was as inconceivable to the former as the idea that men of different ranks might rub shoulders socially. Some career officers regarded fraternization with enlisted men as a form of intercourse more unconscionable than that between GIs and "furlines." In previous wars, officers had been forbidden outright from drinking with NCOs or enlisted men, and at least some still carried that mindset into World War II and beyond. These simmering tensions came to a boil in January 1946. The GI protests gave expression to fury that had been steadily escalating since the war ended. In turn, the fact that soldiers had taken their "'Wanna go home' racket" (in Eichelberger's phrase) to the streets exacerbated commanding officers' contempt for the riffraff who, as they saw it, had been swept en masse into an irregular "people's army."[52]

As the demonstrations spread, another cause célèbre reached its climax in January 1946. The case of Joseph Hicswa further illuminates the ways in which ideas about class, race, and justice differently informed the mentalities of American civilians and military commanders overseas. Although Private First Class Hicswa makes no appearance in most recent studies of occupied Japan, he became briefly well known soon after the war ended. One instant history noted that Americans' "confused mental montage" of the occupation was limited to "General Tojo bleeding on his sofa, jeeps, fraternization, Private Hicswa and the braid on General MacArthur's hat." The notorious soldier made front-page news in the United States for a particularly regrettable reason: he had stabbed two Japanese civilians to death in November 1945, fueled by a lethal cocktail of alcohol and malice, or so a court-martial determined. Many Americans, however, found the most regrettable aspect of Hicswa's case not the grisly crime itself but what they believed to be its disproportionate punishment. The twenty-year-old from Wallington, New Jersey, was sentenced to be "shot to death with musketry." "Well, that's the army for you," Hicswa wrote in a letter to his buddies from the stockade at Yokohama, channeling the zeitgeist.[53]

But supporters at home were determined not to let the army have its way. Hicswa's family, along with staff and pupils at his old high school, joined forces with the Foreign Legion to mobilize support. Mass letter-writing drives lobbied local politicians and petitioned Truman, while Hicswa's mother penned an emotional appeal to MacArthur, begging for clemency on behalf of her son. The general replied, through audibly gritted teeth, that although this plea "moved me deeply . . . there is no manner wherein I can intercede in this matter." Meanwhile, Hicswa's supporters deployed a shifting set of arguments as to why he should be pardoned. At first, family members tried to insist that their nice boy couldn't have committed the murders. They then changed tack to propose that Hicswa must have attacked his victims while "crazed" by drink, making "Liquor, Inc." the real killer (as the *Christian Science Monitor* put it). Later still, an uncle claimed that the epileptic private was "mentally unbalanced" after a head injury sustained twelve years earlier. As protestations of innocence gave way to claims of limited liability, Hicswa's supporters included in their litany of mitigating circumstances the fact that he had been indoctrinated by the army to "hate Japs." If he had slain two after the war, this merely proved how effectively the army had turned an innocent young boy into a programmed killer.[54]

Hicswa, meanwhile, protested his innocence. In a letter to an eighteen-year-old girlfriend in New Jersey he divulged that he'd "gotten in a fight with some Japs" on the night in question, but since he didn't have a knife, he surely couldn't have committed the murders. (Prosecutors claimed that Hicswa had used a bayonet blade, which he'd then hidden in a urinal at his barracks.) Besides, the Japs with whom he'd fought were "still moaning" when he left the scene of the fight. In his own eyes, Hicswa was a scapegoat—"because someone has to be held responsible." Petitioning his uncle, Hicswa insinuated a connection between his fate and the death penalty concurrently pronounced on Japanese war criminals. "I think my sentence has been put to extremes compared to some war criminal cases," Hicswa wrote his uncle. "But what can I do? I am just a minor item to the big boys, and their word is law."[55]

Supportive sections of the press followed this thread binding Hicswa's case to that of General Yamashita, who had been sentenced to death on December 7, 1945—a verdict upheld by the U.S. Supreme Court in February 1946, as lobbying efforts on Hicswa's behalf reached their peak. This development prompted the *New York Herald Tribune* to argue that Hicswa had been offered up for sacrificial slaughter by a military justice system excessively eager to demonstrate—to the world in general, and Japan in particular—that it punished alleged crimes by American privates just as rigorously as those committed by Japanese generals. "It would be a tragic mistake, surely, were unwonted inclemency shown toward him in an effort to prove that this country is as fair to its enemies as to its own citizens," the paper editorialized.[56]

Naturally, leaders of the Eighth Army held a contrary opinion. To Eichelberger and his circle, Hicswa personified everything wrong with their conscript army: a drunken lout who had the temerity to blame military "indoctrination" for his unprovoked homicidal spree. Also of note was the fact that, while many of his peers couldn't wait to get out of the military, Hicswa had just reenlisted for an extended tour in Japan. His murderous rampage occurred the night before he was scheduled to head home to New Jersey for a brief furlough: a "homeward bounder" indeed. Byers offered a gloss on the case to friends in Columbus, Ohio:

> He was out with some friends one night and drank a little bit. It couldn't have been much for otherwise he would have been unable to run with the speed he did or use a knife as effectively as was the case. Apparently he had little or no battle experience and suddenly felt called upon to "get himself a couple of Japs." One happened to pass and he rushed over and stabbed the unfortunate one to death. A few minutes later another Japanese was seen and again Hicswa overtook this individual and killed him. The hue and cry over it all back home was raised that this sweet little boy was just following the tendencies taught him by the horrible Army.

Byers concluded his account with an apology for this unpleasant "recital," which he had provided to indicate "how the strange turn of sympathy back home is making it difficult for the army out here to create an atmosphere in which decent people may live comfortably after the dregs of humanity have been put out of the way."[57]

The particular reason why Byers felt moved to apologize, however insincerely, was over his inclusion of certain "indelicate" aspects of the Hicswa case that Eichelberger wanted to circulate—so long as his own fingerprints didn't mark the story. In a more candid, and thoroughly unapologetic, letter to his wife, Byers explained these plot twists as follows:

> Bob developed a very practical idea this morning which I think is going to do much to knock in the head this disgusting, maudlin sympathy which people back home are accepting in connection with this man Hicswa. He made a temporary escape from jail in company with a negro and a Japanese prisoner. The negro has just received a life sentence for rape and I do not know the charge on the Japanese. The negro and Hicswa were re-taken within an hour after their escape in bed with two Japanese women very near to the prison. We're not sure how we'll release this information, but publicize it we're going to do to the limit of our ability. We realize that this will be a horrible shock for his family but the American people must not be permitted to compel the freedom of such an individual.

Relating all this to his own wife, Eichelberger quipped that, although Hicswa's defense rested on a claim that he had been "taught to hate the Japanese," his capture "in bed with a Japanese prostitute" demonstrated that this "hatred was not all-inclusive."[58]

Eichelberger and Byers pounced in glee on the apparent elasticity of Hicswa's views of the Japanese. But by drawing pointed attention to the identity of his fellow escapee—a "negro" convicted of rape—they more slyly sought to play on the inflexibility of many white Americans' convictions about race. Which was worse: Hicswa's choice of male companions or his female consort? Eighth Army commanders clearly hoped to manipulate racial prejudice in all its hydra-headedness. And for a brief period they thought their stroke of PR genius had succeeded. Byers noted with satisfaction reports on March 5 of a "very favorable . . . if very shocked" reaction back home to the latest Hicswa revelations. But if that was indeed the case, the impact was short lived. Just two months later, Truman interceded on Hicswa's behalf. The president commuted his death sentence, replacing it with a term of thirty years' confinement at hard labor. New Jersey senator Albert Hawkes protested that this punishment was still "too severe," but it left Eighth Army generals in Japan fuming over the president's appalling sop to civilian sentimentality.[59]

In the decades since 1945, the same alchemy responsible for transmuting the "worst war in history" into the "best war ever" has also gilded the Americans who fought it. Enshrined in a pantheon of national heroes, these men and women are routinely saluted as the "greatest generation." That these courageous, selfless individuals gave—and gave up—whatever the wartime state required of them has become an article of faith. Subsequent generations of Americans, both those in uniform and those who resisted Washington's wars, have been disciplined by this earlier generation's reputation for uncommon valor. Often they've been found wanting.

Some veterans beatified in this way must surely have mused on the mysterious ways in which retrospect moves. During World War II, a substantial tranche of this generation thoroughly loathed the military, an institution that often seemed to revile those same enlisted men now so revered. The demobilization frenzy that accompanied the first phase of postwar occupation reveals the depth and breadth of popular antimilitarism, subsequently lost to the purifying fire of sanctification. It's salutary, then, to recall that American soldiers and civilians protested, by furious words and deeds alike, the protracted terms of military service. When Charles Hunt wrote home from Japan in January 1946, "Now I hate the Army and everything connected with it with every ounce of hate in my body," he voiced a sentiment shared by an overwhelming number of his peers. To call Hunt and his cohort "uncomplaining"—a stock characterization of the greatest generation—fails to do justice to their belligerence, ignoring the multiple privations that provoked such bitterness.[60]

If it now seems akin to blasphemy to recall that the greatest generation was riven with the capricious and complex emotions that afflict ordinary mortals, it may be similarly shocking to discover how thoroughly the loathing felt by enlisted men was reciprocated by their superiors. Consider Byers's account of the Hicswa case, with its invocation of the "strange turn of sympathy" taken by Americans in and out of uniform. Wanting nothing more than to "bring the boys home" as soon as possible, enlisted men and their loved ones had abandoned all sense of responsibility, along with any appreciation of the discipline required to sustain a functioning military. Now the hapless home front had thrown its weight behind the cause of a double murderer. This was the peculiar gyration of opinion to which Byers referred. But another attitudinal revolution was also underway. When Byers complained that popular fecklessness was "making it difficult for the army out here to create an atmosphere in which decent people may live comfortably after the dregs of humanity have been put out of the way," it was the *Japanese* whom he termed "decent," American GIs the "dregs of humanity." Six months earlier such a statement would hardly have seemed possible. Yet it remains striking how little attention any U.S. commentators paid to the Japanese victims of Hicswa's lethal rampage, whether they sided with or against him. That the court-martial indicted him for stabbing Yasuichi Sugichi, "a human being," and Choji Nishimoto, "a human being," tells its own story. Japanese "humanness" still could not be taken as given but needed to be spelled out, repeatedly.[61]

Byers's demeaning characterization of enlisted men was echoed in the clinical judgment of War Department chief psychiatrist, Brigadier General William C. Menninger. After a tour of the Pacific theater in January 1946, Menninger diagnosed "neuropsychiatric problems" as the root cause of the "morale problem" whose most visible manifestation was the fervor with which men pressed for demobilization. He duly prescribed "an orientation program which would reconcile the soldiers to their duty and convince them of the necessity of occupation service." Other senior figures agreed that "orientation" must have been deficient for demobilization activism to gather such steam. This was, after all, a less alarming conclusion than to acknowledge that men—for a variety of different reasons, personal and political—found occupation duty distasteful.[62]

For the same reason, the War Department shied away from referring to the events of January 1946 as a "mutiny." That term implied a political dimension to a phenomenon senior commanders preferred to ascribe to excessive homesickness and insufficient indoctrination that had left occupation troops "as unprepared for many of their duties as they would have been for combat if they had not been taught how to handle firearms." The problem, then, was how to animate a proper awareness of occupation's necessity among both soldiers and the civilians whose attitudes did so much to shape those of service personnel abroad. For months, the War Department considered mounting an exposition that would tour major U.S. cities, touting the difficulties and achievements of American military government overseas, complete with photo display panels, short films, and GI speakers. Although this venture did not come to pass, influential civilian commentators made it their business to educate Americans about postwar responsibilities. For liberal internationalists, like McCormick, prolonged occupation was a central plank of America's newly expanded global role and must be advocated as such. She and others duly recast occupation soldiering, in more ennobling terms, as "winning the peace." The continuation of war by political means, occupation validated Carl von Clausewitz's dictum by inversion.[63]

For liberals, the most alarming enemy lurked within. "Isolationism," to the internationalist way of thinking, represented a form of myopia to which Americans were particularly prone in war's aftermath—in 1946 as in 1919. Washington's retreat from global leadership would leave the world as rudderless and prone to turbulence as it had been after the last war, they argued, if Americans failed to absorb the lessons of history. "Isolation" could not be tolerated. The wives and mothers who beset Eisenhower had made the same point, albeit with reference to a different kind of domestic isolation. Theirs was an avowedly conservative antimilitarism: another phenomenon obscured with the passage of time. With their emphasis on patriarchal reconstruction, the Bring Back Daddy activists deployed "family values" to critique a military they represented as endangering both marriages and families, leaving children vulnerable, homes unprotected, and wives alone with their nagging fears of male infidelity. Reinforcing their point, one New Jersey congressman warned that "a generation of fatherless children" risked turning the United States into a "second rate power" if demobilization weren't accelerated.[64]

Occupation—that contentious O word—thus found itself entwined with contending I words. Internationalists waged rhetorical war on isolationists, lambasting irresponsibility that might ultimately produce another world war. Meanwhile, the most radical GI protesters wielded another I word to make an alternative case against occupation. Far from securing the peace, prolonged military occupation constituted a form of imperialism, they argued. As such, it would invite resistance and, by extinguishing popular aspirations for social and political justice in the postwar world, ensure another cataclysm. In early 1946, then, the war over occupation was still in its opening phase.

Chapter 7

GETTING WITHOUT SPENDING

In early January 1946, as the demobilization protests reached their peak, celebrated novelist John Dos Passos offered *Life* magazine readers an account of his "mighty sobering" three-month stint in occupied Europe. The title heralded a grim verdict: "Americans Are Losing the Victory in Europe." This reversal of fortune, as Dos Passos appraised it, owed nothing to last-ditch resistance by the Nazi Werwolf units so feared in early 1945. Rather, victory was being dissipated by the victors' own dissolute behavior. The author's sobered state of mind stood in stark contrast to the sozzled degeneracy of America's army of occupation in Germany, where, in the words of one major, "lust, liquor and loot are the soldier's pay." Although Dos Passos rued the absence of a coherent political blueprint for Germany's reconstruction, his most biting criticism was reserved for the foot soldiers of occupation. In particular, he accentuated the issue of theft—not just from occupied populations but from the U.S. military itself. "Never has American prestige in Europe been lower," Dos Passos lamented. "People never tire of telling you of the ignorance and rowdyism of American troops. They say that the theft and sale of Army supplies is the basis of their black market." Just as "fraternization" had come to assume an alternative meaning with precisely nothing fraternal about it, so "liberation" had been transformed from a positive into a bitterly ironic negative. "Before the Normandy landings it meant to be freed from the tyranny of the Nazis. Now it stands in the minds of civilians for one thing, looting." His conclusion was damning: "We have swept away Hitlerism, but a great many Europeans feel that the cure has been worse than the disease."[1]

Other eminent commentators joined Dos Passos in remarking the ease with which victory—not a permanent trophy but a perishable asset—could be squandered. The old adage "To the victor the spoils" failed to capture victory's tendency to spoil the victorious, in both senses of the word. Material overindulgence, fed by a boundless sense of entitlement, had a morally corrupting effect on the victors. Rather than reforming defeated populations, occupation seemed to be doing more to ruin the occupiers, these critics contended. In an all too literal fashion, American forces overseas were being spoiled rotten—with grave geopolitical ramifications. Where earlier reportage had accentuated

GIs' sexual promiscuity, often stressing the predatory agency of German women in initiating these encounters, Dos Passos and others increasingly focused on material profligacy and the rampant growth of illicit economies wherever occupation forces had dug in. "The whole of Europe has become one vast black market," asserted photographer Margaret Bourke-White in her sardonically entitled portrait of postwar Germany, *"Dear Fatherland, Rest Quietly"* (1946). Erotic pleasure and illicit profit were intimately entwined. Sexual services ranked foremost among GIs' black-market purchases, bought with what quickly became the staple occupation currency, thanks to American soldiers' unlimited supply of this addictive substitute for cash: cigarettes.[2]

Over the course of 1946, the drumbeat of negative commentary from Europe and Asia grew steadily louder, much of it focusing on the bad behavior of occupation soldiers. The demoralization of GIs agitating for early discharge seemed to have found expression in a collective lowering of ethical standards as "homeward bounders" acted at their most caddish. American troops in Japan had "not proved themselves the complete Galahads in shining armor," Lindesay Parrott noted with wry understatement. And in the estimation of many pessimistic observers, American soldiers en masse had adopted the attitude that if they couldn't get home quickly, they could at least turn a quick buck. Thus *Newsweek* reported in January 1946 that the biggest gripe of disgruntled GIs in Germany—men who had taken to the streets in protest—was that they had to walk "miles from the post exchange" to a black-market center to "pick up $150 for a carton of cigarettes." The following month, *Collier's* published an essay by prominent military correspondent Drew Middleton, starkly headlined "Failure in Germany."[3]

Verdicts about who had failed how in occupied territory were not unanimous. Middleton's disquisition on the Office of Military Government, United States' patchy efforts at denazification certainly didn't exonerate the Germans from any share of responsibility. Nor were the Japanese exempt from criticism when journalists placed SCAP's first six months under the microscope. The "balance sheet" that Mark Gayn (a reporter considered dangerously pink by Douglas MacArthur's GHQ) drew up in March 1946 partly blamed sly Japanese saboteurs for America's failure either to expunge nationalist militarism from public life or to dismantle the economic primacy of Japan's zaibatsu. Members of the old guard who had determined to "sweat out years of occupation and of alien reform" were waiting patiently in the wings until U.S. troops withdrew before making their revanchist move, Gayn speculated. But he also noted the susceptibility of GIs to bribery with "wine and women" by these scheming old-timers. And it was, in his view, Americans' characteristic "dread of civil unrest" that had prompted them to preserve so much of the existing machinery of Japanese government, with worrisome implications for the country's longer-term democratization. "For much that has gone wrong, Washington is to blame," Gayn bluntly announced.[4]

Others placed greater weight on the dangerous consequences—political, strategic, and ethical—of breakneck demobilization for America's occupations. As high-points men were released, followed by throngs of lower-scoring soldiers when a besieged Truman upped the tempo of "reconversion" in early 1946, units that had survived the war intact fell apart almost overnight. Influential civilian commentators took a dim view of the young recruits arriving in Europe and Asia to replace discharged veterans—a judgment they had in common with (and perhaps in some measure acquired from) the occupations' military commanders. The kid brothers of men not yet collectively known as the "greatest generation" appeared a sorry lot—"young boys without any skilled trades," Robert Eichelberger noted with chagrin. "Instead of the spick and span army, such as defeated the German Army, the occupation forces give the impression of being made up of a miserable, unhappy, homesick bunch of boys," scoffed the *New York Times'* Cyrus Sulzberger in the first of a high-profile series of reports from Germany that also emphasized the black market as emblematic of occupational failure. Deficient in every regard, these teenage troops were "superficially impressed by German plumbing and roads," Sulzberger opined. "Furthermore many newly arrived soldiers have had no previous romantic experience. Not only are the fraeulines of a supine Germany bountifully generous with their dumpy pulchritude but, even worse, many a simple, well-brought-up occupying soldier, with eight weeks of training, feels he must marry the first object of his affection."[5]

More than a decade before William J. Lederer and Eugene Burdick's novel popularized the archetype of the "ugly American" abroad, intimations of ugliness abounded in diverse reports on the occupations just months after the war's end. Roi Ottley, who wrote for the *Pittsburgh Courier* among other publications, voiced the "general impression" that "America has come out of the war as the most hated country and that the American GI, by his manner and general conduct, has contributed to this greatly." Ottley wasn't alone in seeing ugliness as an amalgam of boorish behavior and noxious beliefs. It wasn't just alcohol that primed soldiers to act up; racism also prompted them to act out viciously.[6]

Occupation soldiers' violent enactment of racist animosity was not confined to Europe. An informed account from Japan, published in April 1946, offered a scathing critique of white Americans' behavior in Asia:

> Yanks are undesirable in large numbers in foreign lands. They herd by themselves and reverberate each others' prejudices more loudly. . . . Already prejudiced, they make public appearances in large groups, and they always have liquor. Yanks seem to enjoy falling down drunk publicly in an enemy land. Then they approach every woman within a hundred yard range. . . . In this mood of roving drunkenness, Yanks scatter cigarettes and money lavishly, with no thought of how they are lofting price-levels for themselves. Yanks in large numbers overseas are a boastful arrogant crew of drunken stumblebums. They trample delicate customs; they never comprehend the minds of the natives; and they reduce all intercourse to the lowest plane of drink and women.

The author, who noted the irony that white GIs exhibited a greater animus against "the American Negroes who had suffered alongside them" than toward their erstwhile Japanese enemies, was not one of those left-progressive journalists so loathed by Japan's occupation authorities. Hargis Westerfield was the official historian of the U.S. Army Forty-First Infantry Division, and he had served in the South Pacific before terminating his tour in Japan.[7]

In June 1946, questions about the ethics of occupation were posed in the most melodramatic fashion by a headline-hogging story about stolen royal jewels in which "lust, liquor, and loot" all figured prominently. The scandal broke when newspapers announced that a staggering haul of treasure, spirited out of Friedrichshof Castle in Kronberg, Germany, had been retrieved by army investigators from a dime-in-the-slot locker in Chicago's Illinois Central Station. The cache included hundreds of pearls, sapphires, diamonds, rubies, and emeralds, many prized from their original settings. Other items later retrieved included letters between various European royals and a gold-bound Bible, inscribed by Queen Victoria for her daughter as a wedding gift.[8]

Before they wound up in a Chicago locker, the Hessian crown jewels (and further valuables estimated at $2.5 million, never subsequently recovered) had been discovered in the basement of an eighty-room castle near Frankfurt. Like many other substantial German properties, Friedrichshof had been appropriated as an army officers' club. When beady-eyed corporal Roy Carlton, scouring the cellar for hidden caches of alcohol, noticed a patch of suspiciously fresh concrete, he set to work to discover what it might conceal. The ensuing excavation unearthed objects far more precious than vintage wine. Dutifully, Carlton informed WAC captain Kathleen Nash, who ran the club, about his discovery. She in turn hatched a plan with her boyfriend, army colonel Jack Durant (a Department of the Interior attorney in civilian life) to steal the priceless treasures. Greed quickly swallowed both common sense and conscience. "We first decided to turn them in," Nash's confession stated. "Then we thought we would take only a few pieces and then we decided we would take all of it."[9]

The theft apparently came to light only when Hessian princess Sophia quizzed army officials about the gems' whereabouts in search of a tiara to wear at her wedding. Her inquiry came too late, however. Nash and Durant had already removed the treasure wholesale from Friedrichshof, selling some jewels in Switzerland, passing others to a former girlfriend of Durant's in Ireland, and mailing packages home to siblings before the couple returned to the States and married. But the thieves, notorious for their drunken binges, were insufficiently skillful crooks to have fathomed how to turn stolen crown jewels into liquid assets. When army investigators closed in on their quarry, led by Colonel A. C. Miller, a former Penn State professor of romance languages, they found Nash's sister in Wisconsin using a thirty-six-piece solid gold table set in her kitchen. Durant's brother had buried his share near Route 7 in Falls Church, Virginia. The newlyweds themselves were arrested at Chicago's luxurious La Salle Hotel just hours before it ignited in a blaze that claimed sixty-one lives: a coincidence that drew yet more attention to this spectacular illustration of how hazardous occupational rewards might prove.[10]

None of the principals emerged unscathed from the scandal as first Nash, then Durant, was extradited to Germany to face court-martial. American press commentary exhibited little sympathy for the Hessian royals who had been robbed. If the family's exorbitant wealth did nothing to endear them to most Americans, their alleged Nazi connections did even less. Although this bond between royalty and the Third Reich didn't let Nash and Durant off the hook, it hinted at a vexed question in all occupied territory: Where was the boundary between legitimate confiscation of the ill-gotten gains of a deposed ruling class and illegitimate theft? Convened in August 1946, Nash's court-martial brought to light a host of murky issues about property and propriety in occupied Germany. It occurred under a glare of publicity unusual for military judicial proceedings—often rather perfunctory affairs attended by a mere handful of participants with a direct stake in the proceedings. Most courts-martial, however, did not feature as exhibit A an eighteen-foot-long table groaning under the weight of jewel-encrusted tiaras, diadems, necklaces, pendants, bracelets, rings, silverware, and gold.[11]

Reporters characterized Nash in uniformly unflattering terms. Her attempts to court sympathy by arguing that army investigators had held her in an "insane asylum" for interrogation and subjected her to a strip search—particularly degrading for a female detainee—did nothing to assist her cause. More noteworthy, for many press commentators, were the defendant's own violations of normative gender conventions. The "stocky" forty-three-year-old had lied about her age on enlisting, claiming to be thirty when she was thirty-nine; and not only had she left two children to join the Women's Army Corps, she'd then taken up with a man seven years her junior, Colonel Durant. Irrespective of the fact that she'd been caught red-handed, Nash did not submit meekly to indictment. Her defense rested on the claim that she was to be made a "scapegoat" for the crimes of American troops who had also taken German property. "Thousands of others have done the same thing," argued her attorney, Colonel John Dwinnell. "It is unjust to point a finger at this woman and say: 'You will now pay the penalty for something that the whole world knows many, many people have done with immunity.'" This logic did not prevail, however, for while countless American soldiers had indeed looted others' possessions, no one else had stolen three million dollars' worth of crown jewels. The captain was duly sentenced to five years' imprisonment at hard labor and dishonorable discharge, while the colonel, perceived as the crime's mastermind, received a stiffer fifteen-year term.[12]

Thousands of wrongs did not, the prosecuting officer asserted, make a right. But these wrongs had never been more glaringly exposed hitherto. Perhaps most damning for the army of occupation was a further revelation that surfaced during the court-martial of an alleged accomplice, Major David Watson. He insisted that he had done nothing wrong in pocketing a modest token of Hessian treasure. After all, Watson pointed out, Durant's own commanding officer, Major General James Bevans, had "accepted" a silver pitcher from the cache. That a general had been bought off in this way raised the suspicion that, even at the highest levels, military government personnel either turned a blind eye to postwar profiteering or themselves took a cut. Bevans subsequently received a rebuke from military governor General Lucius D. Clay for his "extremely poor judgment" but was spared a trial that risked injuring the army's reputation yet further. However, three successive courts-martial in the Hessian crown jewels case more than sufficed to establish a picture of pervasive graft—from petty pilfering to larceny on the grandest of scales. Press coverage devoted to this mesmerizing saga of dumb greed opened space for further tales of officers stealing artwork and diverting whole boxcars of army supplies for black-market sale. When Major Watson's prosecutor countered that millions of soldiers *resisted* the temptation to "take things which did not belong to them," the assertion was less resonant than his admission that "abnormal conditions" prevailed in occupied Germany.[13]

Popular culture reinforced this impression of tawdriness, conjuring a twilight zone of shadowy transactions in fittingly monochromatic tones. The black-market milieu called for innumerable shades of gray, and racketeering formed a staple fixture of noirish representations of occupied Europe, a point most memorably conveyed by Marlene Dietrich's chanteuse in Billy Wilder's *A Foreign Affair* (1948). The breathy delivery of her signature number, "Black Market," leaves no doubt that when she entreats the soldier audience at Berlin's Femina nightclub to "enjoy these goods/for boy, these goods are *hot*," she is not referring to a Meissen figurine. Carol Reed's *The Third Man* (1949), scripted by Graham Greene from a longer novella, gives the subterranean murk of occupation yet more literal form. Set in occupied Vienna— carved, like Berlin, into quadripartite sectors—its climactic scenes play out in the city's underground network of sewer pipes, where antihero Harry Lime (played by Orson Welles) has fled on discovery of his illicit penicillin smuggling operation. "Everyone in Vienna" is "mixed up in some racket," one of Greene's characters claims in self-exoneration—a line that might have been pilfered from Captain Nash.[14]

American analysts reached no consensus about the nub of the problem. Did conquest inescapably corrupt the conquerors, or was it corrupt individuals who degraded the democratizing aspirations of occupation? Different authors switched the mantle of villainy between occupiers, occupied, and the poisonous "abnormality" of occupation itself. A character in one of Kay Boyle's

New Yorker stories set in occupied Germany likened it to a "lepers' colony, an infected island which free men conquered, and who have, because of this, become ailing and evil and no longer free." But however they diagnosed the ailment, a growing number of columnists and novelists shared the view that membership of an occupying army was a morally hazardous proposition. Just as a war could be won and the ensuing peace lost, so soldiers could survive battle only to be snared by postwar's lethal traps. One veteran, Walter J. Slatoff, writing in the *New Republic* in May 1946, described how a buddy who had emerged from combat "without a scratch" became a "casualty in Berlin nearly a year after the war's end"—"the victim of a city in which vice, corruption and callousness have reached a point that defies description." "Imagine your own 18 or 19-year-old son removed entirely from your supervision," entreated Slatoff, "given an almost unlimited supply of money, granted a power over women equal to that of Van Johnson or Clark Gable, fed a steady diet of lies and stories calculated to inspire suspicion, hate and cynicism, and placed among a people who had lost all moral standards." Was it any wonder that the ruined and ruinous former German capital was claiming so many GI casualties?[15]

Military commanders were, of course, well aware of the traps into which youthful recruits—to say nothing of their officers—might readily tumble, and not simply in Berlin where the black market had become coextensive with the city itself. They devoted increasing time to the business of remoralizing their troops as the occupations lengthened. But the relationship between morale and morality was more slippery than their lexical proximity suggested. Although demoralized troops showed a marked tendency toward immorality, inducements to high morale didn't always produce a salutary effect on soldier morals. Indeed, some of the stratagems employed to sweeten the bitter pill of occupation duty contributed, more or less directly, to the very problems that U.S. commanders found themselves confronting: theft, illicit commerce, and the violence with which racketeers' profits were all too commonly "protected."

In the summer of 1945, faced with a vertiginous tailspin in GI morale, military leaders desperately sought to stave off a crisis of disaffection whose symptoms included soaring rates of absenteeism, alcohol poisoning, vehicular misadventure, and the venereal infection that accompanied rampant fraternization. The central planks of this program were consumption, recreation, and travel; the intended outcomes, boosted morale and improved rates of reenlistment. American troops were to be "armed with abundance." This strategy would subsequently be redeployed in Vietnam, as historian Meredith Lair has shown, but it was pioneered in postwar occupied territory. "Our Government has made this the best fed, best clothed and best entertained Army in the world's history," General Eichelberger bragged to his uncle in February 1946. This boast wasn't empty hyperbole. As soon as the war ended, commanding officers devoted considerable attention to distracting, rewarding, and cajoling combat soldiers who found themselves transformed, often against their will, into occupation troops. Time and again, occupationaires were reminded, "You've never had it so good." And perhaps they had not. "We ride everything free, draw our rations free, and all it costs is what we want to spend on souvenirs," gushed a WAC captain in Tokyo. "I'm going to hate to begin paying for things—movies, transportation, food, etc. We are even issued cigarettes here. Right now I have five cartons and four cigars! More fun."[16]

To stave off the tedium that fueled discontent, military leaders emphasized what one army report termed "healthy recreation and entertainment." To that end they ordered the hasty construction or refurbishment of swimming pools, playing fields, athletic tracks, and golf courses. Sports teams competed in tournaments with fellow GIs and, where shared occupational jurisdiction permitted, American athletes tested their prowess against occupation soldiers of other nationalities. (The Soviets earned considerable ill will from the other three powers in Berlin for their unexplained, "unsporting" eleventh-hour withdrawal from a big athletic meet in September 1945—"for no valid reason except that they might not win," John Maginnis surmised.) Some combat veterans gasped at the curious twist of fate whereby their job in the army of occupation became full-time sportsman. Charles Hunt, who spent his first month in Japan playing "torrid bridge games and softball," found himself recruited two months later, in December 1945, to play basketball for his division. "The team has a corner room on the fourth floor of some office building that overlooks the imperial grounds," Hunt told his family. "The food . . . is very good, and we don't have to do a blessed thing but play basketball."[17]

Commanding officers hoped that an exhausting program of swimming, baseball games, tennis matches, and volleyball contests would not only consume enlisted men's idle daytime hours but also divert and deplete energies that might otherwise find less wholesome outlets by night. "Athletics, entertainment and recreation" were quite explicitly conceived as mechanisms to tackle the ongoing prevalence of sexually transmitted infection. "The relaxation that comes with Victory must in no way be extended to include a letdown in the war against venereal disease," urged the Office of the Surgeon of the Fifteenth U.S. Army. In pursuit of victory against infection, military commanders set about the construction of clubs for officers and enlisted men alike, appropriating choice buildings—hotels, castles, and country clubs—for their premises. The lavish setup at Friedrichshof presided over by Captain Nash was but one of hundreds of such establishments across occupied Europe. In Japan, Eichelberger mandated a similar program of construction for the Eighth Army, resulting in dozens of clubs that he considered, not unreasonably, "better than many American small towns could hope to have." These facilities offered a range of attractions, from libraries where books could be read and letters home written in quiet seclusion to bars and dance halls where soldiers could mingle with "respectable" dates at dances under chaperoned conditions. The enlisted men's club at Osaka boasted a "beautiful dance floor where the soldiers dance with their Japanese girls," Eichelberger informed his spouse. Perhaps anticipating her disapproval, he hastily added, "One might doubt the desirability of having soldiers bring their girls to the movies, dances, etc., but that is certainly preferable to other things that might go on. Certain their recreation is supervised and there is none of the rowdiness that one hears about from France."[18]

Senior officers placed considerable faith in the WACs and Red Cross workers who typically staffed these venues to keep fraternization in check. Social interaction with cheerful, attentive, and attractive (but preferably not too sexy) women would, they feebly hoped, bolster men's flagging morale, reminding them of the wholesome girlfriends or matronly wives who awaited their return home: a feminine antidote to the widely touted predicament of GI "loneliness." The "Red Cross girls," Eichelberger noted with avuncular pride, "put their hearts and souls into the problem of decent entertainment."[19]

Leisure became a major industry at every site of occupation, creating different kinds of full-time employment for soldiers with particular skills and talents. Just how big a business recreational pursuits became is indicated, among other things, by the fact that the Eighth Army in Japan boasted a unit whose exclusive assignment was to travel the country repairing pool tables, replacing "sections of table with new green felt covering because of rips, cigar and cigarette burns and liquor stains." Creative, musical, and theatrically oriented GIs, like Jack Rosenfeld, found themselves recruited to full-time work writing and staging shows, musical revues, and talent contests. Movie theaters also quickly sprang up wherever American forces settled for more than a few transitory days. By September 1947, the Eighth Army in Japan presided over 261 motion picture theaters. In some urban locales existing cinemas were simply appropriated and placed under new proprietorship. Elsewhere, large auditoriums were constructed anew, like the 600-seat facilities built in Würzburg and Stuttgart. Screening facilities ranged from the lavish, such as the fabled, six-story Ernie Pyle Theater in Tokyo, to the rudimentary. In remote areas at the tail end of military supply lines, projectors were rigged up in open-air settings. Rambunctious GI audiences watched somewhat dated Hollywood movies not only under the stars but under the curious gaze of local onlookers—a phenomenon first observed by military government officers in North Africa in 1943.[20]

Initiatives to amuse and distract occupation soldiers didn't end with sports, clubs, dances, and movies. Subsidized tourism was a star attraction of postwar recreational programs. Leavening the requirement that troops remain present with frequent permission to be absent, officially sanctioned travel blurred the already rather hazy distinction between work and pleasure in occupied territory. Opportunities to see new places also sharpened soldiers' interest in acquiring cameras, rolls of film, and, for particularly enthusiastic amateurs, developing chemicals. Captain Randolph Seligman wrote home from Hokkaido imploring speedy dispatch of colored film for his movie camera: "Priceless scenes are just begging to be photographed." For his part, Bob LaFollette was equally certain his family would love pictures of Japanese children—"the cutest you ever saw in your life, with their bowl haircuts, enormously fat little cheeks, and miniature clothing and kimonos"—if only they'd send over a "cheap box camera." Navy radioman Alan Sterling, newly arrived in Tokyo in the fall of 1945, found a different reason for valuing photography. Writing to his sister in Schenectady, he offered an appreciation of what the camera necessarily omitted of the olfactory experience of occupation soldiering: "Now that the war is over I would give anything to have a movie camera out here. Even though these islands are practically the same [as others in the South Pacific] the scenery alone would make very good material for movies. The things that your other senses make you aware of is what makes these islands seem so lousy. Pictures alone would be the thing so that you would only receive the good things about the place and not all the rest that goes with them when you are out here."[21]

As these impassioned pleas for photographic backup suggest, for many military personnel photography was little short of a mania. George Cronin devoted almost as much space in the chronicle of his year in occupied Korea to musings about when and whether his camera would arrive from home as he did to when and whether to sleep with Korean girls. Nor was he alone in discerning the camera's value both for recording unfamiliar landscapes and for familiarizing the photographer with locals. Often GIs conceived excursions—whether an afternoon's stroll downtown or a vacation further afield—expressly as opportunities for picture taking. Better yet, possession of a camera could be used to initiate social interactions. Asking a young woman if she'd like her picture taken was a common opening gambit. That the stratagem worked, at least on occasion, is attested by the many snapshots now lodged in U.S. archives that depict Italian, German, Japanese, or Korean women posing for the camera, shyly or more come-hitherly, whether alone, in groups with other women, or alongside American soldiers. Not only cameras but the photographs they produced became prized possessions, things to be mailed home for illustrative purposes or preserved between bound covers as a lasting testament to various foreign conquests.[22]

In Japan, American soldiers enjoyed free "first class" transportation on the country's railroad network, while Japanese passengers crammed into unheated carriages or clung to the sides and tops of overburdened trains. As Eichelberger's diaries make clear, he invested considerable energy in overseeing an elaborate network of rest centers and hotels for Eighth Army use in Japan's most scenic tourist destinations. In turn, many occupation soldiers filled letters home with accounts of their travels and the hospitality they encountered as Japanese hoteliers and chefs whisked the dehydrated rations that military guests brought with them into tempting dishes. During the early phase of occupation, restaurants remained "off limits" to occupation forces in order to preserve scant local food sources, though many Americans had little interest in sampling unfamiliar fare that dissatisfied those who suppressed their repugnance over local fertilization practices long enough to try it. Other local customs held greater appeal than the cuisine, however. Indoor baths, frequented by both sexes, and outdoor hot tubs—together with the back-scrubbing often lavished on occupationaires by female attendants— merited a good deal of inked approbation. On a jaunt to Sapporo, Chuck

FIG. 7.1 An American soldier and his Japanese companion study the arrangements for segregated train travel in occupied Japan in 1946. John Florea/The LIFE Picture Collection/Getty Images [50505223].

Wilhelm expressed surprise over the separate dressing rooms for men and women when there was only one pool. But he didn't grumble about the mixed bathing since the three Japanese in question were "nice looking women too."[23]

In Europe, occupation soldiers enjoyed frequent passes to explore the continent by train, plane, or jeep. Destinations included sites of cultural and religious distinction such as Rome, Salzburg, and Oberammergau, as well as cities that, irrespective of their historic and architectural merits, appealed primarily as erotic hotspots, Paris most particularly. Military tourist circuits were conceived along various lines, from the purely relaxing to the purportedly instructive. In Germany, certain locations indelibly associated with Nazi atrocity were put on display for visitors. Many soldiers duly toured Berchtesgaden, Hitler's mountaintop retreat. They might also inspect a former concentration camp. Visiting Buchenwald in June 1945, Maurice Kurtz observed, "The place is quite a tourist center for GIs. The buildings are all intact, including the crematoriums (slab and all!) but have been disinfected and repainted, new beds (with sheets!), radios and music all over the place, which is today a Displaced Persons Center. Former inmates act as guides to groups. They smoke U.S. cigarettes now . . . smile . . . but frighten easily." Military commanders evidently hoped that such excursions might instill in new recruits a greater appreciation of why Germany's occupation was a necessary long-term undertaking. Similarly, once the war crimes trials opened in November 1945, Nuremberg—erstwhile cradle of National Socialism, now among Germany's more completely razed cities—joined the list of places GIs were encouraged to visit; the tribunal itself was a ticketed event.[24]

Rather than occupying parallel tracks, the lines of these martial tourist trajectories often crossed. In the process, the intended lessons of particular places of pilgrimage became blurred as GIs attached idiosyncratic, frequently irreverent, meanings to itineraries that aspired to cultivate moral awareness. Thus soldiers visiting Berchtesgaden or Berlin's Reichschancellery (before the Soviets put a stop to such visits) often appeared preoccupied with seeing what portable remnants of the Third Reich might still be pocketed, or with leaving a durable trace of their visit by carving initials or Kilroy's legendary tag into wooden or stone surfaces. When Henry Baust described for his spouse the big, octagon-shaped room at the Eagle's Nest where Hitler had held meetings, what he accentuated most was the large, round table in the center: "On it fellows had written their names."[25]

Americans without a relative in the army of occupation read about such things in their newspapers. "By threes and fours in jeeps, and by dozens in 6 by 6s, American soldiers from much of Austria and from all of southern Germany arrive all day long to see the sights and take pictures of each other atop Kehlstein, or framed in the great glassless window of the house where Hitler lived," reported Price Day for the *Baltimore Sun*. Describing the transformation of bombed and burned Berchtesgaden into a "center for GI tourists," he wondered what Hitler would've made of it all. "Never having been to America, he could not know what an American national park is like and that is essentially what the region dearest to his heart has become." Infected by the enveloping ennui, Day concluded, "The place isn't even interesting any more. It isn't even evil now, and if there is a lesson in it, it is merely the old lesson of vanity. This place is now almost intolerably dull."[26]

Likewise, visits to Nuremberg—a "citadel of boredom" in Rebecca West's characterization—did not always fulfill their intended didactic purpose. To some visitors, the courtroom resembled a circus where spectators could peer at the animals behind bars: another occasion to ponder the chasm between bland outer appearance and the concealed malignity within. But not all GIs, even those stationed in Nuremberg, had an interest in the court proceedings. "Honey, I don't hear much about the Nazi[s] they have in jail here and would not get a chance to go [to] the trials anyway," Clarence Davis sourly informed his spouse. "If I did it would probably be in German and I could not understand much of it anyway." In fact, the presiding authorities made sure the proceedings were simultaneously translated into the multiple languages spoken by the various participants and observers so that nothing would be unintelligible to anyone in the courtroom. Davis never found that out, though he did find time to make photographic tours of the city with a German he had befriended, a boy who spoke English "almost as good as we do" and wanted to "get in our air force."[27]

Blame for the slippage between travel's serious and frivolous functions hardly rested with GIs alone. Officers leading visits to Nazi sites sometimes encouraged men to consider these excursions as opportunities for "souvenir-hunting." As such, they became occasions better suited to reveling in military victory than contemplating the bankruptcy of enemy ideology. Meanwhile, some junior officers noted with disdain that their superiors were "goofing off in Nurnberg," as Howard Silbar seethed in a letter to his sister, "on pretext of 'arranging' things for the pending trials there." In his opinion, this cavalier absenteeism reflected the evaporation of any sense of collective responsibility. "Nobody gives a hoot," Silbar lamented. "So much is being done by the Army for the Army and to the Army that little is being done by the Army toward solving the problem (if there is any solution) of what to do with the Germans."[28]

The work of leisure remained as hazy as the mission of occupation soldiering itself. Members of America's "after-armies" were variously, and sometimes simultaneously, guards, police, judges, teachers, aid workers, athletes, actors, tourists, and students. As time blunted the more avowedly

FIG. 7.2 Capt. Florence Rowland *(left)* and Col. Westray Battle Boyce
(second from left) are saluted as they enter the Palace of Justice in Nuremberg
to attend the trial of Nazi war criminals in November 1946. United States Army Signal
Corps/Harry S. Truman Library & Museum [2014–3375].

punitive edge of occupation policy, military officialdom increasingly emphasized troops' ambassadorial function. Rhetorically, occupation soldiers
figured as emissaries of American goodwill: exemplary liberal democrats
whose very presence would inform and uplift occupied populations. To
discharge this responsibility didn't require GIs to proselytize on behalf of
Americanism, liberalism, capitalism, or any other -ism. Military psychologists
generally concurred that the average American soldier was steeped in national
ideology in ways they neither recognized nor could effectively articulate. But
simply by being themselves, and *being there,* occupation troops would dis-

charge their missionary function. Their relaxed demeanor, friendliness, sense of fair play, and generosity would work its own magic on former foes—or so it was hoped.[29]

Yet the expansive repertoire of roles devised for occupation troops was bound to create tensions as individuals attempted to juggle multiple identities. What signal did it send that the army chose to establish a university where 4,000 soldiers on active duty could take courses for college credit not at an ancient seat of learning like Heidelberg, Bologna, or Toulouse but in Biarritz, an exclusive resort on the Bay of Biscay? Relaxed sartorial and behavioral codes scarcely resembled those of university quadrangles, lecture halls, or libraries, and where else, except in fantasy, could a student have hoped to find Marlene Dietrich providing lectures on acting in 1945? Entertainment shamelessly enjoyed a higher premium than education.[30]

At a day-to-day level, the affluence designed to buffer the tedium and isolation of garrison life, as analysts diagnosed the perils of long-term occupation, rested on a foundation of well-stocked post exchanges (PXs). These were constructed in almost every location with a substantial U.S. presence and, at their grandest, resembled well-stocked stateside department stores. Some far surpassed typical American shopping facilities. Military personnel could purchase food, tobacco, alcohol, clothing, gifts for dispatch home, or appliances that would make bunkhouses or billets more comfortable. With more WACs, Red Cross workers, and civilian employees joining the occupation forces, PXs also quickly started to carry products specifically aimed at female consumers. In March 1946, General Eichelberger informed his wife, who would shortly join him overseas, that the enormous, multistory Tokyo PX had recently unveiled "a whole counter of ladies' things from Mum to hair pins, powder puffs, the stuff the gals use on their nails, etc.," ruefully adding that he imagined before long "the GI's will start buying them for their Japanese girls."[31]

In theory, PXs promised simultaneously to satisfy and *contain* GIs' materialism. The "closed shop" system would do less harm to local economies while recycling a portion of soldiers' pay back into military coffers. But in practice, voracious consumption posed challenges to occupational efficacy and ethics alike. Not only did ready access to discounted goods encourage acquisitiveness among occupiers and enviousness among the occupied, PXs also provided the former with bargain-price goods to trade with the latter, stimulating black-market activity. Often occupying very visible locations, post exchanges were bound to draw the attention of local residents. WAC captain Martha Wayman, one of the first seven female officers to arrive in Japan, noted that an "officers' only" store on the Ginza invariably attracted a "big crowd around the window, looking over our clothing, underwear and all!" This curiosity reversed the gaze of occupation personnel who tended to regard it as one of *their* prerogatives to stare brazenly at "the natives" as they anatomized markers of difference. Confusing roles yet further, some PX establishments, like the one in Tokyo, employed local women as "shop girls." Flashily showcased consumption was liable to generate envy when PXs glittered as oases of abundance in landscapes of postwar austerity. Struck by the chasm between American wealth and local poverty, some military personnel strove to give it a positive spin, insisting that jealousy would stimulate reconstructive industry. Exposed to Americans' exemplary consumption, defeated peoples would surely be spurred to close the gap. But not everyone was so optimistic that inequality would stimulate productivity. Those in the military PR business sometimes worried that flaunting the fruits of consumer capitalism might pose awkward questions about what "democracy" meant if it lacked any grounding in economic justice.[32]

Occupied populations were not alone in casting a skeptical, or envious, eye over American affluence. Since supply chains were stretched thin at the outer edges of occupation's archipelago in the Pacific, particularly in Okinawa and Korea, the spoils of postwar were distributed with marked unevenness among the occupiers themselves. The circuits of mobility that kept reshuffling military personnel between one base and another—and from work sites to leisure destinations—meant that GIs were often well aware of how their own situations rated against others'. Soldiers soon found out who had more of what where, and they let interested parties back home know about these disparities in no uncertain terms. As a result, threadbare shelves in Korea attracted the attention of a congressional inquiry conducted by the Military Affairs Committee in 1946. Having visited the peninsula, heard GIs' gripes, and observed the situation firsthand, Representative John Sheridan delivered a stinging rebuke to Eichelberger. "Nowhere, in the entire world, wherein we have inspected the military installations have we received so many complaints, and an inquiry found them wholly justified. The morale here, General, is at the lowest ebb," the congressman wrote in a vituperative letter delivered to

Eichelberger and the press simultaneously. Warming to his theme, Sheridan zeroed in on Korea's parlous PX situation:

> As an instance, the post exchange at the air field command is a misnomer—there is nothing there to exchange. No popular brands of cigarettes are available, in fact no nothing; not even a pair of shoe laces for the Commanding General. Another instance, General, a snack bar was available for our inspection, but we could not touch it because the paint was still wet; they had worked all day and all night to get the bar completed, before our arrival. As a side thought, the bar looks like something which you see back in the States in a back alley, housing a speakeasy. When we compare these so-called facilities with your exchanges and recreational facilities in Tokyo and Yokohama, it only emphasizes their complete deficiencies.[33]

Eichelberger was affronted by the accusation that he had neglected his men. The charge was also misplaced, he insisted, since Korea's U.S. military governor, General John Hodge, was not under Eighth Army command but reported directly to MacArthur. The PX situation in Korea thus lay beyond Eichelberger's purview. "Frankly I could not have been more surprised if I had been publicly censured for conditions in Timbuctoo," he wrote in a letter of self-exculpation to members of Sheridan's committee.[34]

Shopping, not sex, was *the* quintessential leisure pursuit of occupation soldiers. Everyone did it. Acquiring creature comforts, food, or drink was an easy way to spend money and time simultaneously. While some restricted their acquisitions to modest personal items purchased from the PX, others relished the opportunity to acquire "typical" local products as souvenirs, whether lederhosen, carved wood, and beer steins in Germany or kimonos, dolls, and ceramics in Japan. And it was as commercial actors, whether looking to buy, sell, or barter, that GIs most regularly came into contact with local civilians. Some of the latter were seeking simply to subsist, while others hoped to profit more handily from the occupation soldiers' well-paid presence. In Japan, Hunt found that even children—or perhaps children *especially*—were avid entrepreneurs. Writing home to his family in the second month of the occupation, he described one such encounter:

They're always trying to trade me something for chewing gum, and there's one in particular that gives me a hard time. He's a little older than the rest and he can speak a little English—anyway, he comes up to me and says "kind Amelican soldier," then he tries to trade me out of my pants. This goes on day after day, hour after hour, but when I want to get rid of them all I have to do is pull the bolt back on my rifle, let out one yell and they scatter to the four winds, and within two seconds there isn't a kid in sight.

Unself-consciously, Hunt captured the lopsidedness of interactions between occupiers and occupied. The American GI enjoyed the upper hand not only as sole adult but, more particularly, by virtue of being armed. When he became bored with the playful haggling, he could bring it to a precipitate halt by threatening to fire his weapon—a "game" that may have either thrilled or terrified his youthful audience.[35]

Different impulses drove soldiers' acquisitiveness. For military personnel who didn't need to send most of their pay home, accumulating possessions helped mitigate the privations of military life: its regimentation, discipline, lack of privacy, and theft of "own-time." One army veteran, seeking to explain GIs' contribution to runaway inflation in Italy, where the black market ballooned so uncontrollably that the FBI was called in to investigate, attributed avidity to an understandable desire for self-expression. "The mere fact that in making a purchase, even with supplies limited, he can exercise a certain freedom of choice helps him find release from the regimen of camp life," proposed T. E. Beattie. But while acquisition may have offered a way to assert individuality, shopping was often more a social than a solitary pursuit. Men not only routinely visited the PX—or local stores and markets—with buddies, they also frequently bought items for shared use. Beattie discerned a competitive edge to soldiers' efforts to keep up with the GI Joneses by making more, and more impressive, purchases. "There is a strong desire within the men to make their camp as comfortable and as livable as possible. This often borders on buying motives which might be termed those of conspicuous consumption. One tent buys a radio; a neighboring tent sees the radio and wants one just a little better." Eagerness to outdo neighbors, commonly associated with feminine housepride in the domestic realm, appeared a gender-neutral, or even masculine, phenomenon in military life.[36]

Uniformed personnel, both male and female, took pleasure and pride in their ability to snag a bargain. Herman Berger, a nineteen-year-old Jewish corporal from Philadelphia who arrived in Japan in October 1946, devoted significant portions of his correspondence to descriptions of the articles to be found at Tokyo's lavish PX and elsewhere. Constantly on the lookout for deals on silks, ceramics, and jewelry that his female relatives might appreciate, Berger asked his mother to consult with collectors back home about stateside prices for collectible items like cloisonné vases and cultured pearls. When, in January 1947, he heard rumors that the army was about to call in all yen notes—in a bid to curb black-market activity—he went on a spending spree to convert his surplus cash into goods that could be entrusted to the mail. "Everybody was sending home their 'loot' so to speak," Berger noted after a trip to the parcel-choked post office, before gleefully relating his skill at haggling. Transforming a derogatory phrase into a badge of pride, he bragged, "I must have saved 640 yen by 'Jewing' them down. Its an inherited *quality* I guess and I do pretty damn good at it even if I do say so myself." Less confident in her appraising eye or bargaining skill, Wayman placed her faith in the American officer-jeweler who selected pearls—said to be "very good" and 25 percent cheaper than in the States—on behalf of the Tokyo PX.[37]

For serious operators, however, acquisition was less an end in itself than a means to procure merchandise that could then be resold or bartered on the black market. These soldier-entrepreneurs weren't looking to blow a paycheck or find gifts but to multiply their military remuneration by as many times as local conditions and individual savoir-faire permitted. The military's emphasis on consumption provided many incentives for profit maximization. While post exchanges provided a ready supply of cut-price goods, subsidized travel offered more than just a chance to explore new places and enjoy some time off. Tourist destinations served as venues in which to acquire goods that could then be sold or traded on return. Not for nothing did the army attempt to limit personnel traveling to Switzerland to the purchase of one watch apiece—a ban that proved impossible to police. By the reverse token, travel also gave mobile GIs more opportunities to off-load government-issue property at a tidy profit. One ingenious soldier solved his laundry problem by selling his dirty clothing while on leave in Paris, where chic prewar tailoring had been supplanted by refashioned articles of American military apparel.[38]

Disposal of loot was another avenue through which military personnel entered into black-market commerce. There was, presumably, a limit to how many watches, cameras, pistols, or field glasses taken from enemy personnel any one individual needed as mementoes. Keepsakes were, as the name implied, for keeping. But what to do with the surplus? By military order, looted property could not be mailed to the United States, although enforcement of this rule was evidently not rigorous. (Had it been, Captain Nash's sister might never have received her thirty-six-piece set of solid gold cutlery.) Yet however patchy in its application and flimsy as a deterrent to pilferage, the embargo on dispatching home parcels of ill-gotten gains surely encouraged some soldiers to sell or trade property they had amassed, particularly as their scheduled dates for demobilization approached.

When it came to finding buyers for items like watches, Berlin was an especially target-rich environment in the early phase of the city's occupation, when American soldiers still routinely rubbed shoulders with their Red Army counterparts. Soviet occupation troops had just received all their back pay owing for wartime service, amounting to three or four years' wages in some cases, and at generous levels. General Frank Howley noted that Red Army lieutenants were being paid $140 per month. Disbursed as occupation marks, printed with special plates that the U.S. Treasury Department had given their wartime ally, this windfall could not be taken home to the USSR, by strict order of the Red Army. Money therefore had to be spent, and spent quickly. The inevitable result of so much paper chasing so few consumer goods was that inflation soared, rendering the occupation mark almost valueless—but not to U.S. military personnel. For a few months, at least, they were able to exchange this currency for real marks, then convert the latter into dollars that could be remitted home.[39]

American soldiers became key beneficiaries of Red Army spending sprees. Unlike those Berliners who had lost everything in bombing raids, U.S. occupation personnel invariably had something to sell, even if it was just a pack of cigarettes. Since the latter were, by common consent, *the* medium of exchange in occupied Germany, tidy profits could be made from selling packets or cartons bought at heavily discounted rates from the PX. Some six months after V-E Day, Major Maginnis puzzled over the shelf life of a currency seemingly as unstable as it was ubiquitous:

In Berlin we were living in a cigarette economy for cigarettes were money. Black marketers sold them at a reported 1500 marks per carton; US personnel sold them to black marketers; and everyone (US personnel, civilians and other) used them for trading. The mark, supposedly had a value of about 10c but actually it had no such purchasing power except for German purchase of poor food, poorer clothing, payment of rent and similar necessities. . . . Almost all tipping was done in the form of cigarettes. One of the best jobs in Berlin was to be the janitor in one of the Army buildings because each night he was able to collect all the cigarette stubs, from which the remaining tobacco in them would be used to make "new" cigarettes.[40]

Maginnis confined these musings on clandestine transactions to his diary. Other soldiers were more forthright about black-market activity in letters home, relating the exorbitant prices that cigarettes fetched on the black market and, on occasion, requesting relatives to send additional cartons—for a purpose that hardly needed direct explanation. Some men and women in uniform also asked civilian spouses, siblings, or parents to mail them another watch or watches. As the luxury item most desired by Red Army soldiers, timepieces commanded fantastic prices: a reflection not only of their scarcity in the USSR but also of their easy portability. "Most of the Russians have never seen a wrist watch before and they will pay almost anything for one," John Winner informed his mother and sisters back home. From what he'd heard, watches fetched anywhere between $100 and $500, and he claimed to know of GIs in Berlin who'd amassed as much as $30,000 that they were incapable of sending home. Stories soon circulated of Russians wandering Berlin with timepieces arrayed from wrist to elbow. By all accounts, Mickey Mouse watches were particularly sought after—fittingly enough, perhaps, when the paper used to buy them had every appearance of play money.[41]

Berlin in the early months of its four-power occupation became almost synonymous with the black market. The mystique of well-known centers of illicit but highly visible trade—such as the Tiergarten (a large park, largely denuded of trees, by the Brandenburg gate) and Alexanderplatz (later to disappear behind the wall)—turned these sites into tourist destinations for occupation soldiers. Even those who had no intention of becoming operators sometimes wanted to observe the scene or even make an exploratory transaction. Quite apart from the lure of picking up a bargain, dabbling in the black market offered the frisson of the forbidden as well as rich fodder for

FIG. 7.3 GIs vacationing in Lucerne, Switzerland, in August 1945 scrutinize watches available for purchase, perhaps with a view to trading them on Germany's pervasive black market. 3131 Signal Photo Platoon.

anecdote. One couldn't spend time as an occupation soldier in Berlin and *not* have experimented at least once. It would be like visiting Paris without seeing the Eiffel Tower. Thus, Jane DePuy, a WAC sergeant in Berlin, wrote home with lighthearted candor about her foray into black marketing as a date activity. She had gone out with a boyfriend, Bud, looking to find a portable typewriter. At every turn, locals seemed willing to oblige and, before long, the American couple had returned to a German's home to close the deal:

He had a very pleasant wife and the dearest little fox terrier
(wire-haired) pup called Tommy. I liked the machine but they
wanted food and of course I didn't have any and I don't like to sell
my candy because I feel I need it. Bud had a wrist watch on and
Mrs Muller wanted it so finally Dr Muller said we could have [the
typewriter] for the watch and 4 packs of cigarettes. Bud had
gotten the watch for some cigarettes and chocolate somewhere in
Germany and he was willing to give up the watch if I would give
him 15 packs of cigarettes and I readily agreed to that. Of course
he can get 1500 Marks for those cigarettes and I could too but
actually they cost me about 75 cents so you figure it out—did I get
a bargain or not? At least I have the typewriter.

Although DePuy presented herself as more concerned about whether her
date, Bud, was ripping her off than about whether they were giving the
German couple a fair price, her account makes clear that the exchange was
lubricated by acts of reciprocal generosity. Over ersatz coffee ("which was very
nice of them because food is hard to get") DePuy and Bud learned that
Muller's father had been a professor in the university, "killed by the Nazis,"
and that Muller himself was poised to assume editorship of a newspaper published with military government approval. Impressed by this cultured and
gracious couple, DePuy threw a PX lipstick into the deal for Mrs. Muller,
and the initial exchange yielded an invitation to visit again.[42]

In Japan, too, entrepreneurial soldiers sometimes found that cupidity
paid dividends in more than merely economic terms. For those of an inquisitive bent, buying or trading goods formed a point of entry into middle- and
upper-class Japanese homes that Americans might otherwise have found shut.
It took a particularly venturesome spirit to strike up conversation with Japanese strangers out of cross-cultural curiosity alone. LaFollette was one such
curious traveler, eager to befriend young Japanese wherever he went and frequently in despair over his fellow GIs' lack of inquisitiveness. But even gregarious Americans found chance encounters limited by the relatively few
spaces shared by occupiers and occupied. Trains and restaurants were off-
limits to occupation personnel, while requisitioned hotels and rest centers
catered exclusively to military personnel. In some instances, Americans' pursuit of luxury goods generated serendipitous encounters, like DePuy's, that
in turn sparked friendships or even clandestine business partnerships. In

other cases, Japanese civilians initiated contact, extending social invitations to officers in the hope that these visitors might be persuaded to buy jewelry, silk, or porcelain, thus supplementing meager postwar incomes. Wayman described one such dinner to her mother, who evidently disapproved of her daughter's visiting Japanese homes. After serving a meal that Wayman found unappetizing—"sweet potatoes, pickled lotus, lobster, rice with seaweed and hot saki. Yuk!"—the hosts cut to the chase: "The real intention was to show us some of their stuff they have for sale in case we wanted to buy something." Evidently the stuff, "some very nice kimonos and embroidered silk" and lacquerware, was more to Wayman's taste.[43]

Like DePuy and Wayman, few occupation soldiers who engaged in covert trade with inhabitants of the countries they occupied understood themselves to be doing anything wrong, particularly where informal commerce went hand in hand with social informality. Precisely what constituted blackmarket commerce was an open-ended question. In Berlin, General Howley made the counterintuitive claim that there *was* no black market, merely a laissez-faire free-for-all because "the Russians believe in free trade rather than fixed prices." Trying to distinguish the formal economy from its subterranean counterpart was all the more challenging when ostensibly clandestine commerce was hidden in plain sight, if it was hidden at all. "The black market in Berlin was everywhere or anywhere—on a corner, in a park, in some ruins, in a home or just two persons meeting on the street," noted Maginnis. And where barter had become intrinsic to everyday survival, as was undoubtedly the case in Berlin, Naples, Tokyo, Hiroshima, and many other decimated cities, it was easy enough for American soldiers to rationalize their participation in illicit trade as simply unavoidable. One bartered to get by. Although occupation troops undoubtedly injected fresh energy, currency, and products into the economies of occupied territories, boosting both supply and demand, they did not inaugurate the black markets they encountered in Europe and Asia. Last-ditch attempts by the Axis powers to stretch the "sinews of war" to their elastic limits (or beyond) through increasingly stringent rationing had already ensured that overburdened, undernourished citizens would find ways to circumvent state controls on prices and distribution. Mass existence at or below subsistence levels created fertile conditions for unscrupulous suppliers to exploit.[44]

Occupation soldiers could scarcely fail to notice the immiseration of many residents of ruined cities they cohabited on wildly uneven terms. In letters and diaries, American personnel frequently commented on the infants and old people who hovered in wait for their dropped cigarette butts and the discomfiting sight of foragers carefully sorting through GI garbage pails or dining from them on the spot. In Berlin, they found notes pinned to "walls, trees, fences or any similar place, offering something for something else (man's shoes size 43 for 2 serviceable bicycle tires) or something for sale (violin in good condition, 350 marks)." And, in Tokyo, WAC officer Jean Smith found "tragic" the plight of those Japanese on the roadsides who attempted to sell everything from precious heirlooms to shabby belongings that barely passed muster as junk. With desperation everywhere apparent, it's not surprising that compensating a waiter, housekeeper, or repair person with cigarettes for services rendered should have appeared an act of kindness to those Americans who "tipped" with tobacco. Such payments contributed to unregulated trade, aggravating the inflation that threatened to strand those without cigarette-earning potential. But these repercussions remained invisible to most occupation troops. Besides, as Major Maginnis pointed out in his Berlin journal, some Germans simply refused to accept anything else by way of payment. What, then, was an occupation soldier to do?[45]

Not all transactions had even the surface appearance of reciprocal advantage, however. Soldiers tended not to write home about major scams they were either embroiled in or knew about. Despite the lifting of mail censorship, the threat of spot checks on letters' contents remained. But occupation troops did sometimes describe situations in which they, or others, had taken advantage of local traders, capitalizing on their superior physical stature and the monopoly of armed enforcement enjoyed by occupation troops, should backup be required. Sometimes, they related these encounters with no hint of unease, nor any indication that the act of recounting might have been an oblique bid for parental absolution.

Thus Sterling, stationed with the navy in Yokohama, wrote to his mother in October 1946 about small-scale activities trading cigarettes and his search for a kimono at a price he didn't consider extortionate. Adopting an aggrieved tone, he bemoaned the way in which "Jap" traders were profiting from Americans' voracious appetite for souvenirs, expecting that gullible cash-flush foreigners would pay any price. But not Sterling. The strategy he outlined to avoid being fleeced involved handing a token sum of yen to the seller and then simply walking away with the kimono he wanted. "It would be best to have an MP close at hand in case of a fight," he noted. But "they can't do anything if an American does walk off with an article so long as some money is paid so that it wouldn't be called theft," he blithely concluded. Sterling's insouciance in conjuring this act of intimidation—for his mother's exclusive benefit—suggests not only the regularity with which he and other servicepeople engaged in such practices, but also his expectation that folks back home would share his sense of rectitude. "Japs" who tried to extort their occupiers were the villains of the piece in Sterling's telling; and their being in the wrong was confirmed by the MPs' intervention on behalf of Americans who "stood up for themselves" against Japanese swindlers.[46]

Viewed from another perspective, Sterling's vignette sheds light on military police participation in black-market trade—here, as enablers of their compatriots' intimidatory tactics, but elsewhere as direct participants in illicit profiteering. As the occupation authorities stepped up efforts in 1946 and 1947 to stamp out black-market activity, MPs were routinely called on to conduct raids of well-known trading sites, confiscating "hot" property and arresting unlawful traders—whether fellow soldiers or locals. This they sometimes did. But proximity to the action also created opportunities for MPs to resell confiscated goods or demand a cut of the action. In Okinawa, Paul Skuse (the officer in charge of the American military police) noted in 1947 how house-to-house searches ostensibly conducted in order to retrieve stolen U.S. government property were often nothing more than "souvenir hunts." In other words, they were looting parties organized for the purpose of pocketing whatever money and valuables MPs might find in local homes. Skuse found this situation all the more egregious because its formal justification was so woefully deficient. Almost every household contained GI property—given to, not stolen by, a local population rendered homeless and destitute en masse during and after the devastating battle for Okinawa.[47]

Despite the scruples of men like Skuse, who rued both the immorality and the counterproductivity of larcenous soldiers' behavior, those who engaged in black-market activity found numerous ways to justify their activities. Much of Sterling's confidence in his mother's approbation may have rested in a conviction that, just two months after Japan's surrender, she would surely agree that the Japanese could never adequately compensate Americans for the damage they had collectively inflicted on the United States. Weighed against Pearl Harbor, what was a kimono acquired by intimidation? The notion of defeated populations' collective guilt, enunciated as high policy, also found its microapplications in legitimation of black-market activity: reparations extracted "from below."

Shady entrepreneurialism was not, however, simply a barometer of the dim view of defeated populations held by some occupation soldiers. The fact that Germans and Japanese were former foes may well have made it easier to disregard the sentimental (if not also material) value of goods acquired through asymmetric barter or outright theft. But U.S. military personnel commonly found justification for postwar profiteering in what fellow *Americans* had taken from the enemy, or in what they believed was owing to them from the military establishment or civilian society at large.

Stealing was, arguably, a crime of opportunity as much as an outgrowth of enmity. During the war, thievery within the ranks had been a vexing problem for commanding officers, and a persistent irritant for men who found possessions pilfered by their comrades in arms. For light-fingered soldiers, others' portable property was fair game—irrespective of the owners' identity. Similarly, after combat ended, it didn't take long for shrewd operators to parlay their comrades' insatiable craving for war souvenirs into profit. In Okinawa, Skuse was taken aback by the speed with which canny GIs set about manufacturing fake Japanese flags from parachute silk to sell to their gullible peers.[48]

Petty schemes for enrichment could be legitimated with reference to the officer class's much grander swindles. From an enlisted man's perspective, the brass's wholesale requisitioning of palatial residences and fancy limousines readily appeared as theft by any other name. The appropriation of homes was ostensibly time limited and, strictly speaking, did not authorize American occupants to claim the owners' personal property. But this rule was so routinely disregarded that more scrupulous individuals encountered incredulity from fellow officers, shocked by those who did *not* plan to remove Oriental rugs and other desirable furnishings from wealthy Germans' commandeered homes. "I don't know what people are going to do with their 'conquering Army' when it gets back home," quipped WAC officer Betty Olson in Frankfurt. "You'll probably just walk into a neighbor's house, see their new easy chair and say 'I want that' and you'll walk out. That's about what one does—only, of course, it's legal here." Signals from on high suggested that a certain amount—even a significant amount—of "souvenir hunting" was quite acceptable. None other than the Third Army's own commanding general made a characteristically ostentatious display of his personal war trophies. "Gazing in awe at his collection of yachts, stallions and shiny limousines, the people around Munich refer to Patton as 'The Mad King of Bavaria'—after Ludwig II, the deranged monarch who was the patron of

Richard Wagner," noted *Newsweek* in October 1945. "American soldiers subjected to rigid Third Army discipline supply a few other phrases."[49]

The fact that officers were billeted in the best-appointed homes was one
way in which they were better positioned to collect "souvenirs" for keeps or
for trade than were enlisted men. Quartermaster troops aside, officers received privileged access to government-issue property, including a regular
allowance of spirits. Enlisted men, whose propensity for corruption by military life had long been the object of moral crusaders, had to make do with
low-alcohol beer (according to the rulebook, at least). Officers minded to engage in black-market trade were thus well placed to do so. Newly arrived in
Berlin in December 1945, Cornelius DeForest, a civil engineer recruited at
the rank of colonel to assist in restoration of the city's power infrastructure,
informed his wife that the black market "is practiced here to a large extent
and by American officers too." Later letters corroborated his initial impression that "one can by working the Black Market live *very well, at no cost* in
American money if you are inclined to that kind of thing, over here. Many
people just spend their time and energy living easy and making money out
of the tragic situation here." (The flip side to this fine living was that officers
sometimes found their requisitioned homes broken into and robbed by
German black-market gangs, a fate that befell DeForest himself.[50])

Spectacular stories of officers' larcenous activities—none more outrageous than those of Captain Nash and Colonel Durant—surely encouraged
other uniformed compatriots to see nothing awry in capitalizing, at a lower
level, on the easy opportunities occupation afforded for accumulation. This
was spelled out plainly at Major Watson's court-martial when he invoked a
brigadier general's receipt of a silver pitcher to justify his own share of the
Hessian loot. Anger over senior officers' unwarranted privilege kindled soldiers'
sense of entitlement to whatever supplementary compensation could be generated by private initiative. Graft was so pervasive in occupied territory—
with the Soviets carting off everything in sight in Berlin, local entrepreneurs
hiking prices, and GIs swindling fellow soldiers—that it required some determination *not* to engage in enrichment schemes of one sort or another.
One well-placed observer related the frequency with which he had heard
uniformed Americans in Europe remark, "A man was a fool if he didn't
leave the port of Le Havre with at least $1000 in his pocket." And who
wanted to be a fool, in either his own or his buddies' eyes?[51]

However they regarded the brass, many soldiers felt both detached from
and embittered toward American civilians who'd stayed safely home while

others shouldered all the burdens and hazards of wartime and postwar deployment. One military sociologist's study of "The Individual Soldier and the Occupation" (published in 1950) found that GIs commonly rationalized their black-market activity "in terms of the war profits of the 'folks back home,'" fattened on others' sacrifices. Fittingly enough, then, the biggest losers from soldiers' schemes for financial aggrandizement were not occupied populations but U.S. citizens. At least until 1947, occupation troops in Europe and Asia sent home sums of money far in excess of their monthly wages, having converted the fruits of their black-market dealings into dollars issued by the military. In February 1946, troops in the European theater remitted $10 million more than their total collective pay, a surplus that then rose to $14 million in March, $17 million in April, and $18 million in May. "When the Army exchanged more foreign currency than it had disbursed as pay and allowances, the government lost money," noted Walter Rundell, author of a careful study of black-market money. "There were many ways to camouflage such losses and make them appear less consequential than they were, but the fact remains that these losses were eventually and ultimately transferred to American taxpayers."[52]

While military black marketers found various mechanisms for self-justification, those who abstained had quite distinct concerns about what they denounced as immoral behavior. Some occupation personnel who tried their hand at the Berlin black market as a check-box tourist activity felt unnerved by the experience. Anne Alinder, a WAC officer stationed in Frankfurt in the fall of 1945, visited Berlin with an illicit flutter in mind. "I wanted to have some experience on the market—just once—before I left, so I had some blue label cigarettes from the States, and some candy bars also from the States, and a couple of friends and I went down," she wrote in a lengthy round-robin account to friends. This excursion was facilitated by a jeep driver (a former Luftwaffe pilot) who conveyed Alinder and her entourage to the Reichschancellery in the Soviet zone. "Within minutes we were buried in Germans wanting cigarettes and candy. . . . Jack, one of my friends, just didn't care about being a shrewd trader because at that time he felt as I did— that I wished we were a long distance away." The crowd dispersed as rapidly as it had materialized when a gun-waving Red Army soldier triggered alarm that a raid was about to begin. No Soviet military police descended. But still, Alinder wrote, "I was never so happy as when we started off."[53]

Why this episode made Alinder so uneasy she left her readers to deduce: a mixture, perhaps, of claustrophobia, panic, and ethical queasiness. That she followed this account of the aborted black-market visit with a lengthier description of the astonishing lengths to which Berliners—even "well dressed men and women"—would stoop in order to pocket the conquerors' cigarette butts suggests that moral qualms played a role in extinguishing Alinder's enthusiasm for converting her stateside tobacco and candy into desirable souvenirs. In Japan, too, some occupation soldiers' consciences prickled at the thought of Americans amassing others' treasured possessions for a song. In this vein, Harry McMasters mused to his wife that paying only 150 yen for ancient ceremonial swords—as he had observed certain fellow officers do—was "practically stealing" from the Japanese. Conquest did not license daylight robbery, he maintained.[54]

Other Americans, however, fulminated against black-market activity primarily because of who engaged in it, or who they *took* to be primarily responsible. In Japan, Koreans were routinely deemed the worst culprits. Military provost courts dealt with Koreans accused of black-market activity by deporting them: "a hardship on many with Japanese wives and families," noted a 1947 report by the ACLU. Japanese American soldiers also came under suspicion of acting as intermediaries in black-market activity, as they were well positioned to do so by virtue of their bilingualism. Similar logics of ethnicized suspicion informed views of the black market in Germany. While many German civilians and American soldiers found kaleidoscopic self-justifications for their own participation in illicit trade, necessitarian reasoning didn't extend to judgments about *others'* black-market operations. Germans tended to blame hoarding and price hiking on those "outsiders" most noxiously stigmatized by the Third Reich. Thus Germans regularly excoriated the black market as the creation of DPs: Slavs, Poles, and, most particularly, Jews.[55]

Some Americans shared this diagnosis, Brigadier General Jack Whitelaw among them. His rage against fraternizers found a counterpart in intemperate loathing for "carpetbaggers." "I've always been taught that a carpetbagger was the lowest form of American life and I still think so," he huffed to his wife, employing a pejorative that, in white southerners' vernacular, evoked all the perceived ills of Reconstruction, with its dispossession of the plantocracy at the point of Yankee bayonets. In postwar Berlin, the "carpetbaggers" that so infuriated Whitelaw were invariably Jews—or those he presumed to be Jewish because they fulfilled his jaundiced expectations of how Jews looked and acted. One Sunday evening in November 1945, en route to the unveiling of the Soviet war memorial, he had "caught two officers peddling on the ruins of the Mitte," a central Berlin district. "They were two slimey looking Jewish bastards and had musette bags filled with cigarettes and other stuff from the post exchange," Whitelaw informed his wife. He added that he was "preferring charges against them," albeit with no expectation that military justice would be done, since its administration (he believed) was so thoroughly controlled by Jewish military government officers. "They ought to be horsewhipped and then strung up by their thumbs," Whitelaw proposed.[56]

"Getting and spending, we lay waste our powers," William Wordsworth famously lamented in "The World Is Too Much with Us," an excoriation of materialism's corrupting effect on moral sensibility and alertness to natural beauty. Military commanders were well aware that soldiers' "getting and spending" made a substantial contribution to the economic insecurity of occupied countries, presenting some recipients of U.S. government largesse with an irresistible opportunity for exploitation. Worse yet, getting *without* spending was an increasingly common phenomenon in every country under American military government. Senior officers peppered their private correspondence with references to audacious heists: the drunk GI in Berlin rumored to have sold a purloined jeep for $10,000; the young private in Japan who made $45,000 from selling 2,500 pairs of olive drab army fatigues; the nineteen-year-old marine in Tokyo who held up a bank, posing as an inspector in a stolen lieutenant's uniform, and was later apprehended with "an 'Orange Blossom' girlfriend . . . loaded with jewels, silk and yen." "Seems to be a clever lad, but not clever enough to get away with it," mused Benton Decker in relating this foiled escapade to his wife.[57]

Some such stories, illustrative of greed outsmarting the greedy, lent themselves to darkly comedic retelling. But unadorned bureaucratic language perhaps better hints at what military larceny meant in everyday terms for Japanese residents in the ambit of bored and rapacious occupation soldiers. This excerpt from a SCAP Civil Intelligence Section (CIS) report, dated April 17, is fairly typical of "Occupational Trends" digests compiled in the first half of 1946: "In an area [of the remote prefecture of Kagawa] which suffered no friction between soldiers and civilians before 10 March, 24 violations occurred in the last three weeks of that month. Both officers and enlisted men of occupational units in KAGAWA prefecture were violators. Cases included beating civilians, entering homes forcibly, stealing whisky and sake, damaging houses and restaurants, attempting to effect release of prostitutes from police stations, robbing civilians, stealing vitally needed equipment for personal souvenirs and assaulting policemen."[58]

Other prefectures also witnessed rising numbers of rapes, holdups, and break-ins committed by armed occupation soldiers against Japanese civilians. In Yokohama, the point of disembarkation for many occupation troops and home to a substantial number, the CIS found that residents were "becoming afraid to venture from their homes after dark and are afraid to move about the city alone even during the day." But while occupation troops were stealing more brazenly from Japanese locals—everything from chickens to large sums of yen—some officers were simultaneously taking draconian steps to punish residents who dared steal U.S. military property. The CIS report from June 1946 noted that one American officer had "ordered [local] police to beat Japanese civilians charged with stealing Army food supplies."[59]

Against this backdrop, manifestations of Japanese resistance—hitherto so signally lacking—began to emerge. In 1948, as his tour approached its end and he was dictating drafts of a memoir, Eichelberger noted only one significant incident of organized violence directed at occupation soldiers: "In this case, a neighborhood crowd ganged up on two American soldiers en route back to barracks and beat them up for quite a long period." His response had been a robust show of strength. "First, I ran tanks into the area and thoroughly intimidated the people there. About ten were tried and the ringleader was sentenced to life. Twenty years terms at hard labor were given to the rest of the mob." In his published volume, *Our Jungle Road to Tokyo,* Eichelberger offered a more anodyne version of this episode that gave no indication as to what might have provoked the Japanese mob. Locals were simply "annoyed with the visits of Allied soldiers." In the dictated draft, however, he described the location of the attack as a "black market area inhabited by toughs"—an unmistakable clue as to why Japanese civilians and occupation troops had come to blows.[60]

Meanwhile, violent clashes between black and white soldiers were becoming so frequent, and sometimes so lethal, that in April 1946 Eichelberger ordered all African American service companies in Tokyo and Yokohama to be disarmed, other than for guard duty, while MPs would be equipped with machine guns and tear gas. These policies presumed that black soldiers were primarily, if not exclusively, to blame for what Eighth Army commanders referred to as "race riots." The general and his senior staff identified disputes over women as the main flash point of trouble. But while friction undoubtedly did arise over contested sexual territory, this partial diagnosis overlooked African American troops' anger at the separate and shabbier housing and social facilities to which they were consigned: a matter investigated by Truman's special representative, Marcus Ray, in August 1946. Ascribing tension to tussles over "girlfriends" (whom Eighth Army commanders presumed to be prostitutes) also discounted the blunt force with which white MPs policed black enlisted men. In the early months of 1946, Eichelberger delivered frequent dressings-down to massed ranks of black soldiers, rebuking them for disorderliness, higher VD rates, and other signs of indiscipline, prefacing his chastisements with the assertion that he "had absolutely no prejudice against the colored people." "I had grown up with colored people in my own home for whom I have great affection," the general announced. Now, however, he was "getting tired of discriminating in their favor." What his listeners may have deduced was that Eichelberger appreciated well-behaved servants who knew and respected their fittingly humble place.[61]

With tension escalating between Japanese civilians and U.S. soldiers, and across racial lines within American ranks, Eichelberger read the riot act to *all* members of the Eighth Army in June 1946. In a sternly worded message delivered aloud by commanding officers to their men, the general cited a litany of crimes: "There are cases of malicious beating of Japanese by both individuals and groups, of breaking into homes and taking trivial amounts of money from needy natives, of destruction of furniture and windows in districts, of assault of women on the highways and in their homes, and in addition, many indications of deliberate, arrogant bullying on the part of some of our soldiers." It was this swaggering attitude he sought to eliminate. "Some soldiers appear to feel that it is their duty to 'toughen up' the occupation," Eichelberger noted, before reminding Eighth Army personnel that it was MacArthur's job, not theirs, to determine the overall character of the occupation. Embroidering a favorite theme—that might and right were not identical—he cautioned Americans against using their superior size to intimidate "small and undernourished Japanese." This represented quite a turnaround from the surrender ceremony on the *Missouri*. On that momentous occasion, Americans' superior size had been calculatedly underscored. But less than a year later, times had clearly changed. Japan's militarists no longer needed to be shown their subordinate place; now a fragile and impoverished population required American protection. Bullying, Eichelberger warned, would provoke retaliation and harm American purposes. "A drunken man in uniform, fighting, abusing and reviling the people of Japan, offsets the efforts of the great mass of fine, orderly, well-mannered and upstanding soldiers to make the occupation a success."[62]

Eichelberger's admonishment drew renewed American press attention to occupational strife in Japan. But it did not halt the practices he deplored. As commentators continued to remark on the bad behavior of occupation troops and the local resistance engendered by fraternization and black marketeering, the occupations of Germany and Japan were widely understood in the United States as failing projects. Critics on the left deplored the laggardly progress in denazification or, worse yet, the rehabilitation of well-known party members, just as they worried about the affinity between MacArthur's GHQ and Japan's old guard, united in vehement anticommunism. Others accentuated the immorality of America's "immature" occupation troops. By late 1946, the great majority of combat veterans had returned home, to be replaced by a new generation of enlistees, equipped with as little as eight or even four weeks' basic training before dispatch overseas.

How, then, was occupation to be made good? And how were the occupying armies to be remoralized? Transforming soldiers into consumers and tourists may have eased some dissatisfaction with uniformed life, but at a considerable price. Material rewards posed moral hazards. Acknowledging this, military leaders accelerated another developmental model. If occupation soldiers were to be respectable and respectful avatars of Americanism, they would need to be armed with more than just abundance. Henceforth, men would be joined by wives and children—dependents shipped across the Atlantic or Pacific Ocean, along with household goods, pets, and cars. With military communities imported and re-created in Germany, Japan, and Korea, the occupations would be domesticated. Where commanding officers had failed to rein in wayward behavior, spouses and offspring might succeed. To the occupation soldier's already expansive portfolio of identities a further addition was now made: family man.

Chapter 8

DOMESTICATING OCCUPATION

June 24, 1946, was a red-letter day for General Robert Eichelberger, though it began on an inauspicious note. The indoor temperature had already hit eighty degrees by the time Eichelberger got up, as he testily noted in his diary. Air conditioning, or the lack thereof, had vexed the Eighth Army commander since he landed in Japan ten months earlier. But it was particularly important that the house should feel comfortable on this of all days: the much anticipated dawn of his wife's arrival. By seven thirty, Eichelberger was down on the waterfront amid a throng of generals, colonels, majors, captains, lieutenants, and six enlisted men. All were scouring the horizon for a first glimpse of the troop ship *Fred C. Ainsworth* that had transported Miss Em—along with 175 other army wives—across the Pacific from Seattle. "Great excitement everywhere," he noted, both at the dock and, later, back at the residence refurbished in American style by a Red Cross officer who was (as the general archly put it) "supposed to be an interior decorator." With surfaces polished to a high sheen and bottles of champagne readied on ice, everything had been fixed up just so, including Eichelberger's domestic staff. "The house boys were all lined up with clean coats . . . and the house made a big hit." Even the climate cooperated, for once. "Breeze came up so it wasn't so hot after all," the day's journal entry concluded on a satisfied note.[1]

More than just a joyful reunion for Robert and Emalina Eichelberger, the occasion heralded a new phase of postwar occupation. Inevitably, the presence of wives and children altered the complexion of the U.S. military presence abroad, in ways both intended and unexpected. The *Ainsworth* belonged to an armada of troop ships carrying servicemen's families overseas in 1946. It had been preceded three days earlier by the *Charles Carroll,* which landed twenty-two navy wives and two children at Yokosuka. There they were greeted not only by their husbands but by six members of the Yokosuka Women's Association, who assured them that Japanese women had been "waiting eagerly" for their arrival, even as they stole envious glances at the Americans' stockings (or so eagle-eyed correspondent Lindesay Parrott claimed to have observed). Germany had already witnessed differently inflected welcoming ceremonies two months earlier. Arrivals began in late

April, when 224 wives and 130 offspring sailed into Bremerhaven to the strains of "A Sentimental Journey," as rendered by the 311th Infantry regiment band.[2]

These transoceanic voyages—and the many others that followed—announced unmistakably that the occupiers planned to dig in. After months of stepped-up demobilization, the tide was being reversed. Replacements poured into Europe and Asia along with an advance guard of wives and children. With the *Charles Carroll*'s arrival, "the youngest member of the American occupation" in Japan became a two-year-old girl, Parrott wryly informed readers of the *New York Times*. Soon the toddler in question would be robbed of her claim to fame by babies born on the Pacific crossing. But as the occupationaires grew ever younger, the War Department policy of permitting families to join servicemen overseas signaled the longevity of these ventures, announcing to occupiers and occupied alike that the U.S. authorities did not plan to leave precipitately, or (perhaps) at all. The accommodation of "dependents," as wives and children were customarily dubbed in military lingo, demanded a whole new infrastructure. Families needed not only better housing than billets deemed suitable for single male occupancy, but clinics, schools, clubs, and other facilities required to nurture Americans of both sexes and all ages from the cradle to paternal redeployment or retirement.[3]

The family turn marked a significant entrenchment of uniformed U.S. power overseas, consolidating it as a permanent feature of the postwar geopolitical landscape. In the estimation of army historian Earl Ziemke, the inauguration of the first military community—designed to accommodate dependents "in a manner comparable to that on US posts in 1937"—drew wartime to a symbolic conclusion. "Occupation status" now began in earnest—like peacetime, only militarized. In Germany, this transition to conditions intended to approximate prewar American military life occurred just ten months after V-E Day. In Asia, improvised arrangements were also being replaced by more durable settlements adorned with the familiar trappings of American suburbia. Built to last for years, these structures in some cases lasted decades. This longevity might suggest that the War Department had planned all along to make American power more concrete, both literally and figuratively, by embedding garrison communities in former enemy territory. In reality, however, the decision in favor of domestication was more ad hoc. The original blueprints for occupation presupposed that these ventures would be maintained, for however long they might last, by legions of single men. In July 1945, Harry S. Truman pointedly informed *Stars and Stripes* that wives and families would *not* "settle in Europe." Instead, the "problem of soldiers' separated families" would be solved by "getting the soldiers back home."[4]

Numerous concerns about security and logistics militated against the dispatch of families overseas. The shattered cities of conquered Europe and Asia, struggling to shelter millions of people uprooted from their homes or bombed out of them, hardly had housing to spare. To construct military settlements from scratch would represent a huge financial commitment at a time when Truman's administration was under fire for a chronic domestic housing shortage. And even if accommodations could be found or built overseas, there would be the additional expense of shipping families across the Atlantic or Pacific, thereafter maintaining them at an acceptable level of comfort, nutrition, warmth, health, and security in communities signally lacking basic commodities. Despite the subdued state of occupied populations, defeated territories appeared anything but "family-friendly" environments in 1945. For once, the press and the president were on the same page. "To add American families to the burdens already imposed upon [Europe's] inadequate resources would be sheer folly," warned an editorial in the *Washington Post*, speculating that few servicemen would in fact "want their wives and children exposed to the living conditions which prevail there."[5]

Twinned with questions of scarcity, safety loomed large in the initial reluctance to have wives and offspring set sail. Viewed through War Department eyes, the security risks were twofold. American dependents might form tempting, and temptingly soft, targets for local malcontents, made all the more resentful by further rounds of requisitioning. But if military planners feared that the occupied might imperil American civilians, they also suspected that families might jeopardize the occupations' own security. Marital bliss risked eroding martial alertness. Eichelberger took the view that occupation troops would be distracted by domesticity, and he pointed out that U.S. troops were there to fulfill a "certain definite mission and if any trouble breaks out we would not want every soldier to have a wife or sweetheart out in the city someplace and no one in the barracks." Coddled and distracted by the comforts of home, soldiers' combat readiness would surely deteriorate. Prone to pessimistic projections, War Department personnel were becoming increasingly anxious about potential attacks on occupation troops by Soviet forces or the Kremlin's local proxies, who were expected to pounce on any sign of relaxed American vigilance.[6]

Yet despite the many objections to family reunion, the president and Pentagon came under severe pressure to relent—less from enlisted men than senior commanders. The *Post* was right to note that the vast majority of discontented GIs exhibited no desire to prolong occupation duty by settling down with dependents overseas. Most didn't have a family to bring over in any case. In July 1946, the median age of conscripts in Japan was tallied at a tender twenty years and three months. However, several of the occupations' most prominent generals—men who necessarily had to stay put—were loath to do so alone. Just one month after V-E Day, Dwight D. Eisenhower wrote to George Marshall, recommending that any officer or enlisted man of the first three grades who so desired should be permitted to "bring his wife into the European Theater," "contingent upon a showing that satisfactory accommodations can be provided." In pressing his case, Ike emphasized the personal toll that prolonged separation had exacted: "I will admit that the last six weeks have been the hardest of the war. . . . I just plain miss my family." Despite this heartfelt plea, Marshall rejected both the individual request and the broader policy recommendation. "The time has not yet come for such procedure," he countered, expressing further doubts about the wisdom of restricting this perk "to a select group." With criticism of the "caste system" intensifying, Marshall had no desire to stoke discontent by allowing the top brass a privilege that would be denied enlisted men—a point on which he and Ike agreed.[7]

The number of senior commanders adding their voices to the chorus of unhappy husbands grew in the weeks after Japan's surrender. In October 1945, General Jacob Devers, commander of Army Ground Forces in Europe, used a speech in Boston to issue a plea for wives to be permitted to join soldiers in Germany "as soon as quarters can be obtained," underscoring the point by stressing that U.S. troops would remain there "for generations." Douglas MacArthur, who was not in the habit of waiting for higher-ups' permission, had already transported his wife from the Philippines to Tokyo at a strikingly early date. To the consternation of several of the supreme commander's underlings, Jean landed with the advance guard at Atsugi airstrip in August 1945. Soon thereafter the supreme commander began lobbying the Senate to provide funds for all GIs to bring their dependents to Japan—a move Eichelberger greeted with skepticism. "You will recall when we went to Europe once with a lot of Gold Star Mothers that many of these gals didn't want to visit the graves, they wanted to go to Paris," he noted huffily. "It is true that a great part of our GIs are not married but most of them can dig up a dependent mother," he added, though no one had broached the possibility of a maternal invasion of occupied territory. In general, Eichelberger's attitude was that only senior officers either wanted or deserved to be reunited with their spouses in Japan. Too many wives, he feared, would spoil the broth. "Every wife will be watching the wife of another officer or enlisted man to see if some other person isn't getting more than she is. The War Department will show great weakness if it permits wives of all soldiers to come over."[8]

But by early 1946, the War Department had done just that, expanding to all and sundry a perk that Eichelberger had hoped to reserve for the upper echelon. The many cautions against permitting wives and offspring to join spouses overseas were increasingly offset by more compelling rationales for domesticating occupation. Truman's earlier prohibition had failed to anticipate the crisis of plummeting discipline and esprit that quickly engulfed the "after-armies" in the weeks after Germany's collapse and Japan's surrender. Homecoming simply wasn't quick enough to satisfy millions of "displeased persons" in uniform. Yet the helter-skelter speed of demobilization wrought havoc with operational efficiency, as almost every soldier writing home from occupied territory attested in the declining months of 1945. With press attention focused on the seamier sides of occupation—from "fratting" to VD and black marketeering—the problem of elevating both morals and morale gained ever greater urgency. Introducing wives and children into the occupational mix promised to raise soldiers' spirits and standards simultaneously.[9]

In addition to boosting esprit, military planners hoped to improve the caliber of occupation's officer class. As it was, they shared the verdict delivered by numerous low-ranking military government personnel: that their superiors were all too often essentially unfit for service. To make matters worse, the least suitable elements tended to be most attracted to the prospect of prolonged occupation duty: the avaricious and the amorous. With an army investigation in 1946 estimating that one in eight married soldiers had a steady relationship with a German woman, the fact that wives could *not* join husbands overseas may have served as a perverse incentive to stay on. Others were inclined to remain abroad for the opposite reason, having no family life in the United States. One military government officer complained to the *New York Times'* Cyrus Sulzberger that his remaining colleagues were men who "have nothing to go home to. They are failures in civilian life and make more money here than there."[10]

In December 1945, John Winner penned a long diatribe on the subject to his family back in Madison, Wisconsin, based on his experiences in postwar Germany:

> The military government has the greatest collection of incapable men in the American army gathered into a group. When the first Military government was set up, each division was given a quota of men that it had to furnish for the Military government and each division took this opportunity to get rid of all its eight-balls and incompetent individuals. As a result, the majority of the personnel in the Military Government are people that were unable to perform their assigned job in the regular army and were consequently shipped out to the M.G. There are a few exceptions to this rule, but very few. Most of the people in the M.G. are there because they are not interested in working for a living and their only interest is a big home, a lot of liquor and a lot of authority. Very few of them understand what their real responsibility is and what the importance of their job is. Those that had previous training in the States for the job of governing a conquered country were the small time and unsuccessful politicians in the states. Few know anything about international politics.

Amid the rampant inefficiency and venality, Winner could be forgiven for failing to know that the ranks of military government included several individuals who had either already established or would quickly achieve prominence in national and international politics. (Among them were men of such divergent backgrounds as South Carolinian segregationist Strom Thurmond and the twenty-two-year-old, Bavarian-born Heinz Alfred Kissinger.)[11]

With the lure of family reunions and more generous terms of employment, the War Department hoped to arrest the unseemly exodus of trained personnel and improve the caliber of those who stayed on or were freshly recruited for occupation duty. Eligibility hinged on applicants' agreeing to stay put for at least one further year's service. By the end of 1945, plans for families' arrival in Europe were already under way. This development was followed, in February 1946, by an announcement that officers and enlisted men of the first three grades would have the opportunity to bring their families to Japan, irrespective of whether they were regular army personnel, wartime draftees, or postwar recruits. The key determinant was willingness to stay the course, with those who agreed to serve two years receiving priority in the allocation of scarce housing.[12]

Domestication represented one way to encourage principled and conscientious hard workers—men in the altruistic and abstinent mold of John Hersey's Victor Joppolo—to stay on. Senior military personnel also hoped that the intimate proximity of dependents would improve men's bearing and behavior—not just the husbands in question, but all occupation personnel. "Problems contingent upon the extensive fraternization of troops with natives of the occupied area could be alleviated to a noticeable degree by resumption of normal family ties," an army report optimistically proposed in 1947. But while this disciplinary function was ascribed to families' mere presence, the War Department assigned wives and children a more participatory role in the reeducative mission of occupation.[13]

Embodying quintessential American traits—at least in the military's idealized imaginary—families would vivify democratic precepts by their good cheer and good deeds alike. Dependents would help soften the rough edges of occupation by cultivating "deserving elements" among the local population, as one military report put it. With this ambassadorial function firmly in mind, wives and children over the age of fourteen received several hours of indoctrination on their long voyage out, covering such topics as "the necessity for the occupation" and its aims, the "responsibilities of dependents," "the evils of the black market and the need for food conservation." Updated materials produced in 1947 for families heading to Germany reflected the growing emphasis on reconciliation that had by then thoroughly displaced the initial insistence on "collective guilt." Dependents "were told that as they represented the American way of life to a critical German audience, they should exert their best efforts to create a favorable impression on that audience and to illustrate, by their behavior, democracy in action."[14]

However, if the most desirable kind of soldier—and his differently desirable wife—were to be enticed into staying on, certain things had to change. In order to become better, occupation first needed to *look* better. This makeover wasn't easily effected. Cosmetic improvements could only go so far in altering the physical landscape of occupation. Whatever else wives and children encountered in occupied territory, they would be brought face to face with the wholesale destruction—human and material—wrought by years of war and months of aerial bombardment. Senior officers, among them regular army personnel who were veterans of two global conflagrations and sundry other "small wars," found themselves gazing on ruin with an altered perspective, wondering how cratered Berlin or Tokyo and its immiserated inhabitants would strike their loved ones. Since newly arrived civilians were prone to recoil from the stark evidence of what it had taken to effect unconditional surrender, the imminent arrival of families prompted an invigorated program of rubble removal in Yokohama, the main port of disembarkation for new arrivals in Japan. Eichelberger wrote to warn the doughty Miss Em, who was acquainted with the city in its prewar incarnation, that where "miles of houses" had once stood, "we have now just lines of warehouses and hutments for our troops." However unfamiliar, this militarized landscape would be, he assured her, "a much nicer sight for you than to have you see nothing but ruins."[15]

More troubling was the prospect of exposing children to scenes of epic devastation and acute deprivation. Officers who had hitherto regarded razed Japanese cityscapes with grim satisfaction—evidence of the superior job performed by B-29 superfortresses—began to wonder how such obliteration might strike a child. Was the disturbing spectacle of defeat something that ought to be inflicted on infants? Clovis Byers, Eighth Army chief of staff, expressed severe misgivings in letters home to his wife, Marie, anxious about how their young son, Clay, would cope with Yokohama. "There is a very depressing reaction as you pass acre after acre of twisted sheet iron, bricks and broken concrete with reinforcing iron pointing toward the skies in all manner of grotesque figures," he fretted in October 1945, well before the War Department had agreed to authorize family relocations to Japan. Nothing in unscathed America would have prepared Clay for such scenes. "The nearest thing back home that you could see which approaches it is the sight of the small shacks located around any American city dump." Yet despite these troubling thoughts, Byers reassured both himself and his wife that there remained sufficient loveliness in Japan—to say nothing of their own family life—to offset the distressing reminders of what American incendiary bombs had done. "As I brood over these thoughts alone they seem very important," he confessed. "But as usual your cheery outlook has made me realize how beautiful everything will appear when once more we three are able to be together!!"[16]

As the officer responsible for locating suitable residences for Eighth Army personnel, Byers was enviably well placed to shelter his wife and son from at least some of postwar Japan's more disturbing sights. Needless to say, he selected particularly desirables abodes for himself and his boss. Next-door neighbors, the Byerses and Eichelbergers occupied homes that had previously belonged to the assistant manager of Standard Oil and a British gin magnate. Their spacious villas occupied a commanding position on a bluff above Tokyo Bay. Surrounded by "pleasant grounds, grass, shrubs, trees," with a high fence erected to stop Clay from toddling over the precipice, and guards to prevent Japanese thieves sneaking up from the slum neighborhood below, this idyllic spot helped inhabitants forget that reaching it required them to pass through "acres of devastation." "You'll be delighted by the veranda from the master bedroom," Byers enthused, extolling the "unbroken view of the bay." Space aplenty would also provide Marie "a bed-sitting room combination" for "restful privacy."[17]

With Western-style residences at a premium in a country where paper and wood prevailed as construction materials, almost every substantial brick-and-mortar house was appropriated for Eighth Army dependents and the growing number of civilian advisers attached to GHQ. Lavish homes, mostly built for leading industrialists and foreign businessmen, were thoroughly gutted and renovated in conformity with American expectations of convenience and comfort. Out went the tatami mats, shoji screens, charcoal-burning hibachi, and copper sinks; in went the ceramic basins, electric stoves, and—most importantly—flushable toilets. In Germany, housing, much of it appropriated at two hours' notice from its previous occupants, required a less thorough overhaul. Since it was hard to find sufficient furniture and household effects locally, American dependents were permitted a generous luggage allowance, including cars and pets. No wonder, then, that a March 1946 *Washington Post* headline proposed, "The Family Might Even Enjoy the Land Daddy Licked"—despite its also being home to "frauleins and sauerkraut, displaced persons and concentration camps."[18]

Frenetic preparatory activity required large financial outlays as well as huge amounts of labor. In Germany, an estimated "100,000,000 man-hours" were devoted between 1946 and 1948 to the erection of what the army termed "permanent"-type installations: "of a high quality implied by an occupation expected to be of long duration." Appropriated German buildings were transformed into commissaries, post exchanges, chapels, and administrative

FIG. 8.1 "Wife & daughter of U.S. soldier sitting in first class dining car of train looking out window at German expellees traveling in boxcars from Silesia to Westphalia . . . probably somewhere between Berlin & Bremerhaven, Germany," runs the original caption to Walter Sanders's photograph from early 1946. The LIFE Picture Collection/Getty Images [50611799].

offices. Meanwhile in Japan, by September 1947, the Eighth Army's engineering units, making substantial use of local laborers, had constructed or rehabilitated housing for all troops plus some 9,623 families. In addition, they had built seventeen hospitals and established eighty acres of hydroponic farms, giving Americans access to fruit and vegetables cultivated without the benefit of Japanese "night soil." As for who would foot the bill, that circle had been squared with a decision that the Japanese government would pay. The occupied thus absorbed the costs of "familiarizing" U.S. occupation, including the expense of refurbishing requisitioned local residences as well as constructing brand-new facilities for military personnel and their dependents. In Japan these expenses were estimated at 30 percent of the national budget in 1946. Similarly, occupation's expanded circumference was charged to Germany's bill of reparations, with a significant proportion of labor on new military installations being provided by German civilians, POWs, and DPs.[19]

Occupation authorities were thus able to engineer substantial improvements to the built environment. While officers soon to be joined by families concentrated on sprucing up their own digs, even the lowliest form of military housing for enlisted men—corrugated metal Quonset huts, like "a large barrel cut in half long ways," as one unimpressed GI occupant put it—received a fresh lick of paint and curtains in readiness for their new female inhabitants. Some enlisted men also associated the appearance of wives with a renewed emphasis on spit and polish in their daily routines, as soldiers were gussied up for display purposes—at spouses' behest (or so the disgruntled readily imagined). "The wives all like to see their husbands saluted, so their is a big campaign on military courtesy, the wives like to see soldiers dressed up pretty, so their is a big campaign on uniforms and one has to wear a blouse almost all the time," snarled Winner, writing home from Germany in May 1946. "The wives like to look at big military parades and so we are either practicing for a parade or else having a parade most of the time."[20]

It was easier, however, to shift rubble and shine shoes than to reshape the moral contours of occupation. Off-duty debauchery proved harder to remediate than physical discomforts or sloppy attire. One of the ironies of a policy aimed at making good was that the spouses in question would necessarily be exposed to the very symptoms of malaise that their presence was intended to mitigate, if not eradicate altogether. Worse yet, dissolute male behavior was sufficiently ubiquitous—and so very visible—as to constitute a disincentive to wives' joining the occupation forces at all: a catch-22, if ever there was one.

Many officers and enlisted men alike hesitated to recommend that spouses join them overseas, deterred less by the depressing condition of the defeated than by what victory had done to the conquerors. *Stars and Stripes* printed one sergeant's disquisition on the reasons why more enlisted men hadn't requested travel and quarters for dependents, suggesting that if the brass were curious they need look no further than the sidewalk antics of GIs "who acted like supercharged wolves in OD." In Berlin, Cornelius DeForest worried that available accommodations, which "might do for 'War Brides,'" as he harrumphed, were hardly fit for middle-class matrons. But his more persistent concern was that American morals were excessively loose. "The life here, army officers, WACS and 'what have you' is a fast one, and you would just have to live apart from it, let it flow on around you and not bother," he cautioned his spouse. Because regular civilian travel had not yet been authorized, no possibility existed of living *entirely* apart from the occupation and simply drinking in the splendor of the Bavarian Alps, as keen amateur painter Mrs. DeForest would have liked. Any American in the U.S. zone of Germany was necessarily a military dependent, often in more ways than one: reliant on the armed forces for food, fuel, transportation, and personal security.[21]

DeForest's concerns about exposing his wife to the multiple forms of fraternization on abundant display in Berlin were common currency among Americans contemplating conjugal life in occupied territory. So too were his anxieties about the rigors of the voyage over. Anyone with a friend or relative who had served overseas knew that travel aboard transport ships typically tested human endurance to its outer limits. The prospect of subjecting loved ones to conditions belowdecks—the cramped quarters, infernal heat, hellish noise, inadequate bathing and toilet facilities—was more than some high-ranking commanders could countenance. MacArthur and Eichelberger repeatedly pressed for air transportation to convey senior officers' spouses from the States. Fearing charges of favoritism, however, the War Department rejected these entreaties. Eichelberger was left to warn Miss Em of what she might expect at sea, including the alarming possibility that her possessions would be pilfered by the ship's crew or fellow travelers. As a precaution, he recommended that she have iron bands attached to the trunk she would bring.[22]

The imminent arrival of spouses and families required more than an acceleration of rubble removal. It also demanded a new emphasis on respectability—hence on the politics of appearances. In particular, the ubiquity of "fratting," openly conducted in the streets and parks of Germany and Japan, had to be tackled, since nothing was deemed more likely to antagonize spouses than the sight of "wolfish" GIs entangled with local women. If this point wasn't already apparent to senior commanders, a scandal that erupted in Frankfurt in March 1946 drove the message home. Triggered by a British woman's accusation that "overnight wives" were a regular fixture at billets for USFET personnel, the clamor intensified when Major General

Miller G. White confirmed that female visitors were indeed permitted entry. Although they had to be signed in, and were denied entry after 10:30 p.m., nothing prevented early birds from staying overnight. It didn't help the army's reputation that one such officially registered female guest had apparently been just fourteen. Nor were civilian concerns alleviated by confirmation from other military sources that German maids and waitresses who worked at the compound could in theory stay "forever," if they found someone to provide food and quarters. Reaction in the stateside press was immediate, indignant, and clamorous. The *Daily Boston Globe*'s Iris Carpenter announced that parents of young men serving overseas confronted a prospect every bit as worrisome as "the thought that their son might be shot or blown up by a mine." Military chaplains, meanwhile, had been driven to "such a pitch of hopelessness that many of them want to throw in their hand." Flailing to douse the flames of outraged opinion back home, Major General White claimed that there was nothing *inherently* dubious about the presence of female visitors. Besides, there was "no more [a] way of preventing that type of fraternizing than flying to the moon." Shipping wives and offspring across the Atlantic seemed considerably less challenging. And that was exactly what Carpenter urged as the only surefire way to "lift the ceiling of moral tone in our Army overseas—send the men's own womenfolk over but fast!"[23]

SCAP faced an analogous scandal three months later. The stateside circulation of photographs depicting "GIs dancing and taking baths with Japanese girls" caused a "violent uproar." The *Chicago Daily Tribune*'s Walter Simmons reported from Tokyo that, after a six-week-long hiatus in overseas mail delivery, "nearly every man got a bitter letter reproaching him for behavior shown in the widely printed pictures. Scores of divorces and broken engagements ensued." With wives' arrival uppermost on senior commanders' minds, Byers duly issued a directive in March 1946 to the Eighth Army prohibiting whistling or calling aloud to females. Such behavior, he asserted, was "in poor taste" anywhere, but especially unbecoming the uniform in an occupied country—a message somewhat at odds with SCAP's concurrent attempts to encourage kissing and public displays of affection among the Japanese themselves. "A thousand years from now, perhaps" speculated the *Des Moines Register*, "historians will say that the greatest achievement of the MacArthur occupation of Japan was—the kiss."[24]

Having tried to silence catcalls and wolf whistles, Eichelberger followed up with an order that outlawed "public displays of affection," defined rather

FIG. 8.2 George Lichty's "Grin and Bear It" cartoon, printed in the *Los Angeles Times* on March 16, 1946, registers home front dissatisfaction with the pampered treatment lavished on U.S. occupation personnel in Japan.

elliptically as "arm-in-arm strolling and similar actions." The ban on PDA generated "plenty of courts martial" in the weeks that followed, the general informed his wife. According to the new dispensation, any soldier found violating the rule was confined to the MP station until his commanding officer could come and get him out. "This helped a lot as naturally any soldier who was responsible for his company commander getting out of bed in the middle of the night would find that the commander took a very poor view of his activities," Eichelberger explained gleefully, perhaps anticipating that his measure might simultaneously curtail commanding officers' own nocturnal liaisons. Not content with leaving the implementation to others, he assumed a personal role in enforcement. With considerable gusto, the general noted an occasion (just three days after the ban's announcement) when he had "seen what looked like a British Chief Petty Officer with his arm around a Japanese girl. She was dressed in a highly colored kimono. I was driving the new Chevy so I pulled up along-side them and I said, 'I don't know what service you belong to or whether you speak English but if you don't get away from that Japanese girl I am going to put you in jail.' He jumped about five yards." Although Eichelberger anticipated a backlash from peevish enlisted men, he nevertheless expected plenty of support back home. "Don't worry about any attack that may be made on me in the press as a so-called brass hat," Eichelberger counseled Miss Em. "If any criticism would arise, all the preachers and women in America would back me up, and that is a large part of the population."[25]

Eichelberger was correct in anticipating that incoming wives would recoil from public fraternization. Less than a month after the first army spouses arrived in Germany, one anonymous "American wife" made headline news when an angry letter she had submitted to *Stars and Stripes'* "B Bag" column found its way into print in stateside newspapers. "If some of the officers who fraternize could only know how we abhor 'rubbing shoulders' with their 'shack jobs' in the local night clubs, they might confine them to their shacks," railed the unidentified but evidently irate author. Perhaps galvanized by this negative publicity, the Third Army announced its own ban on "public petting"—so sweeping as to prohibit American soldiers from walking arm in arm "even with their own wives."[26]

Germany presented an additional challenge relating to soldiers' relentless pursuit of sex: not simply that newly arrived wives would be privy to the disturbing spectacle of GIs publicly ogling, haranguing, groping, or otherwise canoodling with local women, but that American spouses would *themselves* attract unwelcome male attention. Widespread discussion of this prospect, in military circles and civilian reportage, indicates how pervasive soldiers' harassment of local women had become. Once strictly "off-limits," German fräuleins were now evidently considered, at all times and in all places, "fair game." Fretful speculation about GIs directing their whistles and stares—or worse—toward American spouses suggests that, contrary to earlier damning judgments, provocative "furlines" were far less responsible for the crude sexualization of Germany's public spaces than were predatory occupationaires. That these fearful commentators altogether ignored the presence of WACs, Red Cross workers, and female civilian army employees already at work in Germany is also telling. The personal security of American women menaced by soldiers' rapacity was evidently a lesser concern than safeguarding the marital property of other men in uniform. WACs and nurses had long suffered the aggressive predations of male colleagues without this molestation ever achieving the status of an official problem.[27]

Predictions that military spouses would prove indistinguishable from German women were quickly realized. The first story run by the *New York Times* on the arrival of army dependents in Germany noted that there had been "brushes" with guards "on the look-out for fraueleins at Army movies," presumably with a view to expelling them since German civilians were debarred from U.S. military recreational facilities (officers' bedrooms aside). As a result of these brusque encounters, the army decreed that "passports would be adequate identification for American women in civilian clothes," reported Dana Adams Schmidt. But outside MP-patrolled movie theaters the dynamic was reversed. In civilian space, American soldiers weren't looking to evict German women but rather to entice them. "Inevitably, not a few of the American women were mistaken for fraueleins and received suggestive offers of cigarettes and chocolate and were impressed by the difference between American manners at home and abroad."[28]

What was to be done? The army tried to remedy what it took to be a crisis of confused identity by issuing wives with armbands bearing the American flag, a move analogous to earlier attempts to distinguish DPs from Germans by having them wear their nationality on their sleeve. This measure naively presupposed that, had GIs only known that the women they assailed were *American,* they would have left them alone, mindful of their untouchability. The tenuousness of that supposition was exposed in Japan, where race set occupiers and occupied more clearly apart. U.S. military wives were most unlikely to be "mistaken for Japanese," Japanese American women married to Nisei occupation troops aside. Yet readier distinguishability from the local population failed to safeguard army spouses from harassment. A *Chicago Daily Tribune* report of July 1946 related that recently arrived wives were "resentful at troops who subject them to whistles and howls on the streets," just as they "censured" the "sight of American troops with Japanese women." Eichelberger's injunction against PDA had clearly proven less effective than he hoped in shielding American women from both displeasing sights and disturbing affronts.[29]

Germany's military governor Lucius Clay adamantly maintained that domestication worked. Dependents "gave a stability to our Occupation" that he did not believe "we could have gotten any other way. It brought back a much higher moral standard." But no compelling evidence corroborates that the construction of military communities did, in fact, magically cure the "moral malaria" afflicting occupied territory, to borrow a phrase from Billy Wilder's *A Foreign Affair*. To take but one indicator, families' presence certainly failed to reverse rates of infection from sexually transmitted disease. In Japan, the number of cases rose dramatically from one year to the next during the late 1940s. Wilder's black comedy of triangular transgressions in Berlin itself indicates how persistent the nexus between occupation and fraternization remained in 1948, when the movie was released in the United States. The celluloid affairs in question were multivalent and overlapping. An Iowa congresswoman (Jean Arthur) sent to investigate GIs' illicit black-market transactions falls for the same officer (John Lund) who, despite his assigned role in denazification, is involved with a Nazi big shot's former girlfriend (Marlene Dietrich). Celebrating the congresswoman Phoebe Frost's transformation from frigid killjoy into a more alluring, and tolerant, sensualist, *A Foreign Affair* implies that American women might rather embrace than curtail occupation's erotic possibilities. Where Wilder urged lenience, other contemporary cultural producers offered less sanguine visions of postwar Italy, Germany, and Japan as incubators of decadence and dissolution: places where Americans drank too much, talked too loudly, consumed too greedily, and slept with too many partners—whether local women, fellow ex-pats, or both. In the fiction of Kay Boyle, Zelda Popkin, Alfred Hayes, Lionel Shapiro, and others, occupied territory provided a setting in which to explore "the bewilderment of a conquering nation lost in the terrible complexity of victory," as one contemporary reviewer put it.[30]

Press reports pointed to the possibility that, far from straightening occupation into a condition of monogamous sobriety, American women's presence in greater numbers overseas had simply broadened the range of soldiers' sexual possibilities. As more women (many of them single, by requirement) joined the occupations' administrative staff or worked with UNRRA, the Red Cross, and other relief agencies, relationships proliferated between uniformed Americans and compatriot civilians. Eighteen months after the first army wives arrived in Europe, newspapers divulged that some spouses were setting sail again, in the reverse direction, as military divorce rates skyrocketed. In December 1947, a front-page story in the *Washington Post* quoted an army chaplain's judgment that "occupation mistresses" were "making Army wives into grass widows at a scandalously increasing rate." According to other anonymous army spokesmen, 157 applications for transport home had been received in the preceding three months, filed "for the expressed purpose of dissolving marriages." An unknown number of estranged spouses "just slipped home quietly" without telling anyone. Noting that "only an estimated 50 per cent of the mistresses are frauleins," the rest being "Allied civilian employees who have become camp followers," the *Post*'s story ended on a pruriently cautionary note. One wife had arrived from America "to find her husband living in a Frankfurt suburb with two mistresses." Unpleasantly shocked, she had "left for the States as soon as possible." Relationships between civilian women and men in uniform were nothing new. In a letter to Miss Em in March 1946, Eichelberger noted sardonically that an Eighth Army officer was divorcing his wife to marry his secretary, who was "reputed to be a good one." "Clovis tells me that she can take dictation," the general insinuatingly added. But if he hoped that wives' proximity would end such office dalliances, he would soon be disappointed.[31]

Emphasis on adultery and alcoholism heightened the "colonial" aura that occupation acquired in popular commentary. Postwar Germany may have lacked the exoticism of W. Somerset Maugham's stengah-steeped Singapore or Kenya's notoriously uninhibited Happy Valley, with its heady brew of pink gin, big game, and other ex-pats' partners. Nevertheless, accounts of occupational debauchery shared an elective affinity with projections of imperial decadence popularized by interwar fiction and film. Life for colonial elites had long appeared to license an expanded repertoire of erotic peccadilloes and transgressive couplings—across lines of race and respectability— unthinkable "at home." And it was, in part, sexual permissiveness that the

Chicago Tribune hinted at when it assailed the "colonial attitude" of occupation personnel. More broadly, the paper decried the "incongruous country club atmosphere of every American community."[32]

Postwar occupation was open to critique as an imperial venture in more ways than one. For all the new emphasis on families as avatars of Americanism—embodiments of democracy in action—"digging in" lodged hierarchy ever more firmly into the built environment and social fabric of occupation. Precisely as a language of partnership replaced the punitive idiom of conquest, the physical distance between occupiers and occupied widened. "Almost every interaction between victor and vanquished was infused with intimations of white supremacism," John Dower notes in his history of occupied Japan. Separation was the defining feature of occupation's configurations of space, with decidedly colonial practices of appropriation, segregation, and partition finding favor.[33]

Frantz Fanon's schematic assertion that "the colonial world is a world divided into compartments"—the masters' quarters airy and spacious, the native section cramped and squalid—found some reflection in the spatial arrangements of occupation. In Frankfurt and Munich, the two largest administrative centers of U.S. military government in Germany, American forces ring-fenced whole sections of the city for the occupiers' inhabitation—a precursor to Baghdad's "Green Zone" six decades later. Newcomers were often taken aback to find that their armed forces had sequestered substantial urban areas behind razor wire. A surprised Betty Olson wrote home that the cordon sanitaire around the residential neighborhood of Frankfurt encompassing the former I. G. Farben Building (home to the USFET headquarters) aimed "to keep the civilians out and not necessarily the Army in." Paratroopers "with trousers tucked into boots and snow white gloves" made impressive guards. But judging from the overnight-guest furor, they did a less impeccable job of "keeping the civilians out" than Olson imagined.[34]

Elsewhere in Germany, American families initially lived scattered in local communities, wherever buildings had been requisitioned for military use. Enlisted men continued to live in converted Wehrmacht barracks or other repurposed buildings, venturing forth at mealtimes to messes in former hotels or to shop at PXs located in what had hitherto been German department stores. But by the end of the 1940s, as U.S. forces prepared for the next phase of their embedded existence in Germany—beyond the term limit of military occupation—Americans in uniform and their dependents relocated to exclusive, purpose-built bases where they would be "concentrated." The construction of self-contained military communities occurred at a slightly earlier date in Japan. Since fewer intact Japanese structures lent themselves to army appropriation, new housing developments were required from the outset. Military bases were often erected on the periphery of cities, where the Eighth Army could build on a more expansive scale than in overcrowded urban settings. Allowances of space were strikingly generous. In a densely populated country that had lost a huge proportion of its prewar housing stock, the occupiers' preliminary blueprints airily allocated between 900 and 1,500 square feet of living space to each military family. Americans would inhabit two- and three-bedroom "cottages" and duplexes in nicely landscaped grounds, constructed with "varying exteriors" to "prevent the appearance of a 'workman's row.'" Just as prefabricated suburban settlements were mushrooming around postwar U.S. cities, a military version of this phenomenon was transplanted to occupied Japan.[35]

This incongruous disfigurement prompted visiting diplomat George Kennan to remark that he knew "many of the Japs deserve a worse fate than to have the tastes and habits of American suburbia imposed on them," with the oblique insinuation that he could, in fact, conjure few more onerous punishments than the intrusion of American philistinism into this Buddhist land. Out-of-town developments also served a protective function. Here the goal was less to secure American military personnel and their dependents from the Japanese—who had, after all, never physically threatened the occupiers—than to buffer Japanese urban dwellers against the depredations of U.S. troops. Eichelberger hinted at this logic in his diary. On an inspection tour of Hokkaido in October 1946, he noted that new troop and dependent housing, located eight miles outside Sapporo, would "help a lot." Although the general didn't specify exactly what kind of help this settlement would provide to whom, his preoccupation with GIs' "bullying" behavior hints that increased physical separation was intended to reduce antagonism between occupiers and occupied in Japanese cities. With fancy on-site facilities at their disposal, including a golf course at this complex outside Sapporo, soldiers would have less cause to venture out in search of entertainment. Less time spent off base would correspondingly diminish Americans' abrasive contact with the local population.[36]

The isolation of American communities from Japanese was likely to reduce "unfortunate incidents," but increased separation was hardly calculated to facilitate soldiers' vaunted role as reeducators. Similarly, if the Eighth Army's priority were indeed constructive rehabilitation, it was curious that land commandeered by the occupiers should have been named to commemorate the United States' reclamation of the Philippines. One American spouse noted that "many housing and billet areas are given Philippine names—a sort of reminder to the Japanese, I guess. There are Cebu, Leyte, Mindoro, Davao Courts, Luzon Apartments, and the areas of Nasugb Beach and Tagatay Ridge." Similarly, in Tokyo the former headquarters of the Japanese War Ministry—host to the International Military Tribunal for the Far East—was renamed Pershing Heights. The occupiers thus exercised to the full their prerogative to alter not only the physical appearance of space but the very names by which new "American" places were known. In these extraterritorial enclaves, local authority held no more sway than local languages.[37]

Provocative redesignations were surely calculated to offend Japanese sensibilities, aggravating the affront caused by Americans' extravagant claims on space. Yet even when the occupiers eschewed such gratuitous gestures, there was no escaping occupation's glaring disparities between overlords and subalterns. Some American contemporaries—observers and participants alike—were attuned to the imperial cast of this latter-day civilizing mission. Perhaps nowhere was occupational hubris more evident than in Korea, where U.S. military personnel appropriated the residences and personal wealth of the Japanese colonial elite wholesale, as officer Orlando Ward noted in his diary. In Seoul, army engineers even constructed new housing on the hallowed grounds of the king's palace. "The Japanese never had the nerve to build in the king's palace grounds but we did and have," noted one senior American occupationaire. "Now we have what looks a good deal like a city housing project almost among the old historic buildings." In Japan, SCAP's imperial chutzpah was scarcely more muted. Bemoaning the spiritual nullity of U.S. materialism, Kennan likened MacArthur's reign to the latter days of Empress Catherine II in Russia. Americans had "monopolized . . . everything that smacks of comfort or elegance or luxury," he lamented, noting that MacArthur's underlings and their "shrill cackling" wives behaved as though the war's sole purpose had been to provide them with "six Japanese butlers with the divisional insignia on their jackets."[38]

The top brass did indeed live exceptionally well. Having furnished his mansion in Yokohama with "a very fine German grand piano," among other expropriated treasures, Byers's anxieties about raising a child in a largely obliterated city soon melted away. Life with the Eighth Army, he wrote to Lieutenant General Albert Wedemeyer, was "pleasant beyond imagination." "Our existence is as near perfect as ever could be from the personal angle," he rhapsodized in May 1947. If the chasm between American luxury and Japanese scarcity threatened to discomfit the occupiers, incipient unease could be assuaged by recalling that the dispossessed surely deserved to be parted from their possessions. Justin Williams, a legal expert who arrived in Tokyo in October 1946 to oversee revision of the Japanese Diet Law, wrote to friends back in the States that "American families have taken over all comfortable homes in Tokyo, and no one knows or cares what has happened to the thousands of Jap families who have had to move out (they must have been Zaibatsus, so it makes no difference)." Perhaps Williams was parodying, rather than espousing, the unapologetic tone of overseas Americans. But whether his words were intended ironically or otherwise, the pervasive sense of entitlement was just as evident.[39]

Williams was quick to point out that life in occupied Japan was not, in fact, all it was cracked up to be. Like countless other Western travelers in "primitive" places, he chose to narrate his family's adventures overseas as a tale of patience constantly besieged by privation, incompetence, and backwardness. Japanese life only *appeared* lavish from afar. With customary oriental deceptiveness, an outer veneer of civilization masked a cruder reality. Nine months into his Japanese sojourn, Williams bemoaned the sorry lot of the occupationaire: "Toilets won't flush, the water pump is nearly always on the blink, the electric cook stove blows up, the goldfish die in the Italian pool, the servants quarrel amongst themselves over division of labor and when they do attempt anything, it takes them forever." To top it all off, the one grocery store for 20,000 Americans was "usually in short supply of several essential items of food."[40]

Williams was far from alone in emphasizing the vexations of life overseas. The military's initial pronouncements on family reunion in occupied Europe and Asia cast dependents as " 'social pioneers' whose function was to 'spread the American way of life.' " MacArthur sententiously hailed these plucky Americans as representatives of "a type of pioneering reminiscent of the pioneer days of our own West during the nineteenth century." Army wives would restage in the East the drama of those westward-trekking homesteaders who had valiantly expanded the frontier of civilization. "Just as those days developed the best of our womanhood, so it is believed the wives of our officers and soldiers will welcome the opportunity of sharing the hardship with their husbands," the supreme commander announced—words easily uttered from the palatial former embassy in which the MacArthurs resided. (Nicknamed Hoover's Folly, the compound comprised a "huge, white-walled, earthquake proof structure, half Moorish, half pseudo-colonial," complete with courtyard, reflecting pool, swimming pool, and two apartment houses for the staff.) But however flattering to Americans' sense of self—brimming with initiative and undeterred by hardship or danger—rhetoric of this sort evidently failed to persuade reluctant spouses. The number of wives and family members venturing to Germany and Japan in 1946 fell far short of the army's initial projections. By October 1946, after months of frenzied preparation, just 3,780 American dependents had relocated to Germany.[41]

It fell to the military PR machine to reassure spouses that they would not, in fact, inhabit the functional equivalent of a covered wagon, surrounded by tomahawk-wielding savages. Material ease—promised in the occupational mantra "You Never Had It So Good"—was a more compelling enticement than Manifest Destiny. Stories soon began to litter military magazines and journals extolling the comforts of life far from home. Bernadine V. Lee, a captain's wife, contributed a lengthy feature to the *Army Information Digest* in December 1946, elaborating her journey from skepticism to enchantment in Japan, where she'd found "a home ready to live in; a kitchen complete with electric stove and electric refrigerator, toaster, waffle iron, coffee percolator [*sic*], dishes, silver ware, table linen, and even curtains on the windows; two bathrooms, one with a tile bathtub, four bedrooms . . ." Even more surprising was how "courteous and friendly" the Japanese all appeared. "Eager and able students of the English language," the women were also "wonderful with children." Freed from the tedious burdens of housework and childcare, Lee concluded, "This is a vacation." She entreated other wives to "hesitate no longer."[42]

As recruitment propaganda these aspirational appeals were more shrewd. But extolling the blissful ease of occupation was also a risky proposition. While U.S. policy wasn't meant to be too soft on the Japanese or Germans, it couldn't appear too soft for the Americans either—not, that is, if the military wanted to avoid charges of profiteering or "carpetbagging." Thus General Clay took umbrage at a story in the *Saturday Evening Post* entitled, with precisely no ambiguity, "An Army Wife Lives Very Soft—in Germany." In response, Clay delivered a dense three-and-a-half-page rebuttal to Secretary of War Robert Patterson, making concerted efforts to stifle at birth another exposé with a yet more heckle-raising title, "Malice in Blunderland." As for the original offending article, the *Saturday Evening Post*'s illustrated feature reprised elements of Lee's Tokyo odyssey, detailing how Mrs. Lelah Berry, a captain's wife in her twenties, was managing not only to gain pounds in Germany—thanks to all the dairy products and meat shipped in specially for the occupiers' consumption—but to put away $300 in savings every month (more than half her husband's salary). What differentiated this story from Lee's, however, was Berry's uneasiness over the chasm between her family's "embarrassingly luxurious" existence in a nine-room furnished house and the "lives of the Germans around us." Disparate levels of consumption didn't just stand in "staggering contrast" to one another; they were causally connected: American opulence bought at Germans' expense. Perhaps most unnervingly, the elderly couple whose house the Berry family inhabited continued to live nearby—in a concrete-floored garage. "I can't help feeling piggish about it," Mrs. Berry confessed. "I don't want to coddle or whitewash the Germans, and I tell myself over and over, 'After all, they started it, they asked for it.' But I keep wondering how this sort of occupation can teach them our brand of democracy."[43]

How indeed? The military's establishment of "little Americas" at a calculated remove from local communities did more to exaggerate the socioeconomic gulf between occupiers and occupied than to close it. A report prepared for the army's Operations Research Office in 1951 skewered the point precisely. Noting "the creation of insular communities complete with housing, transportation, food, movies, popcorn, Coca Cola, bubble gum etc.," the authors concluded that this "type of community organization, plus limited language competence of the occupation personnel, had distinct and significant effects upon attainment of ultimate occupation objectives." On a prophetic note, the report offered a sweeping indictment of occupations past, present, and future: "It may be expected that when and if Americans go abroad in large numbers again, they will tend to construct the same kind of separate community. This has been characteristic not only of our own overseas activities but of the long-term colonial undertakings of old-world empires. The problem is accentuated by large-scale, war-time destruction which makes reconstruction of one kind or another essential if excessive inroads on the indigenous housing are to be avoided."[44]

Minimal social interaction with the indigenous population was a feature shared with "old-world empires"—one much commented on in popular accounts of the occupations. The army's official history of the occupation of Germany (issued in 1953) noted that contacts between Germans and U.S. personnel were "amazingly few in view of the great number of persons involved." Author Oliver Frederiksen attributed this phenomenon to the self-sufficiency and introversion of "nomadic" American military communities. Reinforcing this tendency, official policy erected significant barriers toward amicable contact between occupiers and occupied.[45]

Despite their attempts to "wage war" on VD, occupation authorities did far more in practice to discourage *social* than sexual intercourse. The occupation was two years old before American families were permitted to invite German guests to dine in their homes. Another twelve months passed before military personnel were allowed to entertain "indigenous" visitors in an army mess—and then no more than two per week. Touring Germany in 1948, Roger Nash Baldwin of the ACLU decried ubiquitous evidence of "Hans Crowism." Segregation of facilities, redolent of the American South, took myriad forms: "Social passes to frauleins, separate exits and entrances for Germans in public buildings, separate amenities, such as toilets, compounds with barbed wire fences in which Americans lived cut off from the Germans, these are all manifestations of this policy." These demeaning exclusions, Baldwin argued, made a mockery of democracy promotion. In Munich, he noted a sign affixed by a disgruntled German to one Americans-only bathroom: *Nür für das Herrenvolk* (Only for the master race). But even if U.S. authorities had attempted to cultivate greater conviviality, lopsided living standards militated against reciprocity. Frederiksen noted that "overcrowding and comparative poverty" made it difficult for Germans to entertain American guests on a "basis of equality." And without equality, social interaction tended only to underscore economic disparity between occupiers and occupied—to the discomfort of one party, if not both.[46]

The asymmetry that characterized social relations in Germany was even more pronounced in Japan. An ACLU report titled *Civil Liberties in Japan*, produced in 1947, noted caustically that "no American can give anything whatever to a Japanese; none can remain in any Japanese home after 11pm," which was a particular hardship for "Nisei with Japanese relatives." More sweepingly, no American "was permitted to patronize a Japanese theatre, restaurant, place of amusement, a public beach, dance hall, hotels, etc." These embargoes, enacted in the name of stamping out black-market activity, had been accompanied by an empowerment of MPs to "invade Japanese homes and public places looking for Americans who violate the orders." Since American personnel commonly took Japanese police along with them, a "system of espionage on Americans" had been established in which the Japanese played a "leading part." These policies, Baldwin pronounced, were "far more objectionable than the practices they seek to overcome."[47]

More open-minded American civilian employees of SCAP who wished to socialize with their Japanese colleagues found official restrictions buttressed by the blunt force of peer pressure. Thus Hubert Armstrong, a Department of the Interior expert in Native American education who worked in SCAP's Civil Information and Education Section, noted that when a Japanese couple had come to call on him, he could not take them to his room but only into the lounge of the billet in which he lived. Although their conversation lasted just a few minutes, it was enough to ruffle other occupants' feathers. "Later one of the military men here complained that there had been Japanese in the billet," Armstrong told his relatives at home. "It is generally felt here that there are many unnecessary restrictions and that it is hard to teach democracy thru a military dictatorship, however liberal in policy it may be." Given the hostility of the unnamed officer, Armstrong presumably meant that illiberal restrictions were "generally" seen as counterproductive by Japanese professionals and progressive Americans like him who regarded them as peers.[48]

Unconstrained by the rules that governed lower-ranking personnel, senior officers of the Eighth Army regularly mingled with the Japanese elite. (MacArthur, for his part, had spoken more than twice with only sixteen Japanese by the time he left the country in 1952.) In Japanese homes, American officers couldn't help but notice the privations that typified life for even the most affluent members of society, or those who had constituted Japan's prewar elite. On numerous occasions, Eichelberger and Byers wondered where, and how, their hosts had managed to come by such exorbitantly priced rarities as steak for the American guests' delectation. They also both observed and felt the tremendous difference in temperature between their well-heated offices and billets and the glacial state of Japanese homes. The hosts' mottled skin issued its own veiled rebuke to the occupiers, who not only monopolized Japan's scarce supplies of coal but were better placed to insulate themselves in a country where clothing was almost as scare as food and fuel. But the general and his chief of staff resolutely refused to feel abashed, even if the chill did bite. After one frigid dinner party, Eichelberger was quick to recall "the reason that they are suffering is because they lost the war and there is no question about how our people would have suffered in Washington if we had lost the war and the Japanese were in Washington." For his part, Byers, despite noting that the thermometer had read forty-three degrees Fahrenheit—and that the "doll-like 6 year old girl's legs were purple with cold"— reassured his wife that "they seemed to think nothing of it." Eichelberger had merely been wiser in remembering to don thermal underwear before this social visit. "Bob wore the long drawers but I did not, and that's where I made my mistake."[49]

———————

The social segregation that accompanied occupation was not, however, complete. American practice in postwar Europe and Asia shared another trait in common with old-world imperialism and new-world Jim Crowism. Officially mandated insularity coexisted alongside intimate familiarity. The latter simultaneously sustained and destabilized the former. For while American families may not have entertained local guests on conditions of equality, they nevertheless lived side by side on terms of manifest inequality—as master and servant. Like the ostensibly "whites-only" spaces of apartheid South Africa, or their counterparts in the American South, protected enclaves of racial privilege were never hermetically sealed except in rhetorical formulations of apartness. It took a good deal of work, after all, to sustain lifestyles of conspicuous leisure and consumption. And someone had to provide the labor, preferably at minimal cost.

Servants abounded in postwar Germany, Japan, and Korea. The myriad houseboys, bellhops, waitresses, maids, nannies, laundresses, and cooks found bustling about in American messes, billets, clubs, and private homes were both levied from and paid for by the occupied population. Aside from high piles of rubble stacked by the roadside, their presence was one of the first things that struck amazed newcomers. Jacob Van Staavaren, a civilian employee with SCAP who arrived in 1946, tallied up the ratio of residents to servants at several premises where occupationaires were billeted. At the

Imperial Hotel, home to sixty of SCAP's highest-ranking military and civilian officials, the staff of 432 provided a level of personal service outstrip-
ping that of the Ritz in Paris, "which boasted a ratio of two employees for
each of its esteemed guests." A later account reckoned that occupation families had employed over 25,000 servants: "five per general, three per colonel,
and one or two for everybody else."[50]

Like other imperial projects, occupation attracted recruits with the lure
of instant upward mobility: an opportunity to earn more and live substan-
tially better than at home. These inflated earnings had the additional advantage of being tax-free. Quizzed by her sister as to why she'd wish to remain
in Tokyo, thirty-year-old WAC captain Martha Wayman explained that her
salary would be $200 a month, plus $90 for quarters and $21 for rations. "Not
bad, eh?" Coming back to her old job as a schoolteacher held no appeal.
"Seems to me like it would be awfully dull back there—isn't it?" On top of
the generous salaries and tax breaks, servants also sweetened the deal. For
senior officers, household servants were doubtless a taken-for-granted fixture
of existence. But for most occupation personnel, living alongside—and being
in charge of—domestic underlings was an unfamiliar situation, especially for
many African American servicemen and their spouses. It was "paradise" when
"Negro soldiers' dependents . . . hit Nippon," gushed Charley Cherokee in
the *Chicago Defender*. "Their dish washing, suds busting, and scrubbing days
are over for a while." That the servants in question spoke another language
and were ignorant of American ways of running a household, preparing food,
and raising children complicated arrangements alien to both parties. The
training and management of servants thus occupied a good deal of time, particularly for army spouses. Not surprisingly, the deeds and misdeeds of servants also provided rich anecdotal fodder for occupationaires who attempted
to convey to folks back home what "life as a conqueror" entailed. They did so
with varying levels of self-consciousness, embarrassment, or satisfaction.[51]

Some Americans derived seigneurial pleasure from their lordly position,
reveling in the sensation of potency that came from inhabiting homes guarded
by uniformed sentries in which personal needs were gratified by a posse of
handpicked domestics. Recounting his experiences in Japan decades after the
fact, Wiley O'Mohundro continued to delight in the sweeping extent of his
household powers and the accompanying inflation of ego. Prior to selecting
Japanese maids, O'Mohundro (a career infantry officer) asked a doctor to

FIG. 8.3 An unidentified American soldier and his wife are reunited in Japan in the late 1940s. Photographs and Prints Division, Schomburg Center for Research in Black Culture, the New York Public Library, Astor, Lenox and Tilden Foundations [1260278].

inspect the "girls" for venereal disease, evidently equating high moral character with sexual abstinence. The physician more than reassured him: "Not only no venereal disease, they are all virgins." O'Mohundro duly picked three who "were young, pretty and very anxious to please us." Few employers went quite so far in verifying their servants' impeccable credentials, or perhaps they merely neglected to document their invasive background checks for posterity. But O'Mohundro was not alone in selecting Japanese women as much for their "decorative" properties as for their practical capabilities, even if military guidance discouraged men from selecting servants who might strike their wives as "too good-looking." Nor was he unusual in stressing the maids' remarkable eagerness to please.[52]

In a register typical of generations of Western travel writers, Americans in Asia filled their letters with anecdotes about droll cross-cultural misunderstandings that paved the road to domestic harmony. When Armstrong was transferred from Tokyo to Seoul, he found the three Koreans who worked for him and his son to be admirably hard workers but prone to confusion. Asked to make cheese, corned beef, and peanut-butter sandwiches, the maid (a schoolteacher refugee from the Russian sector) had combined all three ingredients rather than serving them separately. The houseboy, despite being a "college kid," needed tutoring in the use of adequate soap for scrubbing, unaccustomed to its abundance. And it didn't help, Armstrong wrote home, that Koreans' education in English began with Shakespeare, Bacon, and Emerson, so while they may have possessed prodigious passive vocabularies, the servants were "quite unable to understand a phrase in speech such as . . . 'You'd better slice the bread a little thinner.' "[53]

Olaf Osnes (another civilian expert with SCAP) and his wife similarly filled their letters with stories about their two female maids: how one had clambered into the bathtub to pummel the laundry in her wooden geta, and the other allowed an errant carrot down the plughole where it stopped the outline pipe. But the main point the Osneses sought to convey was that domestic relationships, however deficient in egalitarianism, were still incubators of progressive change. Intimate acquaintance worked its own attitudinal magic on master and servant alike, converting ingrained suspicion into mutual admiration:

> Today, hundreds and hundreds of these housemaids and waitresses (and houseboys too) know for themselves that they were misled and duped by their leaders and they have had to reverse their entire conception of Americans. The loyalty of our maids is absolute and all of our friends say the same about their help. Altho we almost literally roll in a wealth of material things and they have but a few pitiful garments, comparatively speaking, it is not necessary for us to conceal anything from them or check up on our supplies in the kitchen or anywhere. They just won't take a thing. In fact, their loyalty and honesty continues to astonish us.

Osnes went on to detail what had happened when the family took a week-long vacation the previous year. Having left the house well stocked "with plenty of provisions" for the servants' consumption, the American couple was stunned to be presented on return with "an itemized list of everything they'd eaten for each meal—copying names of things from various cans, bottles and packages."[54]

Osnes was particularly keen to stress his personal contribution to modernizing Japan's "feudal" gender norms, which relegated women to private subservience and public invisibility. Not only did domestic service lift young Japanese women out of postwar penury, it exposed them to appealing American ways of doing things, from labor-saving devices to labor-ready husbands. "It no longer astonishes them when I show up in the kitchen and do some of the wimmens-work there but it used to," Osnes joked in one letter. "It was incredible that the lord of the household should even be aware of the existence of the kitchen." "We often marvel at the way in which they have adjusted themselves to the new life which has come to them with the defeat of their country," he continued. "Mentally speaking, they and their kind must have gone thru a couple of revolutions in the last five years." Praise for the maids' adaptive flexibility was thus a surreptitious form of self-congratulation.[55]

Yet no matter how much positive spin the Osneses gave their tutelary role, anxiety infiltrated their indefatigably buoyant correspondence. Latent doubt wasn't occasioned by concerns about the maids' loyalty but whether the occupiers thoroughly deserved it. Thus Mrs. Osnes wondered aloud about the disjointed feelings the Japanese women—paid forty dollars a month for their labor, half the salary of the lowliest American private—might harbor about the many antique vases, chalices, and metal urns in the Osneses' household. These goods had been claimed from "large scrap heaps that visitors can rummage through," paying just a few yen for whatever treasures they might unearth. In Japan and Germany alike, domestic servants were more intimately acquainted than most with the grand scale of "accumulation by dispossession," whereby the occupiers amassed valuables from the occupied at little or no expense. Unease tarnished the surface of Mrs. Osnes's determinedly upbeat account. "I don't know how the Japanese maids feel about being set to work cleaning and polishing the keepsakes and treasures that these Americans now own," she mused in a memoir circulated to friends back in the States, reassuring herself that "perhaps the poorer class Japanese" would remain ignorant of this transfer of assets, having had "nothing of value to give" to wartime metal-collecting campaigns.[56]

In Germany, the scrapheap Osnes described found a corollary in the "Bartermarts" that U.S. military government initiated in an attempt to suppress black-market trade by converting it into something more respectable. One young army wife wrote breathlessly to her former high school teacher in New Jersey about this fantastic arrangement:

> In Frankfurt, the Army has set up a "BarterMarket"! Any GI or dependents can turn in Blue label (state-side) cigarettes or food, clothing, soap etc (all state-side) and in return get Barter units! The Germans do the same and with all these units, you can buy beautiful crystal, china, silver, cameras etc, and the krauts buy your cigarettes and food! As the krauts bring in these beautiful things, they are appraised for so many barter points. They base it on the cost of American Cigarettes in Peace time which was $8.00 a carton. But even that is getting to be a racket! It's really a legal black market![57]

Louise Farrell, a more self-conscious WAC officer, mused on the lopsidedness of a scheme the *Saturday Evening Post* dubbed "looting with consent." Although the Bartermart was ostensibly operated for mutual benefit, "we definitely by far got the better end of the deal," Farrell informed her sister Kate, passing on the rumor that one general's wife had amassed a collection of 600 porcelain figurines of museum quality. "Between the black market and the Barter Marts it's almost beyond the imagination what we must have taken out of Germany," Farrell marveled in February 1947.[58]

Inevitably, the disparity between the occupiers' wealth and the impoverishment of local employees resulted in tension and sometimes in theft. George Pearson (an army officer in Japan) was puzzled by a robbery at his home in which the only items stolen were several white shirts his wife had brought over from the States. On closer investigation, it turned out that the Pearsons' houseboy had taken them for his sisters. Seamstresses who faced a chronic shortage of thread, they had unraveled the shirts for sewing cotton. The situation's poignant dimensions did not, however, spare the servant from a custodial sentence. When Pearson managed to talk the commanding general into releasing the thief, the latter emerged from prison, "uniform all ruined and dirty. He said is this democracy? Is this what you mean by democracy?" If the undemocratic character of military occupation was not lost on some of the occupiers, it could hardly fail to strike the occupied. Few ironies were more pronounced than the occupiers' attempt to package relations of servitude as a dimension of democratization. Being a good servant, after all, meant obedient fulfillment of orders—the very trait that, as the Allies had agreed at Potsdam, required elimination in German and Japanese civilians who had thrown themselves willingly at their leaders' feet. Yet often with complete unself-consciousness, American commentators now routinely lauded the fact that the Japanese, "accustomed to serving," were "not only expert but also contented in the role."[59]

Domestic servitude brought occupiers and occupied into close proximity. But other forms of intimate contact—the varieties euphemistically termed "fraternization"—continued apace, despite attempts to clean up and "normalize" conditions of occupation life for U.S. personnel. After some months, realizing that unauthorized sexual encounters were not susceptible to total eradication, the military adopted a different tack. The politics of respectability that accompanied families' arrival also prompted a new strategy to convert promiscuous sexuality into stable romantic relationships, and even marriage, between GIs and Germans. Legitimizing the more durable of such unions would not only "give the honest soldier a break," as General Joseph McNarney put it, but improve relations with locals upset by rampant "fratting" and the necessarily illegitimate offspring that sometimes resulted—an increasingly visible and embarrassing problem for military government. By the end of the occupation, American servicemen had fathered thousands of babies in Germany, with estimates ranging from 30,000 to 94,000. But well before 1952, the military's initial refusal to permit men to take responsibility for children they had fathered began to appear an untenable contradiction. The occupiers' figurative language of paternalism called for more responsible models of practical paternity.[60]

In Germany, U.S. authorities quickly acknowledged failure in their attempts to prevent GIs from contracting marriages with local women. Even though they violated military orders in so doing, nothing prevented soldiers from finding clergymen to conduct wedding ceremonies. The men in question were ineligible for service thereafter but they remained married nonetheless.

Rumors of unauthorized unions between German women and American men began circulating just weeks after V-E Day. A brief attempt to prosecute the officiants was abandoned when American commanders recognized that the clergy in question had done nothing illegal. Military prohibitions did not carry juridical weight. Moreover, since the wives were lawful spouses, they enjoyed full right to allotments from their soldier-husbands' pay and were also, thanks to the War Brides Act of 1945, eligible for immigration to the United States on a nonquota basis, passage paid by the U.S. government.[61]

Confounded by these loopholes, military government authorities gave up their attempt to outlaw marriage between Americans and Germans, introducing a new rule in December 1946 that men could marry—subject to officers' approval—during the final month of their overseas duty, provided the engagement outlived a three-month waiting period. This delaying mechanism was intended to trip up fiancées with "gold-digging" ambitions and limited attention spans, or, as the army put it, to "discourage German women from taking advantage of the immaturity of many U.S. soldiers by marrying them for the food, clothing and accommodations they might derive in Germany from the marriage." Although this stipulation was quickly dropped, American servicemen who married German women were still obliged to leave the command within ninety days of marriage. They could, however, continue employment in a civilian capacity.[62]

By June 1948, an estimated 3,500 marriages had been contracted between American men and German women. Although public attention rarely focused on American women marrying German men, Bud Hutton and Andy Rooney bucked the trend in their 1947 "report to the American stockholders" titled *Conquerors' Peace*. They noted that "both the congressional act and the Army's decree are worded to include not only fiancées but fiancés, and there is a possibility, at least, that one or more WAC, Army nurse, or other GI Jane may turn up at the gangplank one day this year with a Herr Hans and a wedding ring. When that happens—brother!" Statistics for "occupation husbands" remain in much shorter supply than those for war and postwar brides. With regard to the latter, however, German women made up a substantial proportion of the total. By the decade's end, Germany was, as historian Susan Zeiger notes, "second only to Britain as the country of origin for the largest number of soldier wives admitted under the War Brides Act." Transatlantic liners were thus kept busy shuttling women in both directions, for while significant numbers of German women sailed the Atlantic to make new lives in the United States, approximately 30,000 American military wives and children had traveled to Germany by 1950.[63]

In Japan, by contrast, SCAP's hostility to American personnel marrying Japanese women remained an abiding feature of the occupation. Steeped in racist objection to "miscegenation," this prohibition found formal justification in the fact that Japanese brides were debarred from admission to the United States. The GI Brides Act of 1945 expressly omitted "all persons ineligible for admission"—an allusion to the Oriental Exclusion Law, which since 1924 had worked to keep Asian immigrants out of America. As in Germany, however, it lay beyond SCAP's powers to prevent soldiers from marrying in Buddhist or Shinto ceremonies, and some officers' wives even provided instruction to Japanese brides in how to eat with cutlery (without "holding the bowl under the chin") and in the use of washing machines and mix masters. First dozens, then hundreds, of American soldiers wed surreptitiously, while other star-crossed binational couples resolved the dilemma of forbidden love in a more lethal way. Stories of tragic suicide pacts became an intermittent feature of press reports from occupied Japan.[64]

When Baldwin visited Japan in 1947 to report on the state of civil liberties under occupation, he found the formal obstacles to marriage particularly troublesome. U.S. authorities seemed unmindful of the fact that an American might choose to remain in Japan or go to another country "where he can take his family," rather than returning to the United States. And if the sotto voce objection was not to binational but rather biracial marriages, why should Japanese Americans in the occupation force be prevented from marrying partners of the same ethnicity? Baldwin was further troubled by the way in which current policy—with its stubborn refusal to take certain facts of life seriously—increased the occupation's *lack* of respectability. In particular, SCAP's rigid opposition to marriage left unaddressed the precarious situation of hundreds of American-fathered babies: illegitimate progeny that, as in Germany, U.S. authorities actively forbade the fathers from acknowledging. As a result, servicemen who wanted to legitimize their offspring had no opportunity to do so. This left the infants in vulnerable limbo, and SCAP's assertion of benevolent paternalism a hollow rhetorical gesture.[65]

Five years after Baldwin delivered a damning report on civil liberties' curtailment in Japan, passage of the McCarran Walter Act finally waived Asian exclusion from the United States. After two brief easements during which restrictions had been temporarily lifted, Japanese war brides were allowed to emigrate on a regularized basis after 1952, although their numbers were still limited by the stringent quotas McCarran Walter imposed on Asian immigrants. In a culminating irony, marriage between U.S. servicemen and Japanese women became "normalized" just as the occupation drew to a formal end.[66]

As we know, however, the presence of American troops overseas did not terminate with the creation of a new South Korean state in 1948, the inauguration of the Federal Republic of Germany in 1949, or Japan's resumption of sovereignty (minus Okinawa) in 1952. Structures originally built to last five years remained in place for decades, and some of the germinal military communities established in the late 1940s still exist today. What occurred wasn't the wholesale return home of American servicemen and servicewomen, but rather a change in how Americans thought about overseas occupation. It did not take long for rosier hues to tint the early emphasis on failure, cupidity, and avarice in popular culture and collective memory alike.

THE "GOOD OCCUPATION"?

Ten years, almost to the day, after Japan's delegates signed the instrument of surrender on board the *Missouri,* members of the Drama Advisory Panel of the American National Theatre and Academy (ANTA) sat down to business. This body administered the State Department's Cultural Presentations Program, and at the top of its agenda on September 14, 1955, was the issue of whether to sponsor a tour of John Patrick's Pulitzer-winning play *The Teahouse of the August Moon* through "the Orient." The proposed itinerary encompassed numerous points east. Starting in Yugoslavia, the production would then journey on to "Turkey, Israel, Egypt, Iraq, Iran, India, etc." The State Department was said to be "extremely interested." There were some cavils, however. Did these countries possess sufficient English speakers to furnish adequate audiences? Perhaps this problem could be circumvented by using IBM translating machines recently employed to good effect in Paris, one committee member ventured. "The only fear was that people might take them home as souvenirs," the minutes recorded. But that possibility could be forestalled, a more sanguine colleague countered, by charging a "small deposit." Overall, the mood was buoyant. "The Panel felt that this play has a terrific effect on foreign audiences where it has already been seen, and is wonderful propaganda for us because we laugh at ourselves."[1]

The play in question, based on a best-selling novel by military government veteran Vern Sneider, is a whimsical farce set in Okinawa immediately after the war. It derives humor from the cross-cultural collision between hapless American occupiers and guileful "orientals" who readily run rings around their conquerors. With encounters between victors and vanquished mediated by an ingenuous native interpreter, Sakini, the Okinawans manage to circumvent the Americans' insistence on constructing a pentagonal schoolhouse, the goal of prefabricated "Plan B," which pays no heed to local preferences or vernaculars. Slyly, the villagers beguile Captain Fisbee, an easily led liberal arts professor, into setting up a sweet-potato brandy distillery to help finance a teahouse for the geisha girl Lotus Blossom—the locals' present to him. After much slapstick knockabout, Fisbee learns "the wisdom of gracious acceptance." The villagers, he discovers, are "wonderful people with a strange sense of beauty. And hard working—when there's a purpose." Since they can't be forced to adopt ill-suited, unfamiliar ways, the wisest path is to bow to their wishes and humbly acknowledge the limits of one's own power. "Plan See," flexible adaptation, trumps the rigid imposition of "Plan B." To mutual satisfaction, it transpires that East and West can be harmoniously reconciled. "I don't want to be a world leader," Fisbee concludes at the end, content with what he's inadvertently accomplished, yet happy to be heading home. "I'm making peace with myself somewhere between my ambitions and my limitations," he announces.[2]

When *The Teahouse of the August Moon* opened on Broadway in October 1953—two years after the San Francisco peace treaty with Japan, and three months after the Korean War armistice—it garnered rapturous reviews in the U.S. press. Critics swooned over the teahouse that dropped magically from the rafters during the third act, admiring the unexpected thespian talent of a goat that wandered the set. An "irresistibly winning fantasy," Richard Watts effused in the *New York Post*. The play bestowed honors "chiefly on the side of the East," Watts opined, yet there was also "victory on our side in the play's happy willingness to accept and applaud the things that the amiable countrymen of a Far Eastern island have to teach us." "Rarely has Rudyard Kipling's famous dictum been disproved so effectually," he applauded. An equally rhapsodic John McClain in the *New York Journal American* deemed *Teahouse* "one of the most charming and hilarious productions to be unveiled in these parts since *South Pacific*," locating Patrick's play within a broader cultural field that was "jollifying" the Pacific War in conformity with the tenets of what scholar Christina Klein terms "cold war Orientalism." This cocktail comprised one part gentle self-mockery and two parts "polite" racism. Exoticizing the natives and their colorful customs, *Teahouse* distinguished "good" Orientals as worthy allies against the bad "through a logic of affiliation as well as through one of difference."[3]

American audiences in the mid-1950s evidently found this an alluring projection of self-other relations. When MGM began filming a Cinemascope version in 1956, with Kyoto standing in for Okinawa, Patrick's stage play was celebrating its thousandth Broadway performance, hailed by the *Los Angeles Times'* drama critic as "the most satisfactory drama to emerge in the postwar American theater." The play's staged convergence of American goodness and Okinawan graciousness appealed to an emergent postwar sensibility of same-under-the-skin cosmopolitanism. "At that time they were teaching that there was absolutely no difference between anybody," Kurt Vonnegut remarked of his GI-billed education in anthropology at the University of Chicago. In the same vein, *Teahouse* told theatergoers that on Okinawa one could no longer tell (in Fisby's words) "who's the conqueror and who the conquered"— words made flesh in the Broadway production by actor David Wayne, who performed in yellowface as the Okinawan interpreter, Sakini. MGM reprised this move by casting Marlon Brando in the lead, after many pounds shed and much time in makeup. The studio's prerelease ballyhoo boasted that even the locals had been fooled by this uncanny ethnic imposture during location shooting, though it boggles belief that Japanese extras were more credulous than American movie critics. "Made up to look like a relative of Dr. Fu Manchu, and babbling pidgin English at a great rate, [Brando] never succeeds in hiding the fact that he's really an all-American boy," John McCarten caustically observed in the *New Yorker*.[4]

To the Drama Advisory Panel's members, *Teahouse* winningly demonstrated that Americans could chuckle at certain national foibles, like their well-intentioned insistence on knowing what was best for everyone else, which was lampooned in the character of Colonel Purdy. A buffoonish brass hat, addicted to the "climaxes" supplied by *Adventure* magazine, Purdy is given to exclaiming "What in the name of Occupation!" when frustrated. Determined to teach "these natives the meaning of Democracy," he declares "they're going to learn Democracy if I have to shoot every one of them"—a line obviously intended to elicit laughter.[5]

Not surprisingly, this vision of oriental guile and occidental gaucherie captivated only those in a position to take the comedy seriously: in other words, Americans oblivious to the power relations that *Teahouse* mystified, along with Okinawa's traumatic unburied past. On the island itself, there could be no doubt about the identities of conqueror and conquered, nor any humor in a quip that casually conjured mass death among a population so thoroughly decimated by war. "Leased" by the United States on a semipermanent basis, Okinawa was governed by an American general who enjoyed the unchallengeable right to appoint its chief executive, veto legislative action, and rule by decree. This military absolutism, coupled with the presence of 20,000 air force personnel, 4,000 dependents, and 10,000 marines—all of whom occupied a substantial proportion of the island's agricultural land— fueled increasingly active opposition in the 1950s. Among the many glaring disparities of life under occupation, Okinawans doubtless noticed that

CONC. 1 MGM's screen adaptation of *The Teahouse of the August Moon* preaches "the wisdom of gracious acceptance" of cultural difference, with Marlon Brando playing an Okinawan interpreter.

the U.S. military paid them only ten cents an hour for heavy labor, while Americans performing the same work received twenty times more. Social segregation was so complete that U.S. personnel and Okinawans rarely mingled, and certainly not on terms of equality. Something other than "gracious acceptance" was also signaled by the fact that in the U.S. government building, where Americans occupied the top three floors and Okinawans the bottom two, a padlocked iron grille was pulled down at night to prevent the locals "drifting up." Demonstrations entreating the occupiers to go home were on the rise. Gone, then, were the islanders Sneider claimed to have encountered in 1945, "completely lacking in sham and pretense and filled with wide-eyed, childlike gratitude." In 1956, Okinawans would engage in the ultimate act of Cold War civil disobedience: electing a communist mayor.[6]

This event lay in the future when the Drama Advisory Panel first met to discuss the play's suitability for a tour of the East. But committee members might have done well to heed a lengthy article that had appeared in the *New Yorker* the previous October. Faubion Bowers, an expert on Japanese theater who had served with Douglas MacArthur's GHQ in Tokyo, delivered a pointed "Letter from Okinawa" that (among other things) noted the dismal flop that ensued when the Army Special Services staged *Teahouse* in the island's capital, Naha. Both literally and figuratively, the play's humor defied translation. Rendered in Japanese kanji, the title "Moon-Viewing Restaurant" made no sense. More damningly, one Okinawan professor protested in a local newspaper that the play "represented his people as liars, cheats, and fools."[7]

As this response made clear, fantasies of powerlessness seduced only the powerful. And only those in a position to recast relations of domination as a celebration of subaltern wiliness could assume that "the natives" would be similarly charmed. That other Asians, like the Okinawan professor, might find *Teahouse* a distasteful masquerade slowly became apparent to the drama panel. Reports arrived from U.S. consular outposts that a tour would not be welcome in some ports of call, polls having revealed that Japan, Pakistan, India, and Burma were unenthusiastic about the proposed production. Even though Americans thought *they* were the targets of the play's "gentle and friendly" fun, foreign audiences might see it differently, some diplomats warned. "Orientals do not like to be laughed at," the committee heard in January 1956. By then, however, the State Department had already sent a Spanish-language version through South America. Reception in Montevideo, Buenos Aires, and Santiago was "tepid," the *New York Times* delicately noted, though troupe members ascribed this disappointing reception not to the play itself but to technical failures "blamed on uncooperative local stagehands."[8]

It tells us a good deal about the United States' growing occupational chutzpah in the 1950s that a comic novel, play, and then movie about military government in Okinawa—of all places—should have so beguiled Americans. Yet more telling is the faith State Department personnel placed in *Teahouse* as a genial ambassador likely to win friends and influence people in "the Orient." Only by hard experience did they discover that the play's appeal was not, in fact, universal. "Not easy to learn. Sometimes painful," Sakini warns in his opening monologue.[9]

Distance from both the time and place conjured by successive stagings of *Teahouse* made it easier for Okinawa, or an imaginary place of that name, to host a broad comedy of manners. But occupation had been played for laughs before—on another island populated by roguish natives where the American occupiers made themselves beloved, though flirtation stopped short of consummation. In 1944 *A Bell for Adano* had struck a deeply responsive chord in the United States, blazing the trail from print to stage and screen that *Teahouse* would later follow. Greeted with fervent enthusiasm on the home front, John Hersey's novel was also an export product of dubious value. (Office of War Information staffers poring over the Twentieth Century Fox script cautioned against American characters calling the local wine "dago red" and the Sicilians "spaghetti-pushers" or "wops," fretting that the picture "could be indicative of an American attitude towards 'foreigners' as comic and picturesque."[10]) If Sneider's message that occupiers would do well to heed local preferences had a familiar ring, the echo wasn't coincidental. Sneider acknowledged a substantial debt in the formulation of his philosophy. Of his days as a military government officer, he reminisced, "At that time a factual work on the occupation of the Rhineland in 1917 [*sic*] was considered the guide. . . . But in April of 1945 when we went into Okinawa with the invasion forces, most of us found that instead of a guide it was a piece of fiction that helped us in the villages, among the people—John Hersey's *A Bell for Adano*."

Sneider hoped his own novel would guide future occupation officers in the art of culturally sensitive improvisation. "Perhaps it might show him that if he looks to the wants of the people under him, then tries to satisfy those wants, he will have very little need for barbed wire and guards armed with rifles," the novelist ruminated—though the play and movie completely banished any hint of razor wire or rifles from their depictions of Okinawa. "Perhaps it will also show him, among other things, that what works in Pottawattamie, Iowa, often will not work in Tobiki Village, Okinawa. . . . That the culture and way of life of an occupied country is often very old and, strangely enough, ideally suited to that country." But in a more ironic reverberation, Sneider, like Hersey, was criticized by military government officers with longer field experience for *insufficient* appreciation of local culture. Jim Watkins, the political science professor who presided over Okinawa's first local council, noted that "after the first chapter any resemblance to Military Government on Okinawa is purely fortuitous. Sneider was an army officer at Camp Tobaru until he was detached in August [1945] and sent with the Corps to Korea. He didn't know anything about Okinawan customs and seems to have got his local

color from a reading of Japanese Tourist Bureau booklets on the tea ceremony, geisha, and the like. The play made from the book is also very funny.
But the same criticisms apply."[11]

It was Hersey's novel, not Sneider's, that endured. "Few U.S. war heroes
have made more money or become better known than warm and selfless Major
Victor Joppolo," remarked *Time* magazine in March 1946. Hersey's beloved
creation would be remobilized numerous times over successive decades, assuming different stripes with each postwar reincarnation. In 1956, as the Pacific
War was in the process of all-out jollification, *Adano* was taken up an octave
and transformed into a musical for CBS television viewers. "A Bell for
Adano, sounds like a song that the angels play," chorus the Sicilians, insisting that they "think more of the bell than of the belly," while Adano's
blond belle, a tiny-waisted sweater girl, winsomely implored Mister Major
to teach her all about democracy. Joppolo himself did not sing. "It was felt
that music is such an integral part of the Italian spirit and psychology that
Anglo-Saxon characters should not compete," noted Oscar Godbout in the
New York Times, forgetting Joppolo's parentage. Eleven years later, at the
height of the Vietnam War, NBC's *Hall of Fame* returned to *Adano* for a
vision of "pacification" accomplished. In a production dedicated to "all veterans of all wars," Joppolo now spoke of "a battle for men's hearts and minds
all over the earth"—phraseology Hersey had never employed. This counter-
insurgent Joppolo would be resurrected shortly after the invasion of Iraq in
2003. When influential essayist Robert Kaplan promulgated ten rules to
guide the United States' achievement of "supremacy by stealth," his first commandment decreed, "Produce More Joppolos." Sure enough, in the interests
of producing more Joppolos, the United States Marine Corps added *Adano*
to its professional reading program.[12]

To a remarkable degree, these recent resuscitations have obscured Joppolo's status as a *fictional* character. His approximate double would sue Hersey
for libel in 1946, taking umbrage at *Adano*'s intimations of adultery—or, as
Hersey saw it, wanting a share in the income of America's best-known veteran. Twenty years later, the novelist declined to present Colonel Frank Toscani with the army's inaugural Civil Affairs Trophy, protesting that the latter
had been "untrue to the very sorts of ideals this award has been instituted to
celebrate," creating a "most un-Joppolo-like furore" with an avaricious libel
suit. Joppolo, his creator implied, stood apart from ordinarily grubby mortals as a better-than-life model. The fact that American military personnel

have been urged to familiarize themselves with a palpably idealized creation underscores the indebtedness of the "good occupation" to works of imagination: a structure of feeling presenting itself as a statement of fact. Many published accounts, memoirs, and diaries by occupation personnel—or bleaker novels written by veterans like John Horne Burns—would have better attuned Marine Corps trainees to recurrent occupational hazards: looting, black marketeering, and fraternization in all its many forms. Why, then, return to *Adano*?[13]

An online Marine Corps reading guide interprets the novel as illustrative of "the single battle concept," "specifically the fact that an area of operations must be viewed as an indivisible entity—not separate rear, close and deep operations." In particular, the guide praises Joppolo for allowing mule traffic through Adano. "Without the carts, Adano is a dependent entity, siphoning resources from the expeditionary force." Strikingly, the guide says nothing about Joppolo's pursuit of a bell—an initiative that siphons his own energies from narrowly military concerns yet is fundamental to Hersey's message about how occupiers endear themselves to the occupied. With its entreaty to disobey mulish four-star generals, *Adano* might seem to offer decidedly mixed messages to those heading for Afghanistan or Adhamiya. Perhaps, then, the more compelling (if less self-conscious) reason to recommend Hersey to Marine Corps cadets is less practical than affective. Hersey's novel, in other words, functions less as a source of advice than of reassurance. By encouraging readers to understand occupation as a "good thing," albeit one that bad men can undo, *Adano* performs that magic sleight of hand whereby the *O* word ceases to have any specific gravity, becoming instead a source of levity and gratification.[14]

As military government personnel in Sicily pointed out at the time, Hersey had to omit a good deal to pull this trick off. Brimming with love, his portrait was signally short on squalor. Joppolo flattered a sentimental self-image of Americans "doing things for"—Ernest Hemingway's definition of love in *A Farewell to Arms*, set in Italy in the wake of World War I. *Adano*'s obfuscation of things done to the occupied, along with issues of power and purpose—why, and in whose interests, it would be necessary for "after-armies" to remain in Europe indefinitely—was taken even further in *Teahouse*. Neither the stage play nor screen adaptation offers any clue as to why Americans in uniform would stay put in Okinawa, other than through misplaced enthusiasm for building pentagonal schoolhouses. It's not even clear that the occupiers will remain. The drama ends with Fisby's imminent departure after he discards any world-altering aspirations—a foreshortening of perspective unlikely to have fooled Okinawans in the mid-1950s. The military's construction of durable, typhoon-proof facilities gave every impression of an occupation built to last. If anyone looked likely to depart en masse in the near future, it was the islanders, not the occupiers. In the mid-1950s, American officials explored the possibility of a forcible relocation of Okinawans to Bolivia to clear yet more space for base development; and they did, in fact, deport several hundred Okinawans reputed to be politically troublesome.[15]

Over time, the morally hazardous dimensions of occupation that concerned many Americans in and out of uniform in the 1940s have faded from view, glossed over by pleasing fictions like *A Bell for Adano* and *Teahouse of the August Moon*. At a remove, it may seem surprising that, in the war's early aftermath, stateside newspapers routinely warned that the peace was being lost, decrying the "heels among the heroes." Far from celebrating American wisdom and generosity, a crop of titles like *Failure in Japan, Betrayal: Our Occupation of Germany* and *Again the Goose Step: The Lost Fruits of Victory* typified the first wave of reportage from occupied territory. Early reckonings by scholars, including several doctoral theses produced by military government veterans, tended to be just as scathing—if not more damning yet. Authors criticized the haphazard implementation of denazification in Germany and noted the unmistakable signs of resurgent German anti-Semitism. They skewered the bungled economic policies and faulty currency controls that had done little to halt rampant black-market activity or stem soaring inflation. Almost invariably, they found fault with planning and training for occupation—the preparations that, in recent years, have often been held up as vastly superior to Washington's inadequate preparations for a post-Baathist Iraq. When progressive critics lambasted the reempowerment of conservative economic and political forces in both Germany and Japan, they expressed little ambiguity as to *why* the United States occupied foreign territory. The point of occupation was to bolster American hegemony as the world's leading economic and military power—a pole position Washington had actively pursued by participation in the war, and had no intention of relinquishing thereafter. If the United States expended significant resources overseas, it did so with a view to recouping these outlays at a high rate of return.[16]

Divested of material interests, the "good occupation" of popular memory offers instead an affirmative vision of postwar altruism. Viewed through this rosy prism, military government appears an obligation of world leadership—shouldered with reluctance but executed with beneficence. This was not, of course, how Americans viewed things, or were encouraged to see things, at the outset. Initially, the work of occupation in Germany and Japan was cast in *de*constructive terms that emphasized dismantling and disabling enemies. Policy makers in Washington did not anticipate the Axis powers' rehabilitation as postwar partners. Had they articulated the mission of occupation in the language with which it was evoked in 2003—pump-priming aid in tandem with "constitutions and parliaments"—many Americans would have protested that the United States was assisting those who manifestly didn't merit help, a complaint that greeted the establishment of UNRRA in 1943. By the same token, men in uniform expressed resentment wherever a fuzzy distinction between civil affairs and military government muddied the terms of engagement, as was the case in North Africa and Italy. In these zones of ambiguity, distribution of U.S. products to the locals, packaged as aid, failed to elicit the kind of payment GIs thought was owing. Generosity surely demanded gratitude—if nothing more tangible. Their disgruntlement points to a recurrent conundrum for states in legitimating *interested* policy as disinterested selflessness. While such rhetoric may flatter national vanity, it doesn't always persuade those tasked with distributing what's been billed as largesse, particularly if the distributors don't see themselves as adequately compensated for their efforts.[17]

Occupational "success"—that elusive quarry of recent years—was gauged by a different yardstick in the early postwar period from the one supplied by hindsight. In the late 1940s, Americans were more inclined to relativism than absolutism in appraising their performance as an occupying power. Thus, commentators routinely deemed MacArthur's efforts in Japan superior to those of General Joseph McNarney, while in Germany some consolation could be derived from looking east across the demarcation lines. In the Soviet zones of Germany and Berlin, rapacity was far more pronounced. Comparatively evaluated, every American occupation appeared better run, even to the most jaded or disgusted occupationaire, than anywhere the Germans or Japanese had occupied in the 1930s and 1940s. And, however faltering, American efforts also far surpassed the occupations the Axis powers *would* have inaugurated had they won the war: a counterfactual dystopia servicemen and servicewomen often conjured to reassure themselves that their behavior, even at its grubbiest, wasn't *so* bad.

Soon, however, a different calculus applied. Rapidly escalating tension between Washington and Moscow—heightened by friction between occupation forces in divided Germany, Austria, and Korea—fueled anxiety that a third world war might be imminent, with conservative elements among the occupied populations artfully stoking American anticommunism. In the increasingly febrile atmosphere of the late 1940s, U.S. policy openly embraced an affinity for the Germans that some occupation officers had felt almost from the start. The Berlin blockade of 1948 galvanized this shift. Provoked by a U.S.-led currency reform that severed economic sinews between East and West, the crisis was roundly attributed to Soviet aggression in the American press: an ominous portent that Moscow aimed to bring the entire city of Berlin (and perhaps all of Germany) into Stalin's orbit. The ensuing American airlift, undertaken to provision Berliners who had been cut off by the Soviet blockade of rail and road access to the western sectors, consolidated West Germans' new image in the United States as endangered victims of "Red aggression." As plucky underdogs in this confrontation between unarmed democrats and armed dictators, Berliners appeared thoroughly deserving of Americans' sympathy and support—feminized and infantilized, as historian Petra Goedde points out, in this projection of U.S. paternalism. Repackaged as a protective undertaking, occupation shed its last punitive vestiges.[18]

The Korean War further accelerated the transformation of Germany and Japan from enemies to putative allies, then formal partners by treaty. Korea's proxy confrontation between Washington and Moscow—an all-too-proximate conflict between U.S.-led UN forces and Chinese People's Volunteers—cemented the great postwar geopolitical reversal. The newly inaugurated Federal Republic of Germany, just one year old when the Korean War began, quickly became more than a merely prospective ally. Washington's national security establishment urged the rearmament of West Germany, paving the way for its entry into the North Atlantic Treaty Organization in 1955. As a result, even while the occupation was ostensibly winding down in the early 1950s, American armed forces were digging in, simultaneously consolidating the U.S. position on the Cold War's European front line and reconstituting a new West German military establishment. This development would have been unimaginable in 1945, when Germany's complete demilitarization—in perpetuity—had formed one of the few points of agreement unequivocally shared by the Soviets and Americans.[19]

Japan, meanwhile, served as a vital rear staging area for the U.S. war effort in Asia. Many of the first American units sent into Korea, such as the Twenty-Fourth Infantry Division, were hastily mustered from Japan; and, in some accounts, they were ill prepared by the soft life of occupation for the rigors of combat. Soon, however, the cushy trappings of that posting—the hotels and recreation centers established by Robert Eichelberger for Eighth Army occupation personnel—would become R&R destinations for servicemen fighting in Korea.[20]

Soviet and Chinese intentions seemed sufficiently menacing to defuse the hostility many Americans had expressed during the war, and soon thereafter, toward both a sizable postwar military establishment and the prospect of protracted overseas occupation. Anticommunism served to transform prewar isolationism into Cold War internationalism. Erstwhile critics of American "gauleiters" became strident agitators against the "red menace" at home and abroad. And as East-West competition escalated, one-time isolationists no longer charged that it was inimical to national values to maintain a vast standing military or to sustain entrenched occupations. Indeed, in the eyes of the *Chicago Tribune* and its ilk, it was un-American to *oppose* these militarized mainstays of national security—a new postwar buzz phrase. Frenzied calls for postwar demobilization proved short lived. In terms of military spending, the United States never did demobilize after World War II. American troops who came home in 1945 and 1946 were soon replaced by hundreds of thousands more men and women deployed to populate the growing network of U.S. bases around the world. Postwar glided into a state of permanent mobilization.[21]

If the U.S. occupations "succeeded" in Germany and Japan, as received wisdom has it, their accomplishment arguably lay more in meeting objectives reoriented toward a future world war than in redressing the wrongs of the one newly ended. Historian Edward Peterson (himself a military government veteran) terms this recalibration a "retreat to victory" in Germany. In other words, Americans accomplished more when they jettisoned their radically transformative ambitions for a deindustrialized and denazified Germany, instead allowing West Germans greater latitude to reconstruct their own polity and economy. "The evidence could be considered a reaffirmation of the Jeffersonian principle that the government which governs least gov-

erns best," Peterson asserts—restating a dictum drummed into military government trainees at Charlottesville that many of them subsequently found
unworkable. On the ground, conditions of total collapse compelled them to
"govern most," at least in the foundational phase of occupation. "Success,"
in short, is a constantly shifting standard, one that invariably begs the questions, For whom? and For what?[22]

With Cold War alliances consolidated and myriad overseas bases established as a durable fixture of the postwar architecture, Americans in the 1950s
were less inclined to recall that postwar occupation had once occasioned grave
alarm. Anti-imperialism—political ground claimed in decades past by both
Right and Left critics of U.S. expansionism—became associated exclusively
with the Left. So too did antimilitarism, another long-standing national tradition that was radically reframed under Cold War pressure as "un-American."
And in this reoriented world, the lived experience of occupation became ripe
for its own miraculous makeover. Squalor gave way to humor. Enmity dissolved into romance or laughter. When Elvis Presley tunefully lamented in
1960's *GI Blues* that the girls all wore signs saying "Keepen Sie Off Die Grass,"
it was clear that the old postwar Germany—where GIs "fratted" with easily
available "furlines"—had been made safe for even the cleanest teens. As for the
United States' most famous occupation soldier, it was on duty in Germany that
Private Presley met his future bride. Priscilla Beaulieu was just fourteen. But
the "good occupation" had clearly come of age.[23]

Fantasies of romantic reconciliation obscure the boredom, bafflement,
and boorishness that pervaded daily life for occupation's often reluctant foot
soldiers. Conquest is not a natural incubator of compassion. The exercise of
dominance tends instead to foster cupidity and corruption, eased by an as-
surance of entitlement. Understandably, then, in the aftermath of humanity's most catastrophic conflict, the victors struggled to heed Francis Lieber's
Civil War admonition, incorporated into the army's 1940 *Field Manual 27-5*:
"As military government is executed by force, it is incumbent upon those
who administer it to be strictly guided by the principles of justice, honor,
and humanity—virtues adorning a soldier even more than other men for the
very reason that he possesses the power of his arms against the unarmed."
Chafing against the malign fate that had stranded them in Europe or Asia
at war's end, occupation soldiers confronted myriad temptations to exploit
those advantages conferred and assured by force of arms. Occupation's struc-
tural asymmetries generated stronger incentives to vice than virtue. And

where gratification was easily had, the nagging prompts of conscience readily faltered.[24]

These inconvenient truths were not unknown to postwar Americans. Conveyed by soldiers in letters home, the transactional murk of occupation was the quotidian stuff of press reports, popular histories, and fiction in the late 1940s. Unlike our generation, they needed no reminding that occupation wasn't all "sweets and flowers" but something less saccharine and fragrant. It took time and toil to smooth the rough edges of lived experience into the sleek veneer of national legend. Like so much else in the postwar world, the image of occupation itself required radical reconstruction.

ABBREVIATIONS

NOTES

ACKNOWLEDGMENTS

INDEX

ACC	Allied Control Commission [of Italy]
ACLU	American Civil Liberties Union
AHR	*American Historical Review*
AJMLL	Arthur J. Morris Law Library, University of Virginia, Charlottesville, VA
AMG	Allied Military Government
AMGOT	Allied Military Government of Occupied Territories
ANTA	American National Theatre and Academy
ASSSCL	Albert and Shirley Small Special Collection Library, University of Virginia, Charlottesville, VA
ATIS	Allied Translator and Interpreter Service
BRB	Beinecke Rare Book and Manuscript Library, Yale University, New Haven, CT
CATS	Civil Affairs Training School
CDT	*Chicago Daily Tribune*
CIS	Civil Intelligence Section [Japan]
CU	Rare Book and Manuscript Library, Columbia University, New York, NY
DMR	David M. Rubenstein Rare Book and Manuscript Library, Duke University, Durham, NC
ETO	European theater of operations
FDRL	Franklin D. Roosevelt Presidential Library, Hyde Park, NY
GHQ	General Headquarters [Japan]

HIA	Hoover Institution Archives, Stanford University, Palo Alto, CA
HSP	Historical Society of Pennsylvania, Philadelphia, PA
IHS	Indiana Historical Society, Indianapolis, IN
JCS	Joint Chiefs of Staff
KCSC	Kislak Center for Special Collections, Rare Books and Manuscripts, University of Pennsylvania, Philadelphia, PA
LAT	*Los Angeles Times*
LOC	Library of Congress, Manuscript Division, Washington, DC
MARBL	Manuscript, Archives, and Rare Book Library, Emory University, Atlanta, GA
NARA	National Archives and Records Administration, Archives II, College Park, MD
NJHS	New Jersey Historical Society, Newark, NJ
NYPL	New York Public Library, Manuscripts and Archives Division, New York, NY
NYT	*New York Times*
OMGUS	Office of Military Government, United States
OSS	Office of Strategic Services
PBS	Peninsula Base Section
PX	post exchange
RAA	Recreation and Amusement Associations
ROHA	Rutgers Oral History Archive, Rutgers University, New Brunswick, NJ
SCAP	Supreme Commander for the Allied Powers [Japan]
SCRBC	Schomburg Center for Research in Black Culture, New York, NY

SGMML	Seeley G. Mudd Manuscript Library, Princeton University, Princeton, NJ
SHAEF	Supreme Headquarters Allied Expeditionary Force
SHC	Southern Historical Collection, Wilson Library, University of North Carolina, Chapel Hill, NC
SMG	School of Military Government
SML	Sterling Memorial Library, Yale University, New Haven, CT
SUL	Syracuse University Libraries, Special Collections Research Center, Syracuse, NY
UNRRA	United Nations Relief and Rehabilitation Administration
USAMHI	United States Army Military History Institute, Carlisle, PA
USAWC	United States Army War College
USFET	United States Forces European theater
USHMM	United States Holocaust Memorial Museum, Washington, DC
USMC	United States Marine Corps
USMC OHP	United States Marine Corps Oral History Program, Historical Branch, Washington, DC
USNR	United States Naval Reserve
UTK	Special Collections, John C. Hodges Library, University of Tennessee, Knoxville, TN
UWO	University of Wisconsin, Oshkosh, WI [archives accessed at the Wisconsin Historical Society]
UWRF	University of Wisconsin, River Falls, WI [archives accessed at the Wisconsin Historical Society]
VHP	Veterans' History Project, American Folklife Center, Library of Congress, Washington, DC

WAC	Women's Army Corps
WHS	Wisconsin Historical Society, Madison, WI
WP	*Washington Post*
WRA	War Relocation Authority
WVM	Wisconsin Veterans' Museum and Archive, Madison, WI

NOTES

INTRODUCTION

1 *The Mouse That Roared,* directed by Jack Arnold (Los Angeles: Columbia Pictures, 1959).

2 The analogy was first floated in October 2002; see David E. Sanger and Eric Schmitt, "U.S. Has a Plan to Occupy Iraq, Officials Report," *NYT,* October 11, 2002, A1. Not all well-connected Bush advisers agreed. One senior figure, alluding to Douglas MacArthur, reportedly announced that the "last thing we need is someone walking around with a corncob pipe, telling the Iraqis how to form a government"; David E. Sanger and James Dao, "Threats and Responses: The White House, U.S. Is Completing Plan to Promote a Democratic Iraq," *NYT,* January 6, 2003, 1.

3 "President George W. Bush Speaks at AEI's Annual Dinner," American Enterprise Institute, February 28, 2003, http://www.aei.org/publication/president-george-w-bush-speaks-at-aeis-annual-dinner/; "President's Radio Address," White House website, March 1, 2003, http://georgewbush-whitehouse.archives.gov/news/releases/2003/03/20030301.html.

4 On the CIA report, see *Report of the Select Committee on Intelligence on Prewar Intelligence Assessments about Postwar Iraq,* 110th Congress, First Session, Senate, May 2007, 102–103, http://www.cfr.org/iraq/report-select-committee-prewar-intelligence-assessments-postwar-iraq/p13540.

5 For sociological studies of U.S. bases overseas, see Charlotte Wolf, *Garrison Community: A Study of an Overseas American Military Colony* (Westport, CT: Greenwood, 1969); John P. Hawkins, *Army of Hope, Army of Alienation: Culture and Contradictions in the American Army Communities of Cold War Germany* (Tuscaloosa: University of Alabama Press, 2005). On the politics and practices of bases, see C. T. Sandars, *America's Overseas Garrisons: The Leasehold Empire* (New York: Oxford University Press, 2000); Kent E. Calder, *Embattled Garrisons: Comparative Base Politics and American Globalism* (Princeton, NJ: Princeton University Press, 2007); Alexander Cooley, *Base Politics: Democratic Change and the U.S. Military Overseas* (Ithaca, NY: Cornell University Press, 2008); Catherine Lutz, ed., *The Bases of Empire: The Global Struggle against U.S. Military Posts* (London: Pluto Press, 2009); David Vine, *Base Nation: How U.S. Military Bases Abroad Harm America and the World* (New York: Metropolitan Books, 2015).

6 Melissa Willard-Foster, "Planning the Peace and Enforcing the Surrender: Deterrence in the Allied Occupations of Germany and Japan," *Journal of Interdisciplinary History* 40 (2009): 33–56; Yoshiro Miwa and J. Mark Ramseyer, "The Good Occupation? Law in the Allied Occupation of Japan," *Washington University Global Studies Law Review* 8 (2009): 363–378, http://openscholarship.wustl.edu/law_globalstudies/vol8/iss2/13/; Bruce Cumings, *The Origins of the Korean War: Liberation and the Emergence of Separate Regimes, 1945–1947* (Princeton, NJ: Princeton University Press, 1981).

7 Donald Rumsfeld was reported to "demur" at use of the word "occupation" in October 2002; David S. Broder, "Rumsfeld's Rush," *WP,* October 16, 2002, A25; Scott Wilson, "Bremer Adopts Firmer Tone for US Occupation of Iraq," *WP,* May 26, 2003, A13. On the international law of occupation and its application to Iraq, see Eyal Benvenisti, *The International Law of Occupation* (Princeton, NJ: Princeton University Press, 2004), xi–xv.

8 "American Gauleiters," *CDT,* January 8, 1943, 12.

9 Benjamin Akzin, *Data on Military Government in Occupied Areas, with Special Reference to the United States and Great Britain* (Washington, DC: Library of Congress, Legislative Reference Service, 1942); Ralph H. Gabriel, "Preliminary Survey of American Experience with Military Government," February 7, 1944, folder 12, box 8, Ralph Henry Gabriel Papers, SML; Ralph H. Gabriel, "American Experience with Military Government," *American Political Science Review* 37 (1943): 417–438; Ralph H. Gabriel, "American Experience with Military Government," *AHR* 49 (1944): 630–643.

10 John Hersey, foreword to *A Bell for Adano* (New York: Alfred A. Knopf, 1944), v–vii.

11 Paul Fussell, introduction to *The Gallery,* by John Horne Burns (New York: New York Review Books, [1947] 2004), ix. As employed by Studs Terkel, whose compendious oral history bears that name and helped popularize it, the phrase carried a decidedly ironic ring; *"The Good War": An Oral History of World War Two* (New York: Pantheon Books, 1984).

12 Gallup Organization, Gallup poll, November 1944, "What do you think we should do with Japan, as a country, after the war?," USGALLUP, 122044.R02A (Storrs, CT: Roper Center for Public Opinion Research, iPOLL); Nathaniel Peffer, "Occupy Japan?," *Harper's Magazine,* April 1944, 385–390; FDR quoted by William I. Hitchcock, *The Bitter Road to Freedom: A New History of the Liberation of Europe* (New York: Free Press, 2008), 175.

13 This was a matter of public record; "Says Rule by Army Will End on Peace," *NYT,* December 30, 1942, 6. On planning and training for occupation, see Harry L. Coles and Albert K. Weinberg, *Civil Affairs: Soldiers Become Governors* (Washington, DC: Office of the Chief of Military History, Department of the Army, 1964).

14 The treatment of France and Belgium has attracted growing critical attention. See Hitchcock, *Bitter Road;* Peter Schrijvers, *Liberators: The Allies and Belgian Society, 1944–1945* (Cambridge: Cambridge University Press, 2009); Alice Kaplan, *The Interpreter* (Chicago: University of Chicago Press, 2005); Mary Louise Roberts, *What Soldiers Do: Sex and the American GI in World War II France* (Chicago: University of Chicago Press, 2013). On wartime rhetorical anticolonialism, see Elizabeth Borgwardt, *A New Deal for the World: America's Vision for Human Rights* (Cambridge, MA: Belknap Press of Harvard University Press, 2005). On the Allies' postwar treatment of Japan's empire, see Ronald H. Spector, *In the Ruins of Empire: The Japanese Surrender and the Battle for Postwar Asia* (New York: Random House, 2007).

15 For a brief overview, see John Whiteclay Chambers II, "Military Government and Occupation," in *Encyclopedia of the American Military,* vol. 3, ed. John E. Jessup (New York: Charles Scribner's Sons, 1994), 1850–1861.

16 Milo Flaten to Mom and Pop, April 12, 1945, folder 8, box 1, Milo G. Flaten Papers, WVM.

17 On V-E Day there were 3,077,000 U.S. troops in the European theater; Earl F. Ziemke, *The U.S. Army in the Occupation of Germany, 1944–1946* (Washington, DC: Center of Military History, U.S. Army, 1975), 320. Numbers of troops were rapidly reduced in the months thereafter. The initial occupation force of Japan numbered around 350,000; Hajo Holborn, *American Military Government: Its Organization and Policies* (Washington, DC: Infantry Journal Press, 1947), xi.

18 *Mount Up! The History of Company C, 17th Armored Infantry Battalion, 12th Armored Division,* n.d., p. 16, folder 12, box 8, Sherman B. Lans Papers, WWII Collection, MS.2012, UTK; George Patton Diary, May 13, 1945, folder 11, box 3, George S. Patton Papers, LOC. Abruptly terminated wartime histories include Rick Atkinson, *The Guns at Last Light: The War in Western Europe, 1944–1945* (New York: Henry Holt, 2013); Edwin P. Hoyt, *The GI's War: The Story of American Soldiers in World War II* (New York: McGraw Hill, 1988); Peter Schrijvers, *The Crash of Ruin: American Combat Soldiers in Europe during World War II* (New York: New York University Press, 1998).

19 The literature is too vast to cite exhaustively. Notable recent contributions include Tony Judt, *Postwar: A History of Europe since 1945* (New York: Penguin Press, 2005); Atina Grossmann, *Jews, Germans and Allies: Close Encounters in Occupied Germany* (Princeton, NJ: Princeton University Press, 2007); Adam R. Seipp, *Strangers in the Wild Place: Refugees, Americans, and a German Town, 1945–1952* (Bloomington: Indiana University Press, 2013); Tara Zahra, *Lost Children: Reconstructing Europe's Families after World War II* (Cambridge, MA: Harvard University Press, 2011); Anna Holian, *Between National Socialism and Soviet Communism: Displaced Persons in Postwar Germany* (Ann Arbor: University of Michigan Press, 2011); Petra Goedde, *GIs and Germans: Culture, Gender, and Foreign Relations, 1945–1949* (New Haven, CT: Yale University Press, 2003); Jennifer Fay, *Theaters of Occupation: Hollywood and the Reeducation of Postwar Germany* (Minneapolis: University of Minnesota Press, 2008); Hiroshi Kitamura, *Screening Enlightenment: Hollywood and the Cultural Reconstruction of Defeated Japan* (Ithaca, NY: Cornell University Press, 2010); Sarah Kovner, *Occupying Power: Sex Workers and Servicemen in Postwar Japan* (Stanford, CA: Stanford University Press, 2012). Noah Feldman, *What We Owe Iraq: War and the Ethics of Nation Building* (Princeton, NJ: Princeton University Press, 2004), 1; John Dower, "A Warning from History: Don't Expect Democracy in Iraq," *Boston Review,* February/March 2003, http://www.bostonreview.net/BR28/dower.html.

20 James Dobbins et al., *America's Role in Nation-Building: From Germany to Iraq* (Santa Monica: Rand, 2003); Francis Fukuyama, ed., *Nation-Building: Beyond Afghanistan and Iraq* (Baltimore: Johns Hopkins University Press, 2005). For more nuanced comparative analysis, see David M. Edelstein, *Occupational Hazard: Success and Failure in Military Occupation* (Ithaca, NY: Cornell University Press, 2008); Peter M. R. Stirk, *The Politics of Military Occupation* (Edinburgh: Edinburgh University Press, 2009).

21 Insufficient planning constitutes a dominant motif of much commentary on Iraq; Thomas E. Ricks, *Fiasco: The American Military Adventure in Iraq* (New York: Penguin Press, 2006); Larry Jay Diamond, *Squandered Victory: The American Occupation and the Bungled Effort to Bring Democracy to Iraq* (New York: Times Books, 2005); James M. Fallows, *Blind into Baghdad: America's War in Iraq* (New York: Vintage Books, 2006). On the imaginative

production of the "good war," see Paul Fussell, *Wartime: Understanding and Behavior in the Second World War* (New York: Oxford University Press, 1989); Michael C. C. Adams, *The Best War Ever: America and World War II* (Baltimore: Johns Hopkins University Press, 1994); Kenneth D. Rose, *Myth and the Greatest Generation: A Social History of Americans in World War II* (New York: Routledge, 2008); Philip Beidler, *The Good War's Greatest Hits: World War II and American Remembering* (Athens: University of Georgia, 1998). For an example of the enhanced present-day reputation of postwar occupation, see John W. Dower, *Cultures of War: Pearl Harbor, Hiroshima, 9–11, Iraq* (New York: W. W. Norton, 2010).

22 Wolfgang Schivelbusch, *The Culture of Defeat: On National Trauma, Mourning and Recovery* (New York: Metropolitan Books, 2003). See also Jenny Macleod, ed., *Defeat and Memory: Cultural Histories of Military Defeat in the Modern Era* (Basingstoke, UK: Palgrave Macmillan, 2008).

23 A. J. P. Taylor, *A Personal History* (London: Hamilton, 1983), 301; J. D. Salinger, "For Esmé—with Love and Squalor," *New Yorker,* April 8, 1950, 33.

24 Malcolm S. MacLean, *Adventures in Occupied Areas,* typescript memoir, July 1975, p. 127, box 1, Malcolm S. MacLean Papers, USAMHI.

25 Maurice to Laya Kurtz, May 3, 1945, folder 4, box 1, Maurice Kurtz Papers, SHC. On identity-swapping soldiers coming home from war, see Natalie Zemon Davis, *The Return of Martin Guerre* (Cambridge, MA: Harvard University Press, 1983). For a more recent fictional instance, Don Draper, protagonist of the AMC series *Mad Men,* is a Korean War veteran who assumes a dead soldier's identity in the hope of escaping his own burdensome past.

26 Ken Adelman, "Cakewalk in Iraq," *WP,* February 13, 2002, A27. George Packer attributes the "sweets and flowers" phrase to Kanan Makiya, whose projections colored Cheney's claim that U.S. troops would be "greeted as liberators"; *The Assassins' Gate: America in Iraq* (New York: Farrar, Straus, and Giroux, 2005), 96–98.

27 Marion Sanders to T. L. Barnard, April 25, 1945, "Liberated Nations of Europe: Information Problems of the U.S. Government after VE Day," box 2, Charles Hulten Papers, Harry S. Truman Library, Independence, MO.

1. PREPARING TO OCCUPY

1 Malcolm S. MacLean, *Adventures in Occupied Areas,* typescript memoir, July 1975, p. 12, box 1, Malcolm S. MacLean Papers, USAMHI; H. E. Robison, preface to ibid., ii. For biographical information, see "Biographical Sketch of Malcolm S. MacLean (b. 1893)," University of Minnesota Archives, 2002, http://special.lib.umn.edu/findaid/xml/uarc00120 .xml.

2 *New Republic,* August 2, 1943, quoted in War Department, memo for chief, Analysis Branch, "Press Views on Allied Military Government in Operation," August 9, 1943, folder "AMG General File, January–November 1943," box 17, Charles Poletti Papers, CU; "U.S. Is Training Men to Govern Occupied Areas," *CDT,* December 31, 1942, 2; "Yankee Gauleiters," *CDT,* August 14, 1943, 10; "American Gauleiters," *CDT,* January 8, 1943, 12. The idea that

empire overseas would return home to pollute domestic political life was a well-worn theme of conservative anti-imperialism with antecedents in turn-of-the-century debates over empire. See Paul Kramer, *The Blood of Government: Race, Empire, the United States, and the Philippines* (Chapel Hill: University of North Carolina Press, 2006).

3 Susan A. Brewer, *Why America Fights: Patriotism and War Propaganda from the Philippines to Iraq* (New York: Oxford University Press, 2009); Elizabeth Borgwardt, *A New Deal for the World: America's Vision for Human Rights* (Cambridge, MA: Belknap Press of Harvard University Press, 2005). On the influence of colonialist thought on wartime debates over the shape and remit of the United Nations, see Mark Mazower, *No Enchanted Palace: The End of Empire and the Ideological Origins of the United Nations* (Princeton, NJ: Princeton University Press, 2009).

4 Col. Harry A. Auer, JAGD, to Brig. Gen. Wade H. Haislip, G-1, September 5, 1941, G-1 files, 16308-125, in Harry L. Coles and Albert K. Weinberg, eds., *Civil Affairs: Soldiers Become Governors* (Washington, DC: Office of the Chief of Military History, Department of the Army, 1964), 6; Gullion to Brig. Gen. Edwin Watson, secretary to the president, February 6, 1943, in Coles and Weinberg, *Civil Affairs,* 28; Arthur A. Ekirch, *The Civilian and the Military: A History of the American Antimilitarist Tradition* (New York: Oxford University Press, 1956); William M. Leary, "Books, Soldiers and Censorship during the Second World War," *American Quarterly* 20 (1968): 237–245. On the interdepartmental debates, see folder 5136, School of Military Government (Charlottesville, VA) 1942, box 3, Official File 5130, FDRL; Coles and Weinberg, *Civil Affairs,* 3–29; Earl F. Ziemke, *The U.S. Army in the Occupation of Germany, 1944–1946* (Washington, DC: Center of Military History, U.S. Army, 1975), 2–33; Office of the Provost Marshal General, *History of Military Government Training* (Washington, DC: Office of the Provost Marshal General, 1945).

5 Memo, Col. Robert N. Young, October 30, 1942, in Coles and Weinberg, *Civil Affairs,* 23. FDR's preference for civilian rule was well publicized, inter alia by Drew Pearson's "Washington Merry-Go-Round" tattle column; "Roosevelt Skeptical of Army Rule," *WP,* January 5, 1943, B7; Allen W. Gullion, "Military Government," *Cavalry Journal* 52 (1943): 60.

6 On "second string" faculty, see Roosevelt to Stimson, October 29, 1942, in Coles and Weinberg, *Civil Affairs,* 22. Jonathan Daniels to FDR, n.d. [circa late November 1942], folder OF 5136, box 3, Official File OF 5130, FDRL.

7 Wayne Coy to FDR, August 11, 1942, folder OF 5136, box 3, Official File OF 5130, FDRL; Jonathan Daniels to FDR, n.d. [circa late November 1942], folder OF 5136, box 3, Official File OF 5130, FDRL. On Miller's remonstrations, see Jonathan Daniels, diary, November 19, 1942, box 71, Jonathan W. Daniels Papers, SHC. MacLean, *Adventures in Occupied Areas,* 8.

8 Jennings L. Wagoner and Robert L. Baxter, *Higher Education Goes to War: The Impact of World War II on the University of Virginia,* 1992, MS S 13525, ASSSCL; Army Service Forces, School of Military Government, Charlottesville, General Orders No. 4, May 16, 1944, box 1, Records of the SMG, ASSSCL; Frank Kelley, "Course at Virginia University Looks to Postwar World," *WP,* January 3, 1943, S4.

9 The median age of the third class, joined by MacLean, was forty-five; Harold Callender, "Occupation Duties Taught to Officers," *NYT,* April 12, 1943, 42. Anon. letter to

"faculty, family and friends," August 22, 1943, folder 45, box 3, Mina Curtiss Collection, SML.

10 Ziemke, *U.S. Army,* 7; Thomas W. Huntington, "AMGOT—a Symbol for Order," *WP,* August 15, 1943, B1; Miller to Gullion, January 10, 1942, in Office of the Provost Marshal General, *History of Military Government Training,* vol. 1, tab 2; Arnold Wolfers, "How to Treat the Germans," SMG Class III, May 1, 1943, box 1, School of Military Government Records, 1943–1945, RG-6/34.981, ASSSCL.

11 Office of the Provost Marshal General, *History of Military Government Training,* vol. 1.

12 Jessica Reinisch, "Internationalism in Relief: The Birth (and Death) of UNRRA," in *Post-war Reconstruction in Europe: International Perspectives, 1945–1949,* ed. Mark Mazower, Jessica Reinisch, and David Feldman (Oxford: Oxford University Press, 2011), 258–289; Ben Shephard, "Becoming Planning Minded: The Theory and Practice of Relief, 1940–1945," *Journal of Contemporary History* 43 (July 2008): 405–419; Saul K. Padover to Ickes, January 8, 1943, folder OF 5136, School of Military Government (Charlottesville, VA) 1943, box 3, Official File OF 5130, FDRL.

13 Margaret Mead, "Food and Feeding in Occupied Territory," *Public Opinion Quarterly* 7 (1943): 618–628; War Department, "Address by Major General Allen W. Gullion, PMG, U.S. Army, at Convention of the Kentucky Press Association, Louisville, Kentucky, January 28, 1943," press release, box 1, SMG Records, ASSSCL.

14 Office of the Provost Marshal General, *History of Military Government Training,* vol. 1, *The Program—General,* 3, 4.

15 Richard V. Van Wagenen, lecture notes on Major Barber, May 3, 1943, box 1, Richard V. Van Wagenen Papers, USAMHI.

16 Cornelius W. Wickersham, "Military Government," *Federal Bar Association Journal* 5 (May 1943): 43. On these Caribbean and Central American occupations, see Mary A. Renda, *Taking Haiti: Military Occupation and the Culture of U.S. Imperialism, 1915–1940* (Chapel Hill: University of North Carolina Press, 2001); Alan McPherson, *The Invaded: How Latin Americans and Their Allies Fought and Ended U.S. Occupations* (New York: Oxford University Press, 2014). On interwar training, see Office of the Provost Marshal General, *History of Military Government Training,* 3; H. A. Smith, *Military Government* (Fort Leavenworth, KS: General Service Schools Press, 1920); War Department, *Basic Field Manual on Military Government—Field Manual 27-5* (Washington, DC: War Department, 1940); Walter M. Hudson, *Army Diplomacy: American Military Occupation and Foreign Policy after World War II* (Lexington: University Press of Kentucky, 2015), 27–59.

17 Students read David Yancey Thomas's primer, *A History of Military Government in Newly Acquired Territory of the United States* (New York: Columbia University Press, 1904). Ralph H. Gabriel, "American Experience with Military Government," *American Political Science Review* 37 (1943): 420. Scripts of all Gabriel's lectures can be found in his papers at Yale. See, in particular, "Preliminary Survey of American Experience with Military Government," SMG Class VII, February 7, 1944, folder 306, box 16, Ralph Henry Gabriel Papers, SML.

18 Ickes to FDR, December 28, 1942, folder OF 5136, School of Military Government (Charlottesville, VA) 1942, and Padover to Ickes, January 8, 1943, folder OF 5136, School of

Military Government (Charlottesville, VA) 1943, box 3, Official File OF 5130, FDRL. On Roosevelt and Haiti, including FDR's interest in purchasing a plantation while on navy business, see Hans Schmidt, *The United States Occupation of Haiti, 1915–1934* (New Brunswick, NJ: Rutgers University Press, 1995), 110–111.

19 Paul Shipman Andrews, "Liaison," SMG Class IV, May 18, 1943, and Thomas H. Barber, "Functions of a Civil Affairs Staff Team," June 12, 1943, RG 389, PMG, Military Govt. Division, Liaison and Studies Branch Files, 1942–46, 100.2–200.9, box 840, NARA; "Outline of Objectives," May 15, 1943, folder "School of Military Government Memos (1942)," box 41, Hardy Cross Dillard Papers, AJMLL.

20 Gabriel, "American Experience with Military Government," 419; "Preliminary Survey," 1; T. Harry Williams, "An Analysis of Some Reconstruction Attitudes," *Journal of Southern History* 12 (1946): 469–486; Bruce E. Baker, *What Reconstruction Meant: Historical Memory in the American South* (Charlottesville: University of Virginia Press, 2007). For a forthright articulation of one southerner's discomfort, see Leon C. Standifer, *Binding Up the Wounds: An American Soldier in Occupied Germany, 1945–1946* (Baton Rouge: Louisiana State University Press, 1997), 10. Howard Fast, *Freedom Road* (New York: Duell, Sloan and Pearce, 1944), and on the author's intended message, see "Freedom Road," folder 4, box 24, Council on Books in Wartime Records, SGMML.

21 Woodrow Wilson, "The Reconstruction of the Southern States," *Atlantic Monthly,* January 1901, 1–15; William A. Dunning, "Military Government during Reconstruction," in *Essays on the Civil War and Reconstruction* (Gloucester, MA: Peter Smith, [1897] 1969). On how this conception of the past shaped Wilson's attitude toward Germany's postwar treatment, see Gideon Rose, *How Wars End: A History of American Intervention from World War I to Afghanistan* (New York: Simon and Schuster, 2010), 31–32; on race and self-rule, see Erez Manela, *The Wilsonian Moment: Self-Determination and the International Origins of Anticolonial Nationalism* (New York: Oxford University Press, 2007).

22 War Department, *Basic Field Manual, FM 27-5, Military Government* (Washington, DC: Government Printing Office, 1940), 5. The Hunt Report was required reading at Charlottesville; United States Army, *American Military Government of Occupied Germany, 1918–1920: Report of the Officer in Charge of Civil Affairs, Third Army and American Forces in Germany* (Washington, DC: Government Printing Office, [1921] 1943). Gabriel, "American Experience with Military Government," 639; Justin Williams, "From Charlottesville to Tokyo: Military Government Training and Democratic Reforms in Occupied Japan," *Pacific Historical Review* 52 (1982): 416.

23 Jeremi Suri, *Liberty's Surest Guardian: American Nation-Building from the Founders to Obama* (New York: Free Press, 2011); Gregory P. Downs, *After Appomattox: Military Occupation and the Ends of War* (Cambridge, MA: Harvard University Press, 2015). On the bronze statues, see Harold Callender, "Trained to Govern," *NYT Magazine,* May 2, 1943, SM10; "Ode to the Overseas-ers," Yearbook of the Second Class, box 2, Records of the SMG, ASSSCL.

24 "Patterson Says Military Rule Formulated for Occupied Areas," *WP,* December 30, 1942, 13; "Songs of the Third Class," folder "SMG Clippings," box 41, Hardy Cross Dillard Papers, AJMLL.

25 *Inquiry into Army and Navy Educational Program, Hearings before the Committee on Military Affairs, House of Representatives, Seventy-Eighth Congress, Second Session,* January 21 and 25, 1944 (Washington, DC: Government Printing Office, 1944), 14 (testimony of Col. Jesse Miller).

26 Alice Myers, "B. P. W. Told Why Women Are Barred from AMG," *Christian Science Monitor,* March 10, 1944, 5; "4 WACS Take GI Government," *Atlanta Constitution,* July 31, 1944, 9.

27 Gullion, PMG, to chief, Civil Affairs Division, "Plan for Civil Affairs Officers for Duty in Japan," memorandum, December 31, 1943, reproduced in Office of the Provost Marshal General, *History of Military Government Training,* vol. 1, tab 22; James C. McNaughton, *Nisei Linguists: Japanese Americans in the Military Intelligence Service during World War II* (Washington, DC: Department of the Army, 2006), 24; "First AMG Course Is Opened to WACs," *NYT,* July 31, 1944, 16.

28 McNaughton, *Nisei Linguists,* 15–21; Donald Richardson, *Random Recollections,* typescript memoir, 1991, p. 1, MS.2653, Donald Richardson World War II Memoir, UTK.

29 "Mundt Urges Army Run Jap Alien Centers," *WP,* June 27, 1943, M13. Although Mundt's plan came to naught, anthropologists working in WRA camps did supply the military with "intelligence" about Japanese psychology that might facilitate Japan's later occupation; David H. Pryce, *Anthropological Intelligence: The Deployment and Neglect of American Anthropology in the Second World War* (Durham, NC: Duke University Press, 2008).

30 Gullion to chief, "Plan for Civil Affairs Officers for Duty in Japan." Not all of the CATS offered Japanese language instruction. The latter was part of the curriculum at Harvard University, Northwestern University, Stanford University, Yale University, the University of Chicago, and the University of Michigan. The Signal Corps trained students at Stanford, Georgetown, and a special school in Arlington. See McNaughton, *Nisei Linguists,* 159–160. On the "hellhole," see Tamotsu Shibutani, *The Derelicts of Company K: A Sociological Study of Demoralization* (Berkeley: University of California Press, 1978), 87. Eiichiro Azuma, "Brokering Race, Culture, and Citizenship: Japanese Americans in Occupied Japan and Postwar National Inclusion," *Journal of American-East Asian Relations* 16 (2009): 189.

31 Richardson, *Random Recollections,* 6; Kelli Y. Nakamura, "'They Are Our Human Secret Weapons': The Military Intelligence Service and the Role of Japanese-Americans in the Pacific War and in the Occupation of Japan," *Historian* 70 (2008): 60; Tad Ichinokuchi, *John Aiso and the M.I.S.: Japanese-American Soldiers in the Military Intelligence Service, World War II* (Los Angeles: Military Intelligence Club of Southern California, 1988).

32 Richardson, *Random Recollections,* 12–16, 36. Grant K. Goodman, another graduate of Michigan, Camp Savage, and Fort Snelling, includes a photograph of a rehearsal of "Nips in the Bud" in his memoir, *America's Japan: The First Year, 1945–1946* (New York: Fordham University Press, 2005).

33 Anon. letter to "faculty, family and friends," August 22, 1943, folder 45, box 3, Mina Curtiss Collection; George McCaffrey Diary, May 10, 1943, box 1, George Herbert McCaffrey Papers, SUL.

34 William A. Lessa claims to have coined this nickname; *Spearhead Governatore: Remembrances of the Campaign in Italy* (Malibu: Undena, 1985), 16. The rhapsodic description

comes from Maurice Neufeld Diary, June 1, 1943, box 1, Maurice F. Neufeld Papers, LOC; see also George McCaffrey Diary, May 27, 1943, box 1, George Herbert McCaffrey Papers. Henry M. Adams, "Allied Military Government in Sicily, 1943," *Military Affairs* 15 (1951): 157; Theodore J. Shannon, AFC 2001/001/68906, video recording, VHP.

35 Eisenhower to Combined Chiefs of Staff, November 14, 1942, quoted by Andrew Buchanan, *American Grand Strategy in the Mediterranean during World War II* (New York: Cambridge University Press, 2014), 72. On these tremors and Washington's management of them, see Buchanan, *American Grand Strategy,* ch. 4; Steven Casey, *Cautious Crusade: Franklin D. Roosevelt, American Public Opinion, and the War against Nazi Germany* (New York: Oxford University Press, 2001), 110–128.

36 Dean S. Fleming, *The Last "Good" War: A Contemporary, Eye Witness Account of World War II, 1940–1945,* typescript memoir, folio 6, p. 1, box 1, Dean S. Fleming Papers, USAMHI; "The Kernel's Journal," p. 8, box 1, George Herbert McCaffrey Papers; John Horne Burns, *The Gallery* (New York: New York Review Books, [1947] 2004), 49; "The Kernel's Journal," 8; George McCaffrey Diary, June 1, 1943, box 1, George Herbert McCaffrey Papers.

37 Fleming, *The Last "Good" War,* folio 7, 11–12; Rick Atkinson, *The Day of Battle: The War in Sicily and Italy, 1943–1944* (New York: Henry Holt, 2007).

38 Harold Callender, "AMGOT Taking Over as Allies Advance," *NYT,* July 25, 1943, E5; Herbert L. Matthews, "We Test a Plan for Governing Europe," *NYT Magazine,* August 22, 1943, SM3; *Raleigh News and Observer* quoted in War Department, memo for chief, Analysis Branch, "Press Views on Allied Military Government in Operation," August 9, 1943, folder "AMG General File January–November 1943," box 17, Charles Poletti Papers; Benedict S. Alper, *Love and Politics in Wartime: Letters to My Wife, 1943–45* (Urbana: University of Illinois Press, 1992), xix.

39 John Hersey, *A Bell for Adano* (New York: Alfred A. Knopf, 1944); unless otherwise noted, citations refer to this edition. Paul Osborn, *A Bell for Adano: A Play in Three Acts* (New York: Dramatists' Play Service, 1945); *A Bell for Adano,* directed by Henry King (Los Angeles: Twentieth Century Fox, 1945). On the novel's ideological work, see Andrew Buchanan, " 'Good Morning, Pupil!': American Representations of Italianness and the Occupation of Italy, 1943–1945," *Journal of Contemporary History* 43 (2008): 217–240; Susan L. Carruthers, " 'Produce More Joppolos:' John Hersey's *A Bell for Adano* and the Making of the 'Good Occupation,' " *Journal of American History* 100 (2014): 1086–1113.

40 John Hersey, "AMGOT at Work," *Life,* August 23, 1943, 29; Toscani Notebook and Hersey Notebook, box 27, John Hersey Papers, BRB. Hersey referred to his "angry haste" in a preface to the Modern Library edition; John Hersey, *A Bell for Adano* (New York: Modern Library, 1946), v. Hersey, *A Bell for Adano,* 48. Hersey based an episode in which Marvin orders the shooting of a dilatory mule on a well-known instance of Patton's intemperance. He was also unfavorably impressed by Patton's striking a shell-shocked soldier; Carlo D'Este, *Patton: A Genius for War* (New York: HarperCollins, 1995), 533–555. Hersey wrote *Adano* before this incident was publicized in America, but the novel appeared after its disclosure; "Italy Invaded à la American: Fiction Story Based on Facts," *Atlanta Constitution,* February 13, 1944, 6D.

41 Hersey, *A Bell for Adano,* 45, 117, 269.

42 Ibid., vii.

43 Diana Trilling, "Fiction in Review," *Nation,* February 12, 1944, 194–195. More typical was Ben Ray Redman's gushing "A Man of Good Will," *Saturday Review,* February 12, 1944, 8. British diplomat Harold Nicholson lauded Joppolo's Wilsonian qualities; Harold Nicholson, "Marginal Comment," *Spectator,* November 3, 1944, 406. F. Scott and Zelda Fitzgerald's daughter, meanwhile, hailed Joppolo as a Christlike figure; Scottie Fitzgerald to Hersey, March 3, 1944, box 19, John Hersey Papers. John Hersey, "Soldiers Come Home to Adano," *Reader's Digest,* June 1944, 92–94. On the Council on Books in Wartime, see Robert O. Ballou, *A History of the Council on Books in Wartime, 1942–46* (New York: Country Life, 1946). On its efforts to promote *Adano,* see "Council Names Hersey Novel as New 'Imperative,'" *Publishers' Weekly,* March 25, 1944, 1287–1289. Archibald Ogden to Lewis Gannett, March 22, 1944, folder 10, "Imperative Book Plan #5," box 10, Council on Books in Wartime Records, SGMML; Albert Einstein to Hersey, August 6, 1944, box 19, John Hersey Papers.

44 Margaret Clement to Hersey, March 2, 1944, box 27, John Hersey Papers; Cpl. Sam Pillsbury to Hersey, box 19, John Hersey Papers.

45 Maurice Neufeld Diary, January 6, 1944, folder 1, box 1, Maurice F. Neufeld Papers; Hinda to Maurice, February 7, 1944, Maurice to Hinda, March 2, 1944, and Maurice to Hinda, March 27, 1944, folder 7, box 5, Maurice F. Neufeld Papers; Maurice to Hinda, May 7, 1944, folder 1, box 6, Maurice F. Neufeld Papers.

46 Poletti, manuscript chapter, "To Palermo," folder "AMG General File January–November 1943," box 17, Charles Poletti Papers. He also contributed an article to *American Magazine* entitled "Scrubbing Up after the Dictator," November 1944. Deane Keller, "American Impressions of Italians and Italian Customs," lecture, Yale University CATS, September 1943, p. 2, in Office of the Provost Marshal General, *History of Military Government Training,* vol. 3.

47 Maurice to Hinda, November 15, 1943, folder 6, box 5, Maurice F. Neufeld Papers; Hinda to Maurice, March 7, 1944, folder 7, box 5, Maurice F. Neufeld Papers.

48 Philip Broadhead to Mary Broadhead, December 23, 1943, folder 23, box 3, MS.2012, World War II Collection, UTK; Fleming, *The Last "Good" War,* folio 8, p. 7, box 1, Dean S. Fleming Papers; Lt. Col. Poletti, Civil Affairs Report, HQ Seventh Army, July 15, 1943, folder "AMG General File, January–November, 1943," box 17, Charles Poletti Papers.

49 Hersey, *A Bell for Adano,* 148, 115–120; Toscani Notebook, box 27, John Hersey Papers; reports of AMGOT divisions up to November 1, 1943, folder "Part III," box 23, Frank J. McSherry Papers, USAMHI; Maurice Neufeld Diary, July 22, 1943, folder 1, box 1, Maurice F. Neufeld Papers; Thomas H. Barber, "Experiences in Military Government," February 16, 1943, box 1, Records of the SMG, ASSSCL.

50 "Panorama of Sicily" (1944), Excerpts from Charlie's Letters, folder 1, box 1, Maurice F. Neufeld Papers.

51 SHAEF, *Civil Affairs Public Safety Manual of Procedures in Liberated Territories* (n.p., 1944), 7; AMGOT Proclamations for Sicily, box 16, Frank J. McSherry Papers; petition "To the Civil Affairs Officer Marsala," enclosed with Maurice's V-mail to Hinda, January 31, 1944, folder 7, box 5, Maurice F. Neufeld Papers.

52 Maurice Neufeld Diary, July 22, 1943, folder 1, box 1, Maurice F. Neufeld Papers; MacLean, *Adventures in Occupied Areas,* 91.

53 Alan Moorehead, *Eclipse* (New York: Coward-McCann, 1945), 62; Toscani Notebook, box 27, John Hersey Papers; Poletti, Civil Affairs Report, HQ Seventh Army, July 15, 1943, folder "AMG General File, January–November, 1943," box 17, Charles Poletti Papers. See also Charles Poletti, "Bread, Spaghetti, but No Fascisti," *NYT Magazine,* July 16, 1944, SM8.

54 Poletti Notebook, July 17, 1943, folder "AMG General File, January–November, 1943," box 17, Charles Poletti Papers; Poletti, Civil Affairs Report, HQ Seventh Army, July 15, 1943, folder "AMG General File, January–November, 1943," box 17, Charles Poletti Papers; MacLean, *Adventures in Occupied Areas,* 91; Henry M. Adams, "Allied Military Government in Sicily, 1943," *Military Affairs* 15 (1951): 163.

55 Poletti to John McCloy, September 27, 1943, box 17, Charles Poletti Papers. On the revised AMGOT acronym, see Robert M. Hill and Elizabeth Craig Hill, *In the Wake of War: Memoirs of an Alabama Military Government Officer in World War II Italy* (Tuscaloosa: University of Alabama Press, 1982), 17.

56 Leon T. David, "Italy: Special Service Section," October 26, 1943, box 1, Leon T. David Papers, USAMHI; Maurice Neufeld Diary, January 6, 1944, folder 1, box 1, Maurice F. Neufeld Papers.

57 "Mr. Poletti and the AMGOT," *CDT,* July 25, 1943, 14; Poletti to Milton Diamond, August 30, 1944, box 18, Charles Poletti Papers. Other columnists, particularly Herbert Matthews, were significantly more favorable. Royall notebook, folder "Notes on ACC and Military Government," box 21, Kenneth C. Royall Papers, SHC.

58 War Department, memo for chief, Analysis Branch, "Press Views on Allied Military Government in Operation," August 9, 1943, box 17, Charles Poletti Papers. Pressures on immigrants to assimilate were such that many Nisei were not thoroughly bilingual, contrary to popular assumptions; Takashi Fujitani, *Race for Empire: Koreans as Japanese and Japanese as Americans during World War II* (Berkeley: University of California Press, 2011).

59 Maurice F. Neufeld, "The Failure of AMG in Italy," *Public Administration Review* 6 (1946): 137–148.

60 Hersey, *A Bell for Adano,* 14; Anthony Muto to Allyn Butterfield, February 24, 1944, RG 107, Records of the Office of the Secretary of War, Bureau of Public Relations, Correspondence relating to Motion Pictures with Military Themes, Motion Picture Scripts, 1942–1946, box 8, NARA; Neufeld, "Failure of AMG," 137. Henry Adams similarly complained that trainees at Chréa had ignored the detailed planning process and "considered their worldly experience and natural abilities . . . sufficient to handle the job"; "Allied Military Government in Sicily," 158.

61 David W. Ellwood, *Italy 1943–1945* (Leicester: Leicester University Press, 1985), 2; Max Ascoli, "Italy, an Experiment in Reconstruction," *Annals of the American Academy of Political and Social Science* 234 (1944): 37; Callender, "AMGOT Taking Over," E5.

62 Colonel Jesse Miller quoted in "Rotary Hears of Occupation Technique," *WP,* August 12, 1943, B8. "Army authorities" quoted by Callender, "Occupation Duties Taught," 42.

2. "THE LIFE OF CONQUERORS"

1 George Patton Diary, March 24, 1945, folder 11, box 3, George S. Patton papers, LOC. On the call to Bradley, see Rick Atkinson, *The Guns at Last Light: The War in Western Europe, 1944–1945* (New York: Henry Holt, 2013), 558.

2 On the conquest of Germany, see Atkinson, *Guns at Last Light;* Stephen G. Fritz, *Endkampf: Soldiers, Civilians, and the Death of the Third Reich* (Lexington: University Press of Kentucky, 2004); Peter Schrijvers, *The Crash of Ruin: American Combat Soldiers in Europe during World War II* (New York: New York University Press, 1998).

3 Payne Templeton, *A Complete Change of Life: Into World War II,* typescript memoir, n.d., p. 80, box 1, Payne Templeton Papers, USAMHI.

4 "Occupation: Germany; Directive to Commander in Chief of United States Forces of Occupation Regarding the Military Government of Germany," April 1945 (hereafter cited as JCS 1067), reprinted in Carl J. Friedrich et al., *American Experiences in Military Government in World War II* (New York: Rinehart, 1948), 381–402. On U.S. policy toward Germany, see Merle Fainsod, "The Development of American Military Government Policy during World War II," in Friedrich, *American Experiences in Military Government,* 23–51; Melissa Willard-Foster, "Planning the Peace and Enforcing the Surrender: Deterrence in the Allied Occupations of Germany and Japan," *Journal of Interdisciplinary History* 40 (2009): 33–56. For the text of the Yalta agreements, see "The Yalta Conference," Lillian Goldman Law Library website, 2008, http://avalon.law.yale.edu/wwii/yalta.asp.

5 JCS 1067, 385. A roundtable on "Germany after the War" including Margaret Mead, Talcott Parsons, and Erich Fromm insisted that "Germans will try to shirk responsibility for the injuries caused to other nations by the war, and blame others for their own sufferings"; *Journal of Orthopsychiatry* 15 (1945): 405. On German reeducation, see James F. Tent, *Mission on the Rhine: Re-education and Denazification in American-Occupied Germany* (Chicago: University of Chicago Press, 1996); Richard Merritt, *Democracy Imposed: U.S. Occupation Policy and the German Public, 1945–1949* (New Haven, CT: Yale University Press, 1995); Nicholas Pronay and Keith Wilson, eds., *The Political Re-education of Germany and Her Allies after World War II* (London: Croom Helm, 1985).

6 *Your Job in Germany,* directed by Frank Capra (U.S. Army Signal Corps, 1945); Donald E. Pease, "Dr. Seuss in Ted Geisel's Never-Never Land," *MLA Notes* 126 (January 2011): 197–202.

7 Army Information Branch, United States Army, *Pocket Guide to Germany* (Washington, DC: Government Printing Office, 1944), 2, 3, 16, 17. For a fuller discussion, see Petra Goedde, *GIs and Germans: Culture, Gender, and Foreign Relations, 1945–1949* (New Haven, CT: Yale University Press, 2003), 46–51.

8 Fritz, *Endkampf,* 1–22; Perry Biddiscombe, *Werwolf! The History of the National Socialist Guerrilla Movement, 1944–1946* (Toronto: University of Toronto Press, 1998).

9 Quoted by Ferdinand A. Hermens, "The Danger of Stereotypes in Viewing Germany," *Public Opinion Quarterly* 9 (Winter 1945–1946): 420.

10 "Friedl" Anders to Anna Josephine ("Mummel") Anders, April 4, 1945, box 1, Winfred Hanns Anders Papers, USAMHI. The instantly famous phrase, "We come as

conquerors, but not as oppressors," appeared in Eisenhower's first proclamation to defeated Germany. Problems of phraseology and translation are discussed by Earl F. Ziemke, *The U.S. Army in the Occupation of Germany, 1944–1946* (Washington, DC: Center of Military History, U.S. Army, 1975), 88–89.

11 Julian Hayes to folks, March 11, 1945, folder 14, box 1, Julian Mixon Hayes Papers, SHC.

12 World War II soldier to his mom, July 13, 1945, MS.2659, UTK; Maurice to Laya Kurtz, April 9, 1945, folder 3, box 1, Maurice Kurtz Papers, SHC.

13 Maurice to Laya Kurtz, April 9, 1945, folder 3, box 1, Maurice Kurtz Papers; Bogart to family, March 1945, in Leo Bogart, *How I Earned the Ruptured Duck: From Brooklyn to Berchtesgaden in World War II* (College Station: Texas A&M Press, 2004), 89; Clarence to Eve Davis, April 18, 1945, box 1, Clarence W. Davis Letters, DMR.

14 Ziemke, *U.S. Army,* 226; Albert to Leanore Hutler, April 7, 1945, RG-19.028*01, Albert Hutler Letters, USHMM; Bogart letter, April 1945, *Ruptured Duck,* 98; Clarence to Eve Davis, April 27, 1945, box 1, Clarence W. Davis Letters. On the exposed toilet, see Pfc. Lewis W. Hollingsworth, AFC 2001/001/06057, Memoir, VHP. On the aesthetics of defeat, see Stefan-Ludwig Hoffmann, "Gazing at Ruins: German Defeat as Visual Experience," *Journal of Modern European History* 3 (2011): 328–350; Dagmar Barnouw, *Germany 1945: Views of War and Violence* (Bloomington: University of Indiana Press, 1996), 88–135; Werner Sollors, *The Temptation of Despair: Tales of the 1940s* (Cambridge, MA: Belknap Press of Harvard University Press, 2014), ch. 3.

15 The "rubble women"—*Trümmerfrauen*—became a stock image for Germans of their defeat; Elizabeth Heineman, "The Hour of the Woman: Memories of Germany's 'Crisis Years' and West German National Identity," *AHR* 101 (1996): 354–395. On more complex initial responses, German and Allied, to these women, see Atina Grossmann, *Jews, Germans and Allies: Close Encounters in Occupied Germany* (Princeton, NJ: Princeton University Press, 2007), 82–83. John Winner to Mother, Betty Jeanne, and Mema, July 4, 1945, folder 23, box 1, John D. Winner Papers, WVM; Clifton Lisle Diary, July 30, 1945, box 13, Clifton Lisle Papers, USAMHI.

16 Maurice to Laya Kurtz, May 2, 1945, folder 4, box 1, Maurice Kurtz Papers; Bogart letters, May (n.d.) and June 6, 1945, *Ruptured Duck,* 124, 125; Eisenberg to family, May 11, 1945, box 1, Sidney S. Eisenberg Papers, USAMHI; Donald Sheldon, untitled typescript memoir, extract from letter dated May 25, 1945, p. 29, box 1, Donald R. Sheldon Papers, HIA; S.Sgt. Alfred Rogers to Norma Rogers, April 15, 1945, folder 10, box 21, Norma Rogers Selections from the Letters of S/Sgt Alfred Rogers, WWII Collection, MS.2112, UTK.

17 Bogart letter to family, April 7, 1945, box 4, Leo Bogart Papers, DMR.

18 Reddick interview with Capt. Leonard Taylor, January 22, 1946, folder 12, box 1, Lawrence D. Reddick WWII Project, SCM 98-19 MG 490, SCRBC.

19 Bogart letter to family, April 7, 1945, box 4, Leo Bogart Papers.

20 Major General J. Milnor Roberts, USAWC/USAMHI Senior Officer Oral History Program, Project 83-A, 1982, USAMHI; C. Harrison Hill, oral history interview, November 29, 1995, by G. Kurt Piehler and David Tsang Hou, ROHA, http://oralhistory.rutgers.edu/interviewees/30-interview-html-text/530-hill-c-harrison.

21 Paul Mitchell, *After the Guns Have Quietened on the Western Front,* typescript memoir, in Sam Thomas, Diary Excerpts, folder 17, box 18, WWII Collection, MS.1764, UTK.

22 April 1945 marked the liberation of Ohrdruf, Nordhausen, Dachau, Buchenwald, and other camps that lay in the path of U.S. troops. The first German camp Americans encountered was Natzwiller, just outside Strasbourg near the Franco-German border, in December 1944. See Robert Abzug, *Inside the Vicious Heart: Americans and the Liberation of Nazi Concentration Camps* (New York: Oxford University Press, 1985); Dan Stone, *The Liberation of the Camps: The End of the Holocaust and Its Aftermath* (New Haven, CT: Yale University Press, 2015).

23 George Patton Diary, April 12, 1945, folder 11, box 3, George S. Patton Papers; Philip Broadhead Papers, inscription on reverse of loose photograph, folder 21, box 3, WWII Collection, MS.2012, UTK. For a recent account of American soldiers' killings "in cold blood" of SS guards at Dachau, based on the letters of army doctor Capt. David Wilsey, see Steve Friess, "A Liberator but Never Free," *New Republic,* May 17, 2005, http://www.newrepublic.com/article/121779/liberator-never-free.

24 Clifton Lisle Diary, May 10, 1945, box 13, Clifton Lisle Papers; letter from M.Sgt. Joseph Jamison to Evelyna Marable, April 25, 1945, folder 2, box 2, Lawrence D. Reddick WWII Project; Julian Hayes to sister, April 22, 1945, folder 14, box 1, Julian Mixon Hayes Papers, SHC.

25 Letter from M.Sgt. Joseph Jamison to Evelyna Marable, April 25, 1945, folder 2, box 2, Lawrence D. Reddick WWII Project.

26 On these confrontations between bystanders and victims, see Barbie Zelizer, *Remembering to Forget: Holocaust Memory through the Camera's Eye* (Chicago: University of Chicago Press, 1998); Barnouw, *Germany 1945,* ch. 1.

27 Susan L. Carruthers, "Compulsory Viewing: Concentration Camp Film and German Re-education," *Millennium: Journal of International Studies* 30 (2001): 733–759; Leonard Linton, *Kilroy Was Here,* typescript memoir, 1997, p. 75, box 1, Leonard Linton Papers, USAMHI.

28 John Maginnis Diary, April 29, 1945, box 2, John J. Maginnis Papers, USAMHI. For an edited version, see John J. Maginnis, with Robert A. Hart, *Military Government Journal: Normandy to Berlin* (Amherst: University of Massachusetts Press, 1971), 245.

29 Templeton, *Complete Change of Life,* 87; Bogart letter to family, April 14, 1945, box 4, Leo Bogart Papers.

30 Milo Flaten to Mom and Pop, May 18, 1945, folder 9, box 1, MS 1701, Milo Flaten Papers, WVM.

31 S.Sgt. Alfred Wesley Rogers to Norma Rogers, May 3, 1945, folder 10, box 21, Norma Rogers Selections from the Letters of S/Sgt Alfred Rogers, WWII Collection, MS.2112; Albert to Leanore Hutler, June 23, 1945, Albert Hutler Letters.

32 Dan Self to Mrs. Blocker, April 24, 1945, folder 25, box 17, WWII Collection, MS.1764, UTK; Paul N. Haubenreich, *Memories of Service in the Second Platoon, Company K, 407th Infantry, March 1944–Sept. 1945,* typescript memoir, n.d., ch. 10, folder 20, box 7, WWII Collection, MS.2012, UTK.

33 Jack to Mary Whitelaw, May 16, 1945, box 1, John L. Whitelaw Papers, USAMHI; Clifton Lisle Diary, June 5, 1945, box 13, Clifton Lisle Papers.

34 Bogart letter to family, April 7, 1945, box 4, Leo Bogart Papers.

35 Victor J. Fox to Mom and all, March 1945, folder 44, box 6, WWII Collection, MS.2012; Aubrey Ivey to wife, May 4, 1945, folder 60, box 7, WWII Collection, MS.2012.

36 Jack R. DeWitt quotes the army chaplain, "You can see the crucifix in the front room, but *Mein Kampf* is on the bookshelf," *Soldier Memories,* typescript memoir, 1982, p. 123, box 1, Jack R. DeWitt Papers, VWM; Jack to Mary Whitelaw, May 30, 1945, box 1, John L. Whitelaw Papers.

37 Army Information Branch, *Pocket Guide,* 1; John D. Winner to Mother, Betty Jeanne and Menna, May 14, 1945, folder 21, box 1, John D. Winner Papers; Atkinson, *Guns at Last Light,* 544–545; Seth A. Givens, "Liberating the Germans: The US Army and Looting in Germany during the Second World War," *War in History* 21 (2013): 33–54. On the looting of crucifixes, see Ziemke, *U.S. Army,* 147.

38 Marion Davy, untitled memoir, n.d., ch. 11, p. 8, Marion Davy Papers, USAMHI; Henry to Louisa Baust, April 29, 1945, folder "Letters January–April 1945," box 2, Henry Baust, Jr. Papers, USAMHI; Milo Flaten to Mom and Pop, April 14, 1945, folder 8, box 1, Milo G. Flaten Papers.

39 Alexander Gordeuk, oral history interview, April 1, 1996, by G. Kurt Piehler and Richard J. Fox, ROHA. Robert Lowenstein discusses picking up "Hitler's stamps"; Robert Lowenstein, oral history interview, June 3, 1999, by Lynn Marley and Shaun Illingworth, ROHA. William G. Van Allen mentions an officer swiping a major stamp collection; William G. Van Allen, oral history interview, May 10, 1996, by G. Kurt Piehler and Sandra Holyoak, ROHA. Sidney Eisenberg to Silv, Ralph, and Hope, October 3, 1945, and Eisenberg to folks, November 11, 1945, box 1, Sidney S. Eisenberg Papers; Samuel to Jake [Jack] Rosenfeld, n.d. [circa April] 1945, folder 125, box 4, Jack Rosenfeld Papers, KCSC.

40 William H. Puntenney, *For the Duration: An Autobiography of the Years of Military Service of a Citizen Soldier during World War II, June 6, 1941–Dec. 21, 1945,* typescript memoir, n.d., p. 128, William H. Puntenney Papers, USAMHI; Templeton, *Complete Change of Life,* 82; Henry Wales, "Yanks' Looting in Reich Called Major Problem," *CDT,* May 14, 1945, 4; Victor M. Wingate, "GI's Mailing Germany Home to Their Folks," *Baltimore Sun,* June 10, 1945, A3.

41 Reddick interview with Roi Ottley, 1946, folder 11, box 1, Lawrence D. Reddick WWII Project.

42 Clifton Lisle Diary, June 16, 1945, box 13, Clifton Lisle Papers; Linton, *Kilroy Was Here,* 79.

43 "German Civilians Turn to Looting Their Supply Depots," *NYT,* April 10, 1945, 10; Seymour Freidin, "Hannover Looted by Citizens; Volkssturm and Police Join In," *New York Herald Tribune,* April 12, 1945, 1A; Dorothy Thompson, "Revise Occupation Policies," *Atlanta Constitution,* June 8, 1945, 11; Templeton, *Complete Change of Life,* 75.

44 Bogart letter to family, April 7, 1945, box 4, Leo Bogart Papers; Marion Davy, memoir, ch. 11, pp. 9–10, Marion Davy Papers.

45 Kenneth Clouse, *Precious Friends and Vanishing Sights: The Memoirs of Kenneth Lamar Clouse,* typescript memoir, p. 18, Kenneth L. Clouse Papers, USAMHI; Leon C. Standifer, *Binding Up the Wounds: An American Soldier in Occupied Germany, 1945–1946* (Baton Rouge: Louisiana State University Press, 1997), 11; Donald Sheldon, untitled typescript memoir, enclosing excerpt from letter home dated May 14, 1945, Donald R. Sheldon Papers, HIA.

46 On diary writing as a form of martial emotional discipline, see Aaron William Moore, *Writing War: Soldiers Record the Japanese Empire* (Cambridge, MA: Harvard University Press, 2013). See also Jochen Hellbeck, " 'The Diaries of Fritzes and the Letters of Gretchens': Personal Writings from the German-Soviet War and Their Readers," *Kritika: Explorations in Russian and Eurasian History* 10 (2009): 571–606. Bogart letter to family, April 7, 1945, box 4, Leo Bogart Papers.

47 Maurice to Laya Kurtz, May 3, 1945, folder 4, box 1, Maurice Kurtz Papers.

48 Anders to mother, July 16, 1945, box 1, Winfred Hanns Anders Papers.

49 Maurice to Laya Kurtz, June 11, 1945, folder 4, box 1, Maurice Kurtz Papers.

50 Atkinson, *Guns at Last Light,* 623–626. On the emotionalism of this falling out, see Frank Costigliola, *Roosevelt's Lost Alliances: How Personal Politics Helped Start the Cold War* (Princeton, NJ: Princeton University Press, 2012), especially ch. 10.

51 John Maginnis Diary, June 23, 1945, box 2, John J. Maginnis Papers.

52 John Maginnis Diary, July 1, 1945, box 2, John J. Maginnis Papers.

53 Frank Howley, Personal Diary, June 1944–July 1946, vol. 1, pp. 78, 139, box 2, Frank L. Howley Papers, USAMHI.

54 Edward Laughlin, *World War II Memoirs: A Paratrooper's Journey,* typescript memoir, 1999, Edward Laughlin Memoir, WWII Collection, MS.2669, UTK; Clifton Lisle Diary, August 3, 1945, box 13, Clifton Lisle Papers.

3. STAGING VICTORY IN ASIA

1 Nicholas Pope Diary, "My Stay in Japan," September 2, 1945, Nicholas Pope Collection, USAMHI.

2 *Eighth U.S. Army in Japan, 30 August 1945–1 May 1946* (Tokyo: Eighth U.S. Army Printing Plant, Boonjudo Printing Works, 1946), 2.

3 Allan S. Clifton, *Time of Fallen Blossoms* (New York: Alfred A. Knopf, 1951), vii; Robert L. Eichelberger, *Our Jungle Road to Tokyo* (New York: Viking, 1950), 262.

4 MacArthur quoted in "U.S. Occupies Japan," *Life,* September 10, 1945, 29. Eichelberger recorded MacArthur's expressed desire to "live in the Palace in Tokyo or if not there, the Imperial Hotel," Eichelberger Diary, August 15, 1945, box 1, Robert L. Eichelberger Papers, DMR. Eichelberger, *Jungle Road,* 264.

5 William Manchester, *American Caesar: Douglas MacArthur, 1880–1964* (New York: Back Bay Books, 2008), 451; John W. Dower, *Embracing Defeat: Japan in the Wake of World War II* (New York: W. W. Norton, 1999), 41; Clovis Byers to My Precious Ones, September 2, 1945, box 30, Clovis E. Byers Papers, HIA.

6 Dower, *Embracing Defeat,* 41.

7 Kase ("penitent schoolboys") quoted by Manchester, *American Caesar,* 451. Dower, *Embracing Defeat,* 41; Eichelberger Diary, August 20, 1945, box 1, Robert L. Eichelberger Papers. This symbolic deployment of male physique foreshadows the use of African American MPs as guards for the defendants at Nuremberg; Werner Sollors, *The Temptation of Despair: Tales of the 1940s* (Cambridge, MA: Belknap Press of Harvard University Press, 2014), 187.

8 MacArthur quoted in Manchester, *American Caesar,* 444. Russell Brines, *MacArthur's Japan* (Philadelphia: J. B. Lippincott, 1948), 54; Eichelberger Diary, September 2, 1945, box 1, Robert L. Eichelberger Papers; Byers to Precious Ones, September 2, 1945, box 30, Clovis E. Byers Papers.

9 Byers to My Darlings, September 1, 1945, box 30, Clovis E. Byers Papers.

10 Byers to My Darlings, September 1, 1945, and September 2, 1945, box 30, Clovis E. Byers Papers.

11 For a photograph of the souvenir card, see Callie Oettinger, "September 2, 1945: Formal Surrender of Japan in Images," The History Reader, September 2, 2011, http://www .thehistoryreader.com/modern-history/september-2-1945-formal-surrender-japan-images/.

12 Eichelberger, *Jungle Road,* 264; Eichelberger Diary, September 2, 1945, box 1, Robert L. Eichelberger Papers.

13 M.Sgt. John C. Plock to Cpl. Harold Kahlert, September 11, 1945, Harald P. Kahlert Papers, WVM. MacArthur's remark, made after having just descended at Atsugi, was ostensibly directed to Eichelberger, but it was delivered with sufficient theatrical flourish—and at high enough volume—to be widely reported in the press; Eichelberger, *Jungle Road,* 262; "MacArthur Arrives," *Life,* September 19, 1945, 30. Harry to Jinny McMasters, September 15, 1945, Harry L. McMasters Letters to His Wife, HIA.

14 On press censorship, see Eiji Takemae, *Inside GHQ: The Allied Occupation of Japan and Its Legacy* (New York: Continuum, 2002), 67. "M'Arthur Outlines Policy for Japan; Will Let Regime Carry Out Orders, with Troops Ready to Act if Needed," *NYT,* September 10, 1945, 1; Don Caswell, "Don't Display Underwear, or Bare Toes, Girls Told," *Atlanta Constitution,* September 18, 1945, 18.

15 John Curtis Perry, *Beneath the Eagle's Wings: Americans in Occupied Japan* (New York: Dodd, Mead, 1980), xiii; Lee Kennett, *GI: The American Soldier in World War II* (New York: Scribner, 1987), 222.

16 On planning and casualty estimates, see Nicholas Evan Sarantakes, *Keystone: The American Occupation of Okinawa and U.S.-Japanese Relations* (College Station: Texas A&M University Press, 2000), 3. Clellan S. Ford, "Occupation Experiences on Okinawa," *Annals of the American Academy of Political and Social Science* 267 (1950): 175–182. On casualties, see Arnold G. Fisch, *Military Government in the Ryukyu Islands, 1945–1950* (Washington, DC: Center of Military History, United States Army, 1988), 42.

17 On wild shooting, see "Odyssey of Robert Malcolm Titus," August 26, 1945, box 5, William A. Titus Papers, UWO. Draft paper, "About the Okinawans," 24th Corps HQ, April 20, 1945, folder "Fraternization and Relations with Civilians," box 6, James Thomas Watkins Papers, HIA.

18 "MG Headquarters, Morgan MS.," box 4, James Thomas Watkins Papers; note on "Training" (LaMotte), box 20, James Thomas Watkins Papers.

19 Lt. Richard Rendleman to Mother, September 29, 1945, folder 2, box 1, Richard James Rendleman Papers, SHC.

20 Rendleman to Mother, October 23, 1945, folder 2, box 1, Richard James Rendleman Papers.

21 Watkins letter IV, June 13, 1945, letter XI, August 19, 1945, and letter XII, August 29, 1945, box 22, James Thomas Watkins Papers.

22 On "gooks," see James T. Watkins, Reports on Morale, box 20, James Thomas Watkins Papers; on Crist, see "MG Headquarters, Morgan MS.," box 4, James Thomas Watkins Papers.

23 Brig. Gen. Crist to Maj. Gen. John Hilldring, May 1945, box 10, James Thomas Watkins Papers. For a detailed account of Okinawa's devastation written by a former naval intelligence officer, see Daniel D. Karasik, "Okinawa: A Problem in Administration and Reconstruction," *Far Eastern Quarterly* 7 (1948): 254–267. On the nature and number of suicides, see Danielle Glassmeyer, "'The Wisdom of Gracious Acceptance': Okinawa, Mass Suicide, and the Cultural Work of *Teahouse of the August Moon*," *Soundings: An Interdisciplinary Journal* 96 (2013): 398–430.

24 Ben R. Games, *The Guardian Angel: Class 43K; One Member's Autobiography,* typescript memoir, p. 57, box 2, Ben Games Papers, USAMHI; Pfc. John W. Taussig (USMC) to Dearest Folks, April 29, 1945, folder 34, box 3, Mina Curtiss Collection, SML. On deteriorating corpses, see "Odyssey of Robert Malcolm Titus."

25 Lt. John C. Dorfman, AFC/2001/001/64154, video recording, VHP.

26 Fisch, *Military Government,* 44–60; Lt. C. C. Ford (USNR), to Crist, MG HQ Is[land]Com[mand], "Military Government Operations in Northern Okinawa from 21 April to 28 May 1945," box 10, James Thomas Watkins Papers; on magic wands, see LaMotte, MS entry for April 17, 1945, box 20, James Thomas Watkins Papers.

27 Paul to Margaret Skuse, June 19, 1945, and June 23, 1945, box 23, James Thomas Watkins Papers.

28 Paul to Margaret Skuse, June 24, 1945, box 23, James Thomas Watkins Papers.

29 Ibid.

30 MG HQ IsCom, "History of MG Operations on Okinawa, 1 May–31 May 1945," June 10, 1945, box 3, James Thomas Watkins Papers.

31 Paul to Margaret Skuse, June 28, 1945, and July 16, 1945, box 23, James Thomas Watkins Papers.

32 MG HQ IsCom, "History of MG Operations on Okinawa, 1 May–31 May 1945."

33 On destruction of Naha, see Ford to MG HQ IsCom, "Military Government Operations in Northern Okinawa from 21 April to 28 May 1945." Letter from M.Sgt. John C. Plock to Cpl. Harold Kahlert, September 11, 1945, Harald P. Kahlert Papers. On deaths during relocation, see MG HQ IsCom, "Incident Involving Civilians at c-13 on 22 June, 1945," memo, June 25, 1945, box 8, James Thomas Watkins Papers.

34 MG HQ IsCom, "History of MG Operations on Okinawa, 1 May–31 May 1945." On the "face-lift," see Paul Steiner to William Schwartz, December 11, 1947, box 3, James

Thomas Watkins Papers. Steiner judged "too conservative" the military estimate that 95 percent of homes had been damaged or destroyed. On a lost civilization, see Thorlaksson quoted in Watkins Diary, July 1, 1945, box 22, James Thomas Watkins Papers.

35 MG HQ IsCom, "Burning of Native Dwellings" and "Demolition of Tombs and Similar Monuments," May 1945, box 3, James Thomas Watkins Papers. On road widening, see "Notes by Caldwell concerning Planning at Army Level for ICEBERG," n.d., box 4, James Thomas Watkins Papers. On Sobe, see Karasik, "Okinawa," 259.

36 "Okinawa Now," *Saturday Evening Post,* November 17, 1945, 26–27.

37 Watkins Diary, December 31, 1945, box 22, James Thomas Watkins Papers; Crist to Hilldring, May 1945, box 10, James Thomas Watkins Papers; "MG Headquarters, Morgan MS.," box 4, James Thomas Watkins Papers; Watkins Diary, January 13, 1946, box 22, James Thomas Watkins Papers. Japanese corpses were also considered fair game for a certain kind of souvenir hunting; "Odyssey of Robert Malcolm Titus." On the speed with which the museum's collections might be raided, see Watkins Diary, January 13, 1946, box 22, James Thomas Watkins Papers.

38 Army Service Command I, MG HQ Okinawa, Circular No. 159, "Attacks upon Civilians by Military Personnel," August 6, 1945, box 6, James Thomas Watkins Papers; Donald W. Titus to William Titus, June 2, 1945, box 5, William A. Titus Papers; Paul to Margaret Skuse, August 22, 1945, box 23, James Thomas Watkins Papers; Watkins letter X, August 11, 1945, box 22, James Thomas Watkins Papers; Lt. Jack Ahearn to Aunt Florrie, September 23, 1945, box 3, Gaffney-Ahearn Family Correspondence, NYPL.

39 William L. Worden, "These Japs Took to Conquest," *Saturday Evening Post,* June 9, 1945, 24; Villegas quoted by Arthur Vesey, "Okinawa Gives Yanks Taste of Jap Occupation," *CDT,* August 27, 1945, 5; Eichelberger Diary, August 19, 1945, box 1, Robert L. Eichelberger Papers.

40 Walter Lee Diary, August 27, 1945, folder 33, box 12, WWII Collection, MS.1764, UTK. For a similar warning issued to members of ATIS, see Donald Richardson, *Random Recollections,* typescript memoir, 1991, p. 69, MS.2653, Donald Richardson World War II Memoir, UTK.

41 A. E. Schanze, *This Was the Army,* typescript memoir, n.d., A. E. Schanze Papers, USAMHI; Byers to My Precious Ones, August 31, 1945, box 30, Clovis E. Byers Papers.

42 "MacArthur Arrives," *Life,* September 19, 1945, 30; Byers to My Precious Ones, August 31, 1945, box 30, Clovis E. Byers Papers.

43 Cpl. Marvin O. Reichman to Mom, October 25, 1945, box 2, 24th Infantry Division, WWII Veterans' Collection, USAMHI. See also Chuck Wilhelm to Mother, November 18, 1945, Wilhelm Family Letters, WHS.

44 Harry to Jinny McMasters, September 10, 1945, Harry L. McMasters Letters to His Wife.

45 Richardson, *Random Recollections,* 65. On MacArthur's sedentariness, see Dower, *Embracing Defeat,* 205. Eichelberger peppered his diary with comments on MacArthur's immobility, unflatteringly contrasted with his own regular peregrinations around Japan; Eichelberger Diary for 1945, 1946, 1947, box 1, Robert L. Eichelberger Papers.

46 Lt. Gen. Thomas E. Bourke interview with Maj. L. E. Tatem, 1973, USMC OHP; John W. Dower, *War without Mercy: Race and Power in the Pacific* (New York: Pantheon, 1986). On *Our Job in Japan,* see Dower, *Embracing Defeat,* 214–217.

47 Martha Wayman to Mother, October 21, 1945, box 2, Martha A. Wayman Papers, USAMHI. On the V sign, see Randolph V. Seligman to Dearest All, October 10, 1945, Mary Jane Anderson Papers, USAMHI. On the blowing of kisses, see Lt. Gen. George F. Good Jr. interview with Benis Frank, 1974, USMC OHP.

48 Richardson, *Random Recollections,* 47. On "bloomers," see Byers to Precious Ones, October 2, 1945, box 30, Clovis E. Byers Papers.

49 Jean Smith, *General Mac's WACs,* part 3, *Japan, 1946–49: Tokyo, from Fear to Friendship,* typescript memoir, box 1, Jean Smith Papers, USAMHI.

50 Herbert Sparrow, October 14, 1945, in *Letters from Japan: First Month of Occupation (Osaka Area)* (McLean, VA: H. G. Sparrow, 1989), 30, copy in USAMHI.

51 Ibid., 33; Harold R. Isaacs, *No Peace for Asia* (New York: Macmillan, 1947), 10. On miniature dimensions, see Philip H. Hostetter, *Combat Doctor in the South Pacific or Red Beach to Mandog Hill,* typescript memoir, n.d., box 2, 24th Infantry Division, WWII Veterans' Collection, USAMHI; Charles Hunt to Family, October 1, 1945, folder 17, box 1, Charles D. Hunt Papers, IHS.

52 Sparrow, October 4, 1945, in *Letters from Japan,* 19; Lt. Gen. James Berkeley interview with Benis Frank, 1973, USMC OHP.

53 Sparrow, September 27, 1945, in *Letters from Japan,* 5.

54 Byers to My Precious Ones, September 11, 1945, box 30, Clovis E. Byers Papers.

55 Byers to My Precious Ones, October 2, 1945, box 30, Clovis E. Byers Papers.

56 Elliott Chaze, *The Stainless Steel Kimono* (New York: Permabooks, [1947] 1955), vii; Sy Kahn, diary entry for September 15, 1945, in *Between Tedium and Terror: A Soldier's World War II Diary, 1943–45* (Urbana: University of Illinois Press, 1993), 296. In the same vein, Henry Zylstra wrote in a letter from Japan on October 27, 1945, that he guessed "if a poll were taken, it would show that the Americans in Japan, almost without exception, are pleased with the Japanese and quite captivated by them"; Henry Zylstra, *Letters from Occupied Japan* (Orange City, IA: Middleburg, 1982), 64.

57 "The People: Their Nation Is Beaten but They Are Not Bowed," *Life,* September 10, 1945, 32.

58 On the change in plans, see Brig. Gen. Joseph L. Stewart interview with Benis Frank, 1973, USMC OHP. On wading ashore, see Sparrow, September 27, 1945, in *Letters from Japan,* 6.

59 Dower, *Embracing Defeat,* 292–296; Naoko Shibusawa, *America's Geisha Ally: Reimagining the Japanese Enemy* (Cambridge, MA: Harvard University Press, 2006), 96–99.

60 Harry to Jinny McMasters, September 8, 1945, Harry L. McMasters Letters to His Wife.

61 Sparrow, October 14, 1945, in *Letters from Japan,* 30.

4. FROM V-E TO VD

1 "Interpreters and Mistresses," *Time,* October 15, 1945, 30; Jack to Mary Whitelaw, October 20, 1945, box 1, John L. Whitelaw Papers, USAMHI.

2 John Hersey, "AMGOT at Work," *Life,* August 23, 1943, 31. On Morse's photograph, see Mary Louise Roberts, *What Soldiers Do: Sex and the American GI in World War II France* (Chicago: University of Chicago Press, 2013), 68–73.

3 Julian Bach, *America's Germany: An Account of the Occupation* (New York: Random House, 1946), 77; Maurice Neufeld Diary, May 23, 1943, box 1, Maurice F. Neufeld papers, LOC; Milton Bracker, "Venereal Disease Increases in Italy," *NYT,* April 19, 1944, p. 3.

4 Roberts, *What Soldiers Do;* Robert M. Hill and Elizabeth Craig Hill, *In The Wake of War: Memoirs of an Alabama Military Government Officer in World War II Italy* (Tuscaloosa: University of Alabama Press, 1982), 20. On SHAEF's antifraternization propaganda, see Petra Goedde, *GIs and Germans: Culture, Gender, and Foreign Relations, 1945–1949* (New Haven, CT: Yale University Press, 2003), 71–72.

5 "The Germans Crumble in the West," *Life,* March 19, 1945, 29.

6 "German Girls: U.S. Army Boycott Fails to Stop GIs from Fraternizing with Them," *Life,* July 23, 1945, 35. On the *Stars and Stripes* photos, see Ann Elizabeth Pfau, *Miss Yourlovin: GIs, Gender, and Domesticity during World War II* (New York: Columbia University Press, 2008), http://www.gutenberg-e.org/pfau/detail/Bad531301.html.

7 "International: Leave Your Helmet On," *Time,* July 2, 1945, 25. For a critique of this trope, see Susanne zur Nieden, "Erotic Fraternization: The Legend of German Women's Quick Surrender," in *Home/Front: The Military, War and Gender in Twentieth Century Germany,* ed. Karen Hagemann and Stefanie Schüler-Springorum (Oxford: Berg, 2002), 297–310.

8 Percy Knauth, "Fraternization: The Word Takes on a Brand-New Meaning in Germany," *Life,* July 2, 1945, 26.

9 Edward P. Morgan, "Heels among the Heroes," *Collier's,* October 19, 1946, 17.

10 Felix to Dorothea Vann, July 1, 1945, Felix Vann Papers, NJHS. MacArthur's letter quoted by John La Cerda, *The Conqueror Comes to Tea* (New Brunswick, NJ: Rutgers University Press, 1946), 53; Bach, *America's Germany,* 71.

11 On reception of *The Gallery,* see David Margolick, *Dreadful: The Short Life and Gay Times of John Horne Burns* (New York: Other Press, 2013). On *A Foreign Affair,* see Werner Sollors, *The Temptation of Despair: Tales of the 1940s* (Cambridge, MA: Belknap Press of Harvard University Press, 2014), 247–277.

12 Douglas F. Habib, "Chastity, Masculinity and Military Efficiency: The United States Army in Germany, 1918–1923," *International History Review* 28 (2006): 737–757; Erika A. Kuhlman, "American Doughboys and German Fräuleins: Sexuality, Patriarchy, and Privilege in the American-Occupied Rhineland, 1918–23," *Journal of Military History* 71 (2007): 1077–1106. On male soldiers' entitlement to heterosexual sex, see Beth Bailey and David Farber, *The First Strange Place: Race and Sex in World War II Hawaii* (Baltimore: Johns Hopkins University Press, 1992), and on the dual standard for female military personnel, see Leisa D. Meyer, *Creating GI Jane: Sexuality and Power in the Women's Army Corps during World War*

II (New York: Columbia University Press, 1996). Lt. Gen. Frederick Morgan quoted by Earl F. Ziemke, *The U.S. Army in the Occupation of Germany, 1944–1946* (Washington, DC: Center of Military History, U.S. Army, 1975), 98.

13 Oliver J. Frederiksen, *The American Military Occupation of Germany, 1945–1953* (Darmstadt, Germany: Historical Division, Headquarters, United States Army, Europe, 1953), 129; Hilldring quoted by Ziemke, *U.S. Army*, 97.

14 Eisenhower quoted by Ziemke, *U.S. Army*, 98; Goedde, *GIs and Germans*, 56–57.

15 On censorship of photography, see George H. Roeder, *The Censored War: American Visual Experience during World War II* (New Haven, CT: Yale University Press, 1993), visual essay 3. Ryan Mungia, ed., *Protect Yourself: Venereal Disease Posters of World War II* (Los Angeles: Boyo Press, 2014).

16 Payne Templeton recorded a rebuke from his driver for shaking hands with the burgomaster; Payne Templeton, *A Complete Change of Life: Into World War II,* typescript memoir, n.d., box 1, Payne Templeton Papers, USAMHI. John Maginnis Diary, May 22, 1945, box 2, John J. Maginnis Papers, USAMHI.

17 Sidney Eisenberg to Silv, Ralph, Bob, and Hope, May 5, 1945, box 1, Sidney S. Eisenberg Papers, USAMHI.

18 Paul N. Haubenreich, *Memories of Service in the Second Platoon, Company K, 407th Infantry, March 1944–Sept. 1945,* typescript memoir, n.d., folder 20, box 7, WWII Collection, MS.2012, UTK; Jack to Mary Whitelaw, April 8, 1945, box 1, John L. Whitelaw Papers.

19 S.Sgt. Alfred Wesley Rogers to Norma Rogers, n.d., folder 10, box 21, Norma Rogers Selections from the Letters of S/Sgt Alfred Rogers, WWII Collection, MS.2112, UTK. Army technician John Katsu recollected homeowners moving into the gardeners' quarters; John Junji Katsu, AFC 2001/001/89308, DVD oral history interview, VHP. Another GI recalled the proprietors of his billet living in the boathouse; Walter C. Krause, *So I Was a Sergeant: Memoirs of an Occupation Soldier* (Hicksville, NY: Exposition Press, 1978), 83–91.

20 James E. Thompson, letter dated July 22, 1945, in *"Dearest Folks": A Collection of Letters Written Home while in World War II Europe by James E. "Ed" Thompson with "Lots of Love,"* typescript memoir, n.d., folder 1, James E. Thompson Papers, USAMHI; John Wortham, *A Short Account of My Endeavors in World War II for My Daughters, Sue and Jan,* typescript memoir, July 1984, folder 3, box 20, WWII Collection, MS.2012, UTK.

21 On the laundry problem, see Franklin M. Davis, *Come as a Conqueror: The United States Army's Occupation of Germany, 1945–1949* (New York: Macmillan, 1967), 144. On mail censorship, see Pfau, *Miss Yourlovin*, ch. 3. Clarence to Eve Davis, May 23, 1945, box 1, Clarence W. Davis Letters, DMR.

22 Leo Bogart to family, June 6, 1945, box 4, Leo Bogart Papers, DMR; Ivey to wife, May 26, 1945, folder 60, box 7, WWII Collection, MS.2012, UTK. The more widely discussed phenomenon relates to German men's rage over GIs consorting with German women; Perry Biddiscombe, "Dangerous Liaisons: The Anti-fraternization Movement in the U.S. Occupation Zones of Germany and Austria, 1945–1948," *Journal of Social History* 34 (2001): 611–647.

23 Maurice to Laya Kurtz, May 31, 1945, folder 4, box 1, Maurice Kurtz Papers, SHC.

24 Eddy to Charlie, May 21, 1945, and July 8, 1945, folder 17, box 2, Mina Curtiss Collection, SML. On "good-looking babes," see Robert E. Daniels to wife and daughter, June 3, 1945, folder 6, box 1, Robert E. Daniels Papers, SHC.

25 Thompson, letter to dad, July 12, 1945, in *"Dearest Folks."* William Leesemann describes a similar pattern but with DP "camp followers" pursuing men from Germany into Austria; William Leesemann, untitled memoir, n.d., folder 52, box 8, WWII Collection, MS.2012, UTK.

26 Felix to Dorothea Vann, May 21, 1945, Felix Vann Papers; Ziemke, *U.S. Army,* 324.

27 Felix to Dorothea Vann, July 1, 1945, Felix Vann Papers; Alan T. Sterling to sister Ruth, April 2, 1946, folder 3, box 1, Alan T. Sterling Papers, DMR.

28 On the sixty-five-dollar fine, see Haubenreich, *Memories;* S.Sgt. Alfred Wesley Rogers to Norma Rogers, June 1945, folder 10, box 21, Norma Rogers Selections from the Letters of S/Sgt Alfred Rogers, WWII Collection, MS.2112, UTK; John Maginnis Diary, May 28, 1945, box 2, John J. Maginnis Papers; Clifton Lisle Diary, June 11, 1945, box 13, Clifton Lisle Papers, USAMHI.

29 Ziemke, *U.S. Army,* 325. On the chow line condom bowl, see *The Memoirs of Gerald Freedman,* typescript memoir, July 26, 2014, edited by Jeffrey Winkelman (in author's possession); and on the same theme, see Edward C. Arn, *Arn's War: Memoirs of a World War II Infantryman, 1940–1946* (Akron, OH: University of Akron Press, 2006), 206.

30 "German Girls," *Life,* 36.

31 Ziemke, *U.S. Army,* 325. On the failure of denazification, see Goedde, *GIs and Germans,* 76. For one officer's attempts to limit social interaction, see John Maginnis Diary, August 9, 1945, box 2, John J. Maginnis Papers. Clifton Lisle Diary, September 22, 1945, Clifton Lisle Papers.

32 S.Sgt. Alfred Wesley Rogers to Norma Rogers, n.d., folder 10, box 21, Norma Rogers Selections from the Letters of S/Sgt Alfred Rogers, WWII Collection, MS.2112.

33 Jack to Mary Whitelaw, September 17, 1945, and August 20, 1945, box 1, John L. Whitelaw Papers. On the zoot suit and its charged meanings, see Kathy Peiss, *Zoot Suit: The Enigmatic Career of an Extreme Style* (Philadelphia: University of Pennsylvania Press, 2011).

34 Hanns Anders to mother, July 25, 1945, and letters throughout the fall, box 1, Winfred Hanns Anders Papers, USAMHI.

35 Felix to Dorothea Vann, May 21, 1945, Felix Vann Papers; Judy Barden, "Candy-Bar Romance—Women of Germany," in *This Is Germany,* ed. Arthur Settel (New York: William Sloane, 1950), 165; Robert J. Lilly, *Taken by Force: Rape and American GIs in Europe during World War II* (New York: Palgrave Macmillan, 2007), 117–119.

36 Bill Taylor to Mudder and Dad, May 20, 1945, "Dear Mudder and Dad: The WWII Letters of William Wellington Taylor, Jr.," https://wwiiwwtaylor.wordpress.com/letters/may-1945/. The story, denied by U.S. authorities in Germany, received scant press attention. David Darrah, "Stuttgart Pins Raping Blame on Moroccans," *CDT,* July 26, 1945, 7. On rape by the Red Army, see Elizabeth Heineman, "The Hour of the Woman: Memories of Germany's 'Crisis Years' and West German National Identity," *AHR* 101 (1996): 354–395; Norman M.

Naimark, *The Russians in Germany: A History of the Soviet Zone of Occupation, 1945–1949* (Cambridge, MA: Belknap Press of Harvard University Press, 1995), 69–140; Atina Grossmann, "A Question of Silence: The Rape of German Women by Occupation Soldiers," *October* 72 (1995): 42–63; Atina Grossmann, *Jews, Germans and Allies: Close Encounters in Occupied Germany* (Princeton, NJ: Princeton University Press, 2007), 69. For examples of Berlin-based officers' infrequent or nonexistent references to rape, see John J. Maginnis Papers; Frank Howley, Personal Diary, box 2, Frank L. Howley Papers, USAMHI; and John L. Whitelaw Papers. Jack to Mary Whitelaw, April 12, 1945, box 1, John L. Whitelaw Papers.

37 David Brion Davis, "The Americanized Mannheim of 1945–1946," in *American Places: Encounters with History,* ed. William Leuchtenberg (New York: Oxford University Press, 2002), 90. On black soldiers' sexual relations with German women, see Heide Fehrenbach, *Race after Hitler: Black Occupation Children in Postwar Germany and America* (Princeton, NJ: Princeton University Press, 2005); Timothy L. Schroer, *Recasting Race after World War II: Germans and African Americans in American-Occupied Germany* (Boulder: University Press of Colorado, 2007); Maria Höhn and Martin Klimke, *A Breath of Freedom: The Civil Rights Struggle, African American GIs, and Germany* (New York: Palgrave Macmillan, 2010). See also the semiautobiographical novel of William Gardner Smith, *Last of the Conquerors* (New York: Signet Books, 1949).

38 Reddick interview with Roi Ottley, 1946, folder 11, box 1, Lawrence D. Reddick WWII Project, SCRBC. Other of Reddick's interviewees confirmed much the same point about black soldiers' superior success with both German and Italian women. See, for example, interview with Cpl. Horace Evans of Detroit, January 12, 1946, folder 8; interview with Leonard D. Stevens, 1945, folder 12; interview with Cruz and Robinson, 1946, folder 8; interview with Wilbur Young, August 9, 1946, folder 13, all in box 1, Lawrence D. Reddick WWII Project.

39 Jack Rosenfeld to Sylvia Solov, June 3, 1945, folder 328, box 12, Jack Rosenfeld Papers, KCSC.

40 Leland to Claire Hiatt, November 11, 1945, and Leland to folks, November 1, 1945, Leland D. Hiatt Papers, AFC 2001/001/92139, VHP.

41 Draft paper, "About the Okinawans," 24th Corps HQ, April 20, 1945, folder "Fraternization and Relations with Civilians," box 6, James Thomas Watkins Papers, HIA.

42 HQ Tenth Army, Office of the Commanding General, Operational Directive Number 1A, May 2, 1945, box 3, James Thomas Watkins Papers. On the threat to confine offenders to the stockade, see "Fraternization," LaMotte MS, June 11, 1945, box 19, James Thomas Watkins Papers.

43 Note, "Fraternization: The News-Pix Picture," n.d., folder "Fraternization and Relations with Civilians," box 6, James Thomas Watkins Papers; Watkins Diary, June 25, 1945, box 22, James Thomas Watkins Papers.

44 On crisscrossing migration, see Yuichiro Onishi, "Occupied Okinawa on the Edge: On Being Okinawan in Hawai'i and U.S. Colonialism toward Okinawa," *American Quarterly* 64 (2012): 741–765.

45 Notes from LaMotte MS, box 19, James Thomas Watkins Papers; Watkins Diary, July 2, 1945, box 22, James Thomas Watkins Papers.

46 Yukiko Koshiro, *Transpacific Racisms and the U.S. Occupation of Japan* (New York: Columbia University Press, 1999). On the "rape problem," see "Fraternization," LaMotte MS, June 28, 1945, box 19, James Thomas Watkins Papers. Regarding African American troops as primarily responsible for rape, Watkins requested a junior officer, Warner Berthoff, to draw up a memorandum in April 1946 asking for black troops' complete removal from the island, an initiative Berthoff regretted; Warner Berthoff, "Memories of Okinawa," *Sewanee Review* 121 (2013): 150. African American troops in both Europe and Japan were tried and convicted of rape in numbers vastly disproportionate to their contribution to troop strength; Lilly, *Taken by Force.* Watkins Diary, September 30, 1945, box 22, James Thomas Watkins Papers. On Korean "comfort women," see MG HQ IsCom, "Report of MG Activities for October 1945," November 23, 1945, box 3, James Thomas Watkins Papers.

47 Watkins Diary, January 19, 1946, box 22, James Thomas Watkins Papers; M. D. Morris, *Okinawa: Tiger by the Tail* (New York: Hawthorn, 1968), 60.

48 Quoted by Sarah Kovner, *Occupying Power: Sex Workers and Servicemen in Postwar Japan* (Stanford, CA: Stanford University Press, 2012), 36.

49 On the divergent orders officers issued regarding fraternization, see Michael Cullen Green, *Black Yanks in the Pacific: Race in the Making of American Military Empire after World War II* (Ithaca, NY: Cornell University Press, 2010), 41. Harry McMasters to wife, September 23, 1945, Harry L. McMasters Letters to His Wife, HIA.

50 Kovner, *Occupying Power,* 22. Ikeda quoted by Eiji Takemae, *Inside GHQ: The Allied Occupation of Japan and Its Legacy* (New York: Continuum, 2002), 68. On prostitution in occupied Japan, see also John W. Dower, *Embracing Defeat: Japan in the Wake of World War II* (New York: W. W. Norton, 1999), 121–139; Holly Sanders, "Panpan: Streetwalking in Occupied Japan," *Pacific Historical Review* 81 (2012): 404–431; Yasuhiro Okada, "Race, Masculinity, and Military Occupation: African American Soldiers' Encounters with the Japanese at Camp Gifu, 1947–51," *Journal of African American History* 96 (2011): 179–203; Michiko Takeuchi, "'Pan-Pan Girls': Performing and Resisting Neocolonialism(s) in the Pacific Theater: U.S. Military Prostitution in Occupied Japan, 1945–1952," in *Over There: Living with the U.S. Military Empire from World War Two to the Present,* ed. Maria Höhn and Seungsook Moon (Durham, NC: Duke University Press, 2010), 78–108.

51 A. E. Schanze, *This Was the Army,* typescript memoir, n.d., pp. 45–46, A. E. Schanze Papers, USAMHI.

52 Eichelberger Diary, September 11, 1945, box 1, Robert L. Eichelberger Papers, DMR; Kovner, *Occupying Power,* ch. 1.

53 HQ Fifteenth U.S. Army, "Control of Venereal Disease," June 27, 1945, folder "15th Army Medical History," box 2, Harold Richard Hennessy Papers, USAMHI.

54 Robert Eichelberger, "Our Soldiers in the Occupation," dictation, February 21, 1948, folder "Japan: Occupation, Misc. 1945–49," box 64, Robert L. Eichelberger Papers. On the May Act, see Marilyn E. Hegarty, *Victory Girls, Khaki-Wackies, and Patriotutes: The Regulation of Female Sexuality during World War II* (New York: New York University Press, 2008), 37–39. On the military and brothels in France, see Roberts, *What Soldiers Do,* 159–160.

55 Paul A. Kramer, "The Darkness That Enters the Home: The Politics of Prostitution during the Philippine-American War," in *Haunted by Empire: Geographies of Intimacy in*

North American History, ed. Laura Ann Stoler (Durham, NC: Duke University Press, 2006), 366–404.

56 On Korea, see Na Young Lee, "The Construction of Military Prostitution in South Korea during the U.S. Military Rule, 1945–1948," *Feminist Studies* 33 (2007): 453–481; Seung-sook Moon, "Regulating Desire, Managing the Empire: U.S. Military Prostitution in South Korea, 1945–1970," in Höhn and Moon, *Over There,* 39–77.

57 On child prostitutes and sibling pimps, see H. A. Miller, *Vignettes of 12102794,* typescript memoir, n.d., folder 38, box 9, WWII Collection, MS.2012, UTK. The bellicose language comes from a memo issued by HQ, Metropolitan Area, PBS, Office of the Surgeon, "VD Control," April 13, 1944, box 17, Charles Poletti Papers, CU.

58 Editorial, "Venus and the Navy," *WP,* November 13, 1945, 6. First published in the *Des Moines Register* on November 5, 1945, Lacour's letter was reprinted in full, along with extended discussion, in "The Navy Provides Social Protection for Servicemen in Japan," *Journal of Social Hygiene* 32 (1946): 82–89. On "Willow Run," see Mark Gayn, *Japan Diary* (New York: William Sloane, 1948), 213–214.

59 Clyde Edwards, "Japanese Open Tokyo 'USO,'" *Stars and Stripes,* September 8, 1945, quoted by Kovner, *Occupying Power,* 18. See also Frank Kelley, "Geisha Industry Buys Up Girls to Entertain GIs," *New York Herald Tribune,* October 21, 1945, 5.

60 Milo Flaten to Mom and Pop, June 13, 1945, folder 9, box 1, Milo G. Flaten Papers, WVM.

61 Paul to Margaret Skuse, June 19, 1945, box 23, James Thomas Watkins Papers.

62 Harry to Jinny McMasters, September 10, September 17, and October 4, 1945, Harry L. McMasters Letters to His Wife.

63 Eichelberger to Miss Em, April 5, 1946, and May 28, 1946, box 11, Robert L. Eichelberger Papers; Eichelberger, "Our Soldiers in the Occupation."

64 Eichelberger to Miss Em, May 20, 1946, box 11, Robert L. Eichelberger Papers.

65 Noel F. Busch, *Fallen Sun: A Report on Japan* (New York: D. Appleton-Century, 1948), 12; Lindesay Parrott, "Geisha Girl—GI version," *NYT,* November, 25, 1945, 92; Peyton Gray, "Gray Finds Japan's Geisha Girls Are Not Prostitutes," *Afro-American,* November 3, 1945, 14; Walters to My Dearests, October 27 and October 31, 1945, folder 13, box 1, John H. Walters Papers, WVM; Louis to Anna Geffen, December 5, 1945, folder 6, box 14, Louis and Anna Geffen Family Correspondence, MARBL.

66 Seligman to Dearest All, October 25, 1945, Mary Jane Anderson Papers, USAMHI.

67 Clovis to Marie Byers, October 1, 1945, box 30, Clovis E. Byers Papers, HIA; Philip H. Hostetter, *Combat Doctor in the South Pacific or Red Beach to Mandog Hill,* typescript memoir, n.d., box 2, 24th Infantry Division, WWII Veterans' Collection, USAMHI.

68 Seligman to Dearest All, October 25, 1945, Mary Jane Anderson Papers; Clovis to Marie Byers, October 1, 1945, box 30, Clovis E. Byers Papers.

69 Marvin Reichman to mom, November 15 and November 25, 1945, and Marvin to Mark Reichman, December 3, 1945, box 2, 24th Infantry Division, WWII Veterans' Collection.

70 Reichman to mom, April 1 and April 6, 1946, box 2, 24th Infantry Division, WWII Veterans' Collection.

71 Harold J. Noble, *What It Takes to Rule Japan* (New York: U.S. Camera, 1946), 92–93. For similar points with reference to European girls, see Victor Dallaire, "The American Woman? Not for This GI," *NYT Magazine,* March 10, 1946, 8. Bill Hume, *Babysan: A Private Look at the Japanese Occupation* (Tokyo: Kasuga Bokei, 1953).

72 On Shep, see "Speaking of Pictures . . . GIs Blowzy Frauleins Hurt Germans' Feelings," *Life,* June 17, 1946, 12–13; Goedde, *GIs and Germans,* 93–94.

73 Tania Long, "Pro-German Attitude Grows as U.S. Troops Fraternize," *NYT,* September 29, 1945, 1.

74 On Japanese war brides, see Susan Zeiger, *Entangling Alliances: Foreign War Brides and American Soldiers in the Twentieth Century* (New York: New York University Press, 2010), 179–189. On the feminization of Japan more broadly, see Naoko Shibusawa, *America's Geisha Ally: Reimagining the Japanese Enemy* (Cambridge, MA: Harvard University Press, 2006). On "pajamas," see Elliott Chaze, *The Stainless Steel Kimono* (New York: Permabooks, [1947] 1955), 61. Walt Sheldon, *The Honorable Conquerors: The Occupation of Japan, 1945–1952* (New York: Macmillan, 1965), 116.

75 Zeiger, *Entangling Alliances,* 180–189. An expectation of indulgence toward Americans' amorous experiences in Japan also colors retrospective memoirs. "Young and inexperienced boys were initiated into the ways of love," reads the foreword to Vincent W. Allen, *A Very Intimate Occupation* (New York: Vantage Press, 2000), xi.

76 Jacob Van Staaveren, *An American in Japan, 1945–1948* (Seattle: University of Washington Press, 1994), 3. See also Green, *Black Yanks,* 31–32.

77 On the "Dear John" letter, see Gerald F. Linderman, *The World within War: America's Combat Experience in World War II* (New York: Free Press, 1997), 310–311. Paul Fussell, *Wartime: Understanding and Behavior in the Second World War* (New York: Oxford University Press, 1989), 96–114; Maurice to Hinda Neufeld, February 4, 1944, folder 7, box 5, Maurice F. Neufeld Papers.

78 Hostetter, *Combat Doctor.*

79 George Cronin Diary, May 26, 1946, George C. Cronin Papers, SHC.

5. DISPLACED AND DISPLEASED PERSONS

1 John Maginnis Diary, September 16, 1945, box 2, John J. Maginnis Papers, US-AMHI. On U.S. occupation soldiers and expellees, see Adam R. Seipp, *Strangers in the Wild Place: Refugees, Americans, and a German Town, 1945–1952* (Bloomington: Indiana University Press, 2013); Adam R. Seipp, "The Driftwood of War: The US Army, Expellees, and West German Society, 1945–52," *War and Society* 32 (2013): 211–232. On expulsion more broadly, see R. M. Douglas, *Orderly and Humane: The Expulsion of the Germans after the Second World War* (New Haven, CT: Yale University Press, 2012).

2 John Maginnis, "Principal MG Operations of Interest in Berlin," n.d., box 2, John J. Maginnis Papers; George Woodbridge, *UNRRA: The History of the United Nations Relief and Rehabilitation Administration* (New York: Columbia University Press, 1950); Jessica Reinisch, "Internationalism in Relief: The Birth (and Death) of UNRRA," in *Post-war Reconstruction*

in Europe: International Perspectives, 1945–1949, ed. Mark Mazower, Jessica Reinisch, and David Feldman (Oxford: Oxford University Press, 2011); Silvia Salvatici, " 'Help the People to Help Themselves': UNRRA Relief Workers and European Displaced Persons," *Journal of Refugee Studies* 25 (2012): 428–451.

3 For statistics, see Mark Spoerer and Jochen Fleischhacker, "Forced Laborers in Nazi Germany: Categories, Numbers, and Survivors," *Journal of Interdisciplinary History* 33 (2002): 197; Mark E. Caprio and Yu Jia, "Occupations of Korea and Japan and the Origins of the Korean Diaspora in Japan," in *Diaspora without Homeland,* ed. Sonia Ryang and John Lie (Berkeley: University of California Press, 2009), 27. The OSS report, "Aliens in Japan," is quoted by Mark E. Caprio, "Resident Aliens: Forging the Political Status of Koreans in Occupied Japan," in *Democracy in Occupied Japan: The U.S. Occupation and Japanese Politics and Society,* ed. Mark E. Caprio and Yoneyuki Sugita (New York: Routledge, 2007), 182. The term "DP" has come to seem synonymous with Europeans, much recent work dealing exclusively with Europe. Ben Shepherd's *The Long Road Home: The Aftermath of the Second World War* (New York: Alfred A. Knopf, 2011), for instance, makes no mention of "displacement" in Asia. Few authors address Europe and Asia; Pamela Ballinger, "Entangled or 'Extruded' Histories? Displacement, National Refugees, and Repatriation after the Second World War," *Journal of Refugee Studies* 25 (2012): 366–386.

4 On the ascription of nationalist attachments to refugees, see Liisa H. Malkki, "Refugees and Exile: From 'Refugee Studies' to the National Order of Things," *Annual Review of Anthropology* 7 (1995): 495–523; Liisa H. Malkki, "National Geographic: The Rooting of People and Territorialization of Identity among Scholars and Refugees," *Cultural Anthropology* 7 (1992): 24–44.

5 Kendall Moore, "Between Expediency and Principle: U.S. Repatriation Policy toward Russian Nationals, 1944–1949," *Diplomatic History* 24 (2000): 381–404; George Ginsburgs, "The Soviet Union and the Problem of Refugees and Displaced Persons 1917–1956," *American Journal of International Law* 51 (1957): 325–361.

6 Atina Grossmann, *Jews, Germans and Allies: Close Encounters in Occupied Germany* (Princeton, NJ: Princeton University Press, 2007), 1; Gerard Daniel Cohen, *In War's Wake: Europe's Displaced Persons in the Postwar Order* (New York: Oxford University Press, 2012), 126. See also Zeev W. Mankowitz, *Life between Memory and Hope: The Survivors of the Holocaust in Occupied Germany* (Cambridge: Cambridge University Press, 2002); Margarete Myers Feinstein, *Holocaust Survivors in Postwar Germany, 1945–1957* (New York: Cambridge University Press, 2010).

7 Cohen, *In War's Wake,* 15; Gil Loescher and John A. Scanlan, *Calculated Kindness: Refugees and America's Half-Open Door, 1945 to the Present* (New York: Free Press, 1986).

8 Silvia Salvatici, "Between Nation and International Mandates: Displaced Persons and Refugees in Postwar Italy," *Journal of Contemporary History* 49 (2014): 515. On Trieste, see Pamela Ballinger, *History in Exile: Memory and Identity at the Borders of the Balkans* (Princeton, NJ: Princeton University Press, 2003); Alfred Connor Bowman, *Zones of Strain: A Memoir of the Early Cold War* (Stanford, CA: Hoover Institution Press, 1982).

9 On the "priority system" instituted in Korea, see William J. Gane, "Foreign Affairs of South Korea: August 1945 to August 1950" (PhD diss., Northwestern University, 1951),

ch. 3. Lori Watt, *When Empire Comes Home: Repatriation and Reintegration in Postwar Japan* (Cambridge, MA: Harvard University Asia Center/Harvard University Press, 2009); Wayne C. McWilliams, *Homeward Bound: Repatriation of Japanese from Korea after World War II* (Hong Kong: Asian Research Service, 1988); Tessa Morris-Suzuki, *Borderline Japan: Foreigners and Frontier Controls in the Postwar Era* (Cambridge: Cambridge University Press, 2010); Matthew R. Augustine, "Dividing Islanders: The Repatriation of 'Ryūkyūans' from Occupied Japan," in *Japan as the Occupier and the Occupied,* ed. Christine de Matos and Mark E. Caprio (Basingstoke, UK: Palgrave Macmillan, 2015), 206–225; Matthew R. Augustine, "From Empire to Nation: Repatriation, Immigration, and Citizenship in Occupied Japan, 1945–1952" (PhD diss., Columbia University, 2009). On the British Commonwealth Occupation Force, see Ian Nish, ed., *The British Commonwealth and the Allied Occupation of Japan, 1945–1952: Personal Encounters and Government Assessments* (Leiden, Netherlands: Brill, 2013).

10 The "pain in the neck" sentiments were expressed by Jack to Mary Whitelaw, April 8, 1945, box 1, John L. Whitelaw Papers, USAMHI. Templeton, letter from Munich, May 22, 1945, folder "Letters, March 26 to Dec. 31, 1945," box 1, Payne Templeton Papers, USAMHI.

11 Payne Templeton, *A Complete Change of Life: Into World War II,* typescript memoir, n.d., p. 94, box 1, Payne Templeton Papers; Theodore Francis Inman Collection, AFC 2001/001/94947, video recording, VHP.

12 Anne Alinder, circular letter, July 6, 1945, box 1, Anne Alinder Korbel Papers, WVM; Betty Olson to family, August 19, 1945, and September 5, 1945, box 1, Betty M. Olson Papers, USAMHI.

13 SHAEF, G5 Division, Displaced Persons Branch, CA/d9, *Guide to the Care of Displaced Persons in Germany* (rev. May 1945), 8, 9, 25, copy in box 3, RG-19.047.03*05, Samuel B. Zisman Papers, USHMM.

14 Malkki, "Refugees and Exile"; SHAEF, *Guide to the Care,* 25.

15 SHAEF, *Guide to the Care,* 5.

16 Albert to Leanore Hutler, May 7, 1945, RG-19.028, Albert Hutler Papers, USHMM; Albert Hutler, *Agony of Survival* (Macomb, IL: Glenbridge, 1989), 13; Kenneth Clouse, *Precious Friends and Vanishing Sights: The Memoirs of Kenneth Lamar Clouse,* typescript memoir, p. 18, Kenneth L. Clouse Papers, USAMHI; Clifton Lisle Diary, August 31, 1945, box 13, Clifton Lisle Papers, USAMHI.

17 Maurice to Laya Kurtz, June 22, 1945, box 1, Maurice Kurtz Papers, SHC; William H. Puntenney, *For the Duration: An Autobiography of the Years of Military Service of a Citizen Soldier during World War II, June 6, 1941–Dec. 21, 1945,* typescript memoir, n.d., p. 120–122, William H. Puntenney Papers, USAMHI.

18 On public health and DPs, see Jessica Reinisch, *The Perils of Peace: The Public Health Crisis in Occupied Germany* (Oxford: Oxford University Press, 2013).

19 Harold Berge, *The War Years, Nov. 25, 1940–Sept. 17, 1945,* typescript memoir, p. 27, AFC 2001/001/1436, VHP.

20 Terrence Des Pres, *The Survivor: An Anatomy of Life in the Death Camps* (New York: Oxford University Press, 1976); Frank Costigliola, "'Like Animals or Worse': Narratives of Culture and Emotion by U.S. and British POWs and Airmen behind Soviet Lines,

1944–1945," *Diplomatic History* 28 (2005): 768; Mary Douglas, *Purity and Danger: An Analysis of Concepts of Pollution and Taboo* (London: Routledge and Kegan Paul, 1966); SHAEF, *Guide to the Care,* 35.

21 Dan Stone, *The Liberation of the Camps: The End of the Holocaust and Its Aftermath* (New Haven, CT: Yale University Press, 2015), ch. 2.

22 Frederick J. Kroesen, oral history interview, March 16, 1998, by G. Kurt Piehler and Lynn Marley, ROHA; Raymond Daniell, "Released 'Slaves' Troubling Allies," *NYT,* May 18, 1945, 7; Dorothy Thompson, "Revise Occupation Policies," *Atlanta Constitution,* June 8, 1945, 11; Berget to Dad, Mom and All, May 6, 1945, box 2, Wilbur C. Berget Papers, WVM.

23 Center for Military History, *Reports of General MacArthur Prepared by His General Staff,* vol. 1 (Washington, DC: U.S. Army Chief of Staff, 1966), 90–93; A. E. Schanze, *This Was the Army,* typescript memoir, n.d., p. 47, A. E. Schanze Papers, USAMHI.

24 Clovis to Marie Byers, August 31, 1945, box 30, Clovis E. Byers Papers, HIA.

25 Eichelberger Diary, September 4, 1945, box 1, Robert L. Eichelberger Papers, DMR; Clovis to Marie Byers, September 11, 1945, box 30, Clovis E. Byers Papers; Eichelberger Diary, September 8, 1945, box 1, Robert L. Eichelberger Papers. The diary records further visits to greet liberated prisoners on September 10 and September 20, when the final trainload disembarked.

26 *Eighth U.S. Army in Japan, 30 August 1945–1 May 1946* (Tokyo: Eighth US Army Printing Plant, Boonjudo Printing Works, 1946), 3.

27 Clovis to Marie Byers, October 3, 1945, box 30, Clovis E. Byers Papers.

28 Robert Trumbull, "Omori Camp to Get Tokyo War Chiefs," *NYT,* October 1, 1945, 6; "Accused Japanese Begin Camp Rigors," *NYT,* October 6, 1945, 5.

29 Maurice to Laya Kurtz, June 27, 1945, box 1, Maurice Kurtz Papers.

30 SHAEF, *Guide to the Care,* 10–15.

31 Albert to Leanore Hutler, April 3, 1945, and April 12, 1945, Albert Hutler Papers.

32 Albert to Leanore Hutler, May 7, 1945, June 22, 1945, and August 4, 1945, Albert Hutler Papers.

33 Clifton Lisle Diary, June 25, 1945, Clifton Lisle Papers.

34 Murphy quoted by Cathal J. Nolan, "Americans in the Gulag: Detention of US Citizens by Russia and the Onset of the Cold War," *Journal of Contemporary History* 25 (1990): 533. Anna Holian, *Between National Socialism and Soviet Communism: Displaced Persons in Postwar Germany* (Ann Arbor: University of Michigan Press, 2011), 45.

35 Albert to Leanore Hutler, September 7, 1945, Albert Hutler Papers. U.S. occupation soldiers' qualms about forcible repatriation feature more prominently in later recollections than in letters home. Hardening anticommunism may have prompted, or rekindled and validated, doubts as to the justice of U.S. policy, as conservative critics began lambasting the betrayal of unwilling Soviet repatriates by FDR to Stalin. See Mark R. Elliott, *Pawns of Yalta: Soviet Refugees and America's Role in Their Repatriation* (Urbana: University of Illinois Press, 1982). For veterans' expressions of misgiving, see Lt. Gen. Herron Maples, oral history, interviewed by Terry Anderson, June 22, 1981, Texas A&M University, USAMHI; Leon C. Standifer, *Binding Up the Wounds: An American Soldier in Occupied Germany, 1945–1946* (Baton Rouge: Louisiana State University Press, 1997), 87.

36 Moore, "Between Expediency and Principle"; Jan-Hinnerk Antons, "Displaced Persons in Postwar Germany: Parallel Societies in a Hostile Environment," *Journal of Contemporary History* 49 (2014): 92–114; Loescher and Scanlan, *Calculated Kindness,* 1–24.

37 Hutler, *Agony of Survival,* 22; Albert to Leanore Hutler, August 19, 1945, Albert Hutler Papers.

38 "Text of Eisenhower's Letter to Truman on Displaced Persons," *NYT,* October 17, 1945, 8; Templeton, *A Complete Change of Life,* 94.

39 John Wortham, *A Short Account of My Endeavors in World War II for My Daughters, Sue and Jan,* typescript memoir, July 1984, folder 3, box 20, WWII Collection, MS.2012, UTK. On DP sexuality, see Grossmann, *Jews, Germans, and Allies,* ch. 5. On American Jewish military chaplains' responses to DPs' sexual activity, see Julius Carlebach and Andreas Brämer, "Flight into Action as a Method of Repression: American Military Rabbis and the Problem of Jewish Displaced Persons in Postwar Germany," *Jewish Studies Quarterly* 2 (1995): 71. Michael Feldberg, "'The Day Is Short and the Task Is Great': Reports from Jewish Military Chaplains in Europe, 1945–1947," *American Jewish History* 91 (2003): 607–625; Lisa Haushofer, "The 'Contaminating Agent': UNRRA, Displaced Persons, and Venereal Disease in Germany, 1945–1947," *American Journal of Public Health* 100 (2010): 993–1003.

40 "Truman's Letter to Eisenhower and Part of Harrison's Report on Displaced Persons in Europe," *NYT,* September 30, 1945, 2.

41 "Text of Report to the President on Conditions among Refugees in Western Europe," *NYT,* September 30, 1945, 38.

42 Susan L. Carruthers, "Compulsory Viewing: Concentration Camp Film and German Re-education," *Millennium: Journal of International Studies* 30 (2001): 733–759.

43 "Text of Eisenhower's Letter," 8; George Patton Diary, August 29, 1945, folder 12, box 3, George S. Patton Papers, LOC. On the fraught politics of food, feeding, and hunger in postwar Germany, see Alice Weinreb, "'For the Hungry Have No Past nor Do They Belong to a Political Party," *Central European History* 45 (2012): 50–78.

44 George Patton Diary, April 12, 1945, April 15, 1945, and September 17, 1945, folders 11 and 12, box 3, George S. Patton Papers.

45 George Patton Diary, September 15, 1945, and September 21, 1945, folder 12, box 3, George S. Patton Papers.

46 Irving Heymont Papers Relating to Displaced Persons in Landsberg and Other Camps, 1945–1946, RG-19.038, USHMM. The published version of Heymont's letters differs in some significant ways from the originals; Jacob Rader Marcus and Abraham J. Peck, eds., *Among the Survivors of the Holocaust—1945: The Landsberg DP Camp Letters of Major Irving Heymont, United States Army* (Cincinnati: American Jewish Archives, 1982).

47 Irving to Joan Heymont, October 4, 1945, Irving Heymont Papers.

48 Irving to Joan Heymont, November 7, 1945, Irving Heymont Papers.

49 Irving to Joan Heymont, September 19, 1945, September 23, 1945, and October 2, 1945, Irving Heymont Papers. For frank mention of "human excrement," see "Blame UNRRA and Jews for Filth of Camps," *CDT,* December 7, 1945, 16. The *Times,* less damningly, headlined the same AP story, "Army Finds Camp of Jews Crowded," *NYT,* December 7, 1945, 5.

For more sympathetic reportage from Landsberg, see Arthur Gaeth, "A Visit to a Displaced Persons' Camp," *Jewish Advocate,* January 3, 1946, 7.

50 Irving to Joan Heymont, September 20, 1945, and October 12, 1945, Irving Heymont Papers; Frank Howley, Personal Diary, July 1, 1945–July 1, 1946, vol. 2, Kommandatura 14th Meeting, October 8, 1945, p. 120, box 2, Frank L. Howley Papers, USAMHI. On the problematic binary of forcible versus voluntary migration, see B. S. Chimni, "The Birth of a 'Discipline': From Refugee Studies to Forced Migration Studies," *Journal of Refugee Studies* 22 (2009): 11–29.

51 Irving to Joan Heymont, October 30, 1945, Irving Heymont Papers.

52 Marcus and Peck, *Among the Survivors.* Heymont's sympathetic understanding of Jewish DPs' traumatic experience is yet more pronounced in the video oral history for the USHMM; Irving Heymont, oral history interview, February 14, 1995, RG-50.470*0008, USHMM, http://collections.ushmm.org/search/catalog/irn511053. Heymont's limited empathy is criticized by William Hitchcock, who relied on the published version of his letters, to which Hitchcock refers as a "diary"; William I. Hitchcock, *The Bitter Road to Freedom: A New History of the Liberation of Europe* (New York: Free Press, 2008), 325–332. On veterans' shifting memories, see Adam R. Seipp, "Buchenwald Stories: Testimony, Military History, and the American Encounter with the Holocaust," *Journal of Military History* 79 (2015): 721–744.

53 Irving to Joan Heymont, November 1, 1945, and October 30, 1945, Irving Heymont Papers; Leo Schwarz, *The Redeemers: A Saga of the Years 1945–1952* (New York: Farrar, Straus and Young, 1953), 62.

54 "22 Nazis Hanged for War Crimes," *Daily Boston Globe,* May 28, 1947, 21; Irving to Joan Heymont, November 5, 1945, and November 6, 1945, Irving Heymont Papers.

55 Irving to Joan Heymont, October 7, 1945, Irving Heymont Papers; Albert to Leanore Hutler, August 19, 1945, Albert Hutler Papers.

56 Brig. Gen. Fred D. Beans, interview with Major Thomas E. Donnelly, 1976, USMC OHP; Watt, *When Empire Comes Home,* 46; McWilliams, *Homeward Bound,* 16–17.

57 The operational history of repatriation in Korea lists just fourteen officers assigned to U.S. military government's Displaced Persons Division; William J. Gane, *Repatriation from 25 September 1945 to 31 December 1945* (Seoul: U.S. Army Military Government in Korea, n.d.), 1. On Sasebo, see McWilliams, *Homeward Bound,* 18. For a critique of the British Commonwealth Occupation Force's similarly disparaging views of Koreans, see Tessa Morris-Suzuki, "An Act Prejudicial to the Occupation Forces: Migration Controls and Korean Residents in Post-surrender Japan," *Japanese Studies* 24 (2004): 5–28; and for a specimen, see Allan S. Clifton, *Time of Fallen Blossoms* (New York: Alfred A. Knopf, 1951), 157–166. For one enlisted man's recollections of spraying repatriates with DDT in Korea, see Ephraim P. Goodman Collection, AFC 2001/001/15661, audio recording, VHP.

58 Lt. Gen. James Berkeley, interview with Benis Frank, 1973, USMC OHP.

59 "Basic Initial Post-surrender Directive to Supreme Commander for the Allied Powers for the Occupation and Control of Japan," quoted by Caprio, "Resident Aliens," 183. Orlando Ward Diary, October 16, 1946, and October 19, 1946, box 10, Orlando W. Ward Papers, USAMHI.

60 Walt Sheldon, *The Honorable Conquerors: The Occupation of Japan, 1945–1952* (New York: Macmillan, 1965), 215.

61 "Aliens in Japan," quoted by Caprio, "Resident Aliens," 181. Takemae notes another contradiction: that the U.S. Army's *Civil Affairs Guide* called for protection of Koreans while advocating their continued use as "coolie labour" for railway and road maintenance; Eiji Takemae, *Inside GHQ: The Allied Occupation of Japan and Its Legacy* (New York: Continuum, 2002), 447.

62 Bassin quoted by Morris-Suzuki, *Borderline Japan,* 60.

63 Howard Handleman, "Pirates Murder Hundreds in Korean Repatriation Fraud," *Atlanta Constitution,* December 19, 1945, 1.

64 David Conde, "The Korean Minority in Japan," *Far Eastern Survey,* February 26, 1947, 44.

65 Gane, *Repatriation,* 41. SCAP report quoted by McWilliams, *Homeward Bound,* 59. Eichelberger to Miss Em, March 27, 1946, box 11, Robert L. Eichelberger Papers; Berkeley, interview with Benis Frank, 1973, USMC OHP. On Japanese attempts to circumvent property restrictions, see Howard Kahm, "Between Empire and Nation: A Micro-historical Approach to Japanese Repatriation and the Korean Economy during the US Occupation of Korea, 1945–6," *Journal of Contemporary History,* September 2014 (online version), doi:10.1177/002200 9414544772.

66 On the impossibility of getting by, see Gane, *Repatriation,* 88. On lexical slippage between stowaways and smugglers, see Morris-Suzuki, *Borderline Japan,* 55. Beans, interview with Major Thomas E. Donnelly, 1976, USMC OHP; Roland Glenn, *The Hawk and the Dove: World War II at Okinawa and Korea* (Kittery Point, ME: Smith/Kerr, 2009), 184.

67 Conde, "Korean Minority in Japan," 41; Irving to Joan Heymont, November 21, 1945, and November 22, 1945, Irving Heymont Papers. On the rearming of German police, see E. N. Harmon, *Combat Commander: Autobiography of a Soldier* (Englewood Cliffs, NJ: Prentice-Hall, 1970), 279–294. On Germans' views of Jewish responsibility for the black market, see Michael Berkowitz and Suzanne Brown-Fleming, "Perceptions of Jewish Displaced Persons as Criminals in Early Postwar Germany," in *"We Are Here,"* ed. A. Patt and M. Berkowitz (Detroit: Wayne State University Press, 2010), 167–193.

68 Robert Eichelberger, "Memoranda on Japan—Japanese People," dictation, February 22, 1948, box 64, Robert L. Eichelberger Papers; Berkeley, interview with Benis Frank, 1973, USMC OHP; "Some GI's Justify German Attack; Army Poll Shows Little Hostility," *NYT,* January 25, 1946, 5; "Anti-Semitism Is Laid to GIs at Landsberg," *New York Herald Tribune,* May 3, 1946, 3; Stephen G. Fritz, *Endkampf: Soldiers, Civilians, and the Death of the Third Reich* (Lexington: University Press of Kentucky, 2004), 242–243; George Patton Diary, September 17, 1945, folder 12, box 3, George S. Patton Papers; Clifton Lisle Diary, October 2 and September 7, 1945, box 13, Clifton Lisle Papers. Since Lisle was by then stationed in Mannheim, it's conceivable that Hutler was among those whom he slurred.

69 Jack to Mary Whitelaw, August 27, 1945, box 1, John L. Whitelaw Papers.

70 George Patton Diary, September 22, 25, 29, and October 1, 2, 1945, folder 12, box 3, George S. Patton Papers; HQ USFET, PR Division, "Transcript of a Press Conference Given

by Lt. Gen. Walter B. Smith at Frankfurt," September 26, 1945, folder 16, box 3, George S. Patton Papers.

71 George Patton to B., October 22, 1945, folder 17, box 13, George S. Patton Papers; fan mail, box 42, box 43, George S. Patton Papers.

72 Jack to Mary Whitelaw, November 18, 1945, and December 8, 1945, box 1, John L. Whitelaw Papers.

73 Hannah Arendt, "The Aftermath of Nazi Rule: Report from Germany," *Commentary* 1 (1950): 342; George Patton Diary, September 22, 1945, and October 2, 1945, folder 12, box 3, George S. Patton Papers.

6. DEMOBILIZATION BY DEMORALIZATION

1 Truman quoted by David McCullough, *Truman* (New York: Simon and Schuster, 1992), 571. On the "military genius," see Marshall Andrews, "Shrill Task Force Intercepts Ike on Way to Testify in House," *WP,* January 23, 1946, 1. On "irate war mothers," see J. Emlyn Williams, " 'Ike' Says Army Can't Release All Dads," *Christian Science Monitor,* January 22, 1946, 1.

2 In the month of September alone, Truman received approximately 1,000 letters on the subject of demobilization, with members of Congress amassing about 80,000; Ann Elizabeth Pfau, *Miss Yourlovin: GIs, Gender, and Domesticity during World War II* (New York: Columbia University Press, 2008), http://www.gutenberg-e.org/pfau/epilogue.html. On the Bring Back Daddy clubs, see R. Alton Lee, "The Army 'Mutiny' of 1946," *Journal of American History* 53 (1966): 558–559; "GI Wives Unite to Bring Back Their 'Daddies,' " *CDT,* November 10, 1945, 3; "Ask Congress' Aid to 'Bring Back Daddy,' " *CDT,* January 5, 1946, 13. The *Tribune* had reported—and pictured—this club's founding on December 1, 1945; "Bring Back Dad Club Is Formed by 200 Mothers," *CDT,* December 1, 1945, 8. "Baby Shoes Plead for Return of G.I.s," *New York Herald Tribune,* January 9, 1946, 3A.

3 " 'War Brides,' 56,000 Strong, Here by July," *WP,* January 5, 1946, 2; Mrs. Dorothy Galomb quoted by Andrews, "Shrill Task Force."

4 Williams, " 'Ike' Says"; Andrews, "Shrill Task Force"; Thomas J. Hamilton, "Wives of Soldiers Query Eisenhower," *NYT,* January 23, 1946, 1; "Why the GI's Demonstrate," *New Republic,* January 21, 1946, 72. On ubiquitous rumors of Eisenhower's affair with Summersby, see Alvin C. Schottenfeld, typescript memoir, n.d., p. 14, AFC 2001/001/4611, VHP.

5 May quoted by Thomas J. Hamilton, "Wives of Soldiers Query Eisenhower," *NYT,* January 23, 1946, 3. On the demobilization protests more broadly, see the army's official history, John C. Sparrow, *History of Personnel Demobilization in the United States Army* (Washington, DC: Office of the Chief of Military History, Department of the Army, 1951); Jack Stokes Ballard, *The Shock of Peace: Military and Economic Demobilization after World War II* (Washington, DC: University Press of America, 1983), 73–116; Daniel Eugene Garcia, "Class and Brass: Demobilization, Working Class Politics, and American Foreign Policy between World War and Cold War," *Diplomatic History* 34 (2010): 681–698; James T. Sparrow, *Warfare*

State: World War II Americans and the Age of Big Government (New York: Oxford University Press, 2011), 237–242.

6 "Army & Navy—Morale: My Son, John," *Time,* January 21, 1946; "Army & Navy—Demobilization: Home by Spring?," *Time,* January 14, 1946; Lee, "Army 'Mutiny,'" 561.

7 For details of how the point system worked, see Ballard, *Shock of Peace,* 75–76; Lee, "Army 'Mutiny,'" 556; and on Patterson's ignorance, ibid., 562. Howard Silbar to mom, January 12, 1946, box 2, Howard J. Silbar Papers, USAMHI.

8 Silbar to mom, December 11, 1945, box 2, Howard J. Silbar Papers; Bess Katz to Jake [Rosenfeld], May 12, 1945, folder 235, box 9, Jack Rosenfeld Papers, KCSC; Patsy to George Wolf, May 19, 1945, George L. Wolf Papers, USAMHI.

9 Robert Trumbull, "20,000 Manila GI's Boo General; Urge Congress to Speed Sailings," *NYT,* January 8, 1946, 1; "MPs Break Up GIs Marching on General," *WP,* January 7, 1946, 1; "Soldiers Plan Ad Campaign to Oust Patterson," *LAT,* January 9, 1945, 4; "GIs in Philippines Hold Fresh Rally," *NYT,* January 9, 1945, 6.

10 "Soldiers Get Aid of Mrs. Roosevelt," *NYT,* January 12, 1946, 6; Kathleen McLaughlin, "GI's in Frankfort Deride McNarney as They Fail to Get Sailing Dates," *NYT,* January 11, 1946, 4; "GIs Protest on Slow Demobilization," *NYT,* January 13, 1946, E1; Lee, "Army 'Mutiny,'" 562–563.

11 "Caution on Morale Given Eighth Army," *NYT,* January 10, 1946, 4.

12 Byers to My Precious Ones, January 9, 1946, box 10, Clovis E. Byers Papers, HIA.

13 Byers to wife, January 11, 1946, box 10, Clovis E. Byers Papers.

14 Stimson quoted by Michael Sherry, *Preparing for the Next War: American Plans for Postwar Defense, 1941–45* (New Haven, CT: Yale University Press, 1977), 191–192. The photograph of "Homeward Bounders" appears in an illustrated feature story saved by Philip Broadhead; Philip Broadhead Scrapbook, oversize item 9/10, WWII Collection, MS.2012, UTK.

15 Robert Daniels to Dearest Babes, May 29, 1945, folder 6, box 1, Robert E. Daniels Papers, SHC; John Bartlow Martin, "Anything Bothering You, Soldier?," *Harper's,* November 1, 1945, 453–457; Bill Taylor to "Mudder and Dad," August 12, 1945, and November 14, 1945, "Dear Mudder and Dad: The WWII Letters of William Wellington Taylor, Jr.," https://wwiiwwtaylor.wordpress.com/letters/.

16 Samuel A. Stouffer et al., *The American Soldier: Combat and Its Aftermath* (Princeton, NJ: Princeton University Press, 1949), 549–595; Nathaniel Warner, "The Morale of Troops on Occupation Duty," *American Journal of Psychiatry* 102 (1946): 749–757.

17 Edward Laughlin, *World War II Memoirs: A Paratrooper's Journey,* typescript memoir, 1999, Edward Laughlin Memoir, WWII Collection, MS.2669, UTK; Robert Engler, "The Individual Soldier and the Occupation," *Annals of the American Academy of Political and Social Science* 267 (1950): 82.

18 Milo Flaten to Mom and Pop, June 4, 1945, folder 9, box 1, Milo G. Flaten Papers, WVM.

19 Keith Mason to Emily Gosnald, June 29, 1945, folder 15, box 9, WWII Collection, MS.21012, UTK; "Ratio of Negro GI Releases to Be Lower than Whites," *Pittsburgh Courier,*

May 19, 1945, 15; "Discharge Bias Charged," *NYT,* August 19, 1945, 4; Langston Hughes, "Simple and the GI's," *Chicago Defender,* February 9, 1946, 9.

20 Norm to Miss Tait, December 17, 1945, Marion Tait Papers, NJHS; Milo Flaten to Mom and Pop, December 14, 1945, folder 10, box 1, Milo G. Flaten Papers.

21 Earl F. Ziemke, *The U.S. Army in the Occupation of Germany, 1944–1946* (Washington, DC: Center of Military History, U.S. Army, 1975), 403.

22 Chargé in the Soviet Union (Kennan) to the Secretary of State, telegram, February 22, 1946, no. 861.00/2-2246, National Security Archive, http://nsarchive.gwu.edu/coldwar/documents/episode-1/kennan.htm.

23 "Occupation by Volunteers," *Collier's,* August 25, 1945, 86; Eichelberger Diary, September 14, 16, and 19, box 1, Robert L. Eichelberger Papers, DMR. On MacArthur's "unauthorized statement," see Howard B. Schonberger, *Aftermath of War: Americans and the Remaking of Japan, 1945–52* (Kent, OH: Kent State University Press, 1989), 48–49.

24 Eisenhower's testimony delivered on January 15, 1945, quoted by Lee, "Army 'Mutiny,'" 567. "Why the GI's Demonstrate," 73.

25 Bill Taylor to Mudder and Dad, August 18, 1945, "Dear Mudder and Dad," https://wwiiwwtaylor.wordpress.com/letters/august-1945/.

26 Rebecca West, *A Train of Powder: Six Reports on the Problem of Guilt and Punishment in Our Time* (New York: Viking, 1955), 3, 4; Janet Flanner, "Letter from Nuremberg," March 15, 1946, originally published in the *New Yorker* under her pen name, Genêt, reprinted in Irving Drutman, ed., *Janet Flanner's World: Uncollected Writings, 1932–1975* (New York: Harvest/Harcourt Brace Jovanovich, 1979), 116.

27 Hanns Anders to mother, August 18, 1945, box 1, Winfred Hanns Anders Papers, USAMHI.

28 Sidney Eisenberg to Silv, Ralph and Hope, August 13, 1945; Sidney to Silv and Ralph, July 9, 1945; Sidney to Mutterchen, June 12, 1945, all in box 1, Sidney S. Eisenberg Papers, USAMHI.

29 Edward Sausville to Miss Macdonald, March 26, 1946, Marghita Macdonald Papers, USAMHI.

30 Ballard, *Shock of Peace,* 84; Bob Titus to Pop, August 28, 1945, box 5, William A. Titus Papers, UWO.

31 Hal Boyle, "Morale at Lowest Ebb since 1941," *LAT,* January 7, 1946, 4; Anne O'Hare McCormick, "Army of Occupation Faces Grave Problems," *NYT,* November 12, 1945, 20; Anne O'Hare McCormick, "When the Policemen Want to Go Home," *NYT,* January 14, 1946, 18.

32 Undated, unsigned letter from Japan, folder "General Correspondence Jan.–March 1946," box 4, Anne O'Hare McCormick Papers, NYPL.

33 McCormick to James Coveney, March 1, 1946, box 4, Anne O'Hare McCormick Papers; Anne O'Hare McCormick, "Overseas Echoes of Voices at Home," *NYT,* January 19, 1946, 12. Her indictment of irresponsible civilians was shared by other contemporary commentators; Engler, "Individual Soldier," 77–86.

34 Silbar to mom, January 12, 1946, box 2, Howard J. Silbar Papers; Bob LaFollette to family, January 11, 1946, folder 1, box 168, Philip Fox LaFollette Papers, WHS.

35 E. Kirschenbaum to McCormick, January 14, 1946, box 4, Anne O'Hare McCormick Papers; "The GIs and the Brass," *NYT,* March 20, 1946, 20; Robert Neville, "What's Wrong with Our Army?," *Life,* February 25, 1946, 108.

36 Lee, "Army 'Mutiny,'" 556–557; John Winner to Mother, Betty Jeanne and Mema, June 22, 1945, folder 21, box 1, John D. Winner Papers, WVM; Patsy to George Wolf, May 19, 1945, George L. Wolf Papers.

37 Watkins Diary, May 9, 1946, box 22, James Thomas Watkins Papers, HIA.

38 Watkins Diary, January 13, 1946, and February 5, 1946, box 22, James Thomas Watkins Papers.

39 Harry to Jinny McMasters, September 29, 1945, Harry L. McMasters Letters to His Wife, HIA.

40 Venice T. Spraggs, "Forrestal Order Rebukes Flattop Chief," *Chicago Defender,* December 22, 1945, 1. On the "backlog" of soldiers at Le Havre, see Ballard, *Shock of Peace,* 83.

41 Bob LaFollette to family, January 9, 1946, folder 1, box 168, Philip Fox LaFollette Papers; "War Department Denies Jim Crow on Okinawa," *Chicago Defender,* January 19, 1946, 13; Rufus to Vivian, November 26, 1945, folder 4, box 1, Lawrence D. Reddick WWII Project, SCRBC.

42 For a sympathetic, insider account of communist labor organizers' involvement in the GI demonstrations in Hawaii, see Erwin Marquit, "The Demobilization Movement of January 1946," *Nature, Society and Thought* 15 (2002): 5–39. See also Garcia, "Class and Brass," 684–685. Both Lee and Sparrow minimize the role played by communist organizers in the protest movement; Lee, "Army 'Mutiny,'" 561, 568–570; John C. Sparrow, *History of Personnel Demobilization,* 215, 394, 476. On the fate of universal military training, see William A. Taylor, *Every Citizen a Soldier: The Campaign for Universal Military Training after World War II* (College Station: Texas A&M Press, 2014). Negro Soldiers in the Pacific Theater, "To the American People," *Cleveland Call and Post,* February 2, 1946, 4B.

43 Marquit, "Demobilization Movement"; John C. Sparrow, *History of Personnel Demobilization,* 215. On the RAF, see David Duncan, "Mutiny in the RAF: The Air Force Strikes of 1946," Socialist History Society Occasional Papers Series No. 8, 1998, accessed May 8, 2016, http://libcom.org/book/export/html/26188. On the Indian mutiny, see Ronald Spector, "The Royal Indian Navy Strike of 1946: A Study of Cohesion and Disintegration in Colonial Armed Forces," *Armed Forces and Society* 7 (1981): 271–284. On Australian labor unions' support for Indonesian independence, see Heather Goodall, "Port Politics: Indian Seamen, Australian Unions and Indonesian Independence, 1945–47," *Labour History* 94 (2008): 43–68. For the larger context of Japanese imperial breakdown and European colonial reconstruction, see Ronald H. Spector, *In the Ruins of Empire: The Japanese Surrender and the Battle for Postwar Asia* (New York: Random House, 2007); C. A. Bayly and T. N. Harper, *Forgotten Wars: Freedom and Revolution in Southeast Asia* (Cambridge, MA: Belknap Press of Harvard University Press, 2007).

44 On the Atlantic Charter, see Elizabeth Borgwardt, *A New Deal for the World: America's Vision for Human Rights* (Cambridge, MA: Belknap Press of Harvard University Press, 2005). Garcia, "Class and Brass," 693–694; Roi Ottley, "GI Protests Seen Cause for

Alarm to Imperialists," *Pittsburgh Courier,* February 2, 1946, 12. Anti-imperialist critique was also evident in U.S. military newspapers; Garcia, "Class and Brass," 690–691.

45 Garcia, "Class and Brass," 692. On the Marine Corps' venture in China, see E. B. Sledge, *China Marine* (Tuscaloosa: University of Alabama Press, 2002). "Morale," *Time,* January 21, 1946, 21–22; Zeller quoted in memo, 401st CIC Detachment, HQ U.S. Army Forces, Middle Pacific, January 11, 1946, box 7, Robert C. Richardson Papers, HIA.

46 On "communist suspects," see John C. Sparrow, *History of Personnel Demobilization,* 394. Memo, 401st CIC Detachment, HQ U.S. Army Forces, Middle Pacific, January 11, 1946, box 7, Robert C. Richardson Papers.

47 Walter Trohan, "Identify Red as Sparkplug of GI Protest," *CDT,* January 24, 1946, 7. *Time* also quoted Byers's remark that "subversive forces are deliberately at work" in the January protests; "Morale," 21. On HUAC, see James T. Sparrow, *Warfare State,* 238.

48 Robert Eichelberger, "Memoranda on MG," dictation, February 28, 1948, folder "Japan: Occupation, Misc. 1945–49," box 64, Robert L. Eichelberger Papers; "Army Censors Criticism from Manila GI Daily," *CDT,* January 12, 1946, 5; "Army Explains Its Controls on G.I. Paper," *New York Herald Tribune,* January 12, 1946, 7A.

49 George Patton Diary, October 3, 1946, folder 12, box 3, George S. Patton Papers, LOC. A reprise of Willie and Joe's wartime experience is found in Bill Mauldin, *Up Front* (New York: Henry Holt, 1945). Jack to Mary Whitelaw, September 17, September 16, and October 8, 1945, box 1, John L. Whitelaw Papers, USAMHI.

50 Jack to Mary Whitelaw, October 14, 1945, box 1, John L. Whitelaw Papers.

51 Neville, "What's Wrong with Our Army?"; Paul Deutschman, "Second Class Citizens," *Life,* February 25, 1946, 114; Eichelberger to Miss Em, April 5, 1946, folder 2, box 11, Robert L. Eichelberger Papers.

52 Lt. Gen. John A. Heintges, interview with Major Jack A. Pellicci, 1974, Senior Officers Oral History Program, USAMHI; Eichelberger to Miss Em, February 17, 1946, folder 2, box 11, Robert L. Eichelberger Papers.

53 Noel F. Busch, *Fallen Sun: A Report on Japan* (New York: D. Appleton-Century, 1948), 12–13; "Mates of Yank Doomed to Die Speak for Him," *CDT,* January 21, 1946, 15. Hicswa surfaces in Terese Svoboda's account of her uncle's troubled tour in occupied Japan, *Black Glasses like Clark Kent: A GI's Secret from Postwar Japan* (Saint Paul, MN: Graywolf Press, 2008).

54 "Home Town Tries to Save Soldier Condemned for Killing Japanese," *NYT,* January 15, 1946, 15; "Move for Hicswa Grows," *NYT,* January 18, 1946, 5; "M'Arthur to Review GI's Death Sentence," *NYT,* January 19, 1946, 6; "M'Arthur Writes to Hicswa's Mother," *NYT,* January 30, 1946, 4; "Hicswas Plead for Son's Life, Citing Head Injury as Boy," *WP,* March 6, 1946, 14; "Murder by Liquor, Inc.," *Christian Science Monitor,* January 17, 1946, 20.

55 Hicswa letter to Sonia Andryk quoted in "Murder of Two Japs Is Denied by Doomed Yank," *CDT,* January 17, 1946, 3; Hicswa letter to uncle quoted in "Doomed GI Pleads for Civil Trial," *WP,* February 5, 1946, 1.

56 "Yamashita and Hicswa," *New York Herald Tribune,* February 6, 1946, 22.

57 Byers to Esther and Haydn Evan, March 5, 1946, box 5, Clovis E. Byers Papers.

58 Clovis to Marie Byers, March 3, 1946, box 10, Clovis E. Byers Papers; Eichelberger to Miss Em, March 5, 1946, box 11, Robert L. Eichelberger Papers.

59 Clovis to Marie Byers, March 5, 1946, box 10, Clovis E. Byers Papers. His informant may have exaggerated. The story did not receive prominent attention in several major papers. The *Washington Post* ignored it altogether. Meanwhile both the *Times'* and the *Chicago Daily Tribune*'s stories on Hicswa's recapture, based on the same AP report, mentioned only the name, not the ethnic identity of his fellow escapee; "Hicswa Escapes, Caught," *NYT,* March 4, 1946, 10; "Hicswa Escapes Prison in Japan but Is Captured," *CDT,* March 4, 1946, 1. Little attention was given to the location of Hicswa's recapture, the *LA Times* mentioning only en passant that he had been found in a "geisha house"; "Doomed G.I. Breaks Jail in Japan, but Not for Long," *LAT,* March 4, 1946, 5. "Hicswa Sentence Is Cut to 30 Years," *NYT,* May 8, 1946, 10. In 1952, Hicswa's sentence was further reduced to twenty-one years, with an estimated release date announced for March 1960; "GI's Sentence Cut to 21 Years," *NYT,* March 18, 1952, 9.

60 Charles Hunt to family, January 6, 1946, folder 18, box 1, Charles D. Hunt Papers, IHS.

61 War Department, Army Service Forces in the Office of the Judge Advocate General, Washington, DC, *United States v. Private First Class Joseph E. Hicswa,* Opinion of the Board of Review, Moyse, Kuder and Wingo, Judge Advocates, April 9, 1946, in Army Board of Review, *Holdings, Opinions and Reviews,* vol. 59 (Washington, DC: Office of the Judge Advocate General).

62 "Psychiatry Urged on Troops Abroad," *NYT,* January 13, 1946, 16. Lee endorses this conclusion about poor indoctrination, "Army 'Mutiny,' " 565.

63 Engler, "Individual Soldier," 84. On plans for a touring exhibit, see "Outline of Proposed Content of Joint State-War Exhibit of U.S. Occupation of Germany," November 1946, box 5, Roswell P. Rosengren Papers, WHS.

64 Quoted by Sherry, *Preparing for the Next War,* 192.

7. GETTING WITHOUT SPENDING

1 John Dos Passos, "Americans Are Losing the Victory in Europe," *Life,* January 7, 1946, 22–25. See also Dos Passos's longer account in *Tour of Duty* (Boston: Houghton Mifflin, 1946). Edward P. Morgan, "Heels among the Heroes," *Collier's,* October 19, 1946, 16–17.

2 Margaret Bourke-White, *"Dear Fatherland Rest Quietly": A Report on the Collapse of Hitler's "Thousand Years"* (New York: Simon and Schuster, 1946), 158.

3 Lindesay Parrott, "GI Behavior in Japan Questioned," *NYT,* January 28, 1946, 5; *Newsweek,* January 28, 1946, 44.

4 Drew Middleton, "Failure in Germany," *Collier's,* February 9, 1946, 12, 13, 62, 65; Mark Gayn, "Our Balance Sheet in Asia," *Collier's,* March 23, 1946, 12, 13, 81, 83. For his more extended analysis, see Mark Gayn, *Japan Diary* (New York: William Sloane, 1948).

5 Eichelberger Diary, February 17, 1946, box 1, Robert L. Eichelberger Papers, DMR; C. L. Sulzberger, "Educators Stress Needs in Germany," *NYT,* April 1, 1946, 5.

6 William J. Lederer and Eugene Burdick, *The Ugly American* (New York: W. W. Norton, 1958); Reddick interview with Roi Ottley, 1946, folder 11, box 1, Lawrence D. Reddick WWII Project, SCRBC.

7 Hargis Westerfield, "Failures in G.I. Orientation: The Japanese Story," *Free World,* April 1946, 62–63.

8 "Something Borrowed . . . ," *Time,* June 17, 1946, 25.

9 Corporal Carlton was absolved; "Ex-soldier Cleared in Hesse Gem Theft," *NYT,* June 14, 1946, 5. "WAC Loses Fight on Gem Confession," *NYT,* August 28, 1946, 13.

10 Sidney Shalett, "Colonel, Wac Captain Held in German Royal Gem Theft," *NYT,* June 8, 1946, 1; "Something Borrowed," 25; Stephen Harding, "Soldiers of Fortune," *World War II* 24 (May 2009): 62; Geoffrey E. Duin, "Intrigue: A Tale of Purloined Jewels, Moles and Royal Mischief Emerged after World War II," *Military History* 23 (January/February 2007): 15–17.

11 "Wac Contests Hesse Jewel Trial on Basis Army Lacks Jurisdiction," *NYT,* August 23, 1946, 8.

12 "Capt. Durant Gets 5 Years for Theft," *NYT,* October 1, 1946, 9; Harding, "Soldiers of Fortune," 63.

13 "Army Linked to Art Loot," *NYT,* July 21, 1946, 24; "Accomplice in Hesse Jewel Theft Gets Five Years and Dismissal," *NYT,* November 1, 1946, 16.

14 *A Foreign Affair,* directed by Billy Wilder (Los Angeles: Paramount Pictures, 1948); *The Third Man,* directed by Carol Reed (London: London Film Productions, 1949); Graham Greene, *The Third Man,* in Philip Stafford, ed., *The Portable Graham Greene* (New York: Penguin, 2005), 324.

15 Kay Boyle, "Frankfurt in Our Blood," in *The Smoking Mountain: Stories of Postwar Germany* (New York: McGraw-Hill, 1951), 123; Walter J. Slatoff, "GI Morals in Germany," *New Republic,* May 13, 1946, 686–687. Slatoff later became chair of Cornell's English Department.

16 Meredith H. Lair, *Armed with Abundance: Consumerism and Soldiering in the Vietnam War* (Chapel Hill: University of North Carolina Press, 2011); Eichelberger to Herman Gudger, February 26, 1946, folder 2, box 11, Robert L. Eichelberger Papers. For other accounts of this process, see John Willoughby, *Remaking the Conquering Heroes: The Postwar American Occupation of Germany* (New York: Palgrave Macmillan, 2009); Oliver J. Frederiksen, *The American Military Occupation of Germany, 1945–1953* (Darmstadt, Germany: Historical Division, Headquarters, United States Army, Europe, 1953), 99–110; Michael Cullen Green, *Black Yanks in the Pacific: Race in the Making of American Military Empire after World War II* (Ithaca, NY: Cornell University Press, 2010). Martha Wayman to Ruth, December 10, 1945, box 2, Martha A. Wayman Papers, USAMHI.

17 Frederiksen, *American Military Occupation,* 101; John Maginnis Diary, September 23, 1945, box 2, John J. Maginnis Papers, USAMHI; Charles Hunt to family, October 1, 1945, and December 19, 1945, folder 18, box 1, Charles D. Hunt Papers, IHS.

18 HQ Fifteenth U.S. Army, "Control of Venereal Disease," June 27, 1945, folder "15th Army Medical History," box 2, Harold Richard Hennessy Papers, USAMHI; Eichelberger to Herman Gudger, February 26, 1946, folder 2, box 11, Robert L. Eichelberger Papers; Eichelberger to Miss Em, February 18, 1946, folder 2, box 11, Robert L. Eichelberger Papers.

19 Robert Eichelberger, "Our Soldiers in the Occupation," dictation, February 21, 1948, folder "Japan: Occupation, Misc., 1945–49," box 64, Robert L. Eichelberger Papers.

20 Eugene Mercier to Roger S. Durham, September 4, 2006, Eugene Mercier Papers, USAMHI; Jack Rosenfeld to Sylvia Solov, July 19, 1945, folder 329, box 12, Jack Rosenfeld Papers, KCSC; memo, "Operation of the Eighth United States Army," September 21, 1947, folder "Japan: Occupation, Misc., 1945–49," box 64, Robert L. Eichelberger Papers; Willoughby, *Remaking the Conquering Heroes,* 111; George McCaffrey Diary, May 24, 1943, box 1, George Herbert McCaffrey Papers, SUL.

21 Some recent scholarship tackles the phenomenon of military tourism but little attention has been paid to its pre–Vietnam War antecedents. See, for example, Scott Laderman, *Tours of Vietnam: War, Travel Guides, and Memory* (Durham, NC: Duke University Press, 2009); Vernadette Vicuña Gonzalez, *Securing Paradise: Tourism and Militarism in Hawai'i and the Philippines* (Durham, NC: Duke University Press, 2013); and, for a different context, Rebecca L. Stein, *Itineraries in Conflict: Israelis, Palestinians, and the Political Lives of Tourism* (Durham, NC: Duke University Press, 2008). Capt. Randolph Seligman to all, October 10, 1945, Mary Jane Anderson Papers, USAMHI; Bob LaFollette to family, February 23, 1946, folder 2, box 168, Philip Fox LaFollette Papers, WHS; Alan Sterling to Ruth, September 15, 1945, folder 2, box 1, Alan T. Sterling Papers, DMR.

22 See, for example, the collection of photo albums from members of the U.S. Army, 24th Infantry Division, DMR.

23 Eichelberger Diary, 1945, 1946, and 1947, box 1, Robert L. Eichelberger Papers; Chuck to family, November 18, 1945, Wilhelm Family Letters, WHS.

24 Maurice to Laya Kurtz, June 25, 1945, folder 4, box 1, Maurice Kurtz Papers, SHC. On Dachau as "the tourist horror spot," see Bud Hutton and Andy Rooney, *Conquerors' Peace: A Report to the American Stockholders* (Garden City, NY: Doubleday, 1947), 28.

25 Henry to Louisa Baust, July 1, 1945, box 3, Henry Baust Jr. Papers, USAMHI. Rebecca West describes the Chad ("What no Fuhrer?") graffiti in *A Train of Powder: Six Reports on the Problem of Guilt and Punishment in Our Time* (New York: Viking, 1955), 39.

26 Price Day, "Berchtesgaden Chalet Is Center for GI Tourists," *Baltimore Sun,* June 7, 1945, 1.

27 West, *Train of Powder,* 3; Clarence to Eve Davis, August 17, 1945, and August 7, 1945, box 1, Clarence W. Davis Letters, DMR.

28 Silbar to Ruth, October 20, 1945, box 2, Howard J. Silbar Papers, USAMHI; Silbar to mom, December 11, 1945, box 2, Howard J. Silbar Papers.

29 Samuel A. Stouffer et al., *The American Soldier: Combat and Its Aftermath* (Princeton, NJ: Princeton University Press, 1949).

30 For personal recollections, see "The Biarritz American University," BBC, January 17, 2006, http://www.bbc.co.uk/history/ww2peopleswar/stories/09/a8610509.shtml; Hervie Haufler, "The Most Contented GIs in History," History.net, August 19, 1999, http://www.historynet.com/the-most-contented-gis-in-europe-october-99-american-history-feature.htm.

31 Eichelberger to Miss Em, March 9, 1946, folder 3, box 11, Robert L. Eichelberger Papers.

32 Martha Wayman to Ruth, November 25, 1945, box 2, Martha A. Wayman Papers.

33 Rep. John Sheridan to Eichelberger, September 1, 1946, box 16, Robert L. Eichelberger Papers.

34 Eichelberger to Hon. Dewey Short, Representatives Short, Johnson, Feighan, Sikes and Martin, September 9, 1946, box 16, Robert L. Eichelberger Papers. Portions of this letter were published in the U.S. press; "Post-Exchange Facilities in Korea Condemned," *NYT,* September 3, 1946, 8.

35 Hunt to family, October 25, 1945, folder 17, box 1, Charles D. Hunt Papers.

36 T. E. Beattie, "The American Soldier as a Purchaser in Southern Italy," *Journal of Marketing* 9 (April 1945): 385.

37 Herman Berger to mother and sister, December 26, 1946, January 1, 1947, folder 4, box 1, Herman Berger Papers, HSP; Wayman to mother, December 13, 1945, box 2, Martha A. Wayman Papers; Wayman to Ruth, December 20, 1945, box 2, Martha A. Wayman Papers.

38 Robert Lowenstein, oral history interview, June 3, 1999, by Lynn Marley and Shaun Illingworth, ROHA; H. A. Miller, *Vignettes of 12102794,* typescript memoir, n.d., folder 38, box 9, WWII Collection, MS.2012, UTK. Dorothy Vickery, who worked in Europe in 1946 as a publicity officer for the Red Cross, similarly noted that GIs in Paris were making forty to fifty dollars per week by selling their clothing and rations; Dorothy S. Vickery, *Memoirs of Europe after World War II, 1945–47,* typescript memoir, n.d., folder 34, box 14, WWII Collection, MS.2012, UTK.

39 Frank Howley, Personal Diary, vol. 2, "The Inter-Allied Occupation of Berlin, Germany," July 1, 1945–July 1, 1946, p. 39, box 2, Frank L. Howley Papers, USAMHI; John Maginnis Diary, August 24, 1945, box 2, John J. Maginnis Papers. That the Treasury Department had handed over these plates later became something of a Cold War scandal; Walter Rundell Jr., *Black Market Money: The Collapse of U.S. Military Currency Control in World War II* (Baton Rouge: Louisiana State University Press, 1964); Vladimir Petrov, *Money and Conquest: Allied Occupation Currencies in World War II* (Baltimore: Johns Hopkins University Press, 1967); Richard L. Stokes, "The Astounding Soviet Swindle of American Taxpayers," *Reader's Digest,* February 1953, 93–96.

40 John Maginnis Diary, November 5, 1945, box 2, John J. Maginnis Papers.

41 John Winner to Mother, Betty Jeanne and Mema, October 9, 1945, folder 26, box 1, John D. Winner Papers, WVM. Anne Alinder noted in a round-robin letter from Frankfurt, dated November 2, 1945, that Red Army tastes had become more sophisticated, Russians now preferring "black faced dials with jewels"; folder 1, box 1, Anne Alinder Korbel Papers, WVM.

42 Jane DePuy to folks, August 21, 1946, box 1, Jane E. DePuy Papers, DMR.

43 See Bob LaFollette's letters from Japan, box 168, Philip Fox LaFollette Family Papers. Martha Wayman to mother, December 3, 1945, box 2, Martha A. Wayman Papers. For an account of a black-market business partnership, see Paul D. Veatch, *Jungle, Sea and Occupation: A World War II Soldier's Memoir of the Pacific Theater* (Jefferson, NC: McFarland, 2000), 135–151.

44 Frank Howley, Personal Diary, vol. 2, p. 39, box 2, Frank L. Howley Papers; John Maginnis Diary, August 24, 1945, box 2, John J. Maginnis Papers; Laura J. Hilton, "The

Black Market in History and Memory: German Perceptions of Victimhood from 1945 to 1948," *German History* 28 (2010): 479–497; Paul Steege, *Black Market, Cold War: Everyday Life in Berlin, 1946–1949* (New York: Cambridge University Press, 2007); Kevin Conley Ruffner, "The Black Market in Postwar Berlin: Colonel Miller and an Army Scandal," *Prologue* 34 (Fall 2002): 170–183. On Japan, John W. Dower, *Embracing Defeat: Japan in the Wake of World War II* (New York: W. W. Norton, 1999), 139–148; Owen Griffith, "Need, Greed, and Protest in Japan's Black Market, 1938–1949," *Journal of Social History* 35 (2002): 825–858.

45 John Maginnis Diary, August 24, 1945, box 2, John J. Maginnis Papers; Jean Smith, *General Mac's WACs, Part III, Japan, 1946–49: Tokyo, from Fear to Friendship,* typescript memoir, n.d., box 1, Jean Smith Papers, USAMHI; John Maginnis Diary, November 5, 1945, box 2, John J. Maginnis Papers.

46 Alan Sterling to mother, October 26, 1945, folder 2, box 1, Alan T. Sterling Papers.

47 Address by Paul Skuse at Air and Ground Forces Intelligence Officers' Conference, January 15, 1947, box 23, James Thomas Watkins Papers, HIA.

48 Paul to Margaret Skuse, August 22, 1945, box 23, James Thomas Watkins Papers.

49 Jack to Mary Whitelaw, October 16, 1945, box 1, John L. Whitelaw Papers, USAMHI; Betty Olson to family, August 19, 1945, box 1, Betty M. Olson Papers, USAMHI; "Making George Do It," *Newsweek,* October 8, 1945, 50.

50 Since African American troops were largely confined to service roles in the military, they formed a disproportionate presence in quartermaster outfits, and were widely seen as privileged black-market operators with ready access to supplies. Several of Lawrence Reddick's oral history interviewees discussed their own, or others', black-market activities; see, for example, interview with Cruz and Robinson, January 12, 1946, folder 8, Lawrence D. Reddick WWII Project, SCRBC; interview with Cpl. Horace Evans of Detroit, 1946, folder 8, Lawrence D. Reddick WWII Project, SCRBC. Cornelius DeForest to wife, December 24, 1945, and April 10, 1946, box 1, Cornelius W. DeForest Papers, USAMHI.

51 Malcolm R. McCallum, "The Study of the Delinquent in the Army," *American Journal of Sociology* 51 (1946): 482.

52 Robert Engler, "The Individual Soldier and the Occupation," *Annals of the American Academy of Political and Social Science* 267 (1950): 82. Resentment toward civilians and rear echelon personnel who were believed to have enriched themselves was not confined to U.S. soldiers. On parallel sentiments shared by Red Army personnel, see Robert Dale, "Rats and Resentment: The Demobilization of the Red Army in Postwar Leningrad, 1945–50," *Journal of Contemporary History* 45 (2010): 113–133. Earl F. Ziemke, *The U.S. Army in the Occupation of Germany, 1944–1946* (Washington, DC: Center of Military History, U.S. Army, 1975), 442; Rundell, *Black Market Money,* ix–x.

53 Anne Alinder, circular letter, November 2, 1945, folder 1, box 1, Anne Alinder Korbel Papers.

54 Ibid.; Harry to Jinny McMasters, September 16, 1945, Harry L. McMasters Letters to His Wife, HIA.

55 ACLU report, *Civil Liberties in Japan,* June 1947, folder "Japan: Occupation, Misc., 1945–49," box 64, Robert L. Eichelberger Papers. On Japanese Americans' involvement, and

perceived implication, in the Japanese black market, see Tamotsu Shibutani, *The Derelicts of Company K: A Sociological Study of Demoralization* (Berkeley: University of California Press, 1978), 366–368. On Germany, see Steege, *Black Market, Cold War,* 49; Hilton, "Black Market in History and Memory"; Michael Berkowitz and Suzanne Brown-Fleming, "Perceptions of Jewish Displaced Persons as Criminals in Early Postwar Germany," in *"We Are Here,"* ed. A. Patt and M. Berkowitz (Detroit: Wayne State University Press, 2010), 167–193; Kierra Crago-Schneider, "Antisemitism or Competing Interests? An Examination of German and American Perceptions of Jewish Displaced Persons Active on the Black Market in Munich's Möhlstrasse," *Yad Vashem Studies* 38 (2010): 167–194.

56 Jack to Mary Whitelaw, November 13, 1945, box 1, John L. Whitelaw Papers.

57 On the jeep, see Frank Howley, Personal Diary, vol. 2, p. 41, box 2, Frank L. Howley Papers. On the olive drab pants, see Olaf Osnes to General Publicus, May 8, 1948, box 1, Olaf Osnes Papers, USAMHI. On the foiled heist, see Benton to Edwina Decker, April 11, 1946, box 5, Benton W. Decker Papers, HIA.

58 Civil Intelligence Section, SCAP Occupational Trends, April 17, 1946, p. 9, box 49, Robert L. Eichelberger Papers.

59 Civil Intelligence Section, SCAP Occupational Trends, June 5, 1946, p. 9, box 49, Robert L. Eichelberger Papers.

60 Robert Eichelberger, "Memoranda on War Crimes," dictation, March 1, 1948, box 64, Robert L. Eichelberger Papers; Robert L. Eichelberger, *Our Jungle Road to Tokyo* (New York: Viking, 1950), 273–274.

61 Clovis Byers to Col. John Elmore, War Dept. General Staff, August 31, 1946, box 6, Clovis E. Byers Papers, HIA. African Americans' complaints are outlined in a letter to Byers from officers of Camp Rinaldo, February 24, 1947, box 7, Clovis E. Byers Papers. Eichelberger to Miss Em, April 30, 1946, folder 4, box 11, Robert L. Eichelberger Papers.

62 Headquarters Eighth Army, Eichelberger to All Unit Commanders, "Incidents Involving United States Troops," June 26, 1946, box 16, Robert L. Eichelberger Papers; Lindesay Parrott, "Curbs on GI Crimes Ordered in Japan," *NYT,* July 14, 1946, 1; "Revealed Drunken Yanks Beat and Bully the Japs," *CDT,* July 19, 1946, 12.

8. DOMESTICATING OCCUPATION

1 Eichelberger Diary, June 24, 1946, May 2, 1946, and April 11, 1946, box 1, Robert L. Eichelberger Papers, DMR.

2 Lindesay Parrott, "Navy Wives First to Land in Japan," *NYT,* June 22, 1946, 3; Grace Robinson, "224 Wives of U.S. Soldiers Reach Bremen," *CDT,* April 29, 1946, 1.

3 Parrott, "Navy Wives First to Land," 3.

4 Lucius Clay, *Decision in Germany* (New York: Doubleday, 1950), 70; Earl F. Ziemke, *The U.S. Army in the Occupation of Germany, 1944–1946* (Washington, DC: Center of Military History, U.S. Army, 1975), 442; Truman interview with *Stars and Stripes* quoted in "GI's Wives to Stay in Europe," *NYT,* July 30, 1945, 5.

5 Oliver J. Frederiksen, *The American Military Occupation of Germany, 1945–1953* (Darmstadt, Germany: Historical Division, Headquarters, United States Army, Europe, 1953); John Willoughby, *Remaking the Conquering Heroes: The Postwar American Occupation of Germany* (New York: Palgrave Macmillan, 2009), 117–125; Donna Alvah, *Unofficial Ambassadors: American Military Families Overseas and the Cold War, 1946–65* (New York: New York University Press, 2007); "G.I. Wives," *WP,* August 5, 1945, B4.

6 Willoughby, *Remaking the Conquering Heroes,* 120–122; Eichelberger to Miss Em, February 10, 1946, folder 2, box 11, Robert L. Eichelberger Papers.

7 Eichelberger told his wife that "practically none" of the enlisted men with whom he had spoken wished their wives to join them; Eichelberger to Miss Em, February 18, 1946, folder 2, box 11, Robert L. Eichelberger Papers. Lindesay Parrott, "Men in Japan Balk at Inviting Wives," *NYT,* February 24, 1946, 36. On the youth of GIs, see Lindesay Parrott, "Curb on GI Crimes Ordered in Japan," *NYT,* July 14, 1946, 1. Eisenhower to Marshall, June 4, 1945, and Marshall to Eisenhower, June 8, 1945, in *The Papers of Dwight David Eisenhower,* vol. 6, *Occupation, 1945,* ed. Alfred D. Chandler and Louis Galambos (Baltimore: Johns Hopkins University Press, 1978), 134–135.

8 Devers quoted in "GI Wives for Occupation," *NYT,* October 4, 1945, 6. On Jean MacArthur's arrival, see William Manchester, *American Caesar: Douglas MacArthur, 1880–1964* (New York: Back Bay Books, 2008), 513. Eichelberger to Miss Em, February 10, 1946, folder 2, box 11, Robert L. Eichelberger Papers.

9 Martha Gravois, "Military Families in Germany, 1946–1986: Why They Came and Why They Stay," *Parameters* 16 (1986): 57–67; Frederiksen, *American Military Occupation of Germany,* 121.

10 For statistics, see Maria Höhn, "'You Can't Pin Sergeant's Stripes on an Archangel': Soldiering, Sexuality, and U.S. Army Policies in Germany," in *Over There: Living with the U.S. Military Empire from World War Two to the Present,* ed. Maria Höhn and Seungsook Moon (Durham, NC: Duke University Press, 2010), 113. C. L. Sulzberger, "U.S. Psychology Fails in Germany," *NYT,* March 26, 1946, 16.

11 John Winner to Mother, Betty Jeanne and Mema, December 4, 1945, folder 28, box 1, John D. Winner Papers, WVM. Having served as a civil affairs officer in France in 1944–1945, Thurmond later made a vigorous intervention in the 1980s on behalf of the army's beleaguered civil affairs program; Susan Lynn Marquis, *Unconventional Warfare: Rebuilding U.S. Special Operations Forces* (Washington, DC: Brookings Institution Press, 1997). Kissinger's career in army counterintelligence in postwar Germany is documented by Jeremi Suri, *Henry Kissinger and the American Century* (Cambridge, MA: Belknap Press of Harvard University Press, 2009).

12 On Europe, see Frederiksen, *American Military Occupation of Germany,* 120–121. Eichelberger Diary, February 26, 1946, box 1, Robert L. Eichelberger Papers.

13 U.S. European Command, Office of the Chief Historian, *Domestic Economy: Shipment of Dependents to the European Theater and Establishment of Military Communities: Occupation Forces in Europe Series, 1945–46* (Frankfurt-am-Main, Germany: Office of the Chief Historian, 1947), 2.

14 On successive iterations of the information program for dependents, see Historical Division, European Command, *The Relations of Occupation Personnel with the Civil Population, 1946–1948* (Karlsruhe, Germany: Historical Division, European Command, 1951), 4, 7.

15 Eichelberger to Miss Em, March 28, 1946, folder 3, box 11, Robert L. Eichelberger Papers.

16 Clovis to Marie Byers, October 15, 1945, box 30, Clovis E. Byers Papers, HIA.

17 Clovis to Marie Byers, October 15, 1945, and March 14, 1946, box 10, Clovis E. Byers Papers.

18 On evictions, see Willoughby, *Remaking the Conquering Heroes,* 122–124. C. P. Harness, "The Family Might Even Enjoy the Land Daddy Licked," *WP,* March 24, 1946, B3.

19 On man-hours, labor, and costs in Germany, see Frederiksen, *American Military Occupation of Germany,* 122–123. For the Eighth Army's construction accomplishments, see memo, "Operation of the Eighth United States Army," September 21, 1947, folder, "Japan: Occupation, Misc., 1945–49," box 64, Robert L. Eichelberger Papers. On occupation costs, see Eiji Takemae, *Inside GHQ: The Allied Occupation of Japan and Its Legacy* (New York: Continuum, 2002), 126.

20 On Quonset huts, see Ernest Kovats, *All My Love, Son: Letters from Korea* (self-published, 2005), 59. While those with two or more dependents would enjoy a Quonset to themselves, others would share "half a hut," an arrangement that provided scant privacy; "U.S. Families in Japan to Use Quonset Huts," *NYT,* April 24, 1946, 16. Winner to Mother, Betty Jeanne and Mema, May 13, 1946, box 2, John D. Winner Papers.

21 *Stars and Stripes,* April 3, 1946, quoted by Gravois, "Military Families," 61; Cornelius to Julie DeForest, January 21, 1946, and February 9, 1946, box 1, Cornelius W. DeForest Papers, USAMHI.

22 Clovis to Marie Byers, February 7, 1946, box 10, Clovis E. Byers Papers; Eichelberger to Miss Em, June 1, 1946, folder 6, box 11, Robert L. Eichelberger Papers.

23 "No Army Law against Girls in Brass' Rooms," *Atlanta Constitution,* March 5, 1946, 1; Iris Carpenter, "Overseas Soldiers' Wives Should Go Abroad Quickly," *Daily Boston Globe,* March 10, 1946, D1.

24 Walter Simmons, "Teen-Age GI's Prefer Movie to Jap Girls," *CDT,* June 5, 1946, 19. Byers's "poor taste" remark was recorded by Robert Eichelberger, "Our Soldiers in the Occupation," dictation, February 21, 1948, folder "Japan: Occupation, Misc., 1945–49," box 64, Robert L. Eichelberger Papers. On encouragement of kissing as part of a "democratic" practice of courtship, including the insertion of kissing sequences into Japanese movies, see Mark McLelland, "'Kissing Is a Symbol of Democracy!' Dating, Democracy, and Romance in Occupied Japan, 1945–1952," *Journal of the History of Sexuality* 19 (2010): 508–535. "Teaching the Kiss," *Des Moines Register,* reprinted in "Opinions of Other Newspapers," *LAT,* March 20, 1949, A4.

25 "GI's in Japan Warned against Public Necking," *LAT,* March 23, 1946, 5. The Associated Press tallied forty arrests by the month's end; "Jap Courting Ban Pays Off; GI Ardor Nets $10 Fines," *LAT,* March 29, 1946, 5. Eichelberger to Miss Em, March 28, 1946, March 31, 1946, and April 3, 1946, folder 3 (March) and folder 4 (April), box 11, Robert L. Eichelberger Papers.

26 "Army Wife in Germany Hits at Fraternizing," *Hartford Courant,* June 3, 1946, 16; "GI's in Munich Can't Even Hold Arms of Wives," *CDT,* July 7, 1946, 10.

27 On sexual harassment and rape experienced by WACs, see Leisa D. Meyer, *Creating GI Jane: Sexuality and Power in the Women's Army Corps during World War II* (New York: Columbia University Press, 1996), ch. 6.

28 Dana Adams Schmidt, "Soldier Wives and Children Begin New Life in Germany," *NYT,* May 5, 1946, E4.

29 On armbands, see Gravois, "Military Families," 59. "Reveal Drunken Yanks Beat and Bully the Japs," *CDT,* July 14, 1946, 12.

30 Clay quoted by Willoughby, *Remaking the Conquering Heroes,* 128. On rising VD rates, see Public Health Section reports, box 63, Robert L. Eichelberger Papers. *A Foreign Affair,* directed by Billy Wilder (Los Angeles: Paramount Pictures, 1948). Kay Boyle's short fiction set in occupied Germany, first published in the *New Yorker* and elsewhere, has been collected in *Fifty Stories* (New York: Penguin, 1981). See also Alfred Hayes, *All They Conquests* (New York: Howell Soskin, 1946), and *The Girl on the Via Flaminia* (New York: Harper, 1949); Zelda Popkin, *Small Victory* (Philadelphia: J. B. Lippincott, 1947); Wesley Towner, *The Liberators* (New York: A. A. Wyn, 1946); Donald Richie, *This Scorching Earth* (Rutland, VT: Charles E. Tuttle, 1956). Isabelle Mallet, "Perils of Occupation," review of *The Sealed Verdict,* by Lionel Shapiro (New York: Doubleday, 1947), *NYT,* October 19, 1947, 16.

31 "2,011 American Women Work for War Department in Tokyo," *New York Herald Tribune,* July 13, 1947, A5. The same story also noted that, since June 1946, 500 "American girls" had married, according to the American consulate in Yokohama. "Illicit Affairs Increase Zonal Army Divorces," *WP,* December 22, 1947, 1; Eichelberger to Miss Em, March 24, 1946, folder 3, box 11, Robert L. Eichelberger Papers.

32 C. J. C. Duder, "Love and the Lions: The Image of White Settlement in Kenya in Popular Fiction, 1919–1939," *African Affairs* 90 (1991): 427–438; Ronald Hyam, *Empire and Sexuality: The British Experience* (Manchester: Manchester University Press, 1990); John Thompson, "Occupied Germany! Story of Scandal: Lush Living, Immorality Blot Americans' Record," *CDT,* November 30, 1946, 1. For a parallel denunciation of the "colonial atmosphere" in Japan, see Margery Finn Brown, *Over a Bamboo Fence: An American Looks at Japan* (New York: William Morrow, 1951), 54.

33 John W. Dower, *Embracing Defeat: Japan in the Wake of World War II* (New York: W. W. Norton, 1999), 211. Dower characterizes the occupation as a "neo-colonial revolution" (the title of his sixth chapter).

34 Frantz Fanon, *The Wretched of the Earth,* trans. Constance Farrington (New York: Grove, 1963), 36; Rajiv Chandrasekaran, *Imperial Life in the Emerald City: Inside Iraq's Green Zone* (New York: Alfred A. Knopf, 2006); Betty Olson to family, August 19, 1945, box 1, Betty M. Olson Papers, USAMHI.

35 On "concentration" in Germany, see Frederiksen, *American Military Occupation of Germany,* 123–124. On the U.S. military's enduringly cavalier use of space, see Mark L. Gillem, *America Town: Building the Outposts of Empire* (Minneapolis: University of Minnesota Press, 2007). "Japanese Must Build Homes to House Families of Allies," *Christian Science Monitor,* March 8, 1946, 7; Michael Cullen Green, *Black Yanks in the Pacific: Race in*

the Making of American Military Empire after World War II (Ithaca, NY: Cornell University Press, 2010), 47.

36 Kennan, writing in March 1948, quoted by Michael Schaller, *The American Occupation of Japan: The Origins of the Cold War in Asia* (New York: Oxford University Press, 1985), 125; Eichelberger Diary, October 8, 1946, box 1, Robert L. Eichelberger Papers.

37 Edna W. Osnes, "Osnes Odyssey," typescript memoir, n.d., p. 7, box 1, Olaf Osnes Papers, USAMHI; Jacob Van Staaveren, *An American in Japan, 1945–1948* (Seattle: University of Washington Press, 1994), 21.

38 Orlando Ward Diary, October 28, 1946, box 10, Orlando W. Ward Papers, US-AMHI; Hubert Armstrong to unspecified recipient(s), March 14, 1948, folder 3, box 5, Hubert Coslet Armstrong Papers, HIA; Kennan quoted by Schaller, *American Occupation,* 125.

39 Clovis to Marie Byers, March 13, 1946, box 10, Clovis E. Byers Papers; Byers to Lt. Gen. Albert C. Wedemeyer, July 29, 1946, box 5, Clovis E. Byers Papers; Byers to Aunt Mai, July 25, 1947, box 7, Clovis E. Byers Papers; Justin Williams to Walker Wyman, October 9, 1946, box 4, Walker Demarquis Wyman Papers, UWRF.

40 Justin Williams to Walker Wyman, July 18, 1947, box 4, Walker Demarquis Wyman Papers.

41 Margaret Parton, "First Families of Army Men Land in Tokyo," *New York Herald Tribune,* June 25, 1946, 8; MacArthur quoted by Green, *Black Yanks,* 46. On the embassy setup, see Manchester, *American Caesar,* 513. For statistics of arrivals in Germany, see Willoughby, *Remaking the Conquering Heroes,* 120.

42 Gravois, "Military Families," 62–63; Alvah, *Unofficial Ambassadors,* 61–70; Bernadine V. Lee, "Army Wife in Tokyo," *Army Information Digest,* December 1946, 15–22.

43 Mrs. Lelah Berry, as told to Ann Stringer, "An Army Wife Lives Very Soft—in Germany," *Saturday Evening Post,* February 15, 1947, 25; Clay to Patterson, March 5, 1947, box 21, RG 260, Records of the United States Occupation Headquarters, OMGUS, Records Maintained for Military Governor Lt. Gen. Lucius D. Clay, 1945–49, NARA. Clay painted Mrs. Berry as an ingénue who had been manipulated by an experienced dirt digger. The text of Joan S. Crane's "Malice in Blunderland" is located in the same box.

44 "Research in Occupation Administration," prepared by Governmental Affairs Institute, DC, for Operations Research Office, August 1951, p. 28, folder "Military Govt. Reports, misc.," box 53, Robert L. Eichelberger Papers.

45 Frederiksen, *American Military Occupation of Germany,* 137.

46 On the construction of U.S. bases in Japan leading to greater social isolation, see, for example, Walt Sheldon, *The Honorable Conquerors: The Occupation of Japan, 1945–1952* (New York: Macmillan, 1965), 150–151; and on the same phenomenon in Germany, see Davis, *Come as a Conqueror,* 193. Historical Division, European Command, *Relations of Occupation Forces Personnel,* 19–20; "Roger Baldwin Assails U.S. Zone 'Hans Crowism,'" *New York Herald Tribune,* October 5, 1948, 19. On the sign above the toilet, see "Notes on Germany," n.d., folder 8, box 17, Roger Nash Baldwin Papers, SGMML. Frederiksen, *American Military Occupation of Germany,* 137, 138.

47 ACLU report, *Civil Liberties in Japan,* June 1947, p. 4, folder 7, box 18, Roger Nash Baldwin Papers.

48 Hubert Armstrong, undated letter [ca. mid-1947], folder 3, box 5, Hubert Coslet Armstrong Papers.

49 On MacArthur's minimal contact with Japanese, see Dower, *Embracing Defeat,* 204. Eichelberger to Miss Em, March 2, 1946, folder 3, box 11, Robert L. Eichelberger Papers; Clovis to Marie Byers, March 17, 1946, and March 1, 1946, box 10, Clovis E. Byers Papers.

50 Van Staaveren, *American in Japan,* 15–16. On the superabundance of servants, see also Dower, *Embracing Defeat,* 207. Sheldon, *Honorable Conquerors,* 115.

51 Martha Wayman to Ruth, January 2, 1946, box 2, Martha A. Wayman Papers, US-AMHI; Noel F. Busch, *Fallen Sun: A Report on Japan* (New York: D. Appleton-Century, 1948), 25. On African American service personnel and servants, see Green, *Black Yanks,* 51; Charley Cherokee, "Well Shut My Mouth," *Chicago Defender,* March 1, 1947, 13. Servants were a staple feature of press and news magazine commentary; Alvah, *Unofficial Ambassadors,* 107–110.

52 Wiley H. O'Mohundro, *From Mules to Missiles, Part II,* typescript memoir, n.d., p. 70, Wiley H. O'Mohundro Papers, USAMHI; Willoughby, *Remaking the Conquering Heroes,* 127.

53 Armstrong, undated letter from Seoul [ca. 1948], folder 3, box 5, Hubert Coslet Armstrong Papers.

54 Olaf Osnes to Sigval and Phoebe Osnes, November 22, 1947, box 1, Olaf Osnes Papers.

55 Ibid. On the pervasiveness of this trope of American "uplift" of oppressed Japanese women, see Naoko Shibusawa, *America's Geisha Ally: Reimagining the Japanese Enemy* (Cambridge, MA: Harvard University Press, 2006), 44–47.

56 Edna W. Osnes, "Osnes Odyssey," pp. 39, 40, box 1, Olaf Osnes Papers.

57 Mary to Miss Marion Tait, January 14, 1947, Marion Tait Papers, NJHS.

58 Martin Sommers, "Looting with Consent," *Saturday Evening Post,* March 13, 1948, 12; Louise to Kate Farrell, February 4, 1947, Farrell Family Papers, USAMHI.

59 George O. Pearson, oral history interview with Col. Robert G. Sharp, n.d., George O. Pearson Papers, USAMHI; Busch, *Fallen Sun,* 25.

60 McNarney quoted by Bud Hutton and Andy Rooney, *Conquerors' Peace: A Report to the American Stockholders* (Garden City, NY: Doubleday, 1947), 49. Höhn puts the total at 90,000 babies; "'You Can't Pin Sergeant's Stripes on an Archangel,'" 124. On the particular tensions surrounding "brown babies," see Heide Fehrenbach, *Race after Hitler: Black Occupation Children in Postwar Germany and America* (Princeton, NJ: Princeton University Press, 2005).

61 Frederiksen, *American Military Occupation of Germany,* 136.

62 Ibid.; Historical Division, European Command, *Relations of Occupation Forces Personnel,* 20.

63 For marriage statistics, see Frederiksen, *American Military Occupation of Germany,* 136–137. Hutton and Rooney, *Conquerors' Peace,* 55; Susan Zeiger, *Entangling Alliances: Foreign War Brides and American Soldiers in the Twentieth Century* (New York: New York University Press, 2010), 151; Willoughby, *Remaking the Conquering Heroes,* 120.

64 On Asian exclusion, see Zeiger, *Entangling Alliances,* 181. For an account of American wives' training of Japanese brides, see William Neufeld, "Foreign Service—II," handwritten notes of a SCAP officer, February 27, 1976, William Neufeld Papers, HIA. "500 Americans in Jap Weddings," *WP,* February 13, 1946, M3; "GI-Japanese Marriages Pass the 1,000 Mark," *Cleveland Call and Post,* August 18, 1951, 3A. On suicides, see, for example, "GI, Jap Girl Die in Suicide Pact," *Afro-American,* March 15, 1947, 5.

65 ACLU report, *Civil Liberties in Japan,* 5; Malvina Lindsay, "Marriage Melting Pot," *WP,* August 14, 1948, 4.

66 Zeiger, *Entangling Alliances,* 167; Philip E. Wolgin and Irene Bloemraad, " 'Our Gratitude to Our Soldiers': Military Spouses, Family Re-unification, and Postwar Immigration Reform," *Journal of Interdisciplinary History* 41 (2010): 27–60.

CONCLUSION

1 Drama Advisory Panel, International Exchange Program, September 14, 1955, Bureau of Educational and Cultural Affairs Historical Collection, Series 5, MS 468, University of Arkansas Library, Special Collections, Fayetteville.

2 John Patrick, *The Teahouse of the August Moon* (New York: Dramatists Play Service, 1957), 74, 50; Vern Sneider, *The Teahouse of the August Moon* (New York: G. P. Putnam's Sons, 1951). For recent analyses of the book, play, and film, see Danielle Glassmeyer, " 'The Wisdom of Gracious Acceptance': Okinawa, Mass Suicide, and the Cultural Work of *Teahouse of the August Moon,*" *Soundings: An Interdisciplinary Journal* 96 (2013): 398–430; Nicholas Evans Sarantakes, "The Teahouse Tempest: The U.S. Occupation of Okinawa and *The Teahouse of the August Moon,*" *Journal of American-East Asian Relations* 21 (2014): 1–28.

3 Richard Watts, "A Thoroughly Delightful Comedy," *New York Post,* October 16, 1953; John McClain, "Comedy a Colossal Hit," *New York Journal American,* October 16, 1953. Theater critics in the "highbrow" press were just as effusive. Brooks Atkinson, "The Teahouse of the August Moon," *NYT,* October 16, 1953, 32; Brooks Atkinson, "Enchanted Teahouse," *NYT,* October 25, 1953, X1. On the turn to "polite" racism, see Takashi Fujitani, *Race for Empire: Koreans as Japanese and Japanese as Americans during World War II* (Berkeley: University of California Press, 2011), 7. Christina Klein, *Cold War Orientalism: Asia in the Middlebrow Imagination* (Berkeley: University of California Press, 2003), 16.

4 Cecil Smith, "Author at Loss over Success of 'Teahouse,'" *LAT,* November 27, 1955, E4; Kurt Vonnegut, *Slaughterhouse-Five* (New York: Delacorte, 1969), 8; Patrick, *Teahouse,* 74; Ray Falk, "Bivouac at an Okinawan 'Teahouse' in Japan," *NYT,* June 10, 1956, 125; John McCarten, "The Current Cinema: No Time for Subtlety," *New Yorker,* December 8, 1956, 144–145.

5 Patrick, *Teahouse,* 13.

6 Some of these inequities were also apparent to readers of U.S. newspapers and magazines, although coverage was sparse. Robert Trumbull, "Okinawa: 'Sometimes Painful' Lessons for U.S.," *NYT,* April 7, 1957, 225; Faubion Bowers, "Letter from Okinawa," *New Yorker,* October 23, 1954, 139–148; William L. Worden, "Rugged Bachelors of Okinawa," *Saturday*

Evening Post, March 30, 1957, 84–88; Vern Sneider, "Below 'The Teahouse,'" *NYT,* October 11, 1953, X1.

7 Bowers, "Letter from Okinawa," 146.

8 Drama Advisory Panel, committee minutes, January 18, 1956, Bureau of Educational and Cultural Affairs Historical Collection; "'Teahouse' Limps into Montevideo," *NYT,* May 13, 1956, 85.

9 Intriguingly, the play and its derivations were reported to be a huge hit in West Germany. *Das Kleine Teehaus* spawned a radio show, "Captain Fisby's Geishas," and racked up 1,000 performances over twelve months; "Fete Lauds 'Teahouse,'" *NYT,* March 22, 1955, 35.

10 Office of War Information, Motion Picture Division, Feature Script Review, January 21, 1944, RG 208, entry 567, box 3512, NARA; Office of War Information, Motion Picture Review, Olga Weinert, September 18, 1945, RG 208, entry 567, box 3512, NARA.

11 Sneider, "Below 'The Teahouse,'" X3; James Watkins to Maynard Thoreson, March 8, 1955, folder "Correspondence with Enlisted Men," box 10, James Thomas Watkins Papers, HIA.

12 "New York: Too Big," *Time,* March 25, 1946; Oscar Godbout, "'A Bell for Adano' on TV," *NYT,* May 27, 1956, 105; Hal Humphrey, "'Adano' Rings 23 Years Too Late," *LAT,* November 8, 1967, E22. (Viewing copies of both productions consulted at the Paley Center for Media, New York.) Robert D. Kaplan, "Supremacy by Stealth," *Atlantic Monthly,* July–August 2003, 65. Kaplan also quotes from Hersey's foreword at some length as an epilogue to his *Imperial Grunts* (New York: Vintage, 2006), vii. In the interim, Herbert Mitgang disinterred Joppolo as a model for U.S. peacekeepers in Bosnia; Herbert Mitgang, "Chocolate Grenades," *Newsweek,* February 26, 1996, 15. S. D. Griffin, "A Bell for Adano Discussion Guide," USMC Professional Reading Program, Lejeune Leadership Institute, n.d. The novel was also commended to personnel of the U.S. Air Force; Andrew Kovich, "Compassion and the American Soldier," *Air Force Print News,* December 30, 2008, http://www.warren.af.mil /news/story.asp?id=123128532. For an army endorsement, see Patrick J. Donahoe, "Preparing Leaders for Nationbuilding," *Military Review* 84 (2004): 24–26.

13 "'Adano' Suit Upheld," *NYT,* June 28, 1946, 19; John Hersey to Major General T. R. Yancey, April 16, 1966, box 19, John Hersey Papers, BRB.

14 Griffin, "A Bell for Adano Discussion Guide," 1, 3.

15 Kozy K. Amemiya, "The Bolivian Connection: U.S. Bases and Okinawan Emigration," Japan Policy Research Institute, Working Paper No. 25, October 1996, http://www .jpri.org/publications/workingpapers/wp25.html.

16 Robert B. Textor, *Failure in Japan: With Keystones for a Positive Policy* (New York: John Day, 1951); Arthur D. Kahn, *Betrayal: Our Occupation of Germany* (New York: Beacon Service, 1950); Delbert Clark, *Again the Goose Step: The Lost Fruits of Victory* (Indianapolis: Bobbs, Merrill, 1949). For useful short historiographical surveys on Germany and Japan, see Edward N. Peterson, "The Occupation as Perceived by the Public, Scholars, and Policy Makers," in *Americans as Proconsuls: United States Military Government in Germany and Japan, 1944–1952,* ed. Robert Wolfe (Carbondale: Southern Illinois University Press, 1984), 416–434; Carol Gluck, "Entangling Illusions: Japanese and American Views of the Occupation," in *New Frontiers in American-East Asian Relations,* ed. Warren Cohen (New York: Columbia University Press, 1983), 169–236.

17 John Morton Blum, *V Was for Victory: Politics and American Culture during World War II* (San Diego: Harcourt Brace, 1976), 305–307. For further evidence of Americans' preference for harsh occupations, see Jay B. Krane, "Polls, Press and Occupation Policy," *Columbia Journal of International Affairs* 2 (1948): 71–75; H. Schuyler Foster, *Activism Replaces Isolationism: U.S. Public Attitudes, 1940–1975* (Washington, DC: Foxhall, 1983), 53–56, 96–99. For a more recent restatement of this position that occupation "had better be" about profit, so long as the spoils are equitably divided, see Deborah Scranton's documentary about members of the New Hampshire National Guard serving in Iraq, *The War Tapes* (2006).

18 Petra Goedde, *GIs and Germans: Culture, Gender, and Foreign Relations, 1945–1949* (New Haven, CT: Yale University Press, 2003), 167.

19 C. G. D. Onslow, "West German Rearmament," *World Politics* 3 (1951): 450–485.

20 William T. Bowers, William M. Hammond, and George L. MacGarrigle, *Black Soldier/White Army: The 24th Infantry Regiment in Korea* (Washington, DC: Center of Military History, United States Army, 1996).

21 Michael Sherry, *In the Shadow of War: The United States since the 1930s* (New Haven, CT: Yale University Press, 1995); Benjamin Sparrow, *Warfare State: World War II Americans and the Age of Big Government* (New York: Oxford University Press, 2011); Mary Dudziak, *War-Time: An Idea, Its History, Its Consequences* (New York: Oxford University Press, 2012).

22 Edward N. Peterson, *The American Occupation of Germany—Retreat to Victory* (Detroit: Wayne State University Press, 1977), 11.

23 *GI Blues,* directed by Norman Taurog (Los Angeles: Paramount Pictures, 1960).

24 War Department, *Basic Field Manual, FM 27-5, Military Government* (Washington, DC: Government Printing Office, 1940), 4. This entreaty makes no appearance in the reissued 1943 edition of FM 27-5.

ACKNOWLEDGMENTS

Despite its wrenching subject matter, this book's journey into existence has been uncommonly enjoyable. Along the way, I've encountered great interest in the project from colleagues, friends, archivists, and various kindly strangers. The readiness with which many interlocutors volunteered impromptu anecdotes about their own, their parents', or their grandparents' experience of postwar occupation convinced me that I was on to something worth pursuing. This pursuit led me to rich troves of unpublished letters, diaries, and memoirs in more than thirty archives across the country. I read these materials with great appreciation for not only the candor of their authors but also the generosity of those who've made their own, or their relatives', intimate documents accessible to researchers.

My most substantial debt, then, is to those individuals whose experiences I drew on in writing this book, and to the numerous institutions dedicated to preserving written and oral testimony where I conducted my research. I'm extremely grateful to the staff of all the libraries and archives I visited. However, a few archivists who gave of their time and expertise with unusual generosity deserve special thanks: Richard Sommers and Richard Baker at the United States Army Military History Institute; Carol Leadenham at the Hoover Institution Archives; Russell Horton at the Wisconsin Veterans' Museum and Archive; Cynthia Tinker in the Special Collections department of the John C. Hodges Library at the University of Tennessee in Knoxville; and Megan Harris at the Veterans' History Project of the American Folklife Center of the Library of Congress. I appreciate the willingness of Greg Taylor to let me quote his father's letters; Andrea Malmont's permission to use her grandfather's correspondence; and Jeffrey Winkelman's generosity in sharing his grandfather's memoir with me.

In addition to primary source materials, historians' other biggest requirements are time and space in which to write. I've been immensely fortunate in this regard too. The project began to germinate while I was a fellow at the Woodrow Wilson International Center for Scholars in 2010–2011, and it reached completion in the hospitable environs of Princeton's Shelby Cullom Davis Center, where I spent the fall of 2015 in residence. I'm indebted to both institutions for funding my work and for providing such stimulating settings in which to engage in scholarly conversation and production. At the Woodrow Wilson Center, thanks are due to then director Lee Hamilton and many friends: Jojo Abinales, Lindsay Collins, Kimberly Connor, Martin Dimitrov, Don Doyle, David Freund, Lucy Jilka, Mel Leffler, Lori Leonard, Ioana Macrea-Toma, Marjorie Spruill, Ron Steel, and Melissa Stockdale. Janet Spikes and the staff of the center's library were models of helpfulness and good cheer, while Tom DeMaio provided stellar research assistance. At the Shelby Cullom Davis Center, Philip Nord proved an exceedingly gracious host to a delightful coterie of fellows: Pierre Fuller, Marie Kelleher, Emma Kuby, and Arnaud Orain. Jennifer Gould couldn't have taken more attentive care of us, and other friends in Princeton ensured that the fall of 2015 was an especially enjoyable one. Thanks, then, are due to Eva Giloi and Severin and Sebastian Bremner for making Tuesday evenings such fun, and to Shel Garon for his camaraderie.

I received a number of invitations to present portions of this project as it was under construction, and I extend thanks to Tarak Barkawi, Linda Gordon, William Roger Louis, and Aviel Roshwald for invitations to speak at the New School, NYU, the Washington History Seminar, and Georgetown University, respectively. Members of the U.S. bases symposium at Temple University in October 2015 offered especially productive commentary. My appreciation goes to Andy Buchanan, Cynthia Enloe, Gretchen Heefner, Richard Immerman, Jana Lipman, Marilyn Young, and other participants in that venture.

For longer-range support and encouragement, I'm thankful to Richard Aldrich, Andy Buchanan, Mary Dudziak, Linda Gordon, Emily Rosenberg, and Ellen Schrecker. I owe particular debts of gratitude to Thomas Doherty and, above all, to Marilyn Young for her indefatigable letter writing and loyal friendship over many years. Meanwhile, at Rutgers University–Newark, I appreciate the willingness of Dean Jan Lewis and History Department Chair Karen Caplan to sanction my leaves of absence. I'm immensely grateful to Christina Strasburger for her friendship and all her incredibly hard work on behalf of everyone in the History Department. Other RU–N friends and colleagues deserve recognition for their comradeship, a long list headed by Fran Bartkowski and Gary Roth. Graduate students in my "Postwar" seminar in the spring of 2015 delivered a truly memorable classroom experience, for which I offer thanks. I'm also grateful to graduate students Nicholas Turner and Garrett Weedon for their research assistance.

At Harvard University Press, Joyce Seltzer has been an impeccably attentive editor whose enthusiasm for the project has been most heartening throughout. Brian Distelberg; Kathi Drummy; Deborah Grahame-Smith; and Ashley Moore, with her sharp eye and light touch, also deserve thanks for their roles in helping turn the manuscript into this book.

Deep appreciation and love go to my parents, John and Paddy Carruthers, along with other family members in Galway: Siobhán, John, Maura, Julia, and John Patrick Morrison (my "favorite nephew"). The last and largest debt, however, is owed to Joe Romano, to whom this book is dedicated—with thanks for making life so joyful, and with much love. Always.

Maplewood, NJ
January 10, 2016

INDEX